*Flag: Thanks

*Back: Happy

KOYOHARU GOTOUGE

Hello! I'm Gotouge. I am truly thankful to everyone happy about the *Demon Slayer* anime as if it were their own good news! All the kind and congratulatory words, gifts and happiness massaged me and blew away my stiff shoulders and headaches. My nose is still running though. I'm sorry I can't reply individually or give you anything back. I'm blessed by much good fortune and the aid and encouragement of nice people helps a lot. I am always praying from the bottom of my heart for the health and happiness of people who are kind to me.

DEMON SLAYER:
KIMETSU NO YAIBA
VOLUME 12
Shonen Jump Edition

Story and Art by
KOYOHARU GOTOUGE

TRANSLATION John Werry
ENGLISH ADAPTATION Stan!
TOUCH-UP ART & LETTERING John Hunt
DESIGN Jimmy Presler
EDITOR Mike Montesa

Printed in Italy

Published by VIZ Media, LLC
P.O. Box 77010
San Francisco, CA 94107

10
First printing, May 2020
Tenth printing, April 2022

ratings.viz.com RATED T TEEN

PARENTAL ADVISORY
DEMON SLAYER: KIMETSU NO YAIBA is rated T for Teen and recommended for ages 13 and up. This volume contains realistic and fantasy violence.

VIZ MEDIA
viz.com

SHONEN JUMP

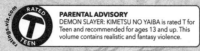

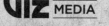

DEMON
SLAYER
KIMETSU NO YAIBA

12

THE
UPPER
RANKS
GATHER

KOYOHARU
GOTOUGE

CHARACTERS

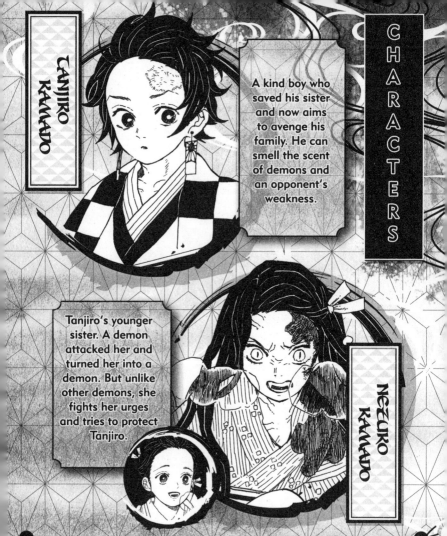

TANJIRO KAMADO

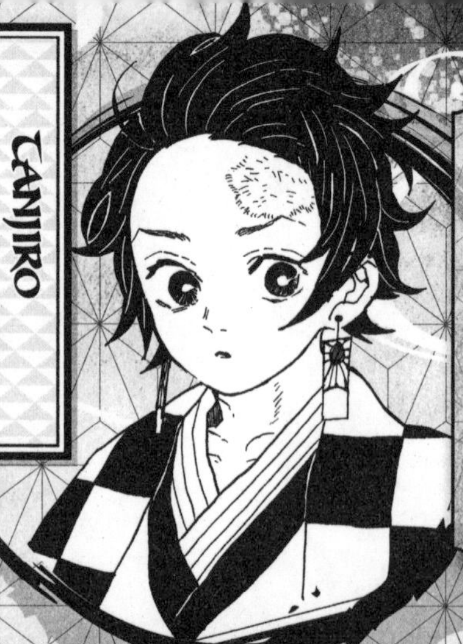

A kind boy who saved his sister and now aims to avenge his family. He can smell the scent of demons and an opponent's weakness.

NEZUKO KAMADO

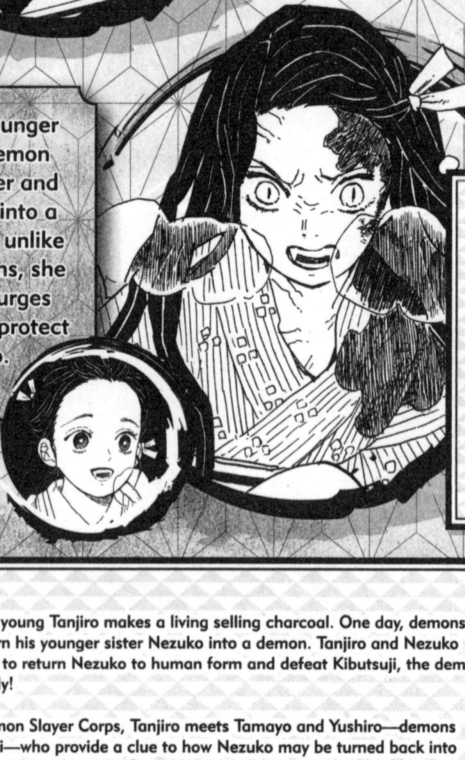

Tanjiro's younger sister. A demon attacked her and turned her into a demon. But unlike other demons, she fights her urges and tries to protect Tanjiro.

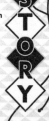

STORY

In Taisho-era Japan, young Tanjiro makes a living selling charcoal. One day, demons kill his family and turn his younger sister Nezuko into a demon. Tanjiro and Nezuko set out to find a way to return Nezuko to human form and defeat Kibutsuji, the demon who killed their family!

After joining the Demon Slayer Corps, Tanjiro meets Tamayo and Yushiro—demons who oppose Kibutsuji—who provide a clue to how Nezuko may be turned back into a human. On a new mission, Uzui the Sound Hashira, Tanjiro and others confront a brother-and-sister pair of demons who are Upper Rank 6. The sibling demons repeatedly get the better of them, but our heroes show indomitable perseverance and defeat the demons at great cost. Meanwhile, the first death of an upper-rank demon in over a hundred years has an impact on the remaining upper-rank demons.

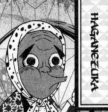

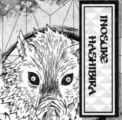

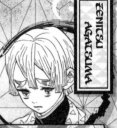

ZENITSU AGATSUMA

He went through Final Selection at the same time as Tanjiro. He's usually cowardly, but when he falls asleep his true power comes out.

INOSUKE HASHIBIRA

He also went through Final Selection at the same time as Tanjiro. He wears the pelt of a wild boar and is very belligerent.

HAGANEZUKA

The swordsmith who made Tanjiro's katana. He has the soul of an artist, so he gets angry when a blade is treated poorly.

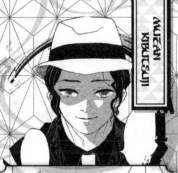

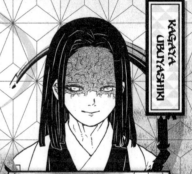

KAGAYA UBUYASHIKI

The leader of the Demon Slayer Corps who seeks to defeat Muzan Kibutsuji. His body is weak, but he is very charismatic.

MUZAN KIBUTSUJI

Kibutsuji turned Nezuko into a demon. He is Tanjiro's enemy and hides his nature in order to live among human beings.

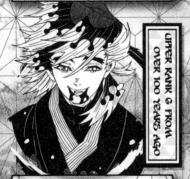

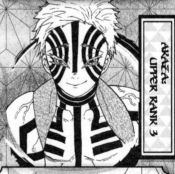

AKAZA: UPPER RANK 3

Upper Rank 3. The demon who killed Kyojuro Rengoku, the Flame Hashira of the Demon Slayer Corps. He burns with desire for revenge against Tanjiro.

UPPER RANK 6 FROM OVER 100 YEARS AGO

The demon who turned Gyutaro and Daki—who were until recently the Upper Rank 6 demons—into demons.

CONTENTS

DEMON SLAYER

KIMETSU NO YAIBA

12

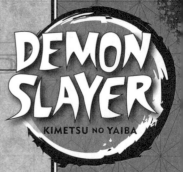

THE UPPER RANKS GATHER

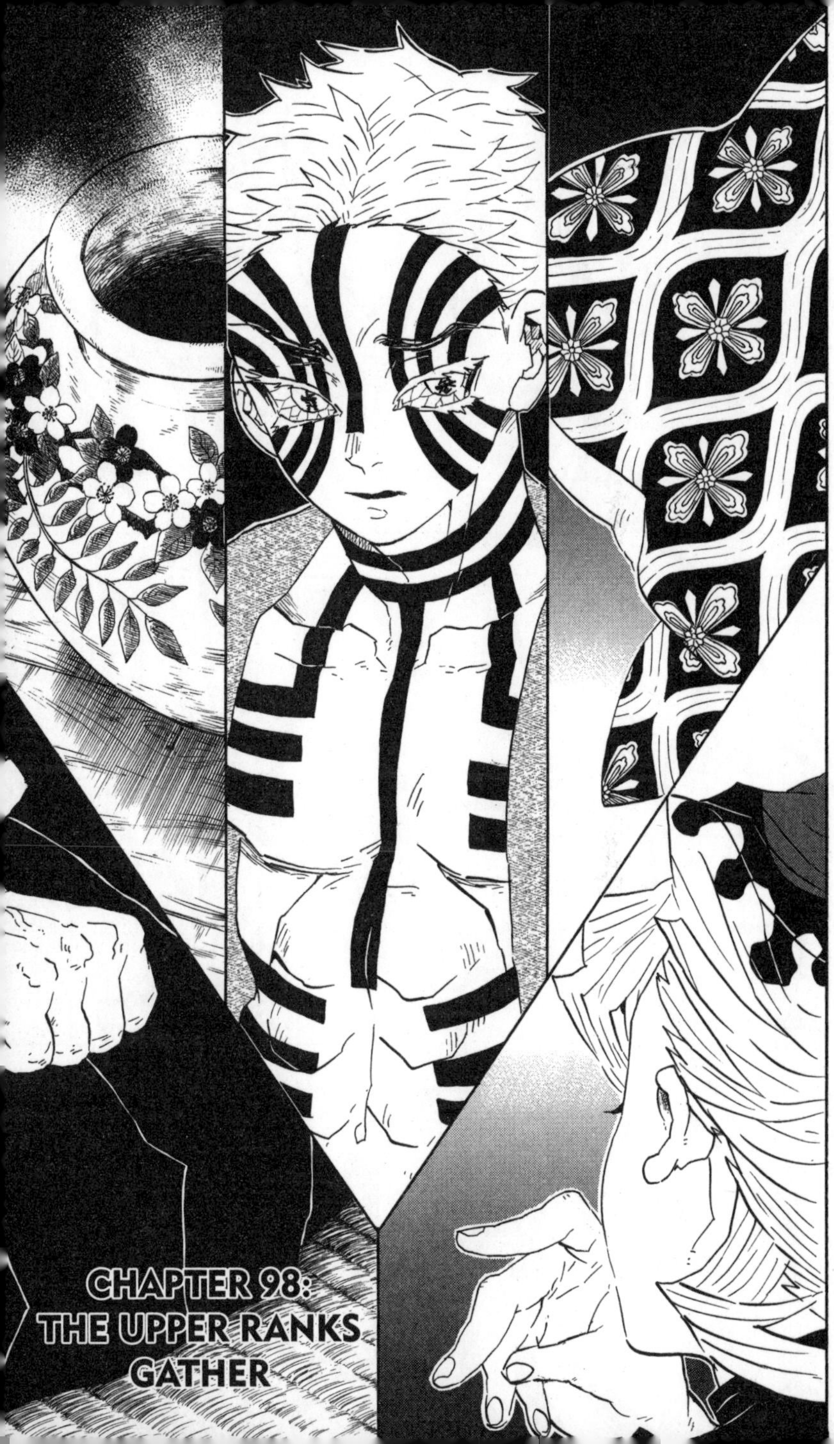
CHAPTER 98:
THE UPPER RANKS
GATHER

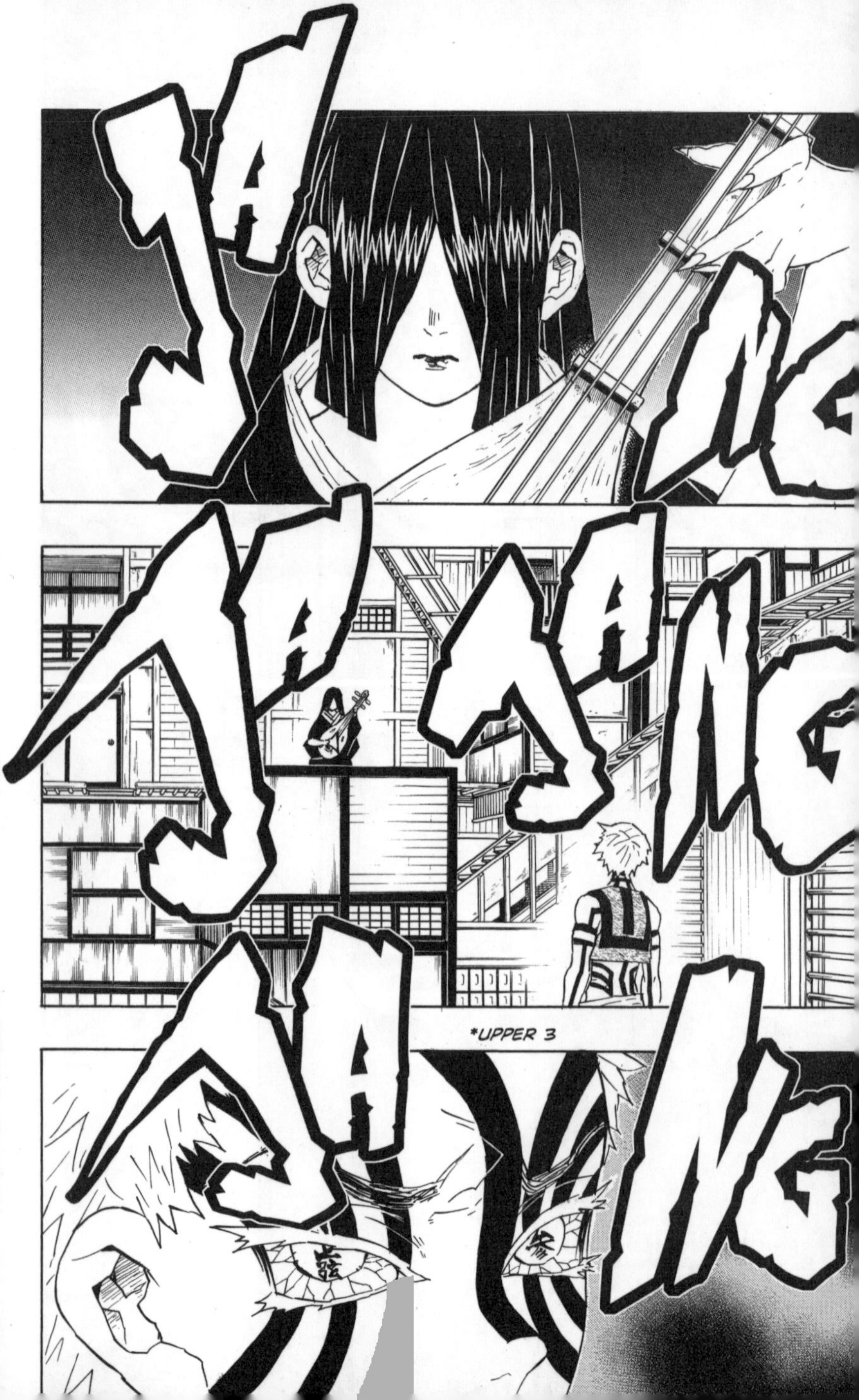
JANG
JAJANG
*UPPER 3
JAJANG

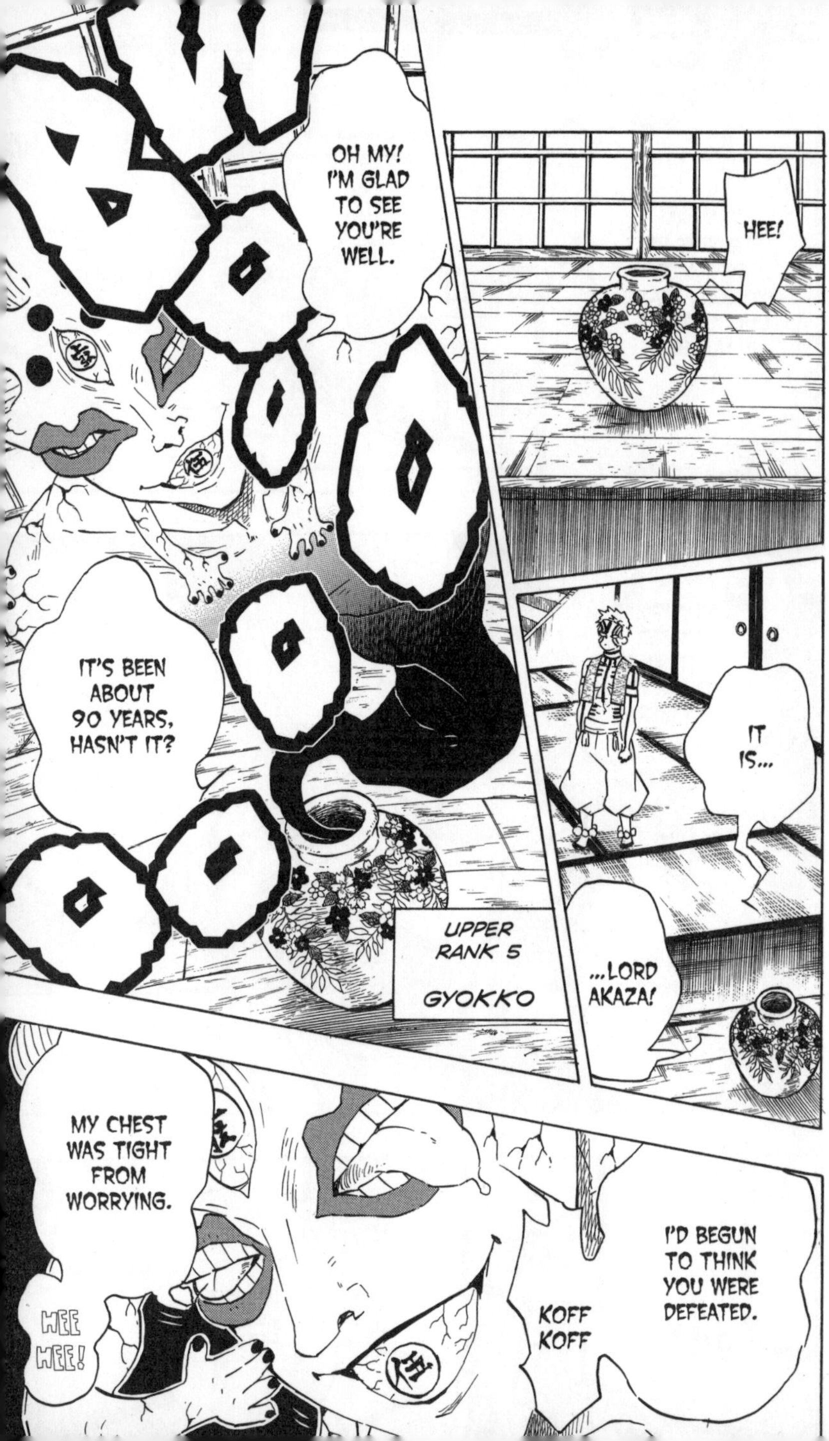

HEE!
IT IS...
...LORD AKAZA!
OH MY! I'M GLAD TO SEE YOU'RE WELL.
IT'S BEEN ABOUT 90 YEARS, HASN'T IT?
UPPER RANK 5
GYOKKO
MY CHEST WAS TIGHT FROM WORRYING.
I'D BEGUN TO THINK YOU WERE DEFEATED.
KOFF KOFF
HEE HEE!

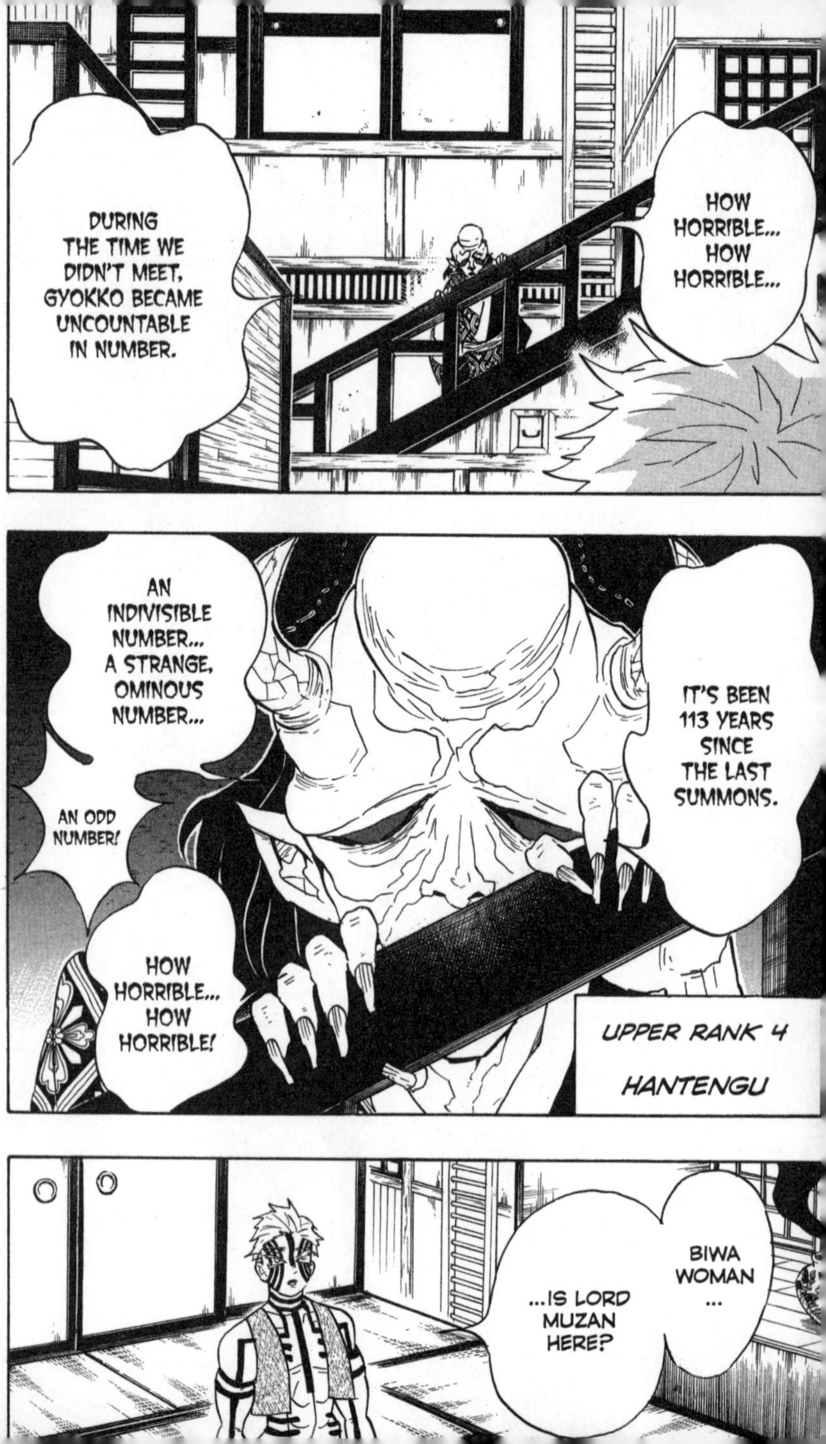
HOW HORRIBLE... HOW HORRIBLE...
DURING THE TIME WE DIDN'T MEET, GYOKKO BECAME UNCOUNTABLE IN NUMBER.
IT'S BEEN 113 YEARS SINCE THE LAST SUMMONS.
UPPER RANK 4
HANTENGU
AN INDIVISIBLE NUMBER... A STRANGE, OMINOUS NUMBER...
AN ODD NUMBER!
HOW HORRIBLE... HOW HORRIBLE!
BIWA WOMAN ...
...IS LORD MUZAN HERE?

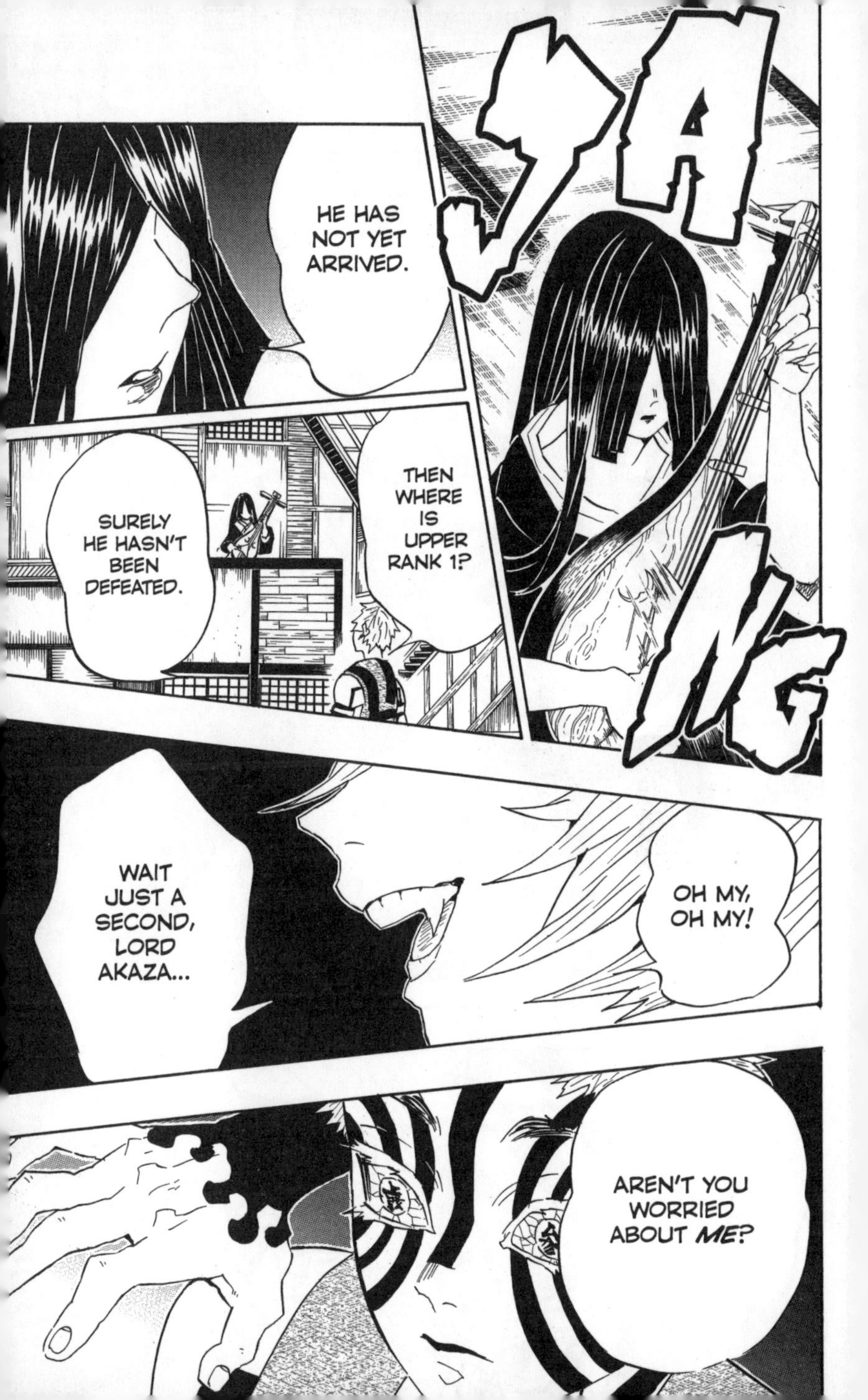
JYANG
HE HAS NOT YET ARRIVED.
THEN WHERE IS UPPER RANK 1?
SURELY HE HASN'T BEEN DEFEATED.
OH MY, OH MY!
WAIT JUST A SECOND, LORD AKAZA...
AREN'T YOU WORRIED ABOUT *ME*?

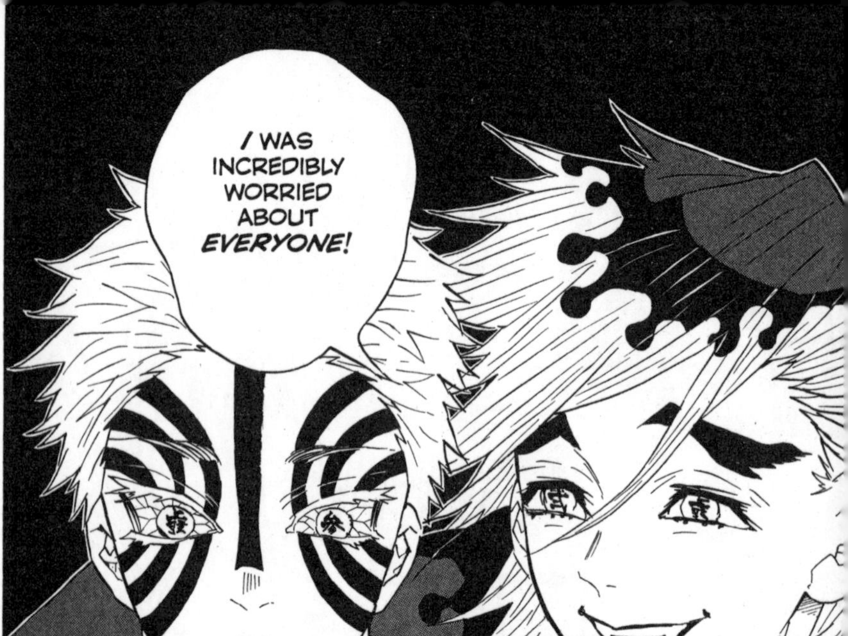
I WAS INCREDIBLY WORRIED ABOUT *EVERYONE*!

*DOMA'S EYES: UPPER 2

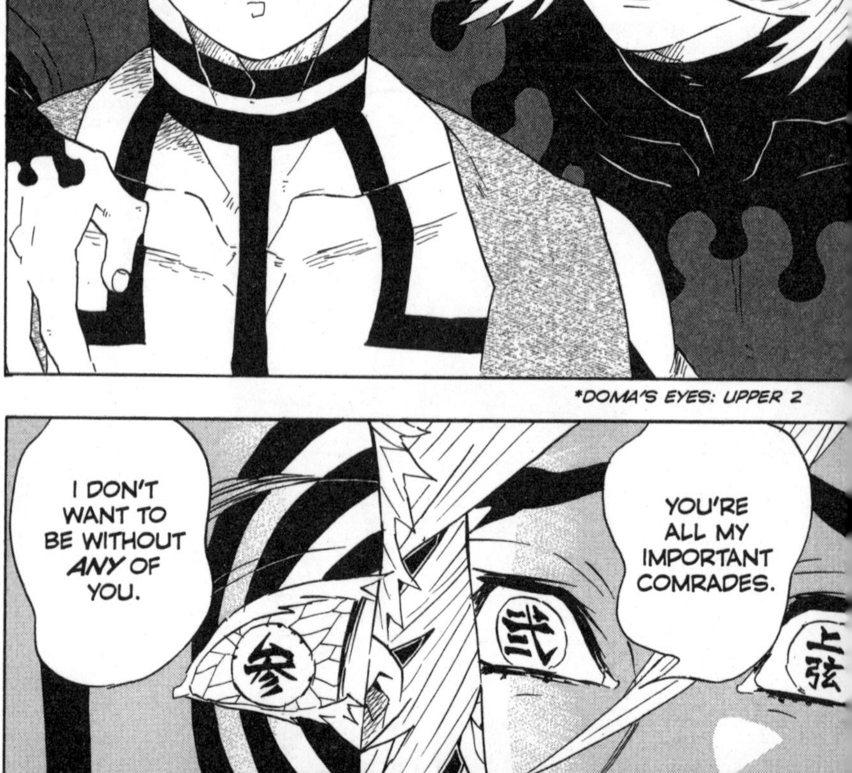
YOU'RE ALL MY IMPORTANT COMRADES.
I DON'T WANT TO BE WITHOUT *ANY* OF YOU.

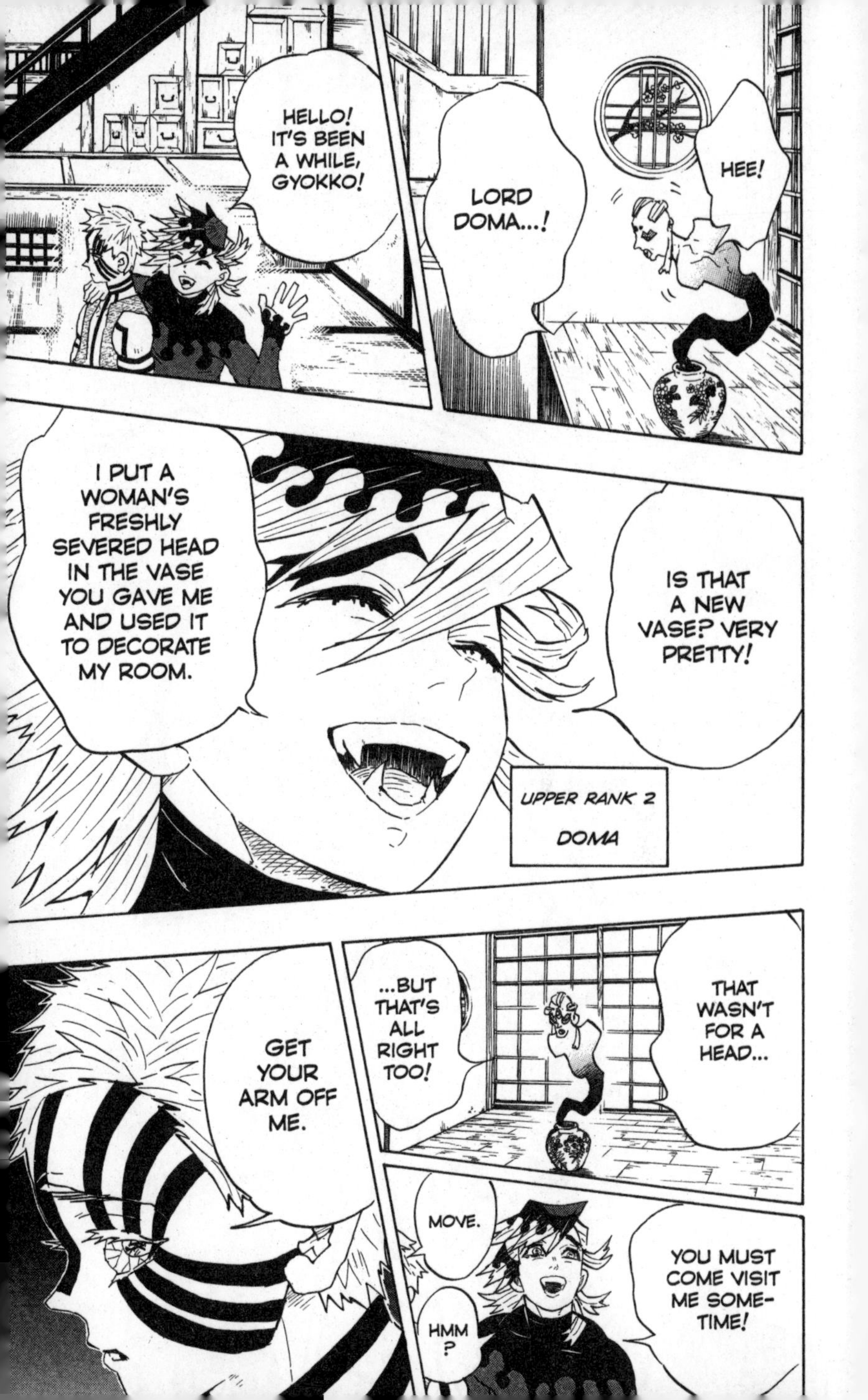
HEE!
LORD DOMA...!
HELLO! IT'S BEEN A WHILE, GYOKKO!
IS THAT A NEW VASE? VERY PRETTY!
UPPER RANK 2
DOMA
I PUT A WOMAN'S FRESHLY SEVERED HEAD IN THE VASE YOU GAVE ME AND USED IT TO DECORATE MY ROOM.
THAT WASN'T FOR A HEAD...
...BUT THAT'S ALL RIGHT TOO!
YOU MUST COME VISIT ME SOME-TIME!
MOVE.
HMM?
GET YOUR ARM OFF ME.

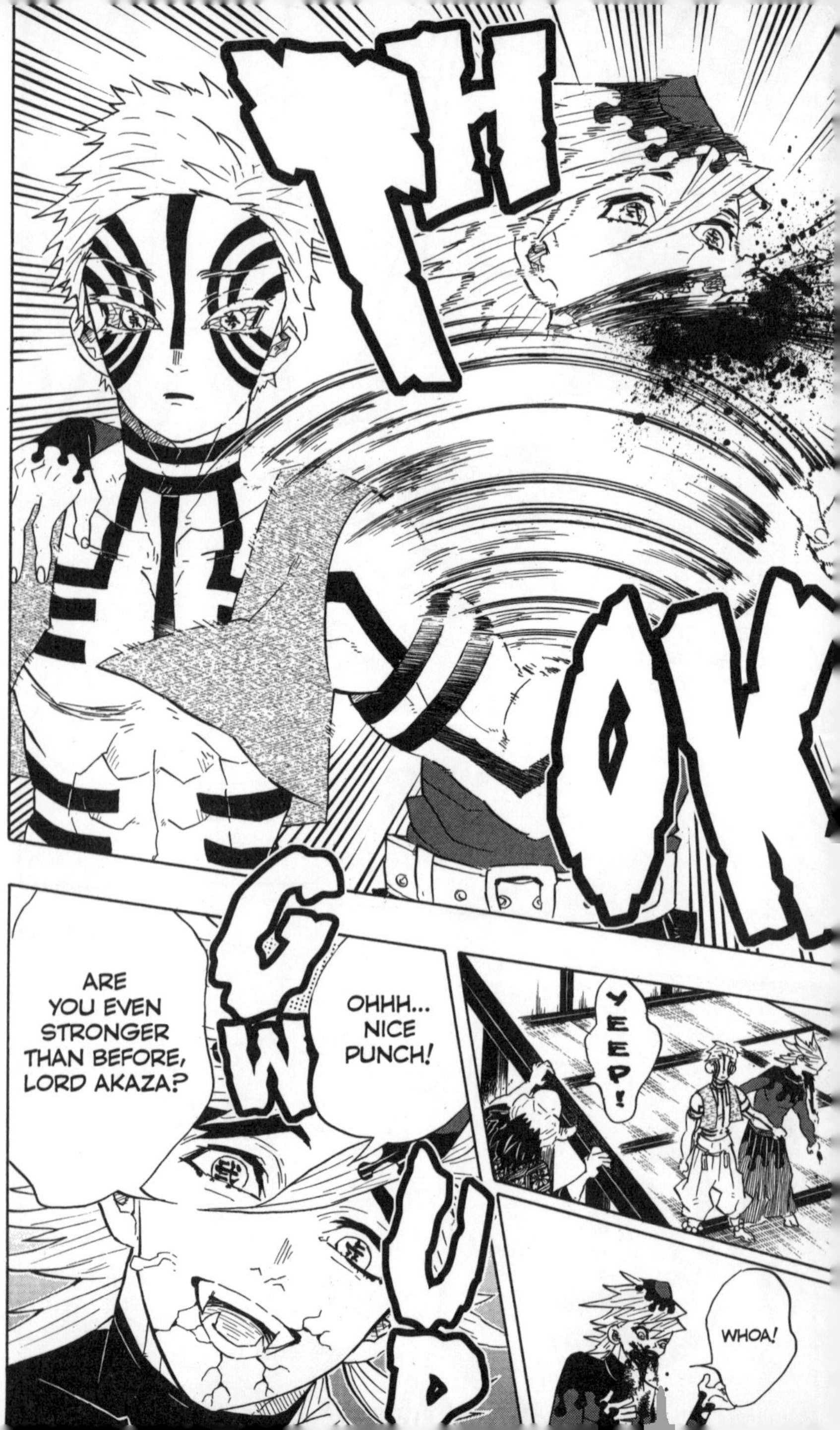
THOK
YEEP!
WHOA!
GWU
OHHH... NICE PUNCH!
ARE YOU EVEN STRONGER THAN BEFORE, LORD AKAZA?

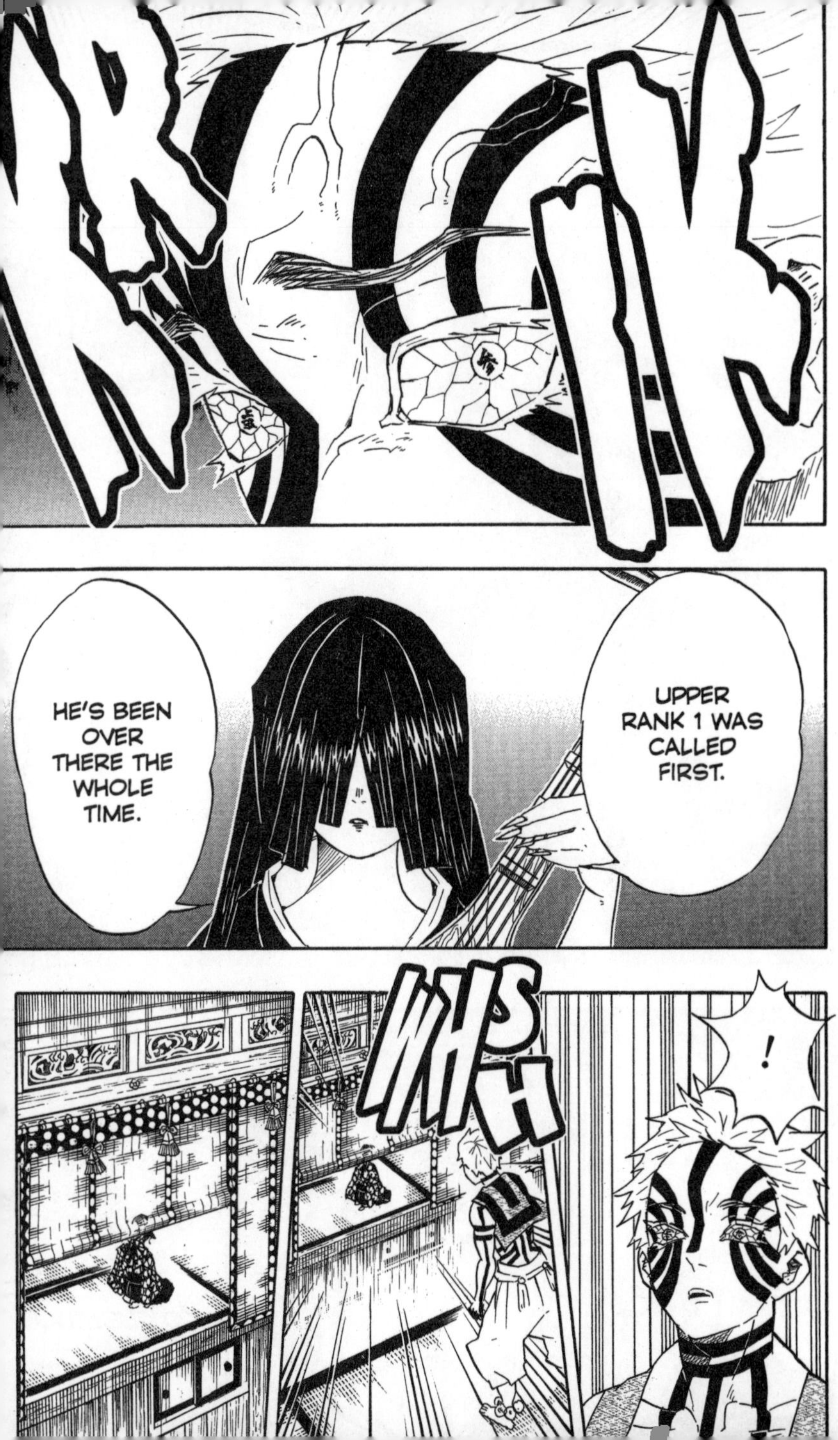
UPPER RANK 1 WAS CALLED FIRST.
HE'S BEEN OVER THERE THE WHOLE TIME.
!
WHSH

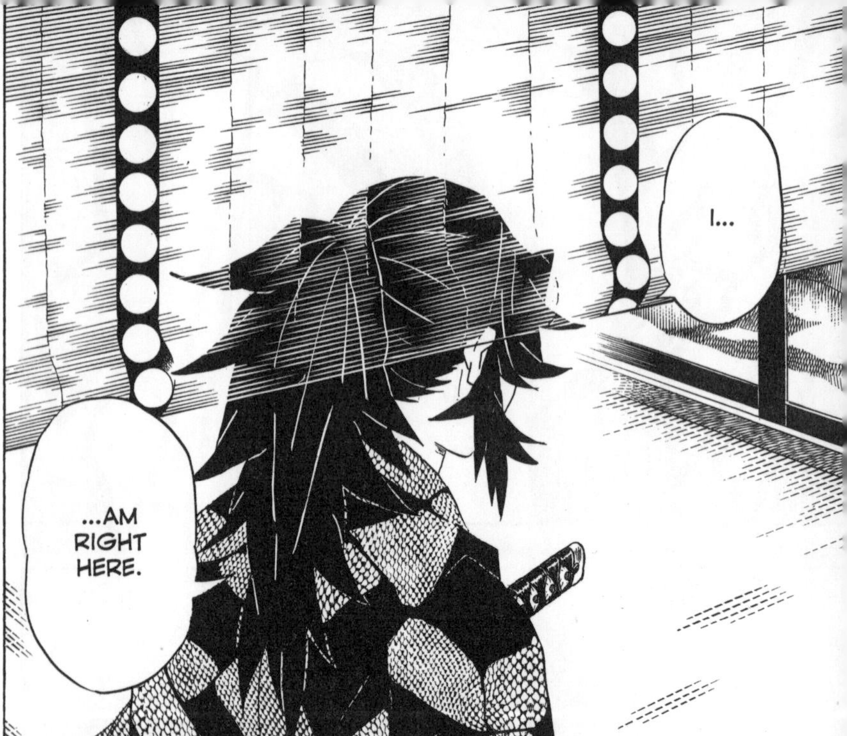
I...
...AM RIGHT HERE.

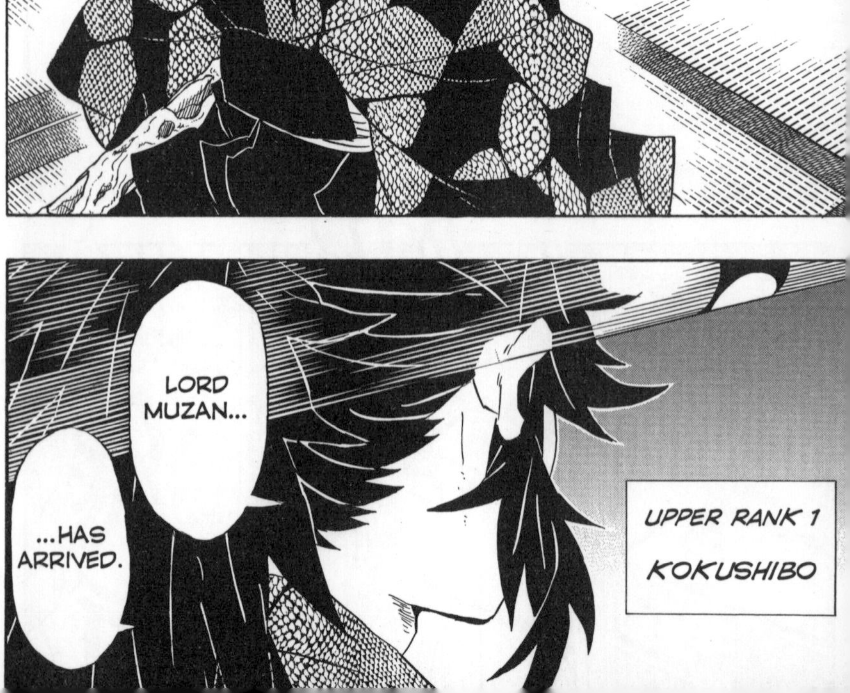
LORD MUZAN...
...HAS ARRIVED.
UPPER RANK 1
KOKUSHIBO

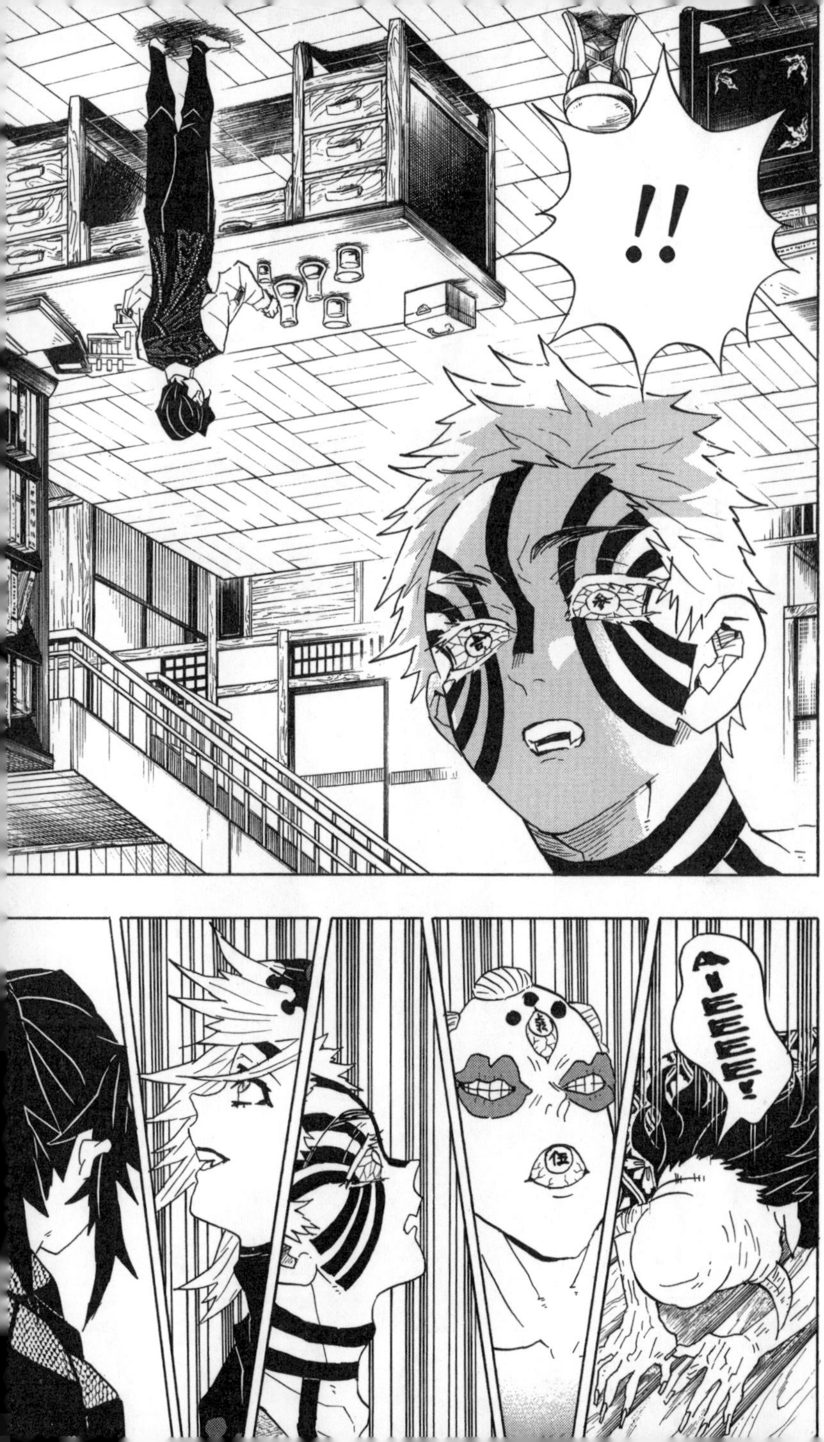
!!
AIEEEEE!

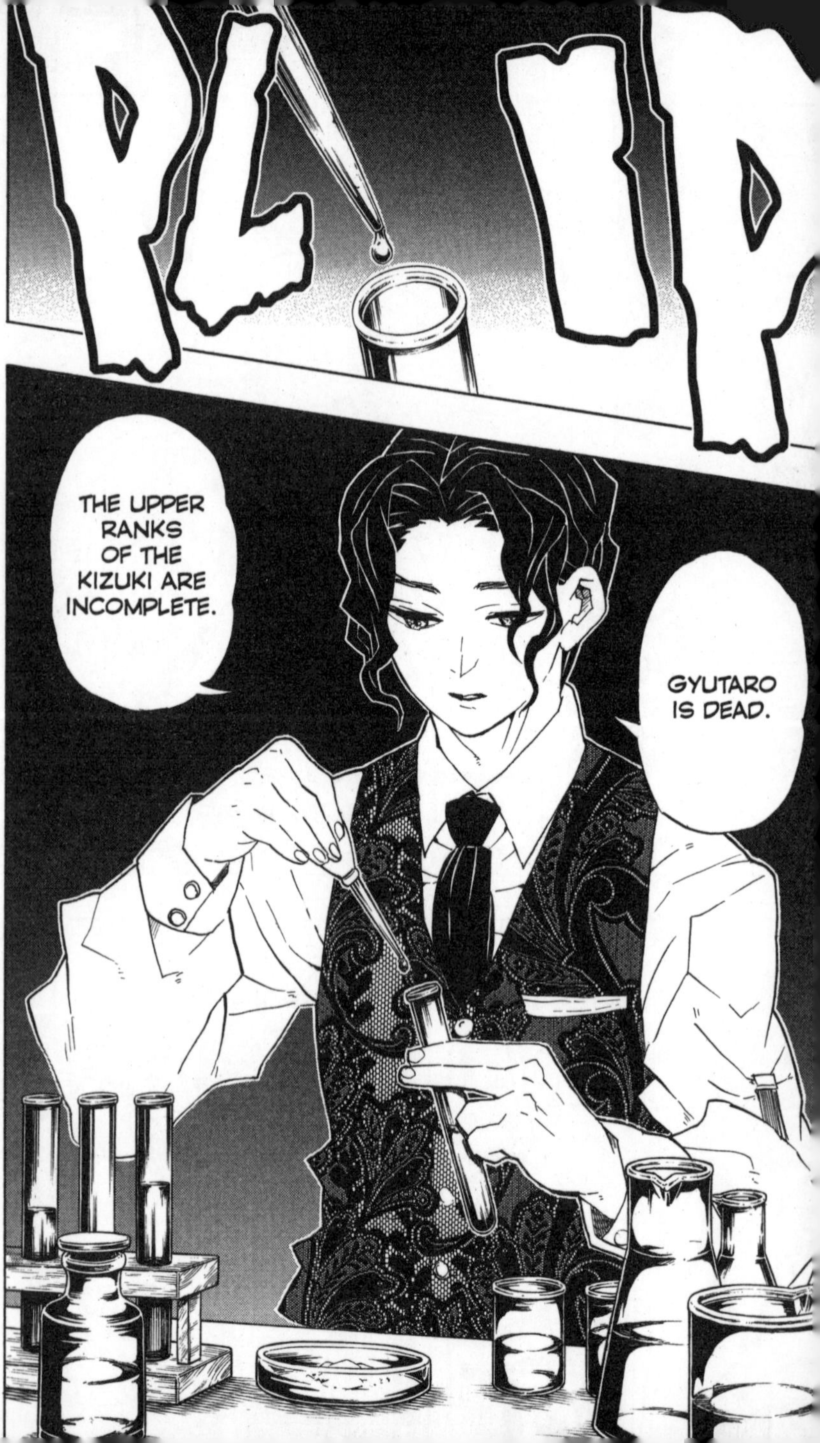
PLIP
GYUTARO IS DEAD.
THE UPPER RANKS OF THE KIZUKI ARE INCOMPLETE.

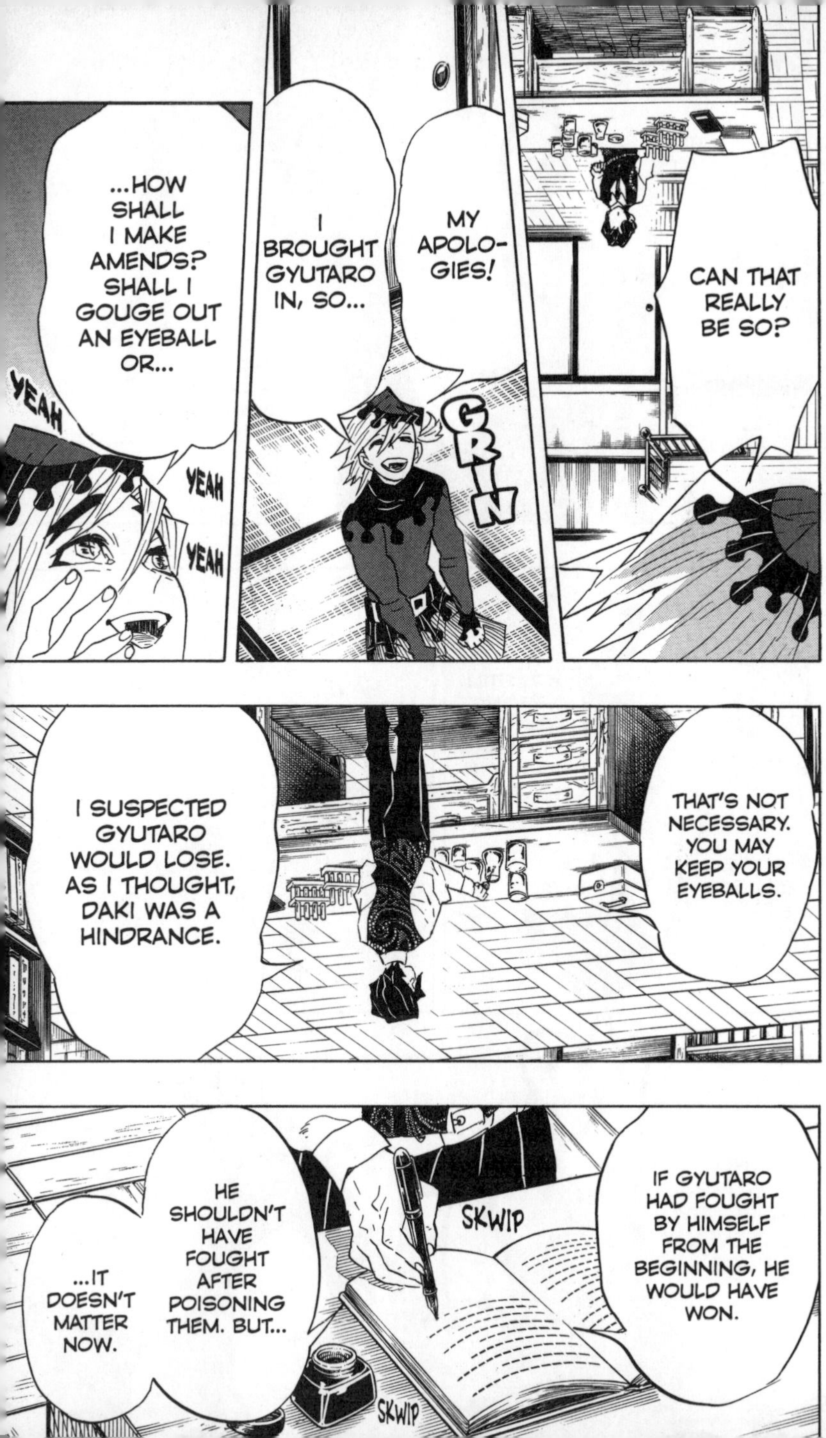
CAN THAT REALLY BE SO?
MY APOLOGIES!
I BROUGHT GYUTARO IN, SO...
GRIN
...HOW SHALL I MAKE AMENDS? SHALL I GOUGE OUT AN EYEBALL OR...
YEAH
YEAH
YEAH
THAT'S NOT NECESSARY. YOU MAY KEEP YOUR EYEBALLS.
I SUSPECTED GYUTARO WOULD LOSE. AS I THOUGHT, DAKI WAS A HINDRANCE.
IF GYUTARO HAD FOUGHT BY HIMSELF FROM THE BEGINNING, HE WOULD HAVE WON.
SKWIP
HE SHOULDN'T HAVE FOUGHT AFTER POISONING THEM. BUT...
...IT DOESN'T MATTER NOW.
SKWIP

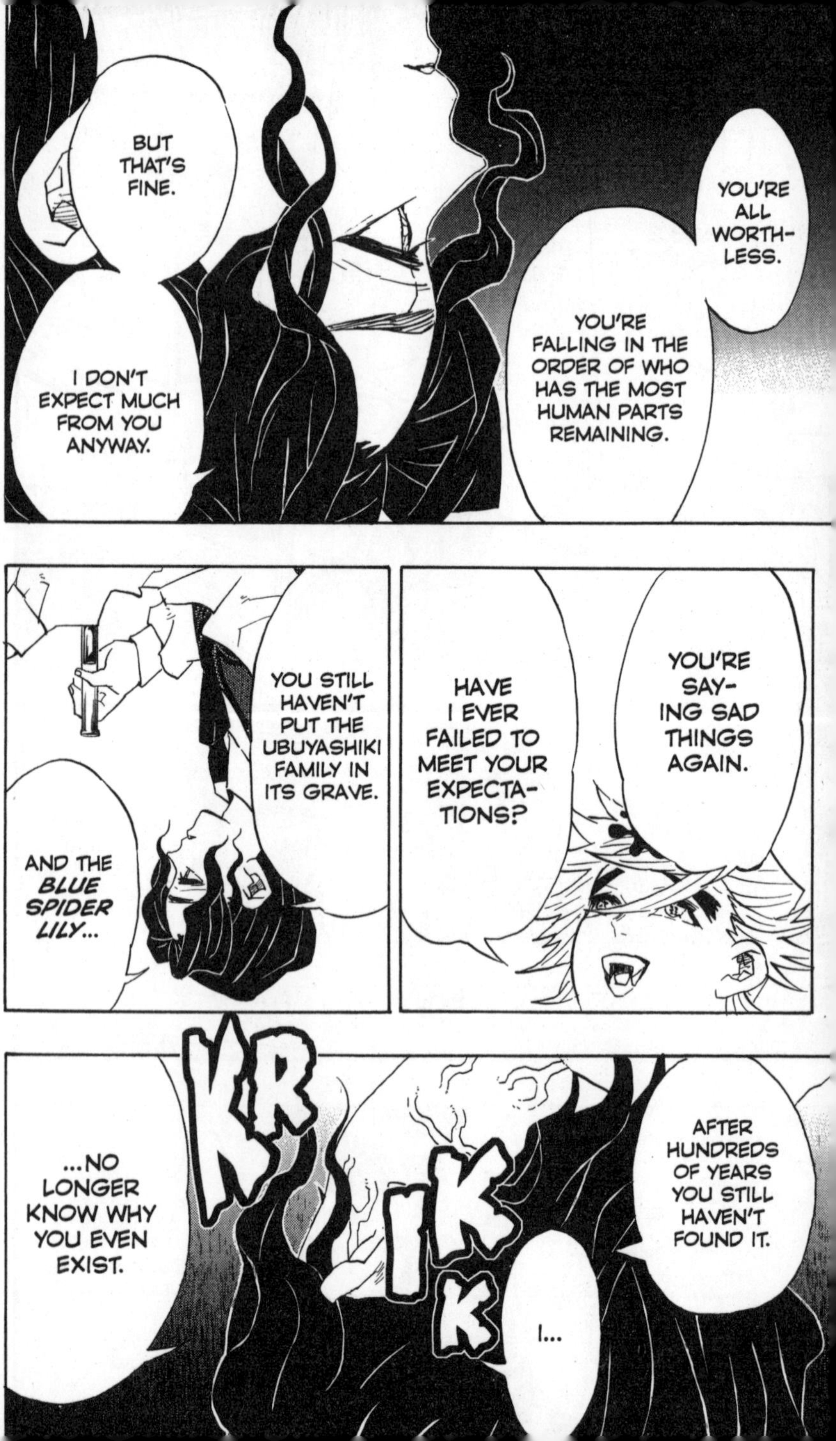
YOU'RE ALL WORTHLESS.
YOU'RE FALLING IN THE ORDER OF WHO HAS THE MOST HUMAN PARTS REMAINING.
BUT THAT'S FINE.
I DON'T EXPECT MUCH FROM YOU ANYWAY.
YOU'RE SAYING SAD THINGS AGAIN.
HAVE I EVER FAILED TO MEET YOUR EXPECTATIONS?
YOU STILL HAVEN'T PUT THE UBUYASHIKI FAMILY IN ITS GRAVE.
AND THE *BLUE SPIDER LILY*...
AFTER HUNDREDS OF YEARS YOU STILL HAVEN'T FOUND IT.
I...
KRIKK
...NO LONGER KNOW WHY YOU EVEN EXIST.

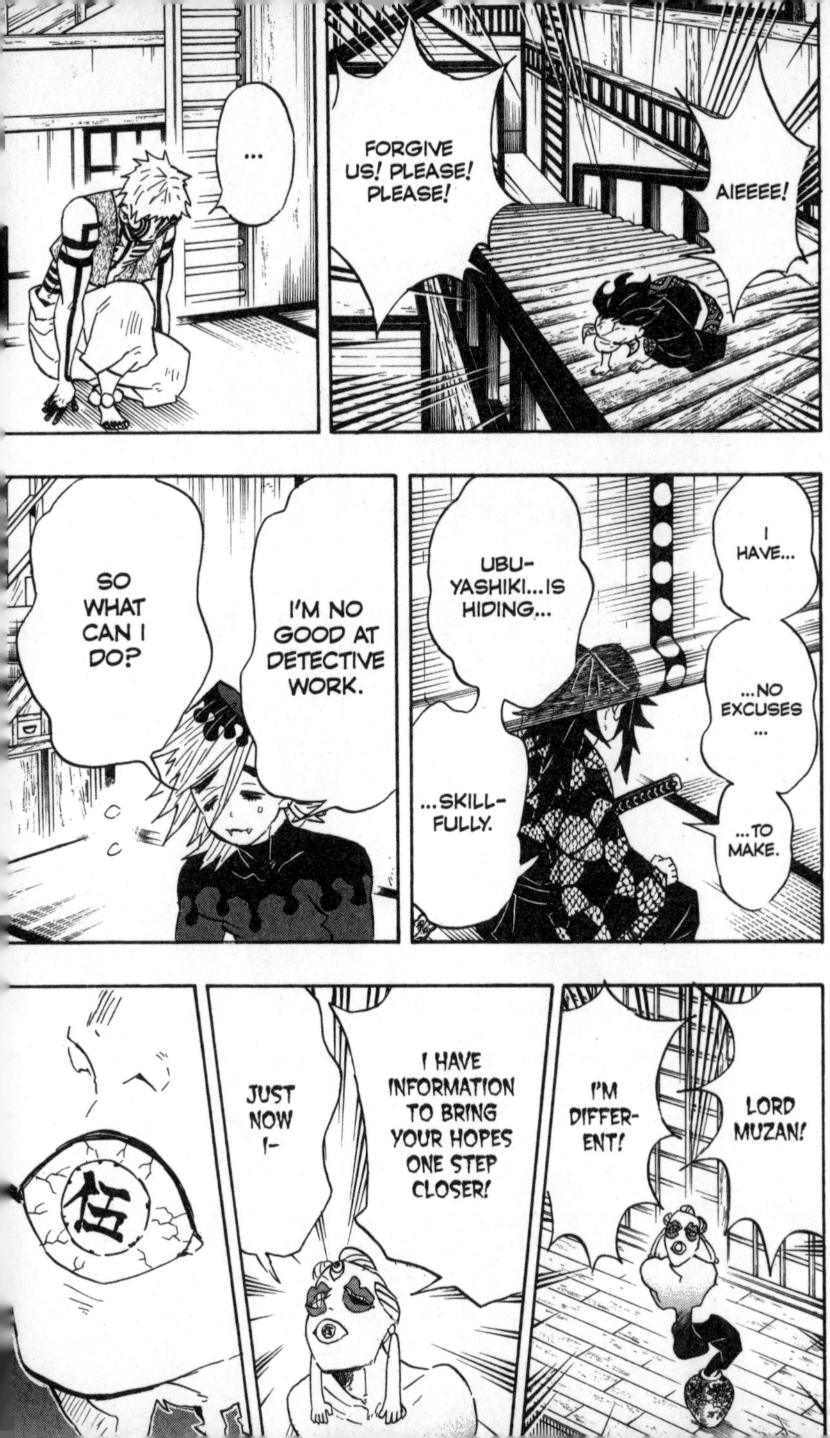
AIEEEE!
FORGIVE US! PLEASE! PLEASE!
...
I HAVE...
...NO EXCUSES ...
...TO MAKE.
UBU-YASHIKI...IS HIDING...
...SKILL-FULLY.
I'M NO GOOD AT DETECTIVE WORK.
SO WHAT CAN I DO?
LORD MUZAN!
I'M DIFFER-ENT!
I HAVE INFORMATION TO BRING YOUR HOPES ONE STEP CLOSER!
JUST NOW I-

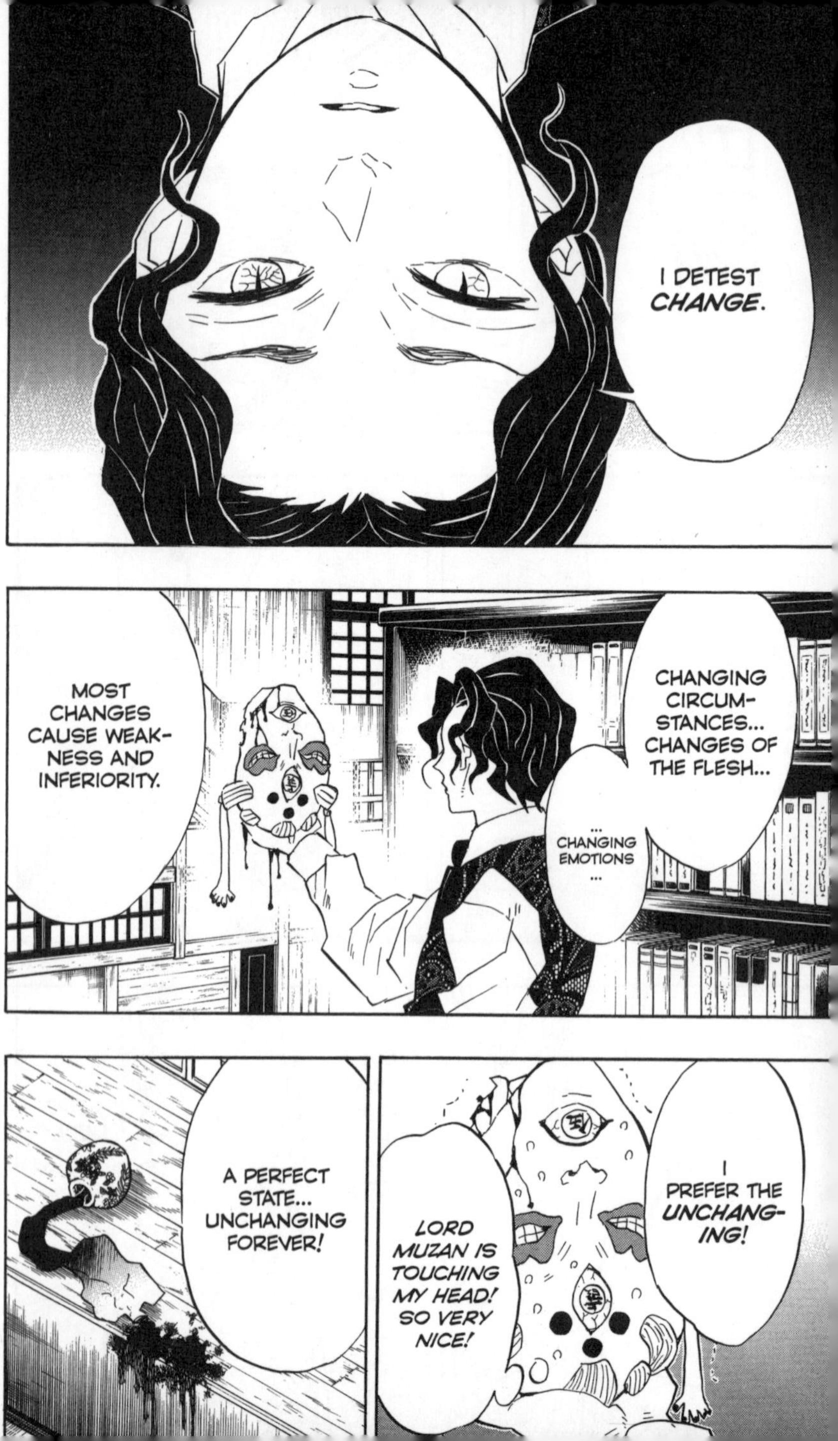
I DETEST *CHANGE*.
CHANGING CIRCUM-STANCES... CHANGES OF THE FLESH...
... CHANGING EMOTIONS ...
MOST CHANGES CAUSE WEAK-NESS AND INFERIORITY.
I PREFER THE *UNCHANG-ING*!
LORD MUZAN IS TOUCHING MY HEAD! SO VERY NICE!
A PERFECT STATE... UNCHANGING FOREVER!

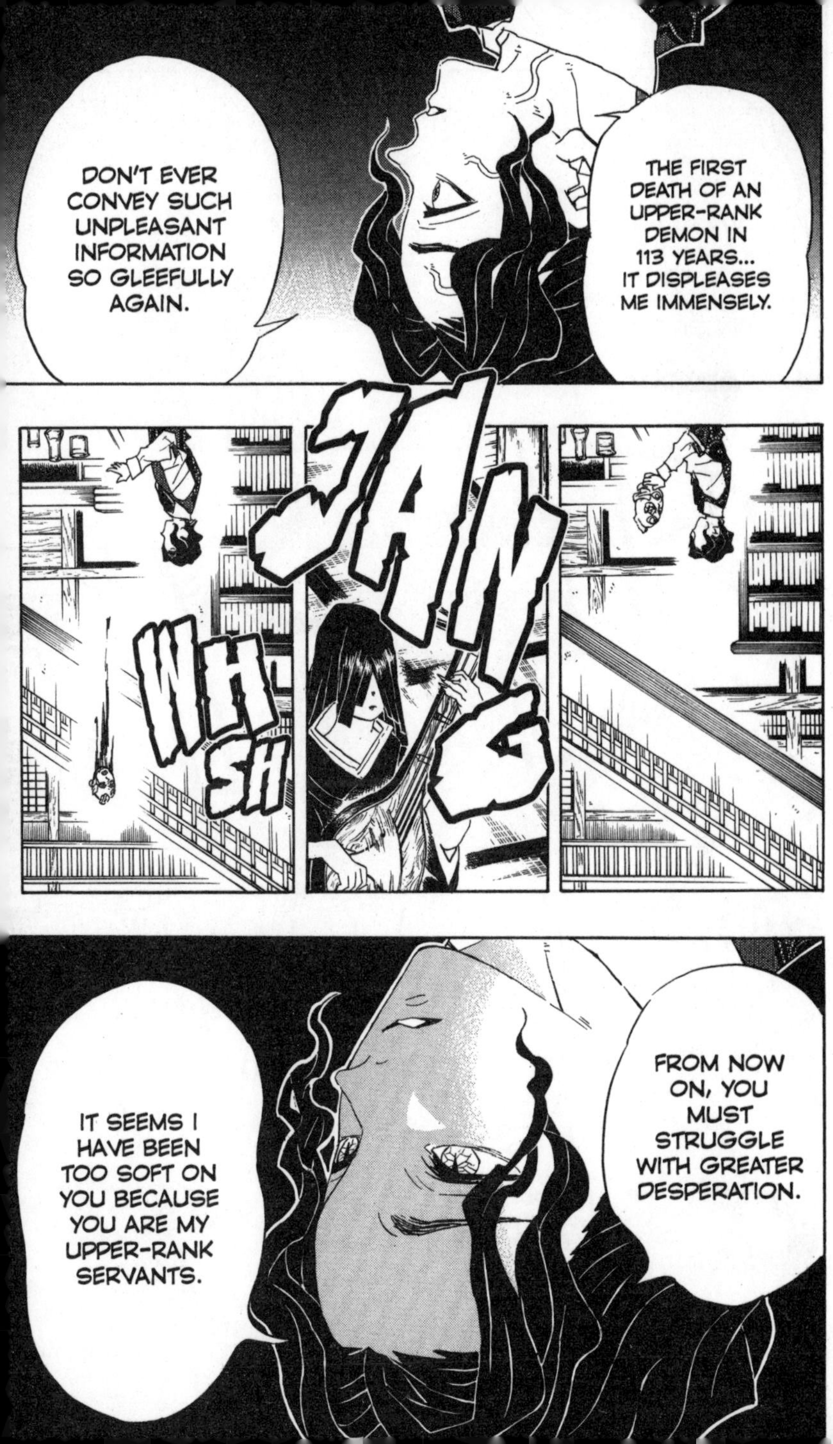
THE FIRST DEATH OF AN UPPER-RANK DEMON IN 113 YEARS... IT DISPLEASES ME IMMENSELY.
DON'T EVER CONVEY SUCH UNPLEASANT INFORMATION SO GLEEFULLY AGAIN.
JANG
WHSH
FROM NOW ON, YOU MUST STRUGGLE WITH GREATER DESPERATION.
IT SEEMS I HAVE BEEN TOO SOFT ON YOU BECAUSE YOU ARE MY UPPER-RANK SERVANTS.

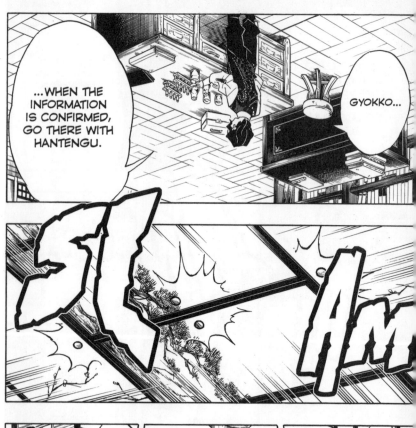

...WHEN THE INFORMATION IS CONFIRMED, GO THERE WITH HANTENGU.

GYOKKO...

SLAM

SHMP

LORD GYOKKO!

!

BUT I GOT THE INFORMATION!

OUTRAGEOUS! BUT THAT'S ALL RIGHT...

...!

TK

CHK

TWK

AS YOU WISH!

AIEEE!

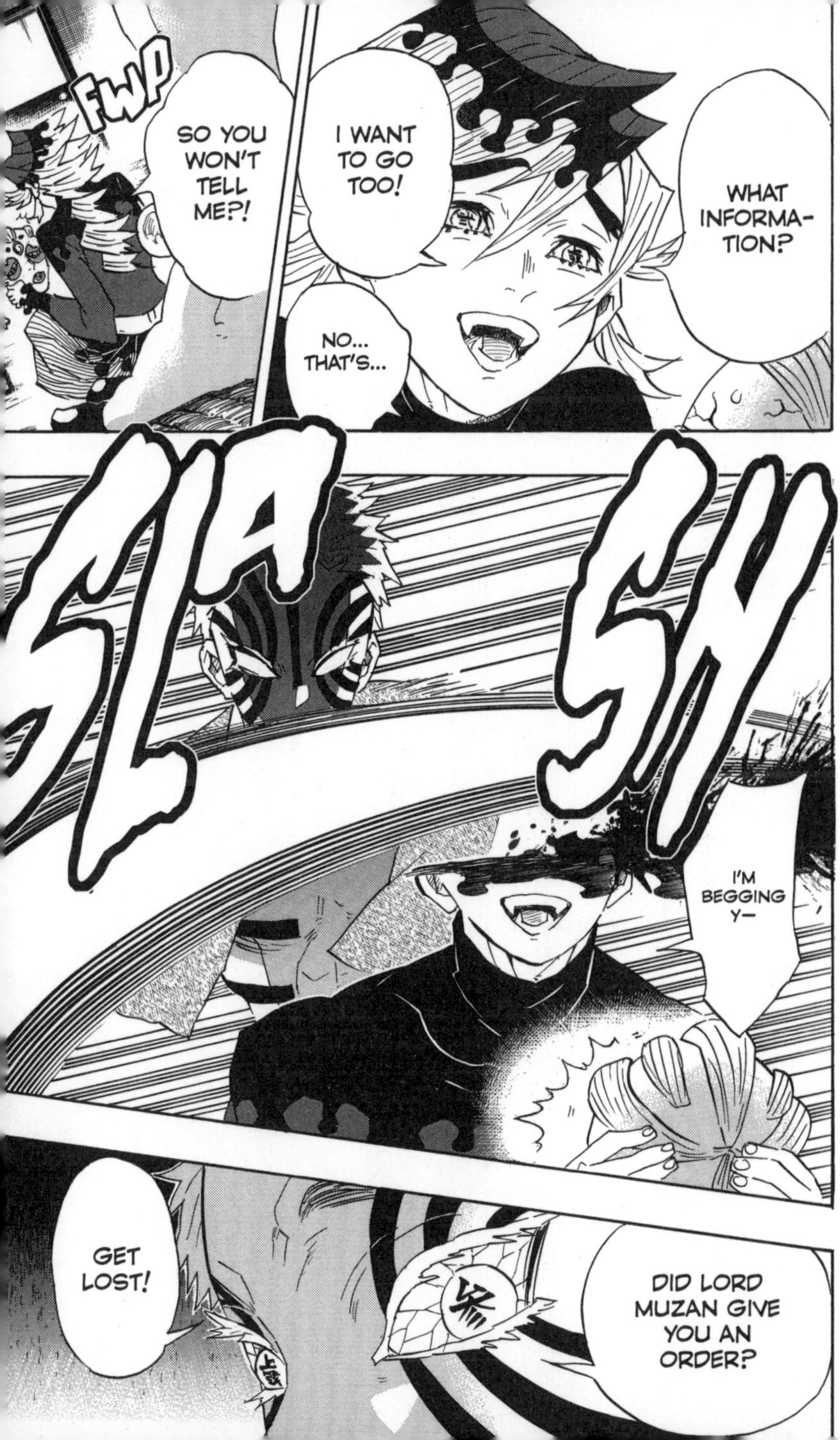
WHAT INFORMATION?
I WANT TO GO TOO!
NO... THAT'S...
FWP
SO YOU WON'T TELL ME?!
SLASH
I'M BEGGING Y—
DID LORD MUZAN GIVE YOU AN ORDER?
GET LOST!

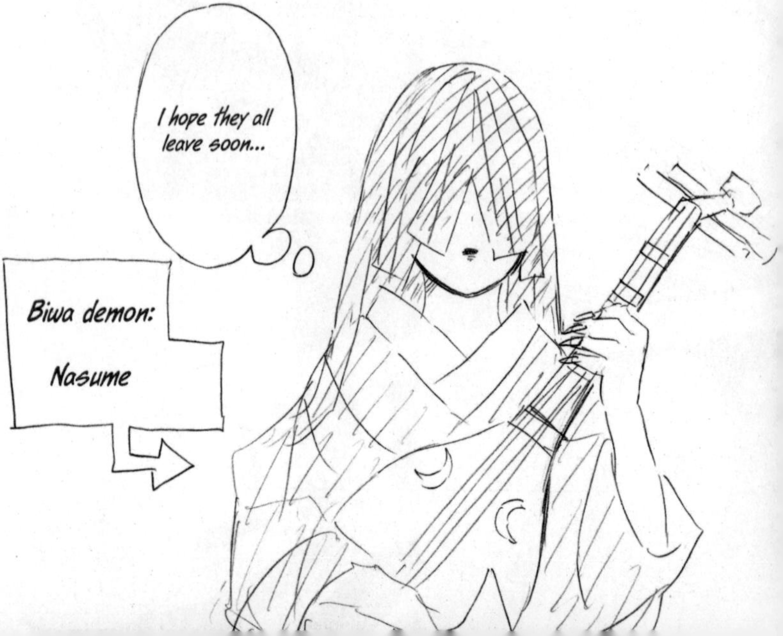
I hope they all leave soon...
Biwa demon:
Nasume

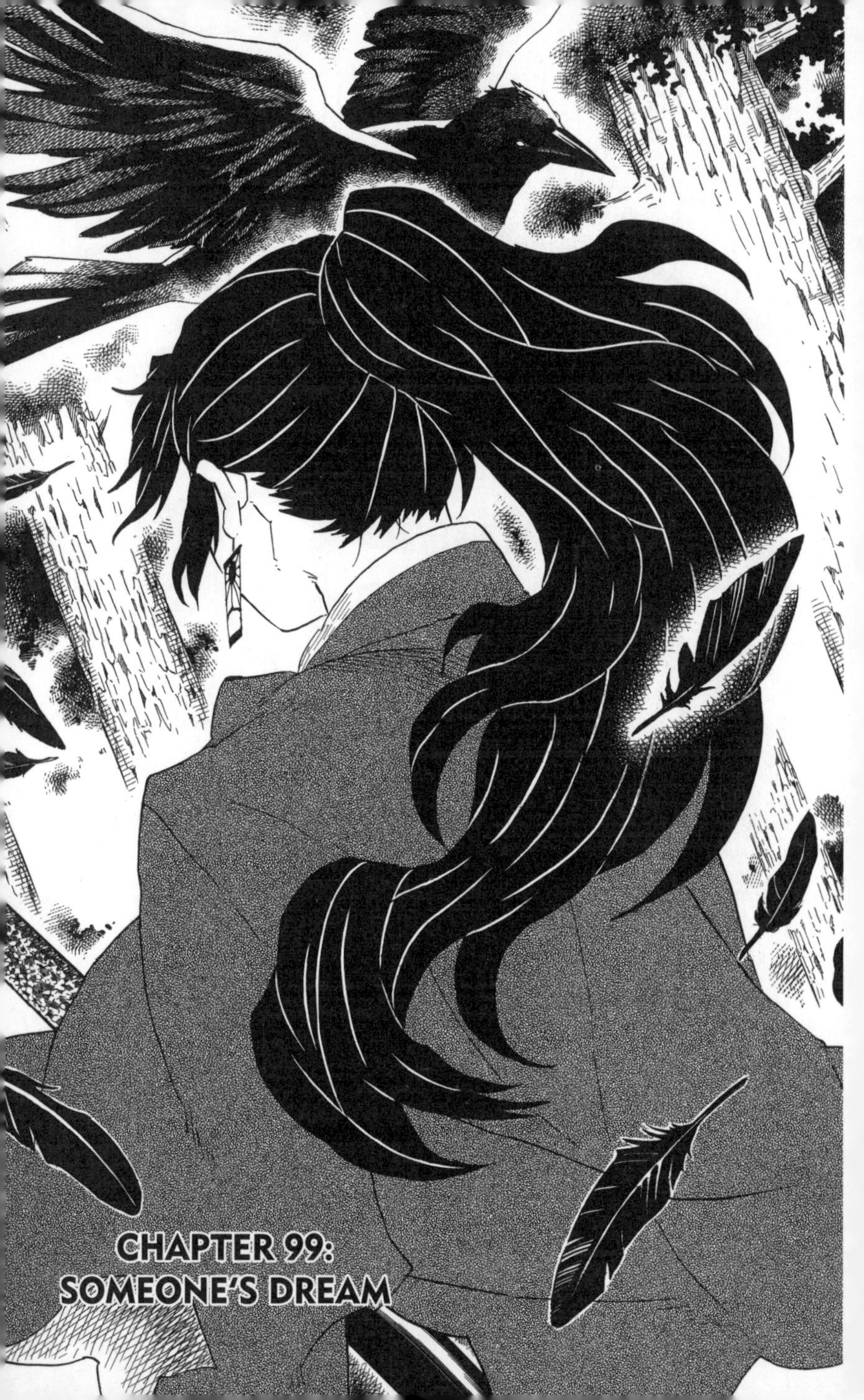
CHAPTER 99:
SOMEONE'S DREAM

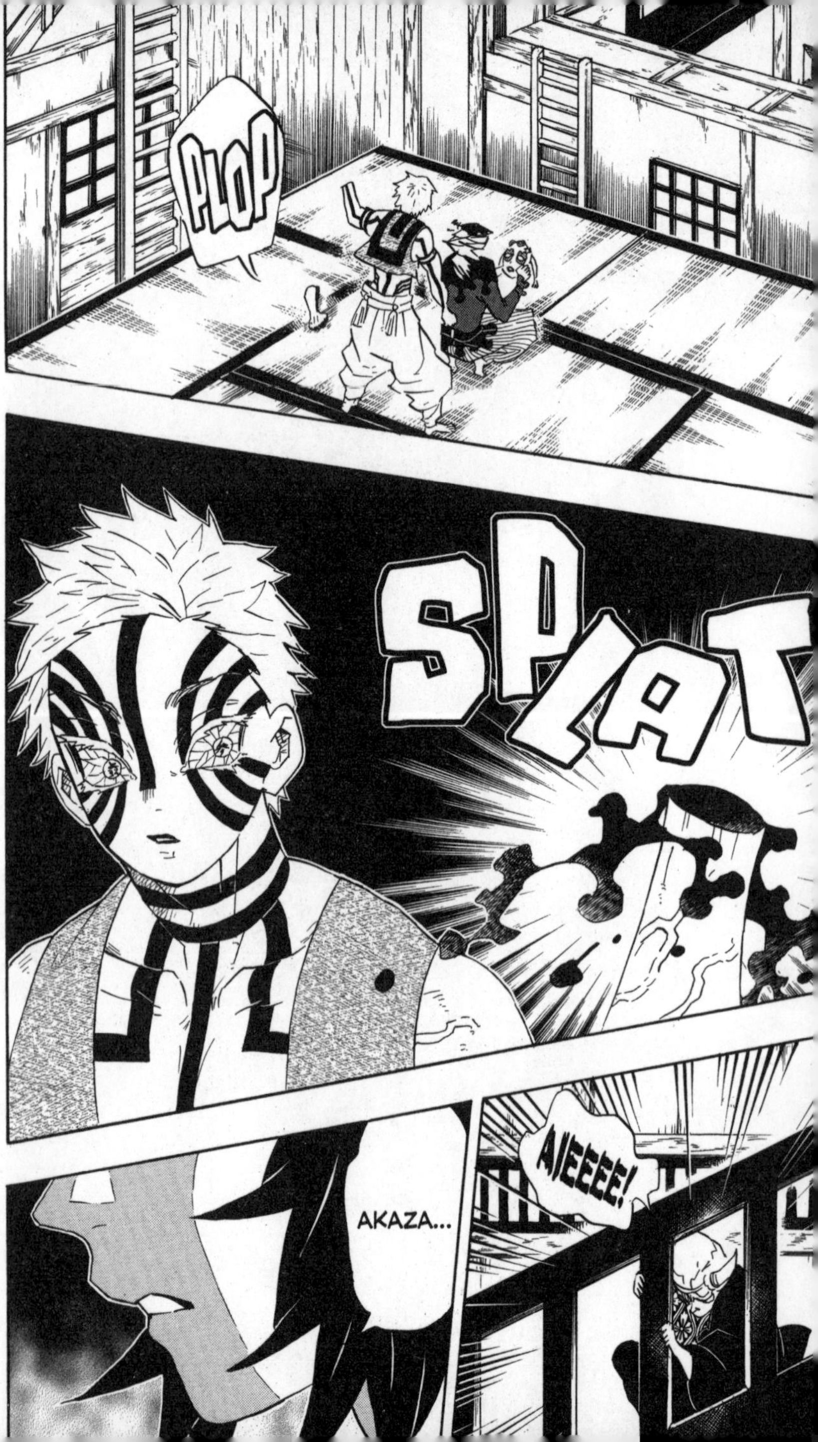
PLOP
SPLAT
AIEEEE!
AKAZA...

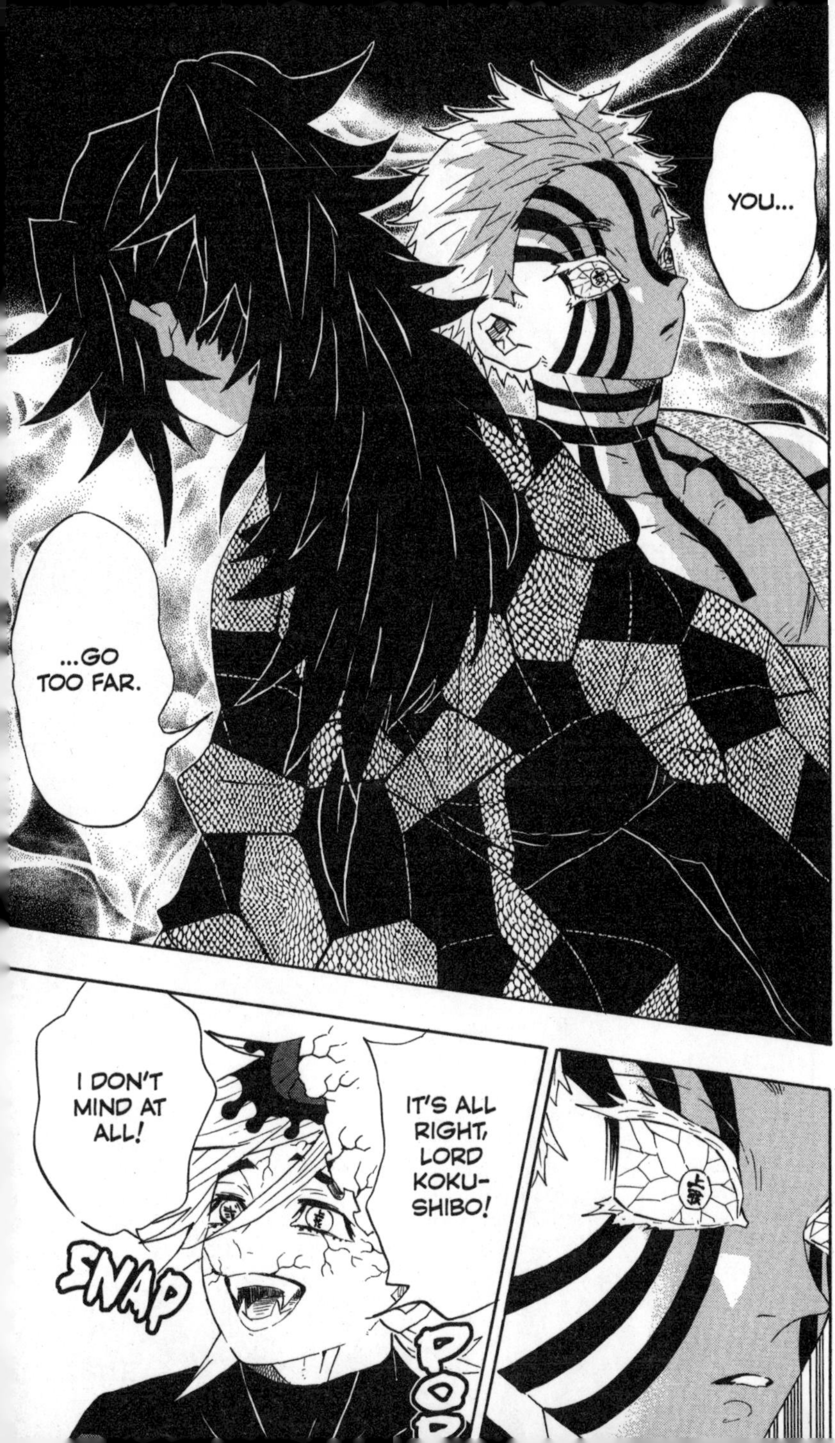
YOU...
...GO TOO FAR.
IT'S ALL RIGHT, LORD KOKU-SHIBO!
I DON'T MIND AT ALL!
SNAP

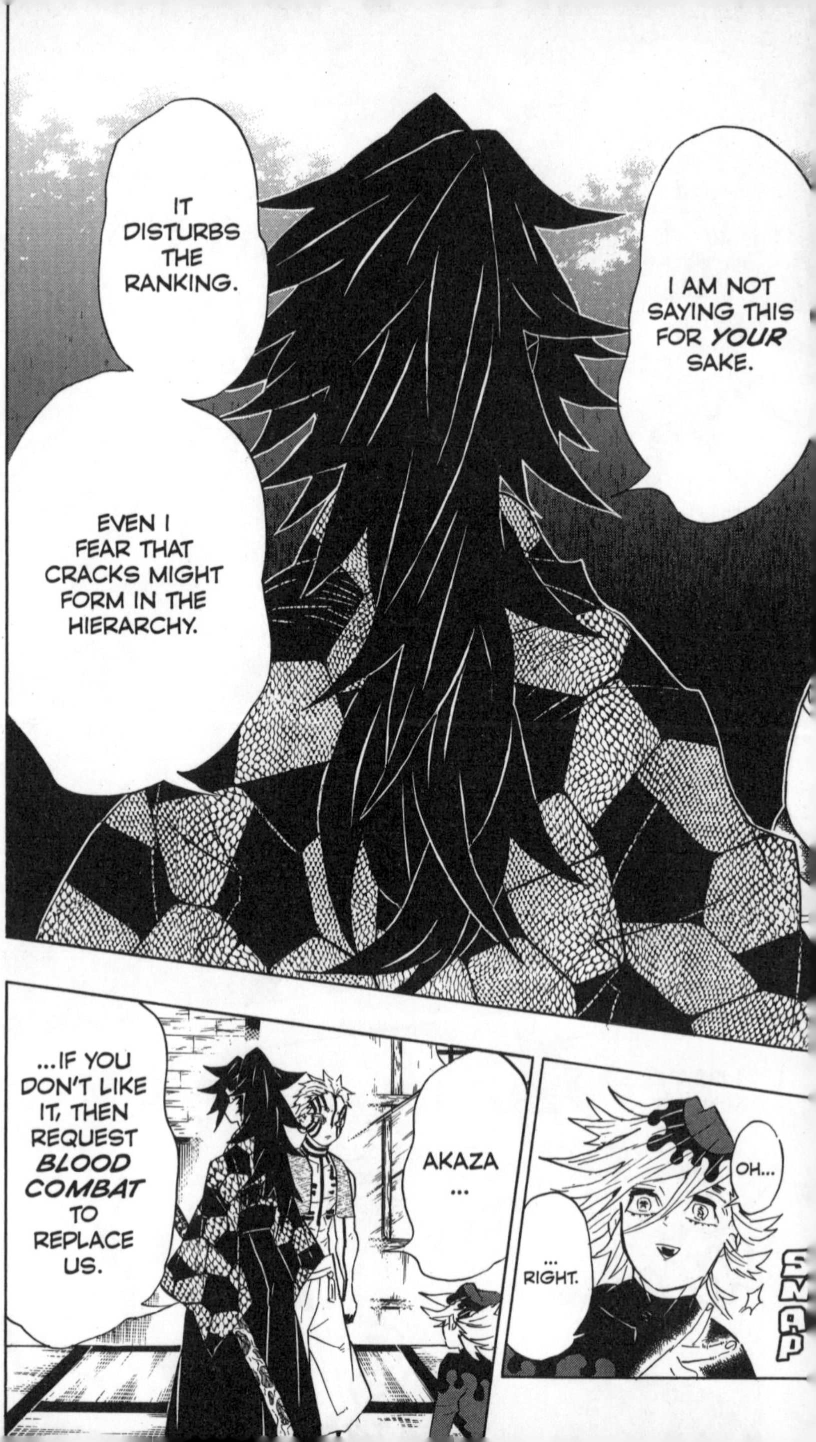
I AM NOT SAYING THIS FOR *YOUR* SAKE.
IT DISTURBS THE RANKING.
EVEN I FEAR THAT CRACKS MIGHT FORM IN THE HIERARCHY.
OH...
... RIGHT.
SNAP
AKAZA ...
...IF YOU DON'T LIKE IT, THEN REQUEST ***BLOOD COMBAT*** TO REPLACE US.

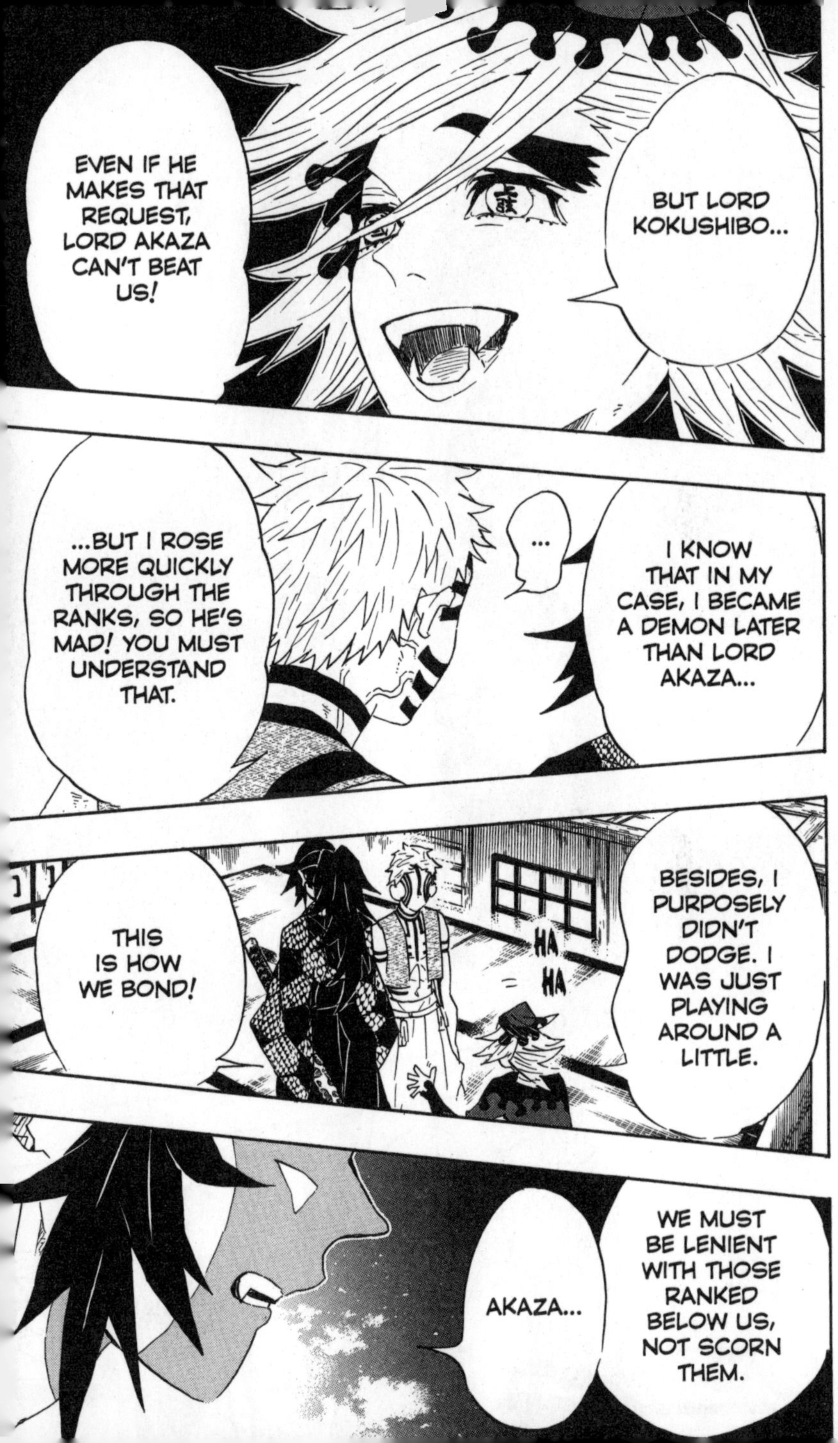
BUT LORD KOKUSHIBO...
EVEN IF HE MAKES THAT REQUEST, LORD AKAZA CAN'T BEAT US!
I KNOW THAT IN MY CASE, I BECAME A DEMON LATER THAN LORD AKAZA...
...
...BUT I ROSE MORE QUICKLY THROUGH THE RANKS, SO HE'S MAD! YOU MUST UNDERSTAND THAT.
BESIDES, I PURPOSELY DIDN'T DODGE. I WAS JUST PLAYING AROUND A LITTLE.
HA HA
THIS IS HOW WE BOND!
WE MUST BE LENIENT WITH THOSE RANKED BELOW US, NOT SCORN THEM.
AKAZA...

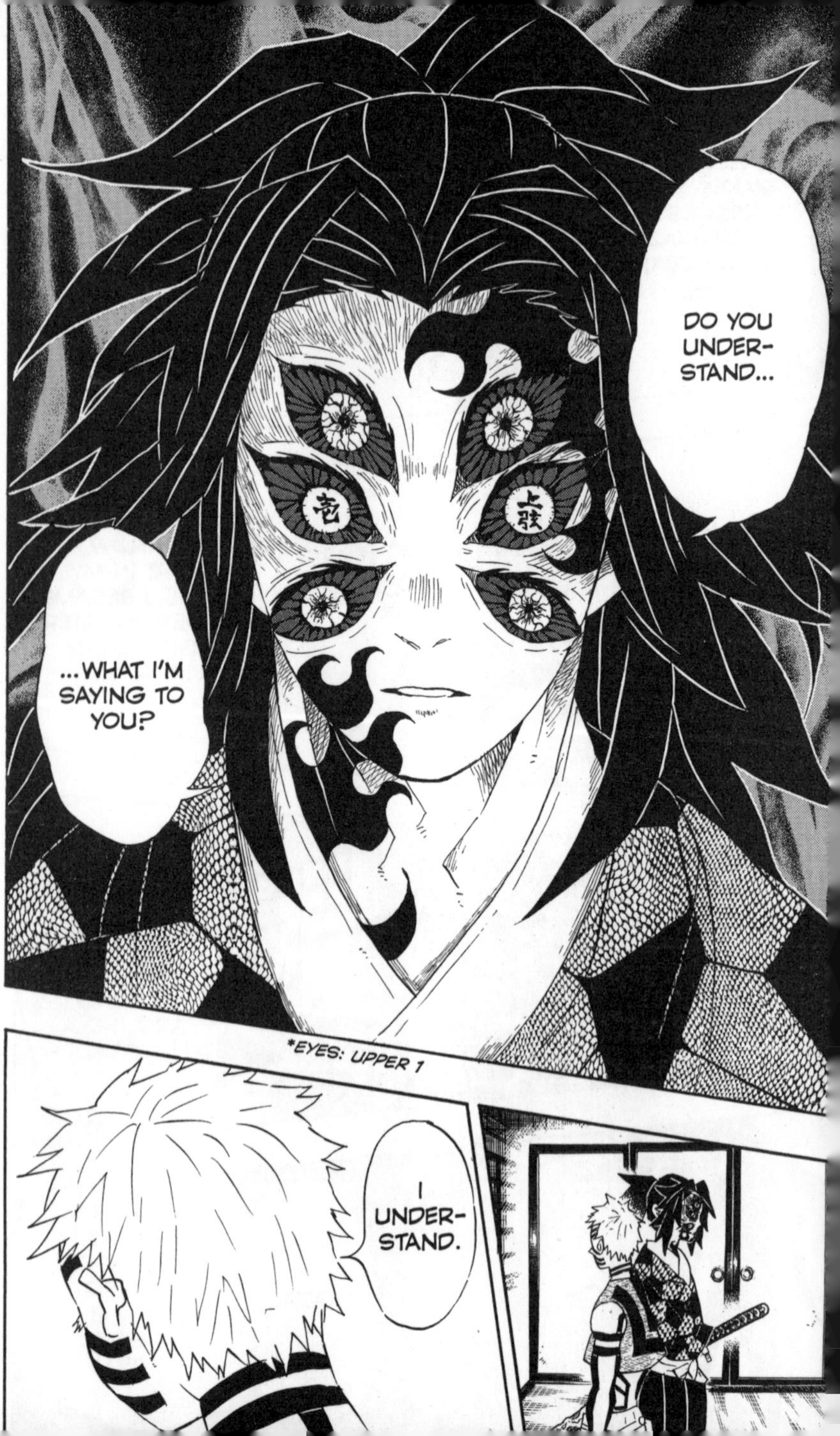
DO YOU UNDER-STAND...
上弦
壱
...WHAT I'M SAYING TO YOU?
*EYES: UPPER 1
I UNDER-STAND.

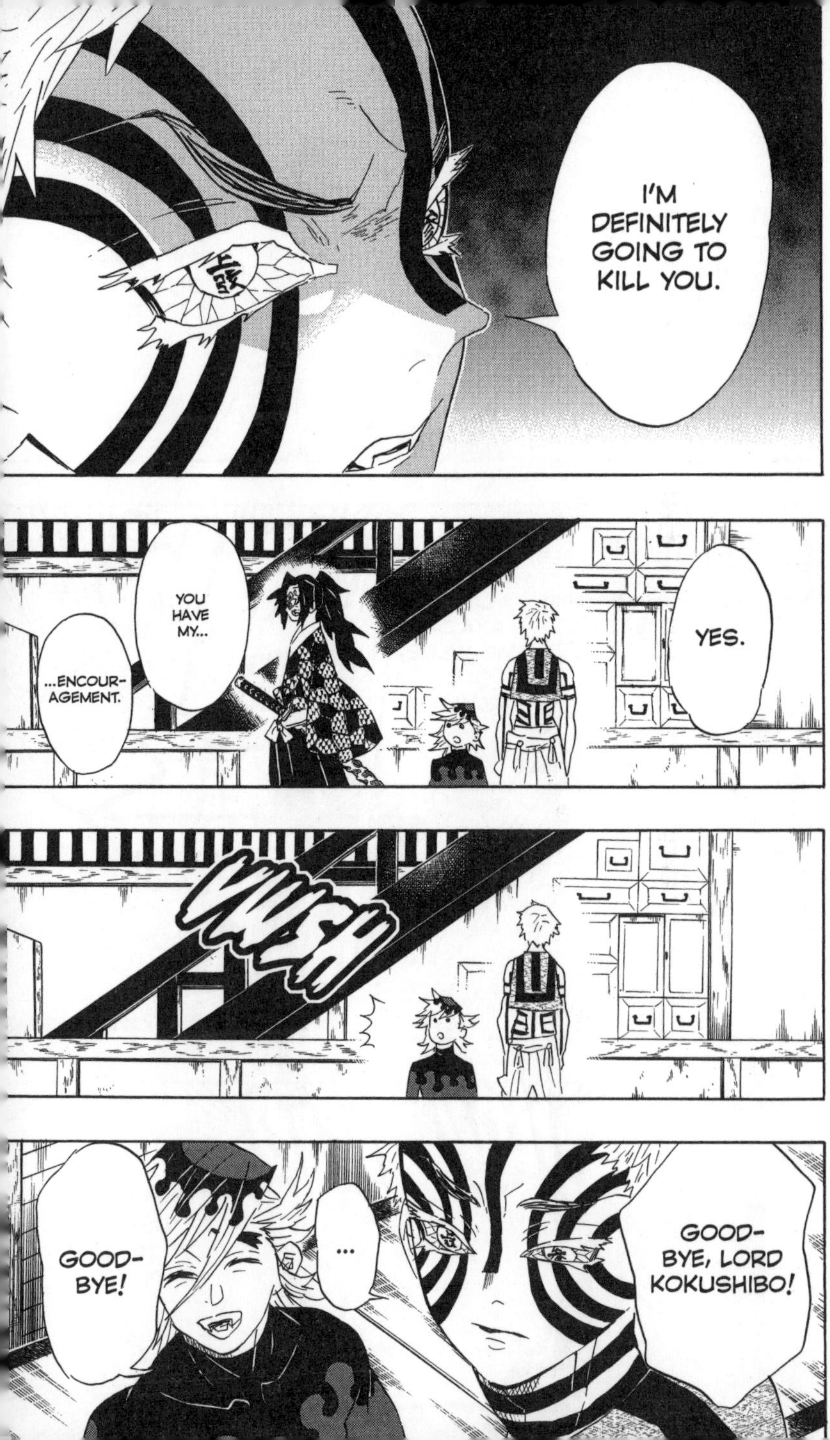
I'M DEFINITELY GOING TO KILL YOU.
YES.
YOU HAVE MY...
...ENCOURAGEMENT.
VWSH
GOOD-BYE, LORD KOKUSHIBO!
...
GOOD-BYE!

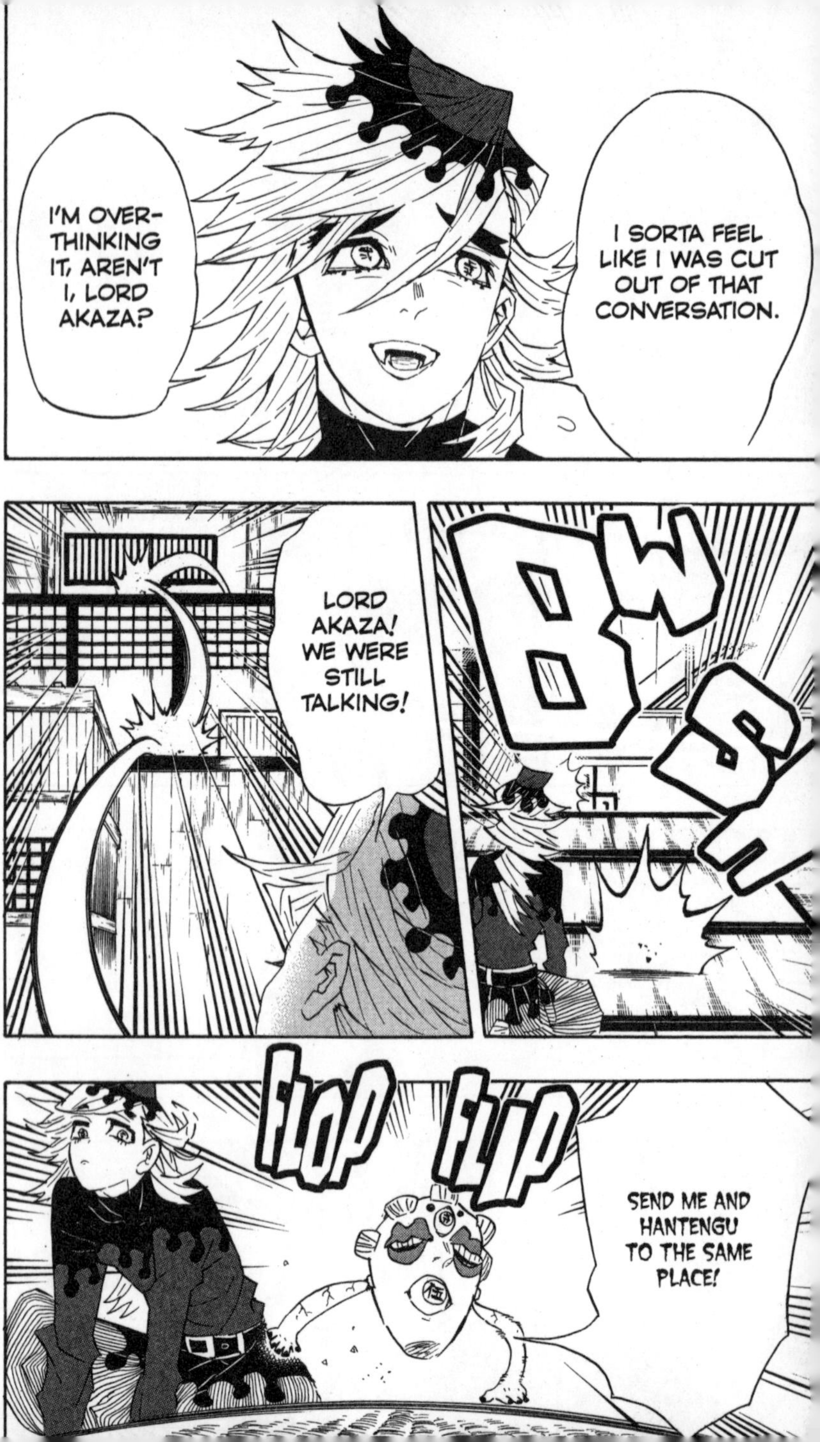
I SORTA FEEL LIKE I WAS CUT OUT OF THAT CONVERSATION.
I'M OVER-THINKING IT, AREN'T I, LORD AKAZA?
BWSH
LORD AKAZA! WE WERE STILL TALKING!
SEND ME AND HANTENGU TO THE SAME PLACE!
FLOP FLIP

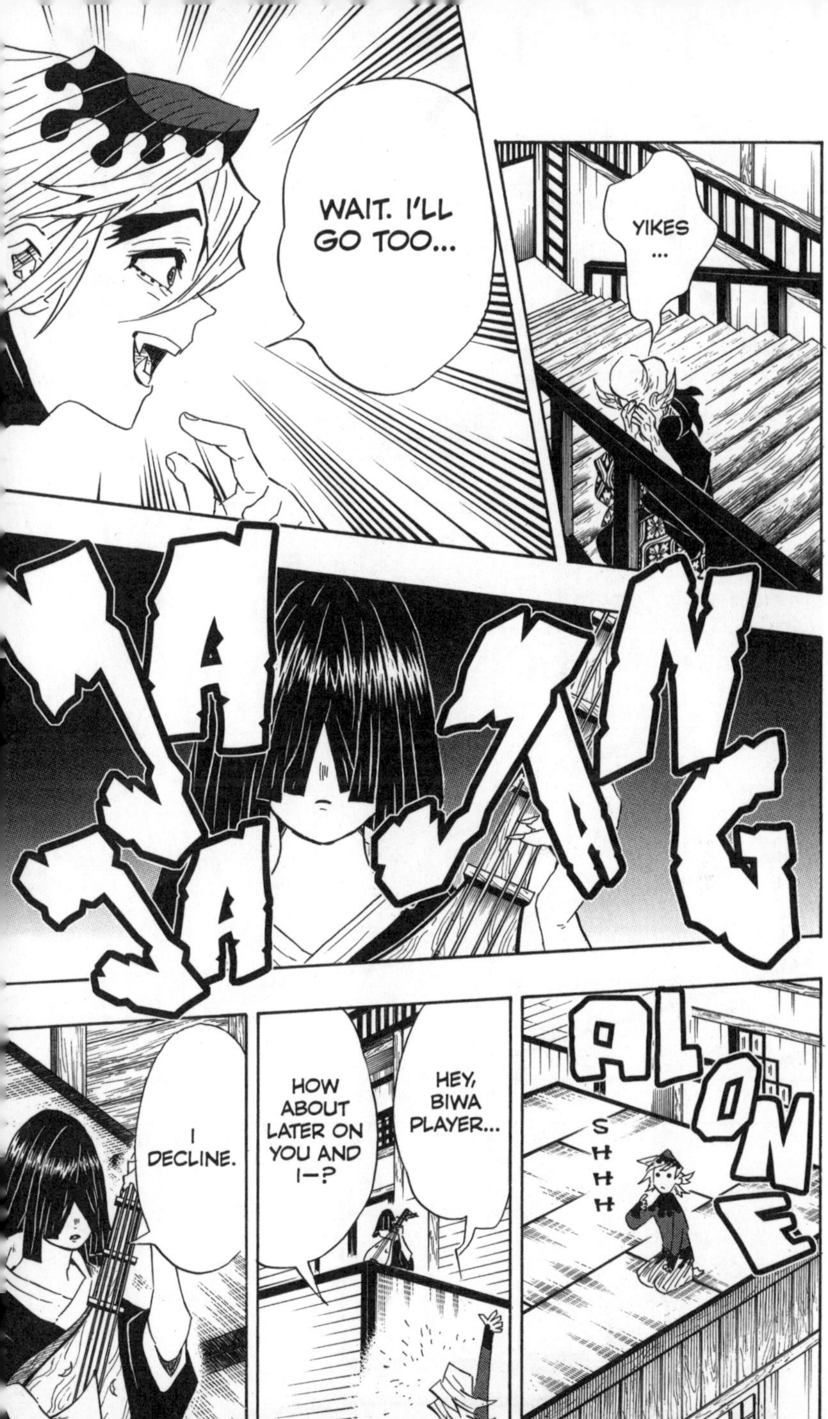
YIKES ...
WAIT. I'LL GO TOO...
ALONE
SHHH
HEY, BIWA PLAYER...
HOW ABOUT LATER ON YOU AND I—?
I DECLINE.

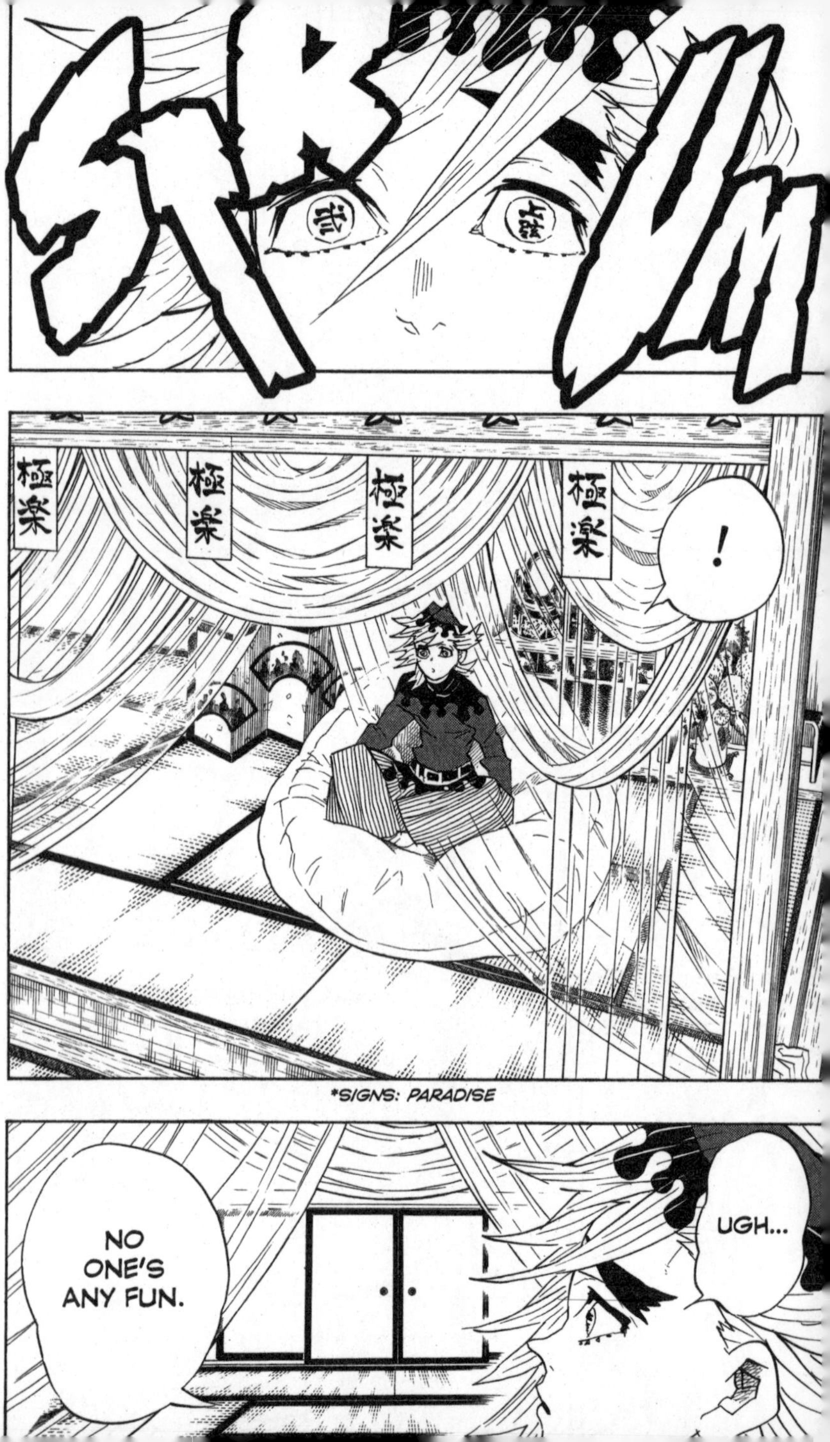
!
極楽
極楽
極楽
極楽
*SIGNS: PARADISE
UGH...
NO ONE'S ANY FUN.

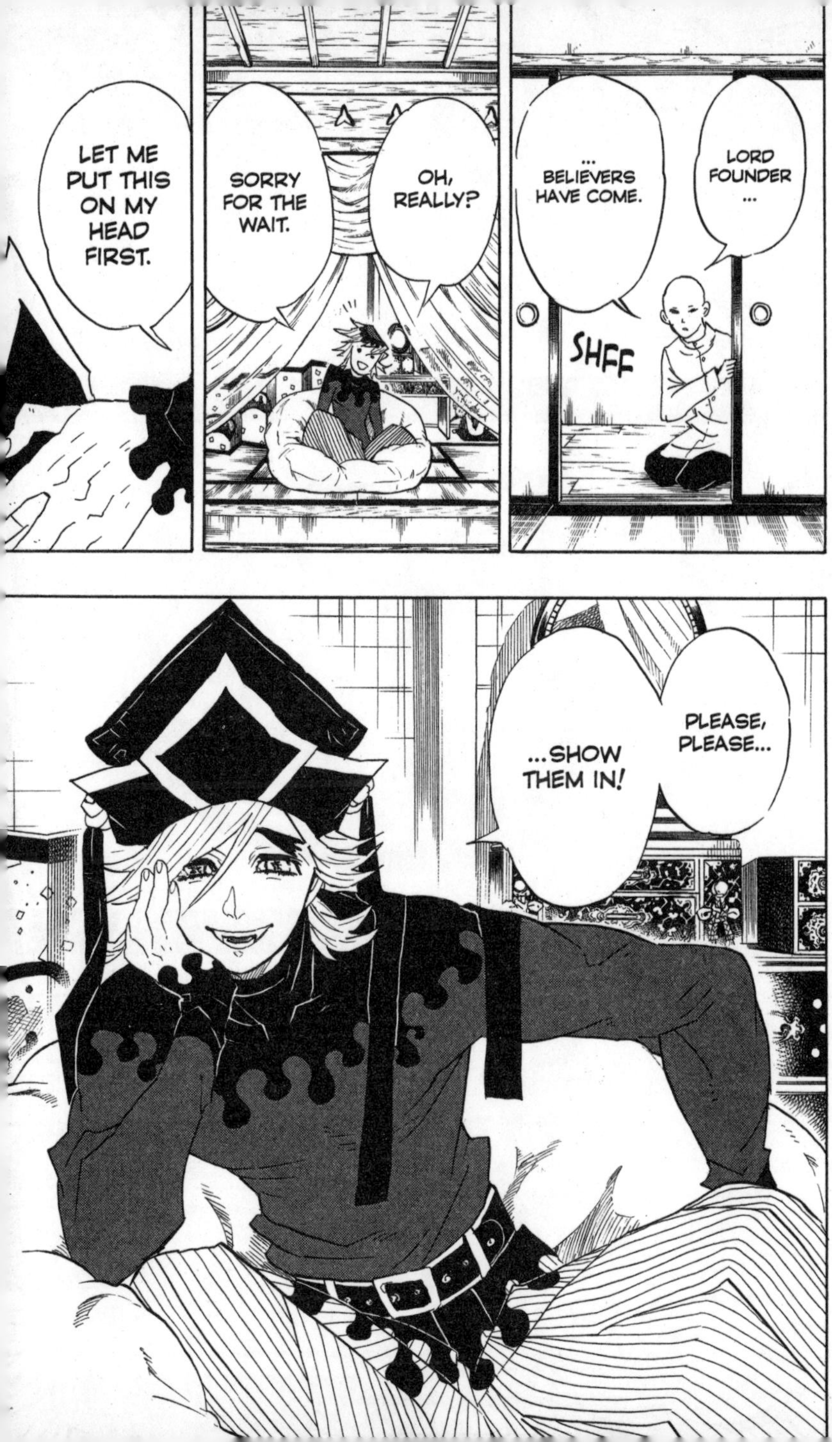
LORD FOUNDER ...
... BELIEVERS HAVE COME.
SHFF
OH, REALLY?
SORRY FOR THE WAIT.
LET ME PUT THIS ON MY HEAD FIRST.
PLEASE, PLEASE...
...SHOW THEM IN!

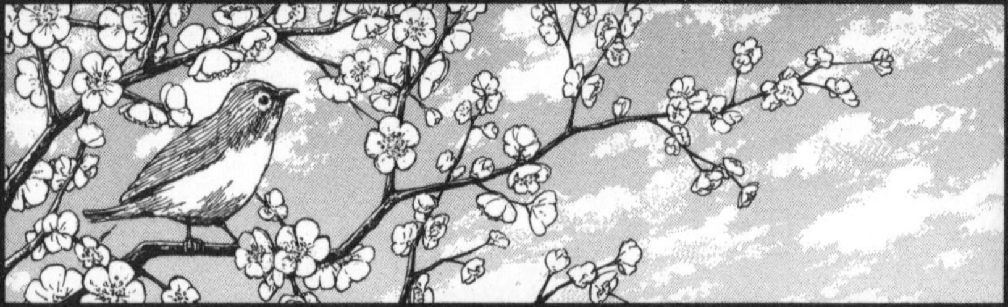

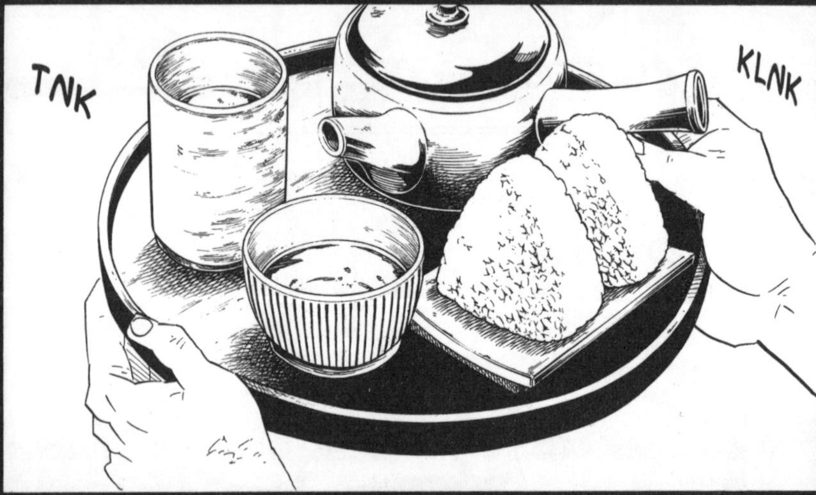
KLNK
TNK

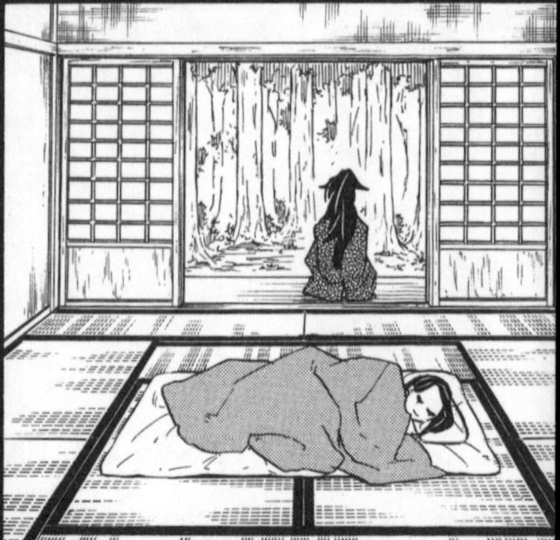

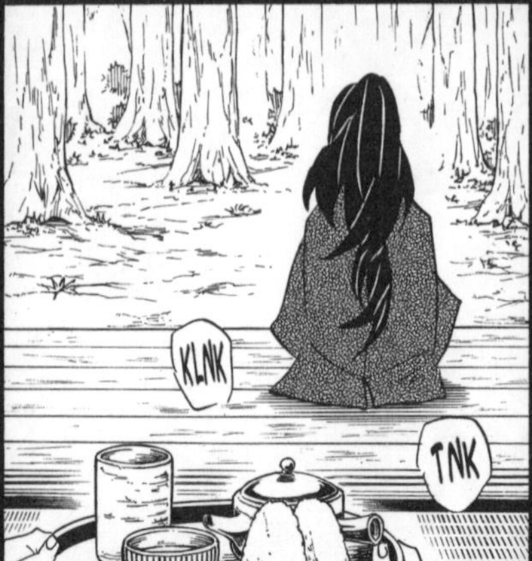
KLNK
TNK

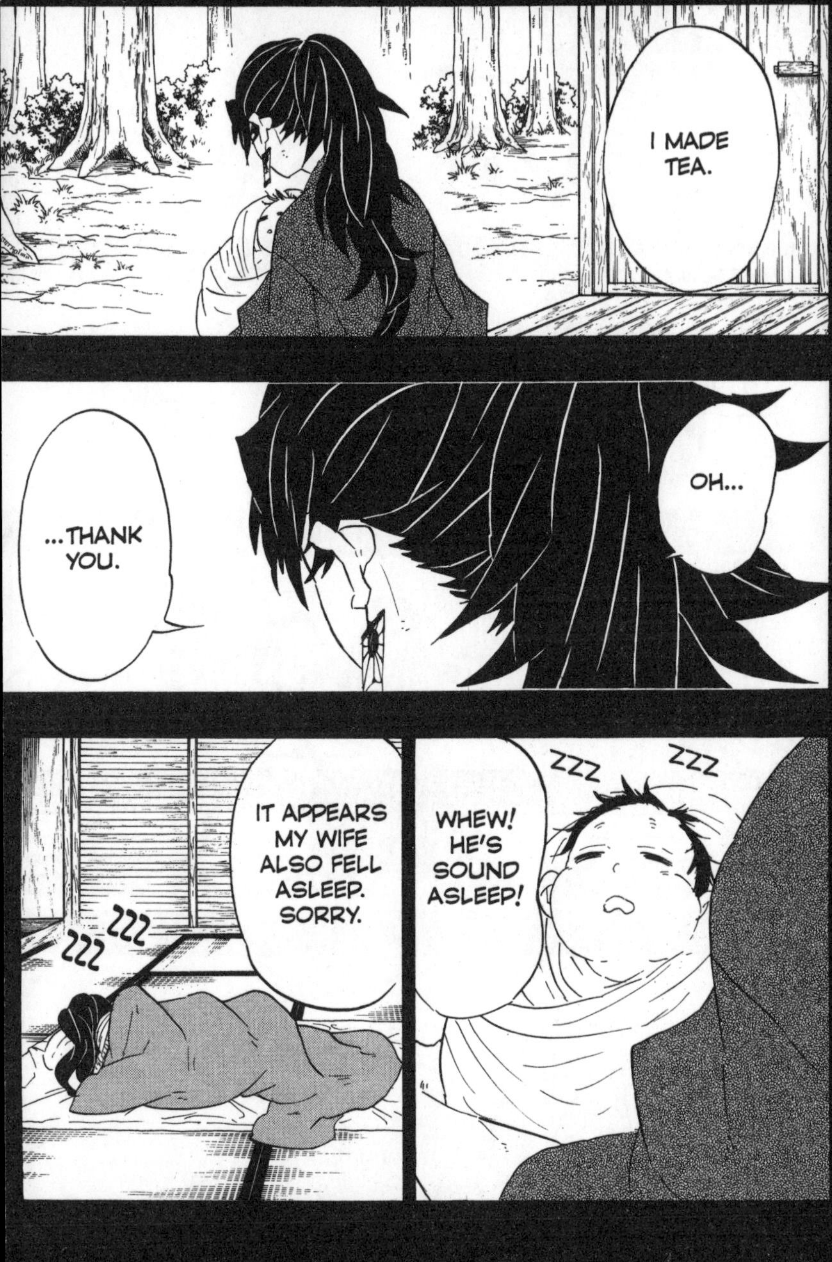
I MADE TEA.
OH...
...THANK YOU.
ZZZ
ZZZ
WHEW! HE'S SOUND ASLEEP!
IT APPEARS MY WIFE ALSO FELL ASLEEP. SORRY.
ZZZ
ZZZ

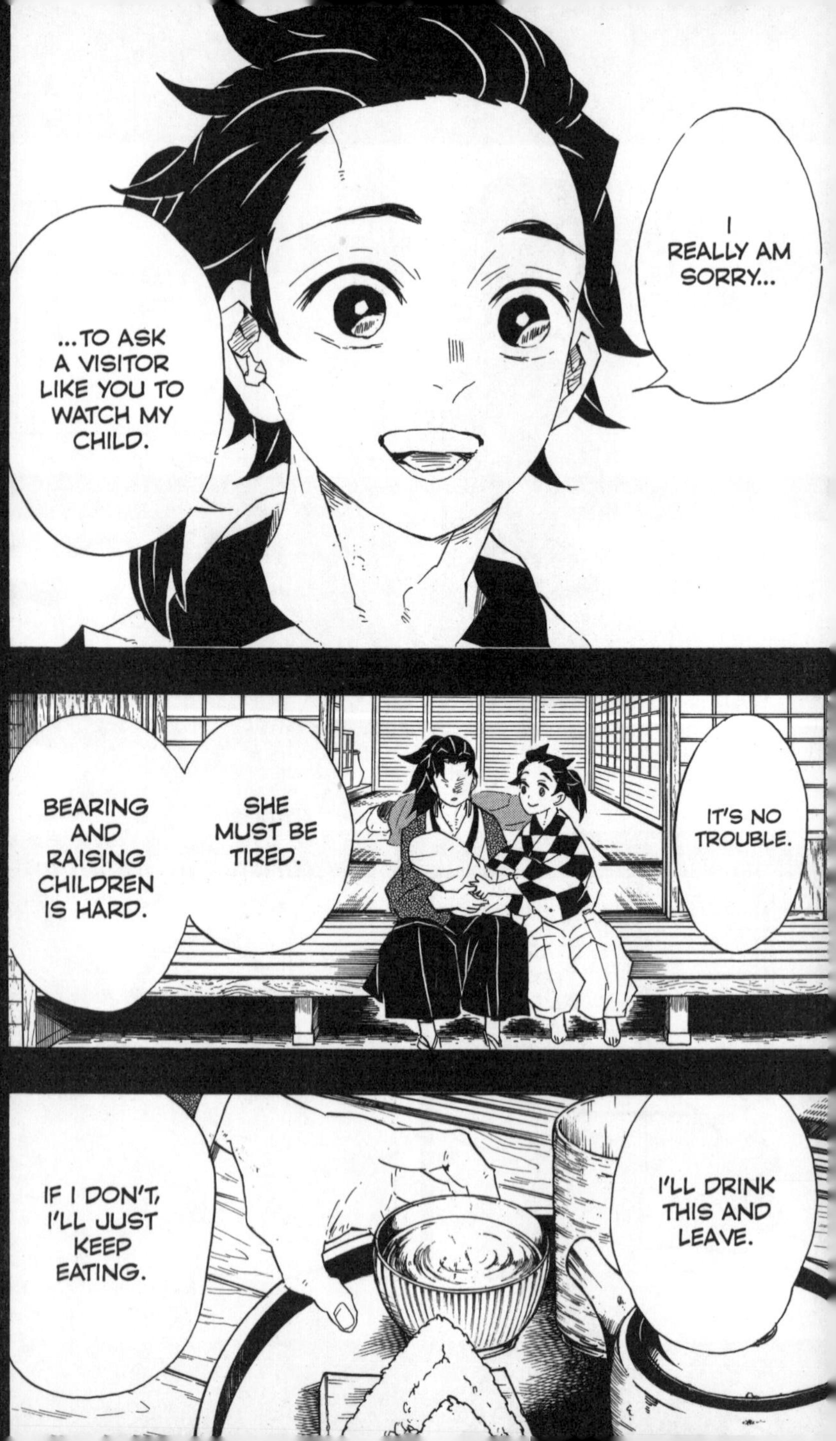
I REALLY AM SORRY...
...TO ASK A VISITOR LIKE YOU TO WATCH MY CHILD.
IT'S NO TROUBLE.
SHE MUST BE TIRED.
BEARING AND RAISING CHILDREN IS HARD.
I'LL DRINK THIS AND LEAVE.
IF I DON'T, I'LL JUST KEEP EATING.

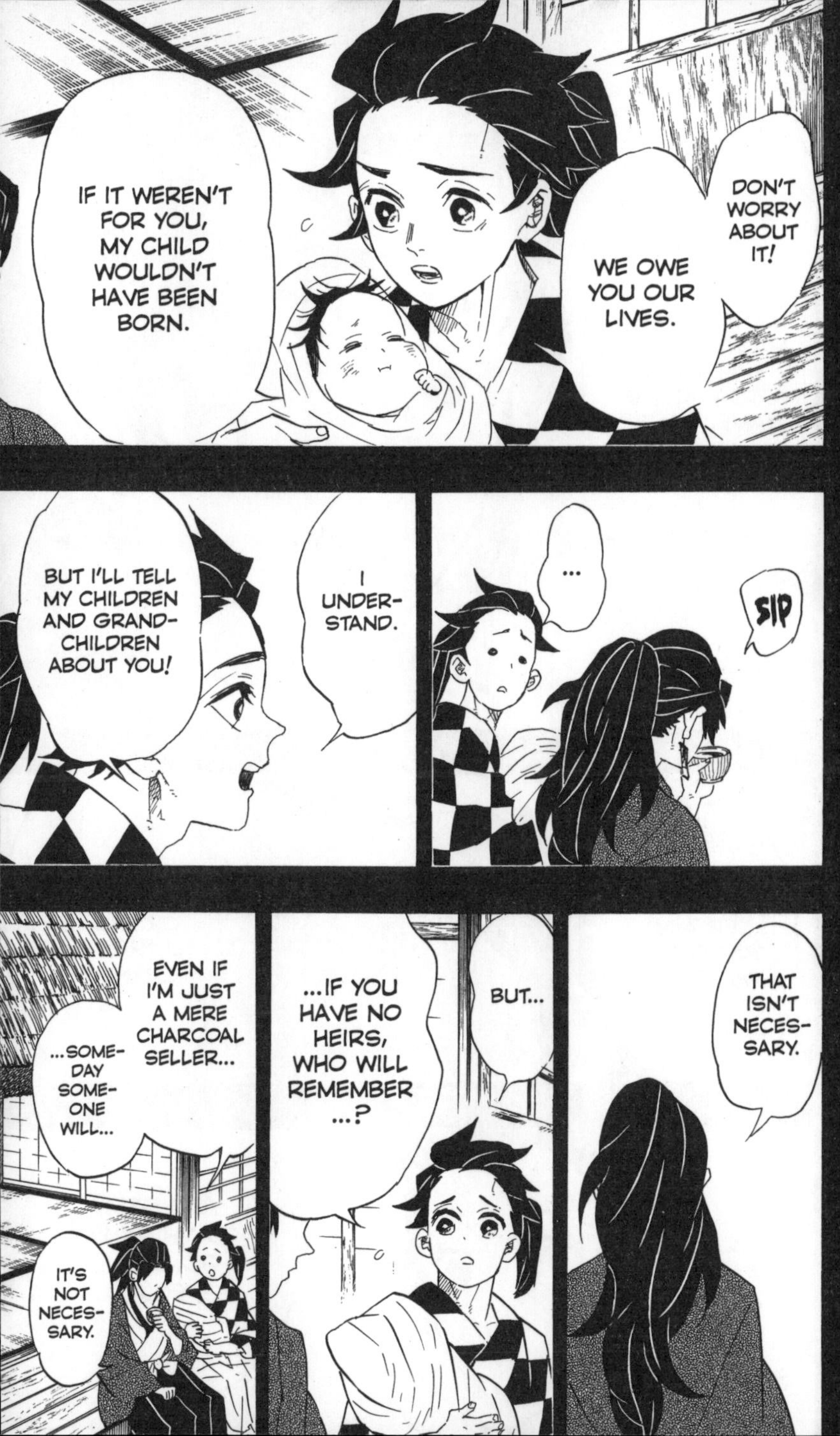
DON'T WORRY ABOUT IT!
WE OWE YOU OUR LIVES.
IF IT WEREN'T FOR YOU, MY CHILD WOULDN'T HAVE BEEN BORN.
...
SIP
I UNDERSTAND.
BUT I'LL TELL MY CHILDREN AND GRANDCHILDREN ABOUT YOU!
THAT ISN'T NECESSARY.
BUT...
...IF YOU HAVE NO HEIRS, WHO WILL REMEMBER...?
EVEN IF I'M JUST A MERE CHARCOAL SELLER...
...SOMEDAY SOMEONE WILL...
IT'S NOT NECESSARY.

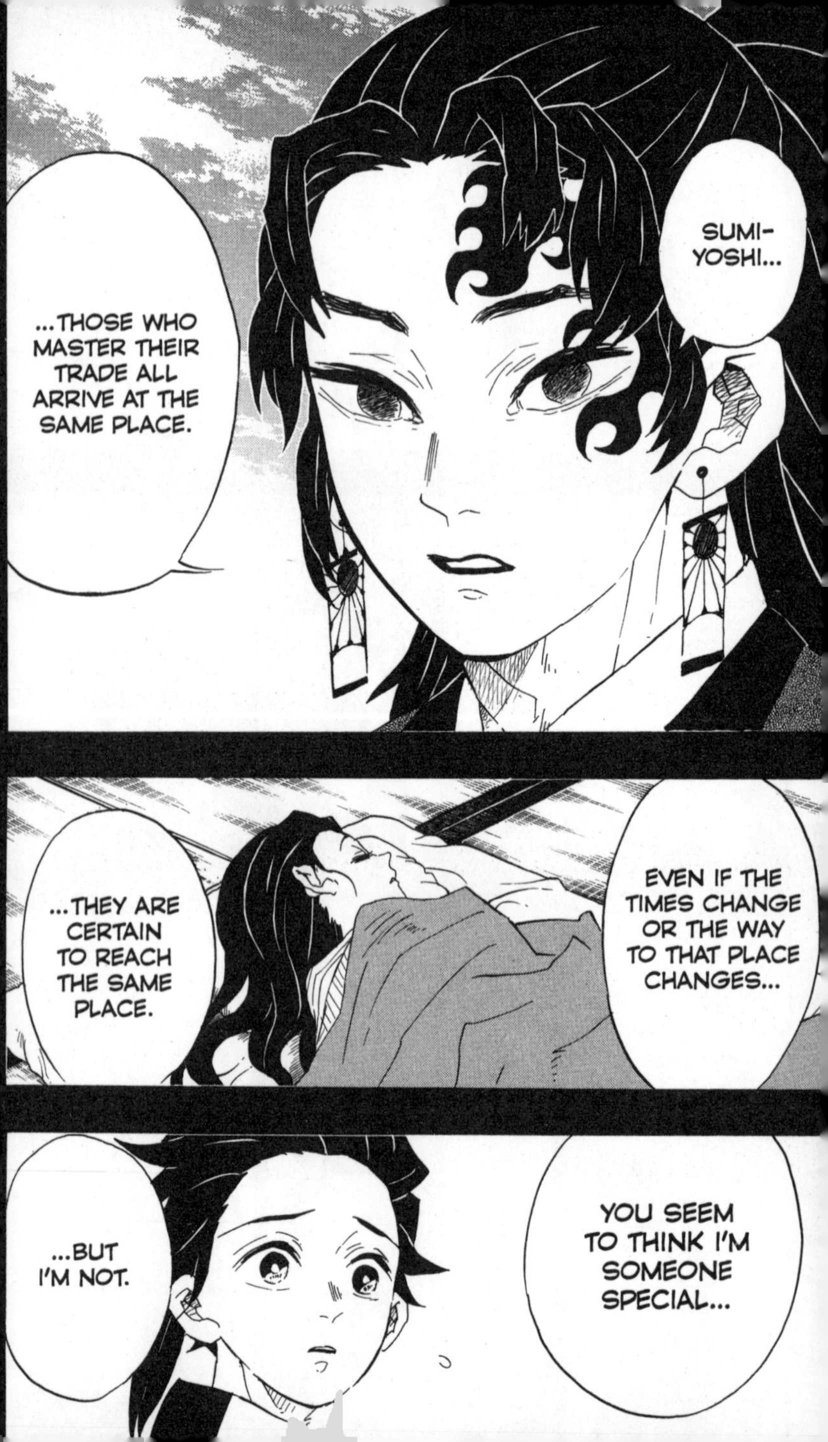
SUMI-YOSHI...
...THOSE WHO MASTER THEIR TRADE ALL ARRIVE AT THE SAME PLACE.
EVEN IF THE TIMES CHANGE OR THE WAY TO THAT PLACE CHANGES...
...THEY ARE CERTAIN TO REACH THE SAME PLACE.
YOU SEEM TO THINK I'M SOMEONE SPECIAL...
...BUT I'M NOT.

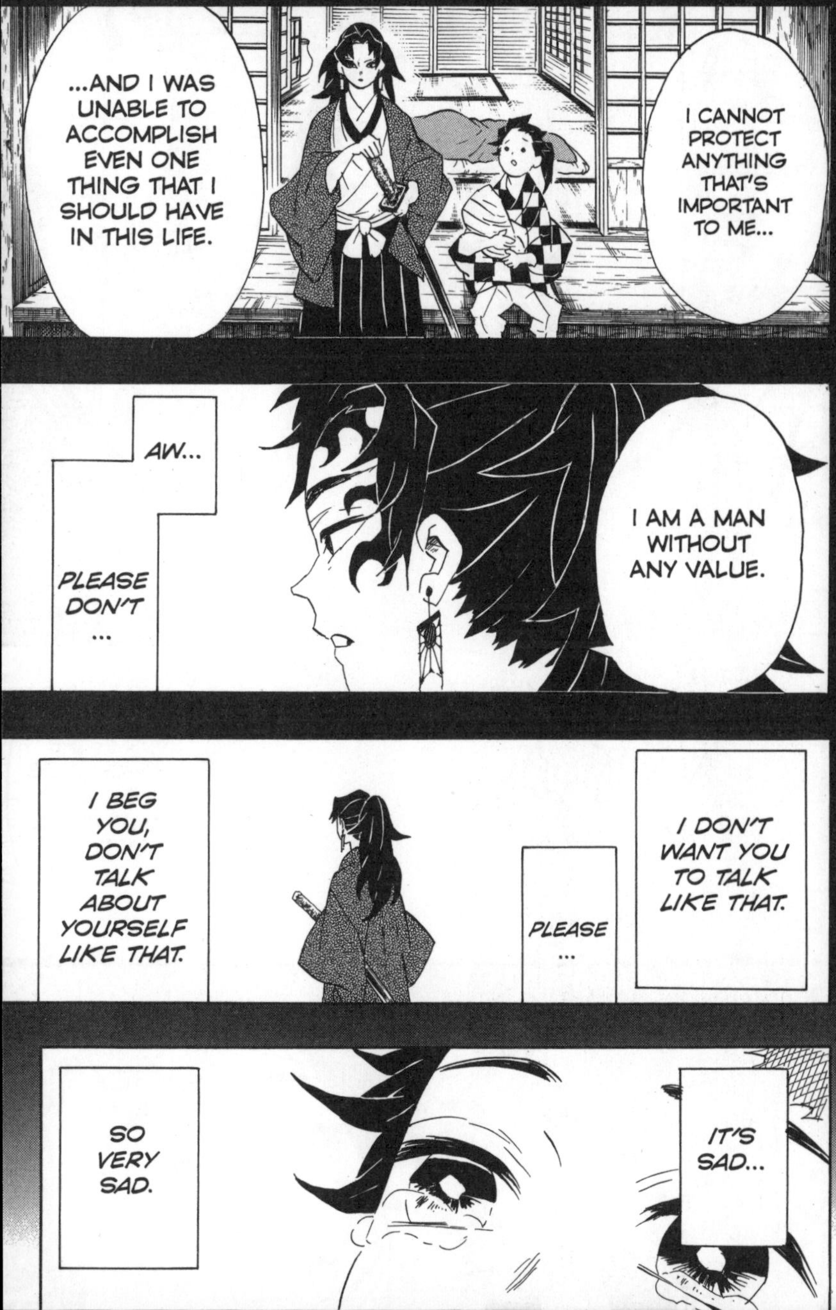
I CANNOT PROTECT ANYTHING THAT'S IMPORTANT TO ME...
...AND I WAS UNABLE TO ACCOMPLISH EVEN ONE THING THAT I SHOULD HAVE IN THIS LIFE.
I AM A MAN WITHOUT ANY VALUE.
AW...
PLEASE DON'T ...
I DON'T WANT YOU TO TALK LIKE THAT.
PLEASE ...
I BEG YOU, DON'T TALK ABOUT YOURSELF LIKE THAT.
IT'S SAD...
SO VERY SAD.

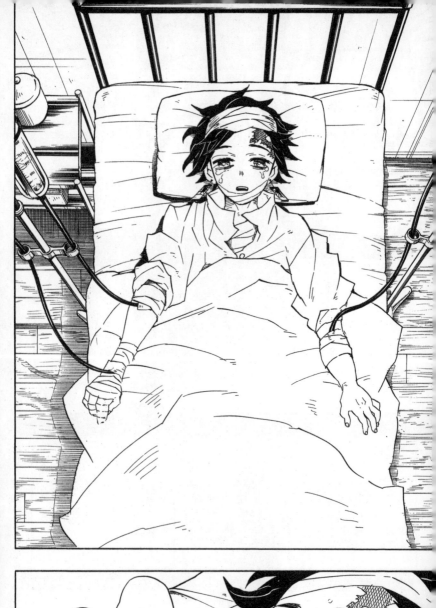

WAS THAT...A DREAM?

WHERE... AM I?

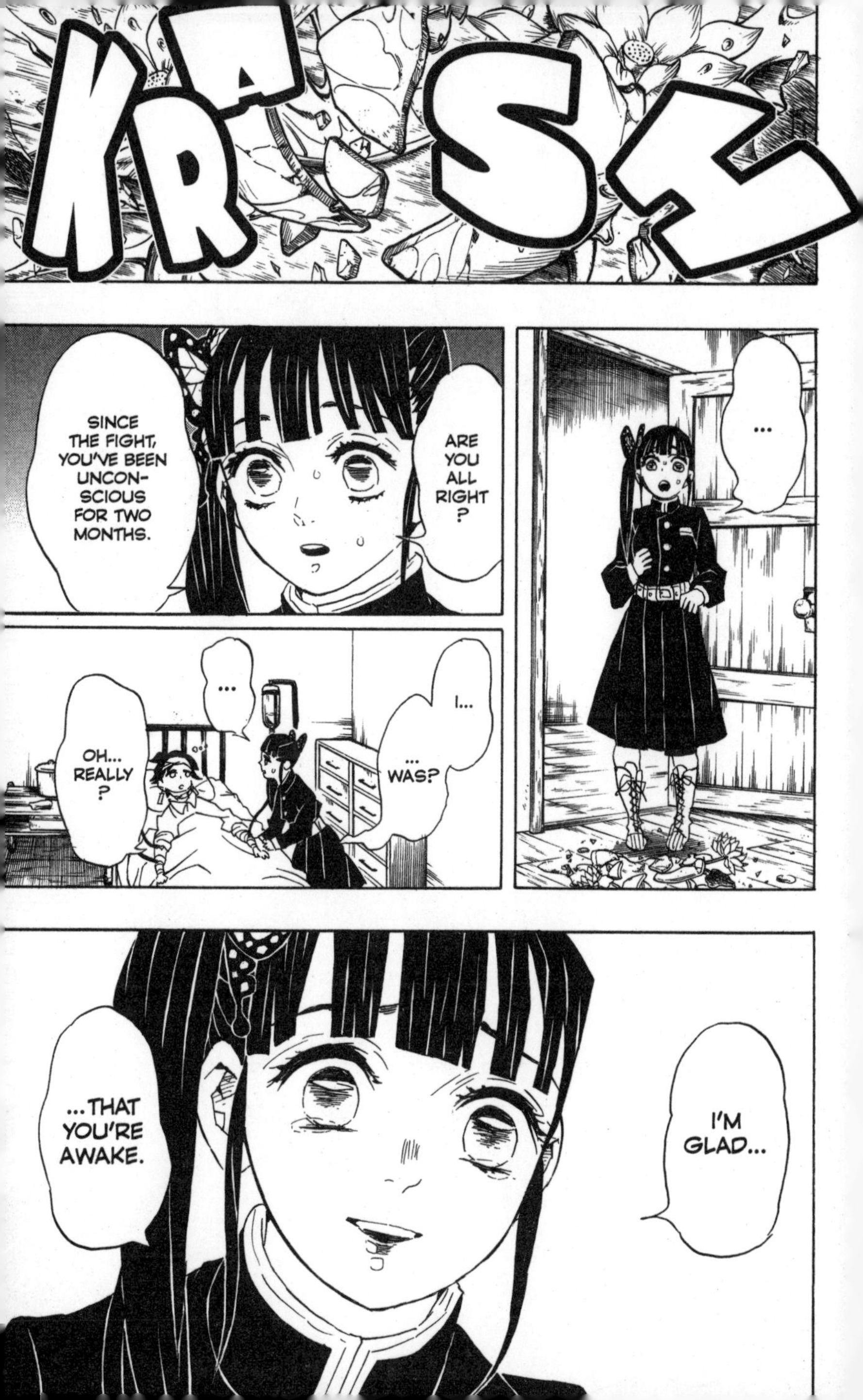
KRASH
...
ARE YOU ALL RIGHT?
SINCE THE FIGHT, YOU'VE BEEN UNCONSCIOUS FOR TWO MONTHS.
I... ...WAS?
...
OH... REALLY?
I'M GLAD...
...THAT YOU'RE AWAKE.

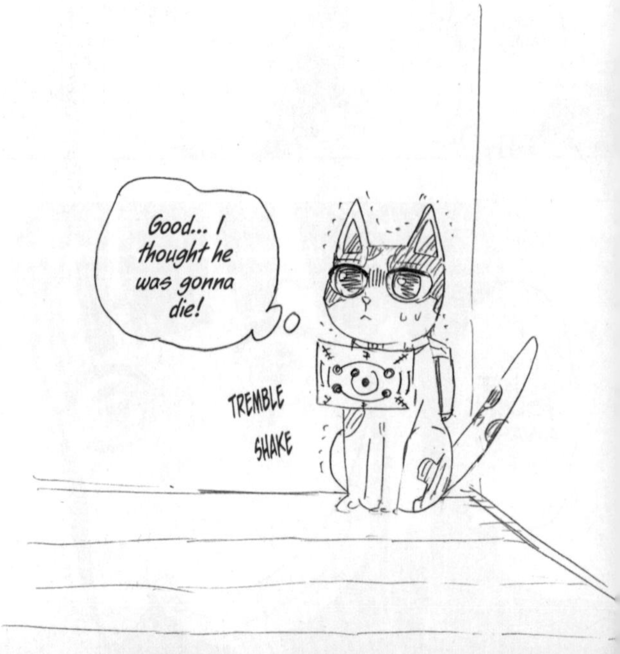
Good... I thought he was gonna die!
TREMBLE
SHAKE

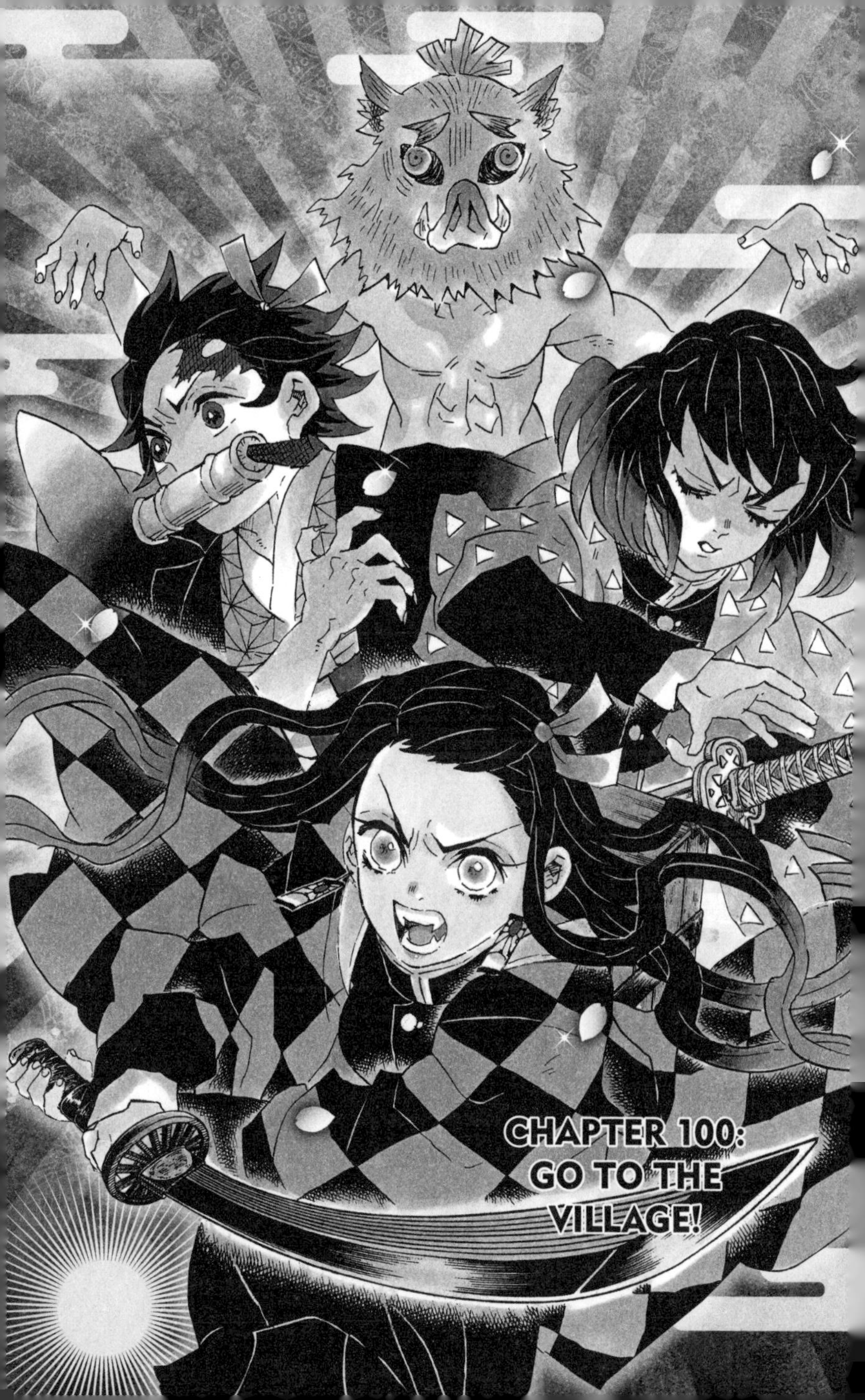
CHAPTER 100:
GO TO THE
VILLAGE!

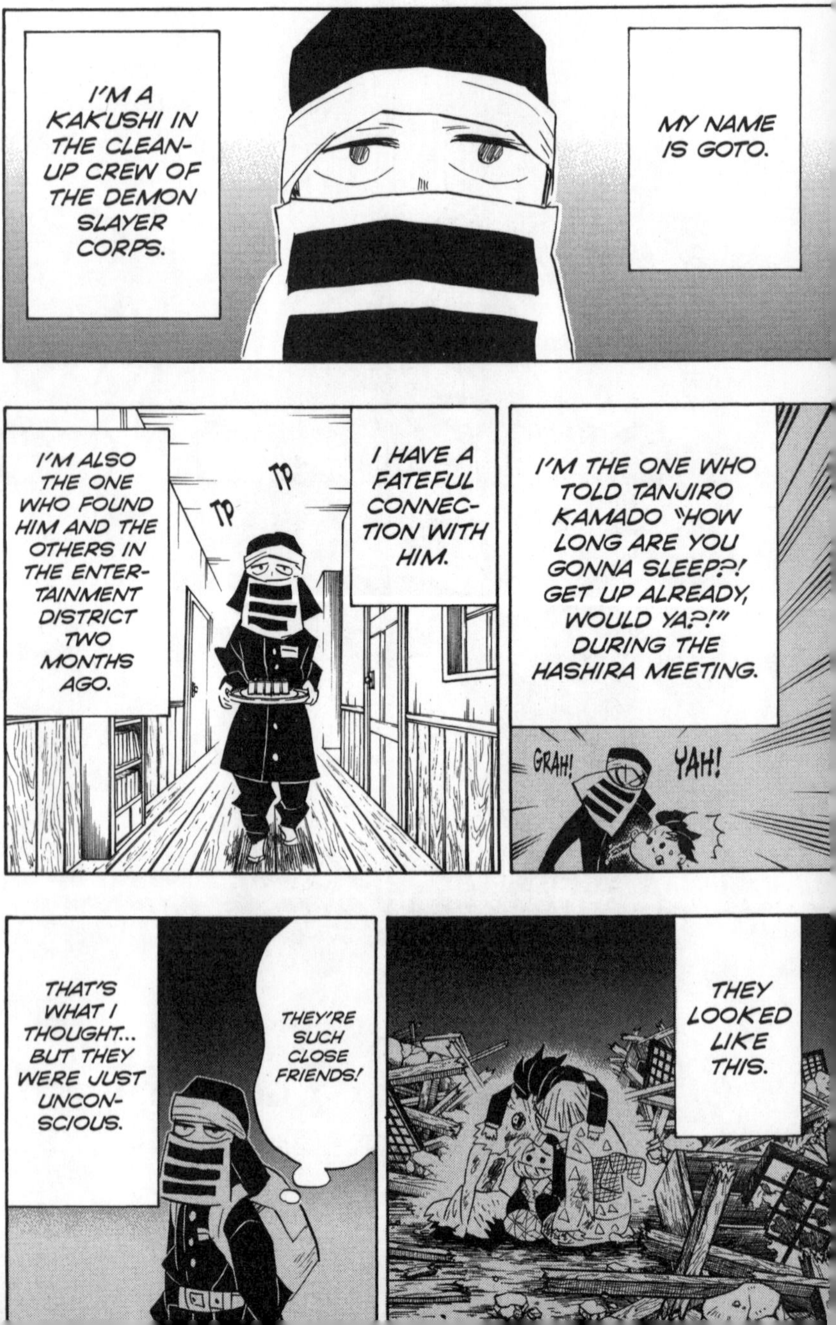
MY NAME IS GOTO.
I'M A KAKUSHI IN THE CLEAN-UP CREW OF THE DEMON SLAYER CORPS.
I'M THE ONE WHO TOLD TANJIRO KAMADO "HOW LONG ARE YOU GONNA SLEEP?! GET UP ALREADY, WOULD YA?!" DURING THE HASHIRA MEETING.
YAH!
GRAH!
I HAVE A FATEFUL CONNEC-TION WITH HIM.
TP
TP
I'M ALSO THE ONE WHO FOUND HIM AND THE OTHERS IN THE ENTER-TAINMENT DISTRICT TWO MONTHS AGO.
THEY LOOKED LIKE THIS.
THEY'RE SUCH CLOSE FRIENDS!
THAT'S WHAT I THOUGHT... BUT THEY WERE JUST UNCON-SCIOUS.

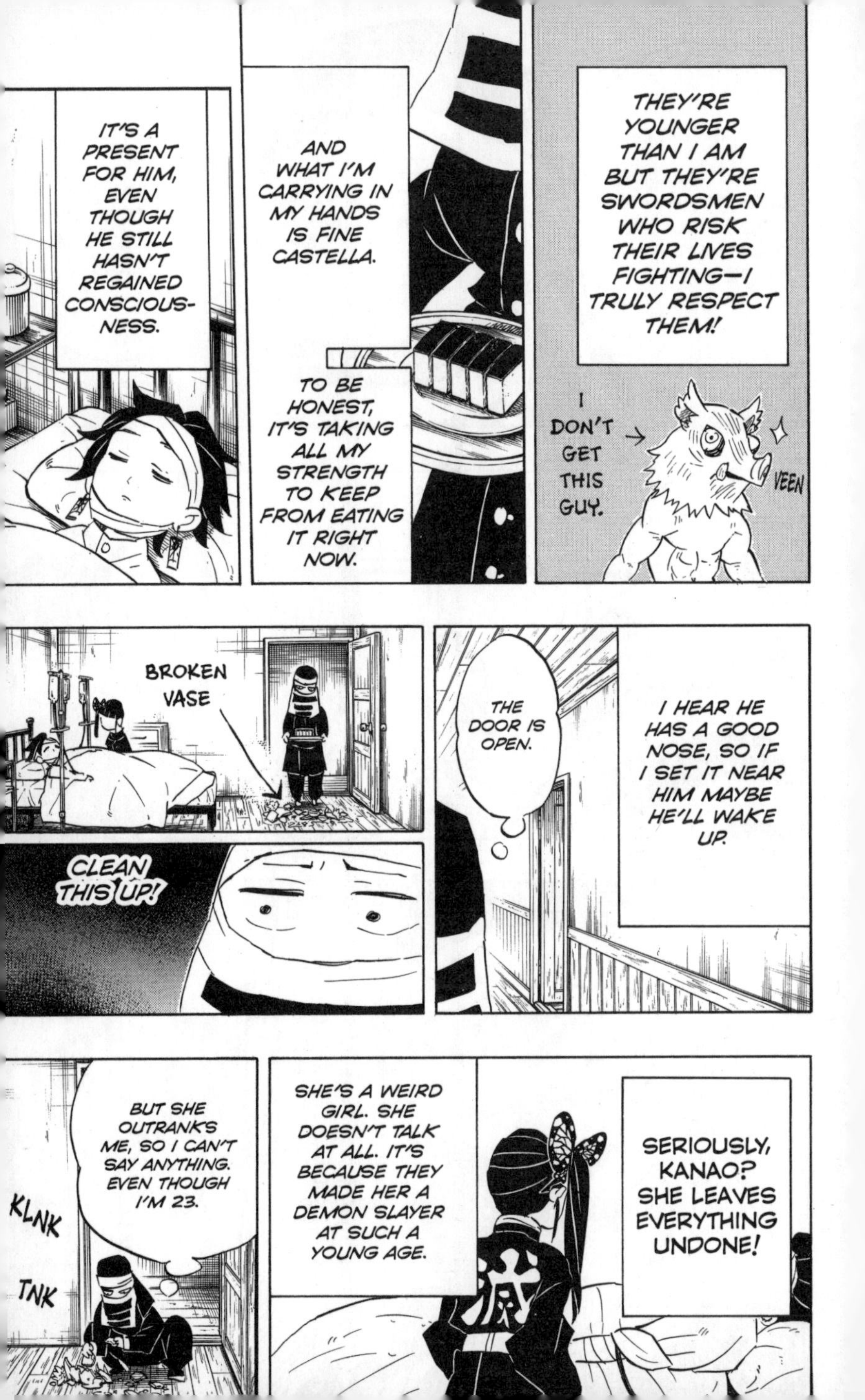
THEY'RE YOUNGER THAN I AM BUT THEY'RE SWORDSMEN WHO RISK THEIR LIVES FIGHTING—I TRULY RESPECT THEM!
I DON'T GET THIS GUY.
VEEN
AND WHAT I'M CARRYING IN MY HANDS IS FINE CASTELLA.
TO BE HONEST, IT'S TAKING ALL MY STRENGTH TO KEEP FROM EATING IT RIGHT NOW.
IT'S A PRESENT FOR HIM, EVEN THOUGH HE STILL HASN'T REGAINED CONSCIOUS-NESS.
I HEAR HE HAS A GOOD NOSE, SO IF I SET IT NEAR HIM MAYBE HE'LL WAKE UP.
THE DOOR IS OPEN.
BROKEN VASE
CLEAN THIS UP!
SERIOUSLY, KANAO? SHE LEAVES EVERYTHING UNDONE!
SHE'S A WEIRD GIRL. SHE DOESN'T TALK AT ALL. IT'S BECAUSE THEY MADE HER A DEMON SLAYER AT SUCH A YOUNG AGE.
BUT SHE OUTRANKS ME, SO I CAN'T SAY ANYTHING. EVEN THOUGH I'M 23.
KLNK
TNK

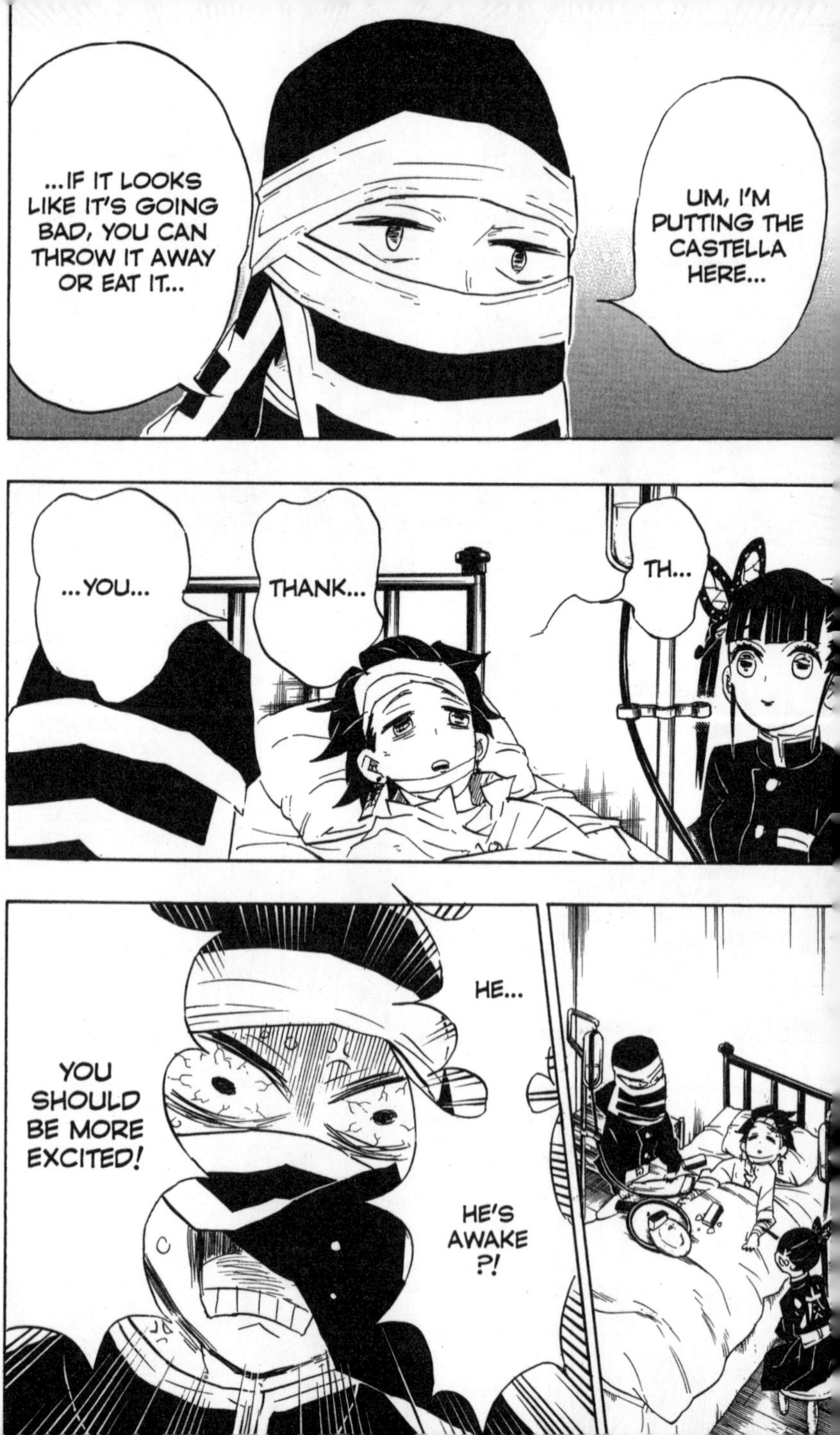
UM, I'M PUTTING THE CASTELLA HERE...
...IF IT LOOKS LIKE IT'S GOING BAD, YOU CAN THROW IT AWAY OR EAT IT...
TH...
THANK...
...YOU...
HE...
HE'S AWAKE ?!
YOU SHOULD BE MORE EXCITED!

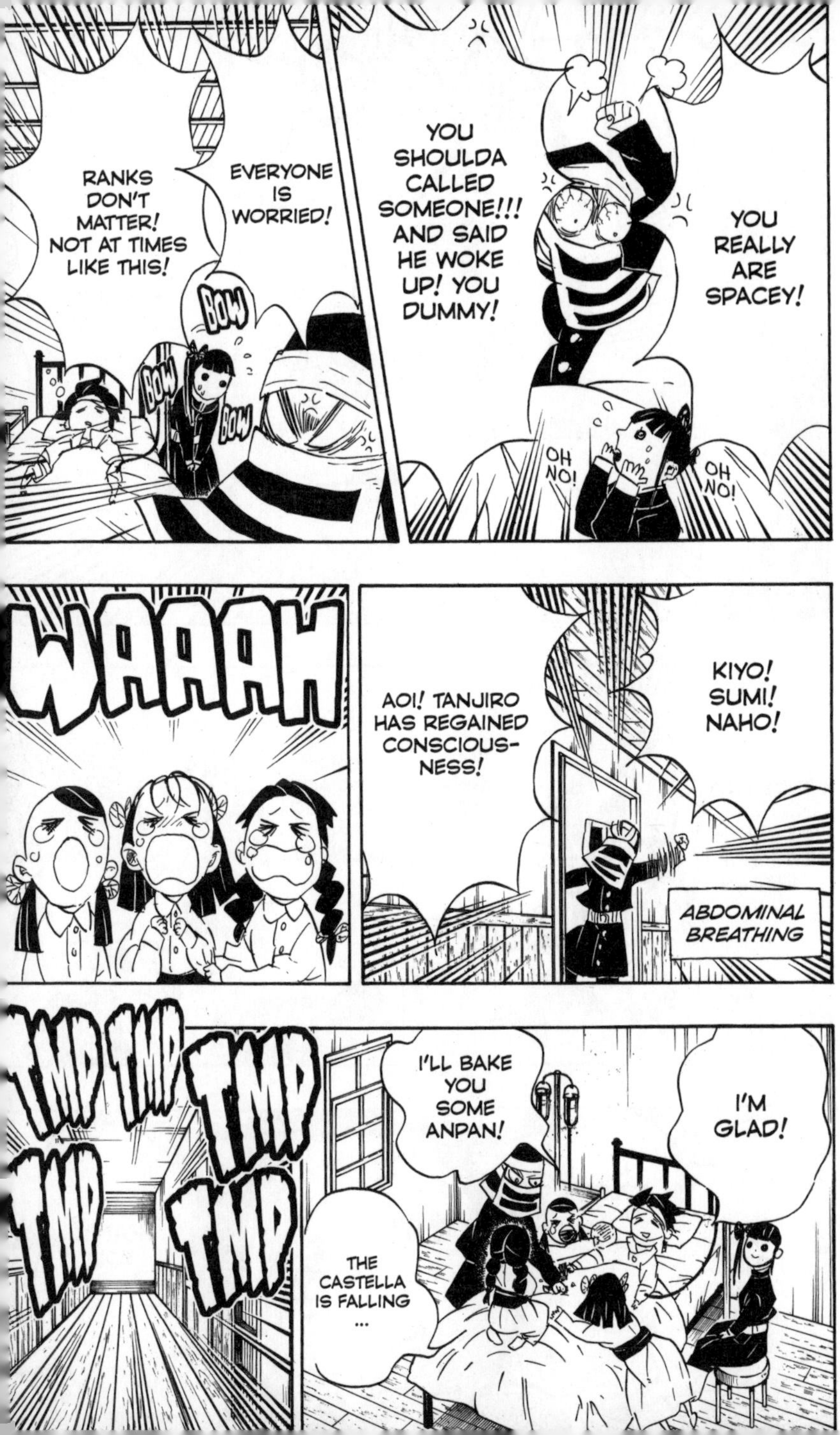
YOU REALLY ARE SPACEY!
YOU SHOULDA CALLED SOMEONE!!! AND SAID HE WOKE UP! YOU DUMMY!
OH NO!
OH NO!
EVERYONE IS WORRIED!
RANKS DON'T MATTER! NOT AT TIMES LIKE THIS!
BOW
BOW
BOW
KIYO! SUMI! NAHO!
AOI! TANJIRO HAS REGAINED CONSCIOUS-NESS!
ABDOMINAL BREATHING
WAAAH
I'M GLAD!
I'LL BAKE YOU SOME ANPAN!
THE CASTELLA IS FALLING ...
TMP TMP TMP TMP TMP

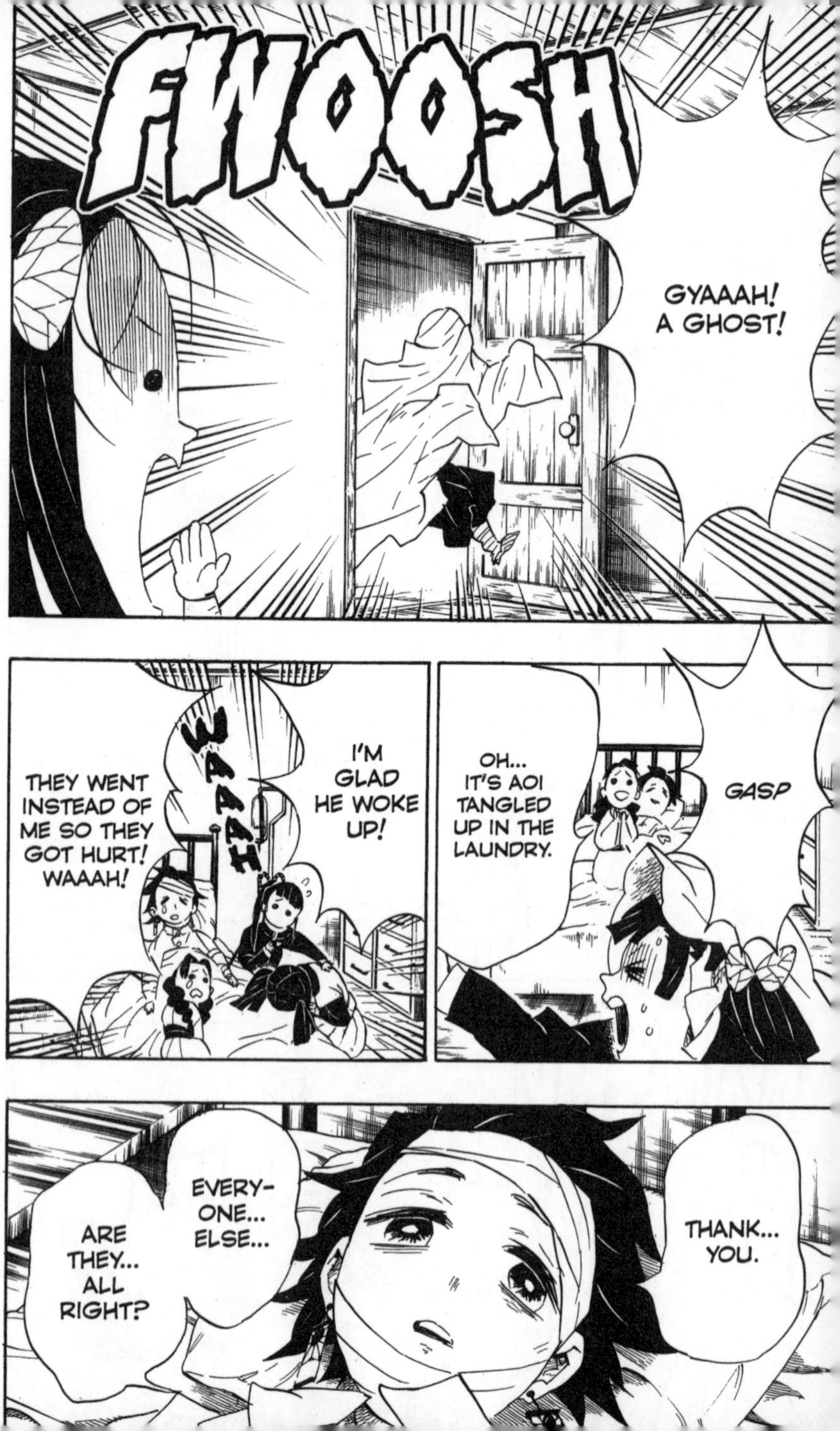
FWOOSH
GYAAAH! A GHOST!
GASP
OH... IT'S AOI TANGLED UP IN THE LAUNDRY.
I'M GLAD HE WOKE UP!
WAAAAH
THEY WENT INSTEAD OF ME SO THEY GOT HURT! WAAAH!
THANK... YOU.
EVERY-ONE... ELSE...
ARE THEY... ALL RIGHT?

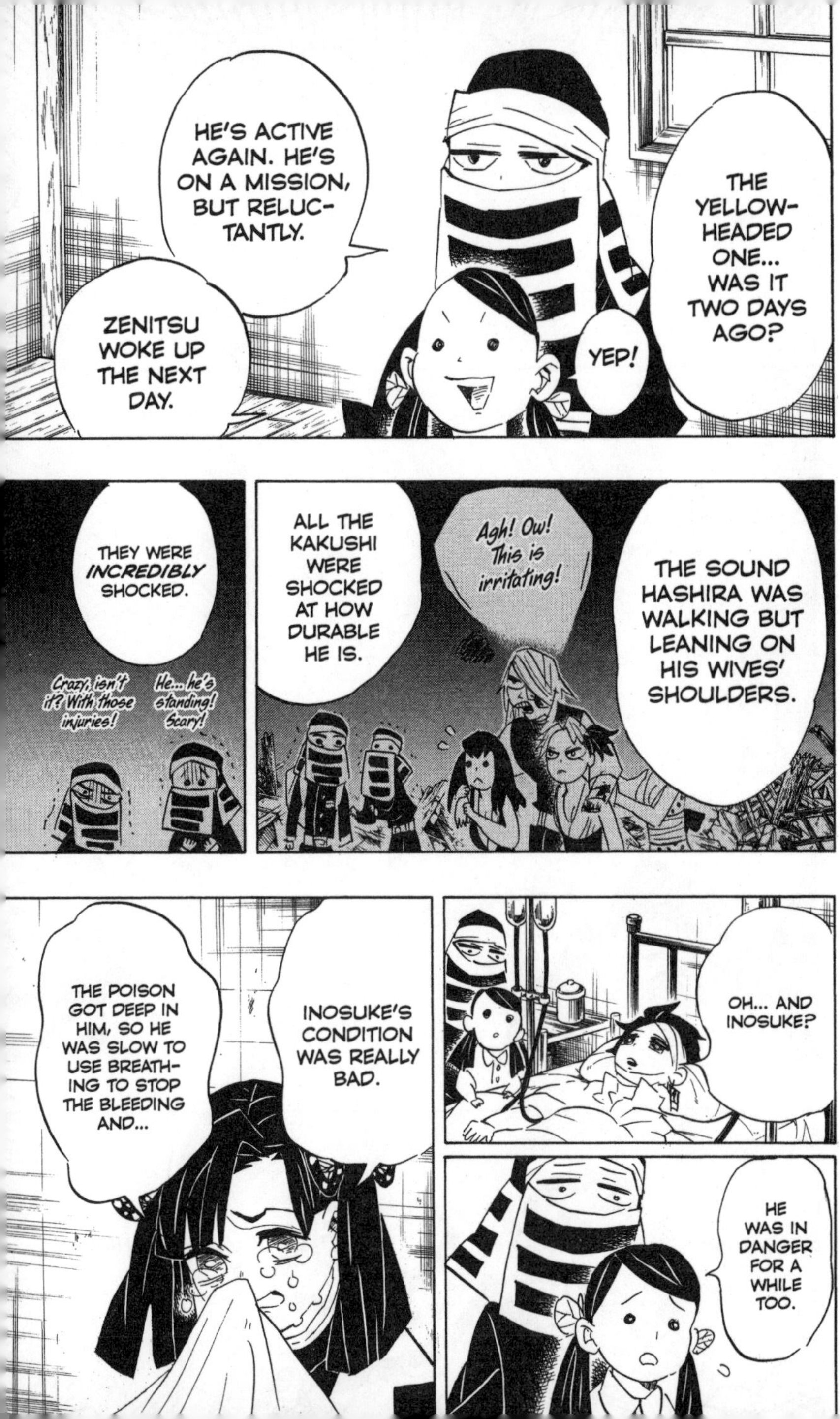
THE YELLOW-HEADED ONE... WAS IT TWO DAYS AGO?
YEP!
ZENITSU WOKE UP THE NEXT DAY.
HE'S ACTIVE AGAIN. HE'S ON A MISSION, BUT RELUC-TANTLY.
THE SOUND HASHIRA WAS WALKING BUT LEANING ON HIS WIVES' SHOULDERS.
Agh! Ow! This is irritating!
ALL THE KAKUSHI WERE SHOCKED AT HOW DURABLE HE IS.
THEY WERE ***INCREDIBLY*** SHOCKED.
He... he's standing! Scary!
Crazy, isn't it? With those injuries!
OH... AND INOSUKE?
HE WAS IN DANGER FOR A WHILE TOO.
INOSUKE'S CONDITION WAS REALLY BAD.
THE POISON GOT DEEP IN HIM, SO HE WAS SLOW TO USE BREATH-ING TO STOP THE BLEEDING AND...

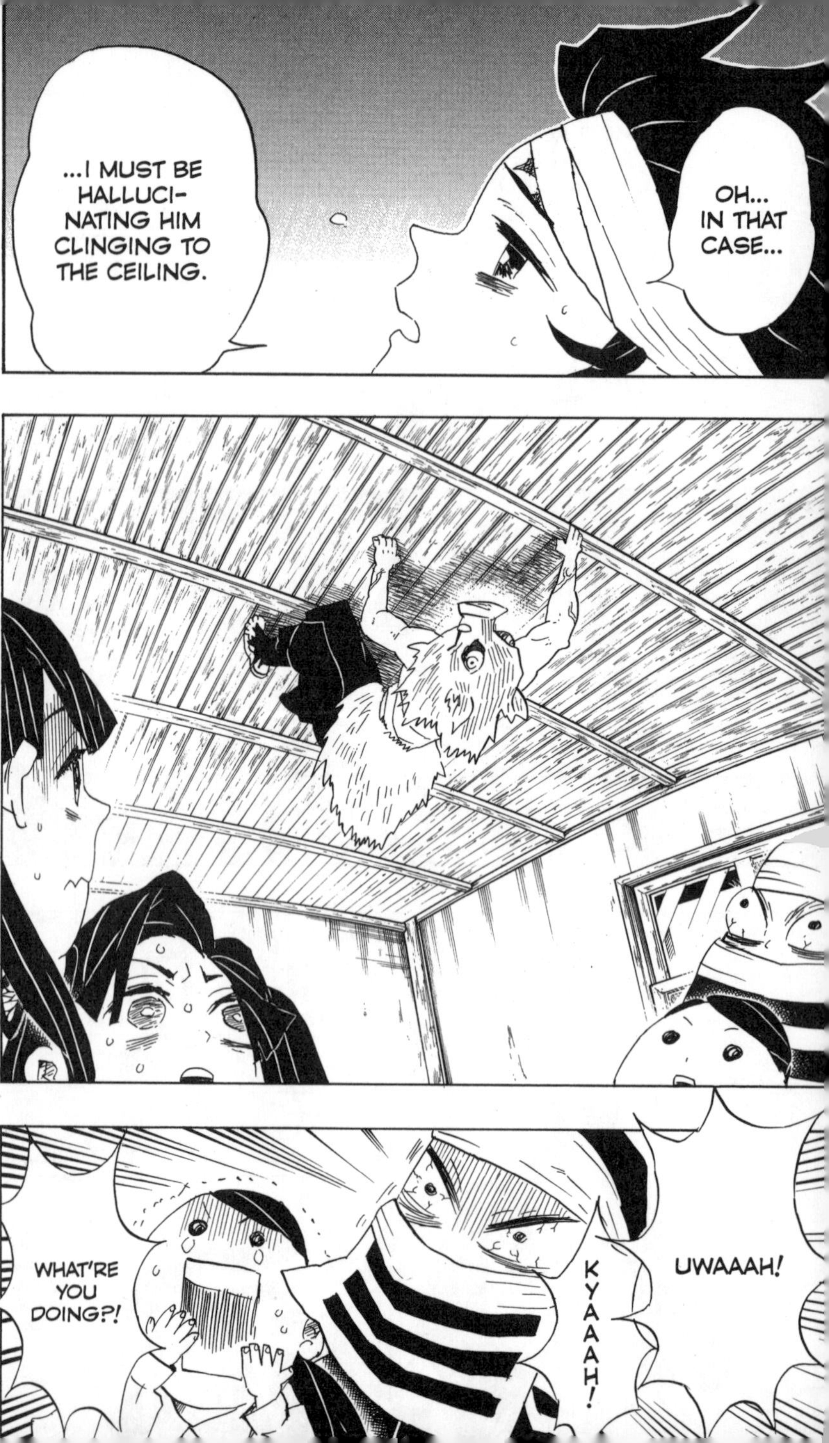
OH... IN THAT CASE...
...I MUST BE HALLUCI-NATING HIM CLINGING TO THE CEILING.
UWAAAH!
KYAAAH!
WHAT'RE YOU DOING?!

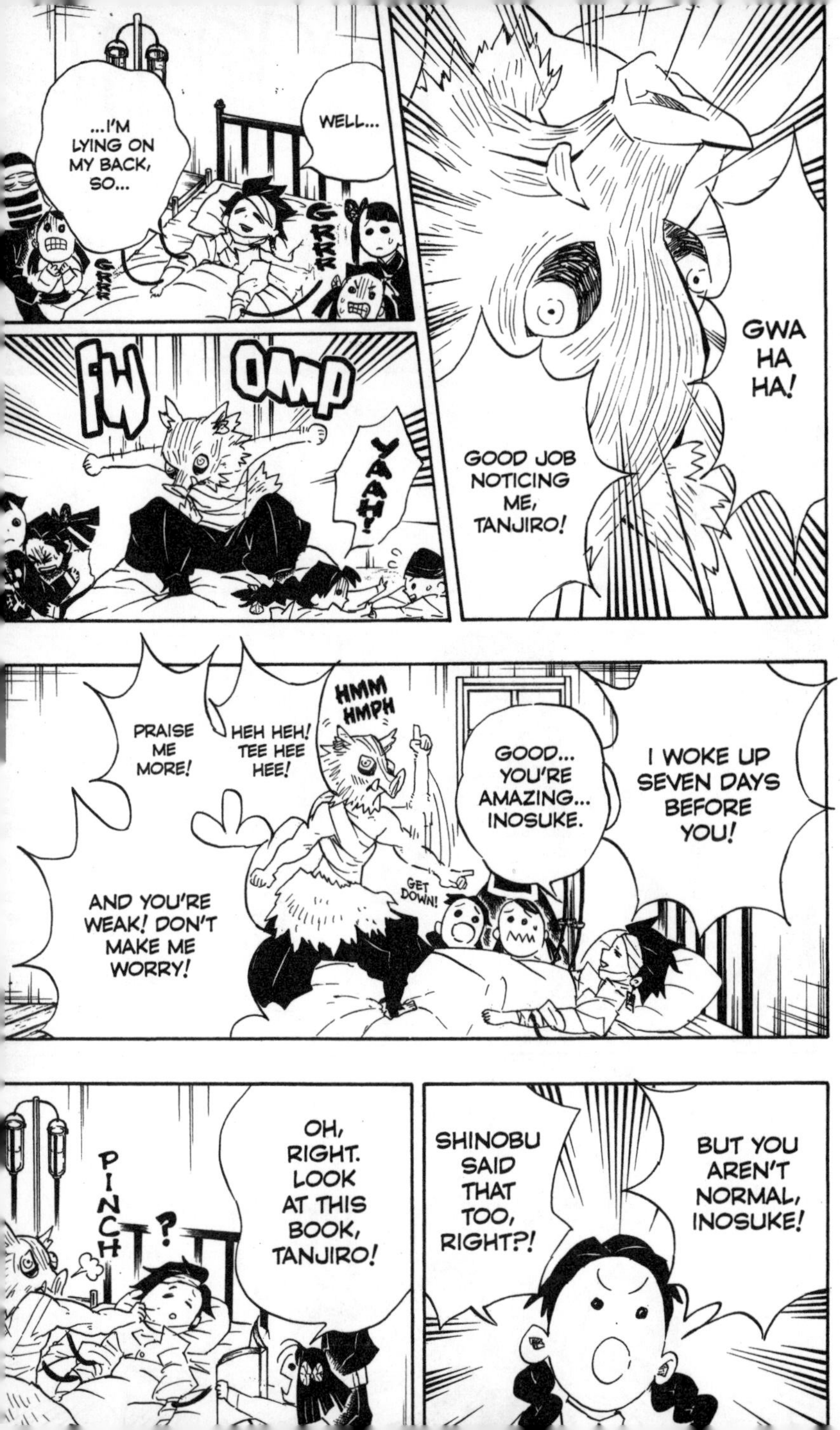
GWA HA HA!
GOOD JOB NOTICING ME, TANJIRO!
WELL...
GRRR
...I'M LYING ON MY BACK, SO...
GRRR
YAAAH!
FWOMP
I WOKE UP SEVEN DAYS BEFORE YOU!
GOOD... YOU'RE AMAZING... INOSUKE.
HMM HMPH
HEH HEH! TEE HEE HEE!
PRAISE ME MORE!
GET DOWN!
AND YOU'RE WEAK! DON'T MAKE ME WORRY!
BUT YOU AREN'T NORMAL, INOSUKE!
SHINOBU SAID THAT TOO, RIGHT?!
OH, RIGHT. LOOK AT THIS BOOK, TANJIRO!
?
PINCH

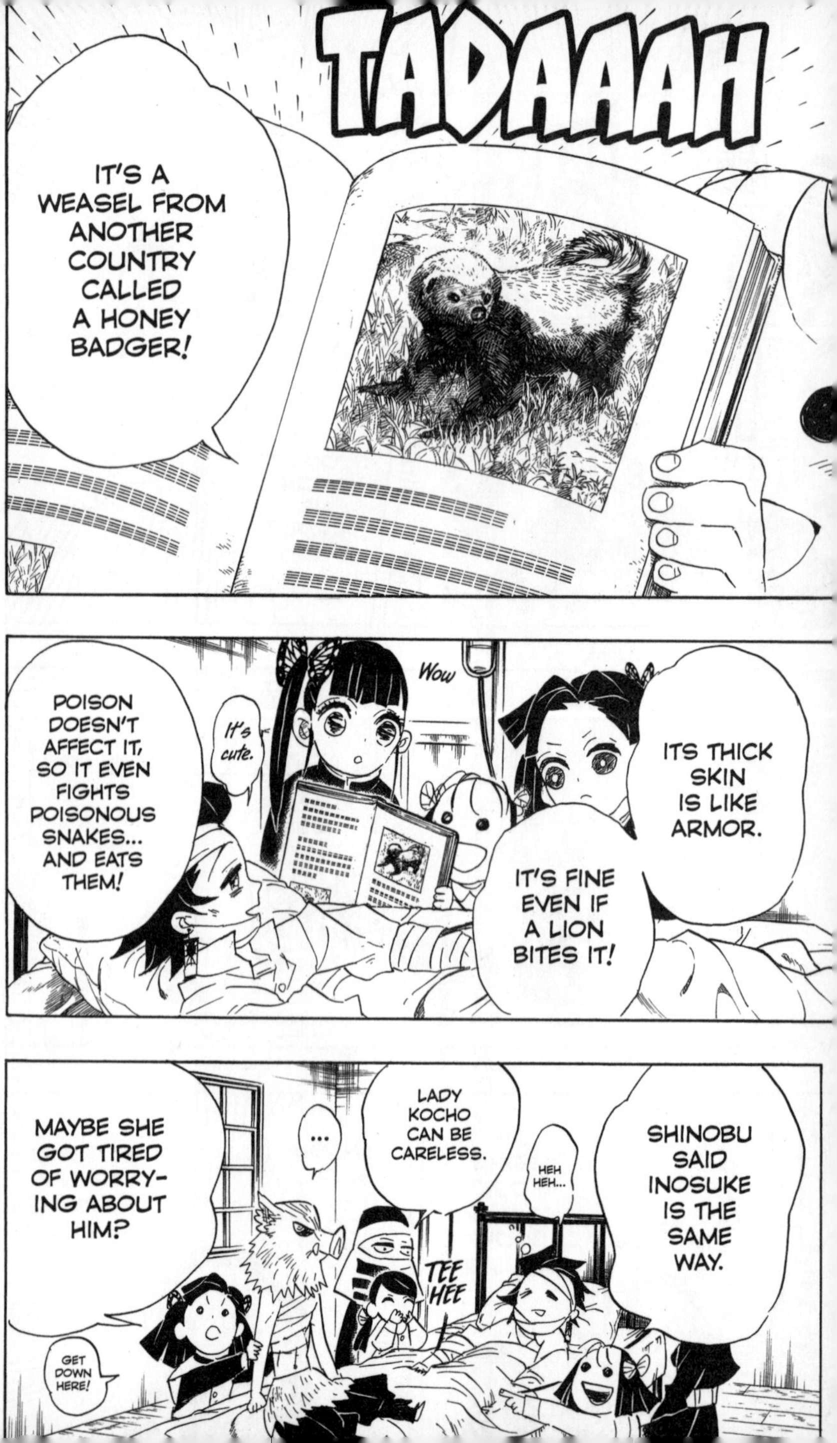
TADAAAH
IT'S A WEASEL FROM ANOTHER COUNTRY CALLED A HONEY BADGER!
ITS THICK SKIN IS LIKE ARMOR.
IT'S FINE EVEN IF A LION BITES IT!
Wow
It's cute.
POISON DOESN'T AFFECT IT, SO IT EVEN FIGHTS POISONOUS SNAKES... AND EATS THEM!
SHINOBU SAID INOSUKE IS THE SAME WAY.
HEH HEH...
LADY KOCHO CAN BE CARELESS.
TEE HEE
...
MAYBE SHE GOT TIRED OF WORRYING ABOUT HIM?
GET DOWN HERE!

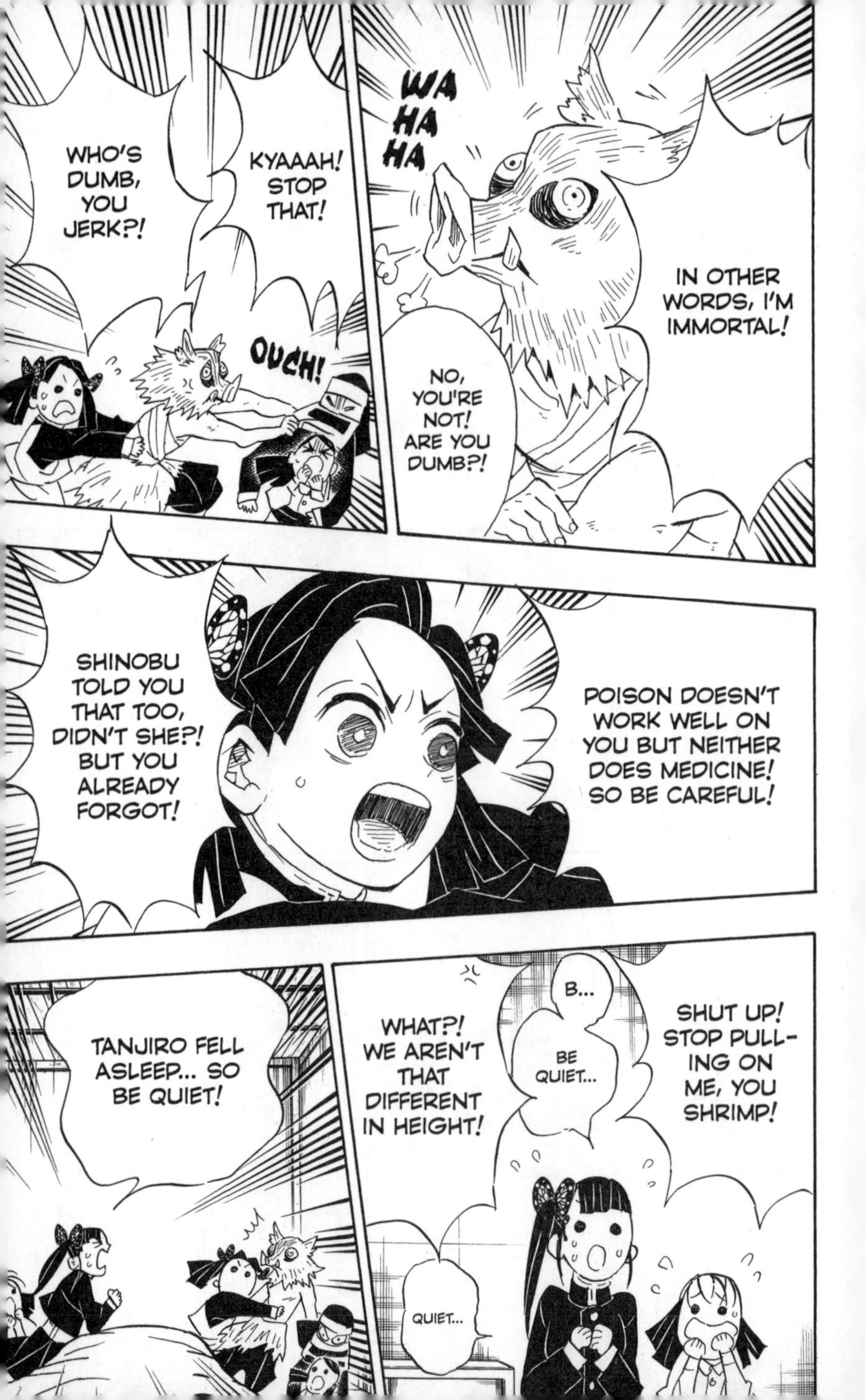
WA HA HA
IN OTHER WORDS, I'M IMMORTAL!
NO, YOU'RE NOT! ARE YOU DUMB?!
KYAAAH! STOP THAT!
WHO'S DUMB, YOU JERK?!
OUCH!
POISON DOESN'T WORK WELL ON YOU BUT NEITHER DOES MEDICINE! SO BE CAREFUL!
SHINOBU TOLD YOU THAT TOO, DIDN'T SHE?! BUT YOU ALREADY FORGOT!
SHUT UP! STOP PULL-ING ON ME, YOU SHRIMP!
B...
BE QUIET...
WHAT?! WE AREN'T THAT DIFFERENT IN HEIGHT!
QUIET...
TANJIRO FELL ASLEEP... SO BE QUIET!

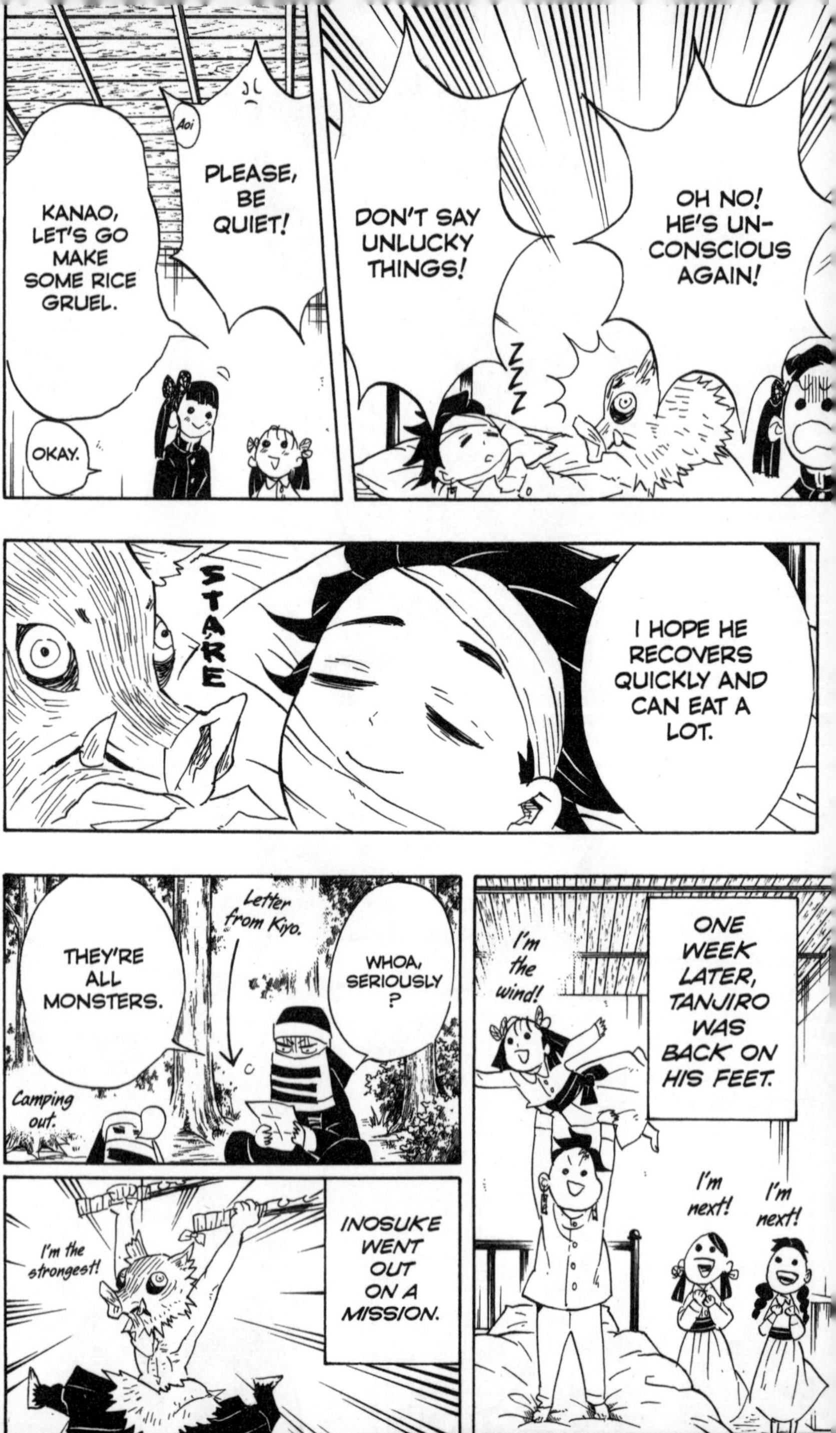
OH NO! HE'S UN-CONSCIOUS AGAIN!
DON'T SAY UNLUCKY THINGS!
ZZZ
Aoi
PLEASE, BE QUIET!
KANAO, LET'S GO MAKE SOME RICE GRUEL.
OKAY.
I HOPE HE RECOVERS QUICKLY AND CAN EAT A LOT.
STARE
ONE WEEK LATER, TANJIRO WAS BACK ON HIS FEET.
I'm the wind!
I'm next!
I'm next!
WHOA, SERIOUSLY?
Letter from Kiyo.
THEY'RE ALL MONSTERS.
Camping out.
INOSUKE WENT OUT ON A MISSION.
I'm the strongest!

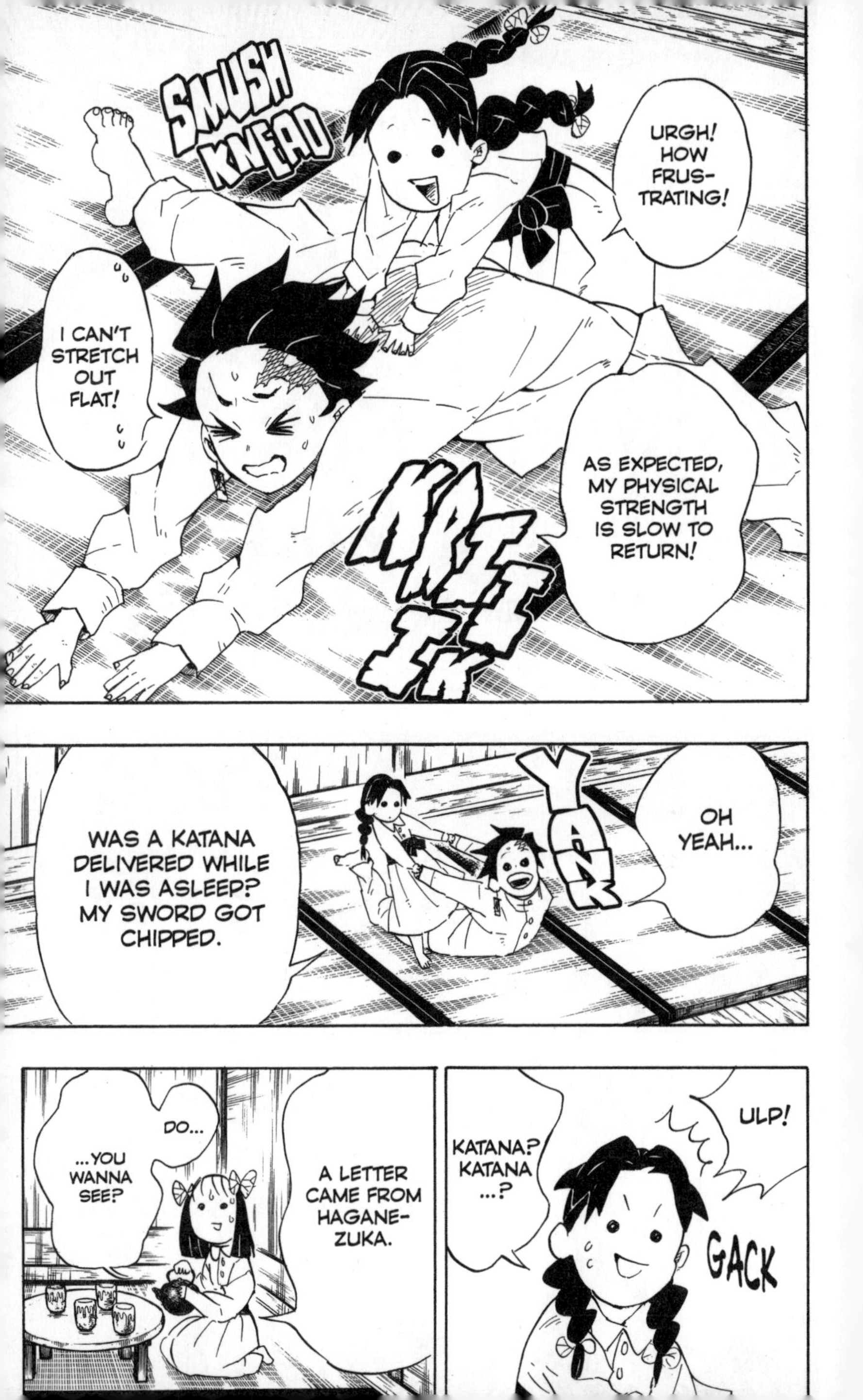
URGH! HOW FRUS-TRATING!
SMUSH KNEAD
AS EXPECTED, MY PHYSICAL STRENGTH IS SLOW TO RETURN!
I CAN'T STRETCH OUT FLAT!
KRIIIK
OH YEAH...
YANK
WAS A KATANA DELIVERED WHILE I WAS ASLEEP? MY SWORD GOT CHIPPED.
ULP!
KATANA? KATANA ...?
GACK
A LETTER CAME FROM HAGANE-ZUKA.
DO...
...YOU WANNA SEE?

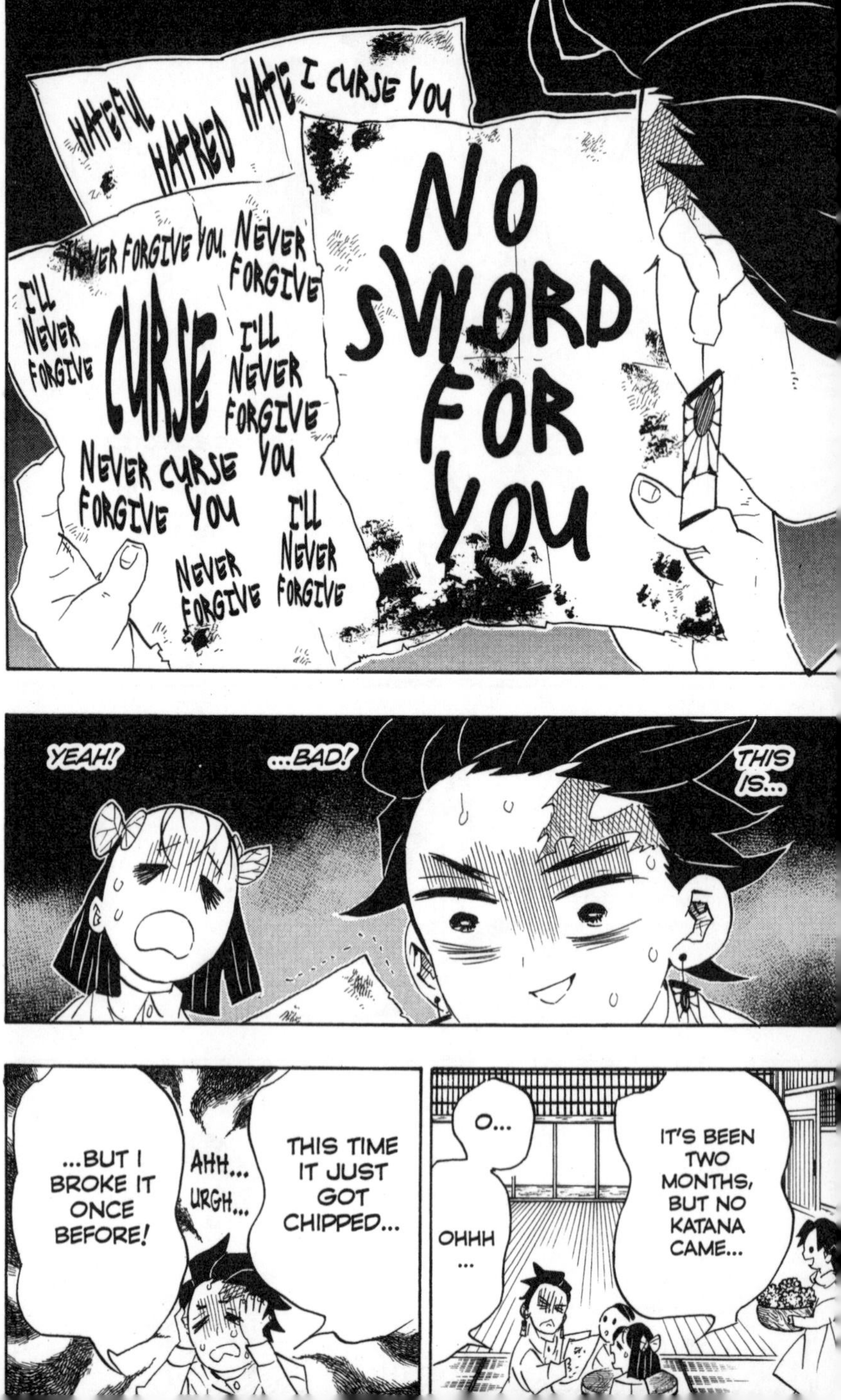
NO SWORD FOR YOU
I CURSE YOU
HATE
HATRED
HATEFUL
NEVER FORGIVE
NEVER FORGIVE YOU.
I'LL NEVER FORGIVE YOU
CURSE
I'LL NEVER FORGIVE
NEVER CURSE FORGIVE YOU
I'LL NEVER FORGIVE
NEVER FORGIVE
THIS IS...
...BAD!
YEAH!
IT'S BEEN TWO MONTHS, BUT NO KATANA CAME...
O...
OHHH ...
THIS TIME IT JUST GOT CHIPPED...
AHH... URGH...
...BUT I BROKE IT ONCE BEFORE!

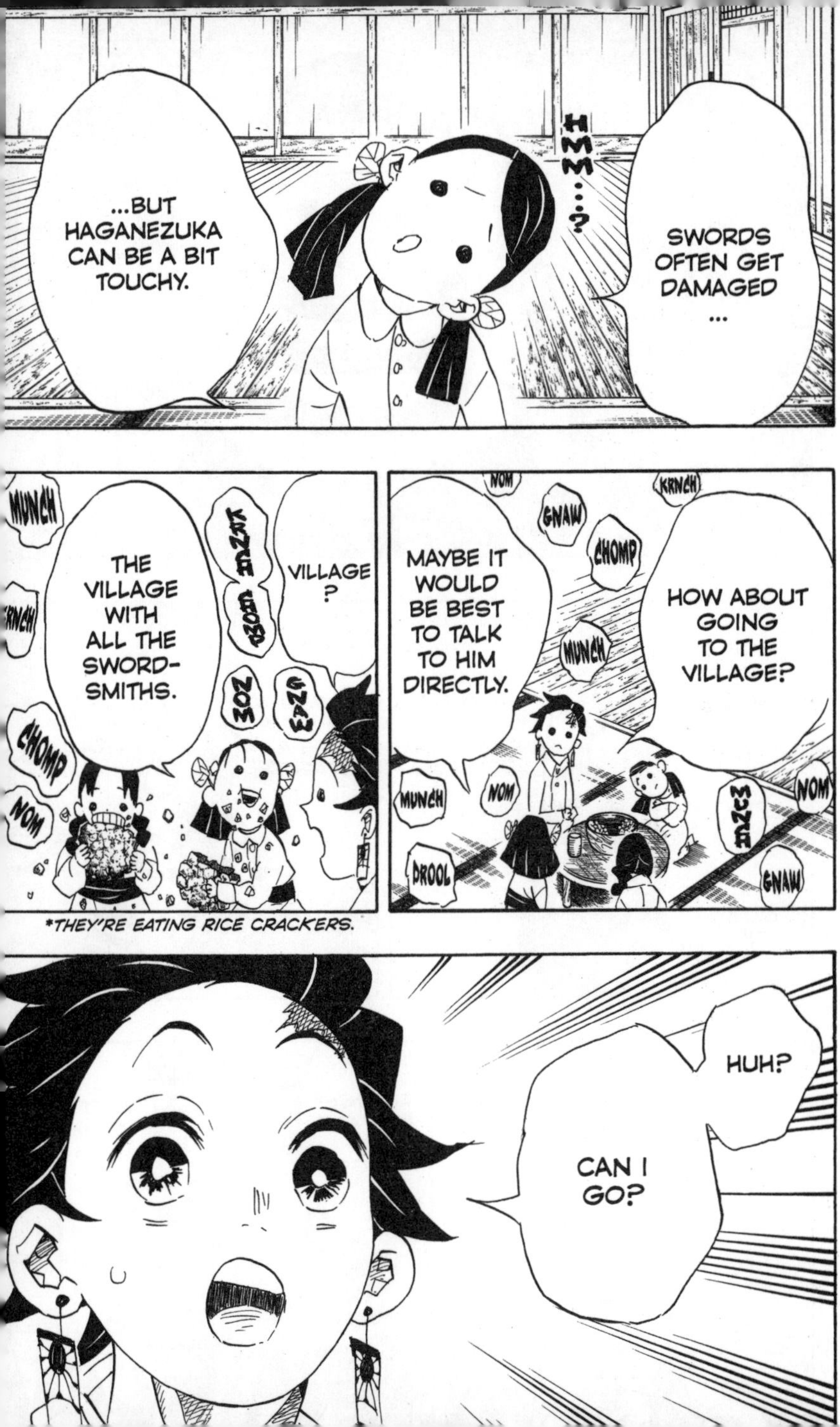
SWORDS OFTEN GET DAMAGED ...
HMM...?
...BUT HAGANEZUKA CAN BE A BIT TOUCHY.
KRNCH
GNAW
CHOMP
NOM
HOW ABOUT GOING TO THE VILLAGE?
MAYBE IT WOULD BE BEST TO TALK TO HIM DIRECTLY.
MUNCH
NOM
MUNCH
NOM
GNAW
MUNCH
DROOL
VILLAGE?
KRNCH CHOMP
GNAW
NOM
THE VILLAGE WITH ALL THE SWORD-SMITHS.
MUNCH
KRNCH
CHOMP
NOM
*THEY'RE EATING RICE CRACKERS.
HUH?
CAN I GO?

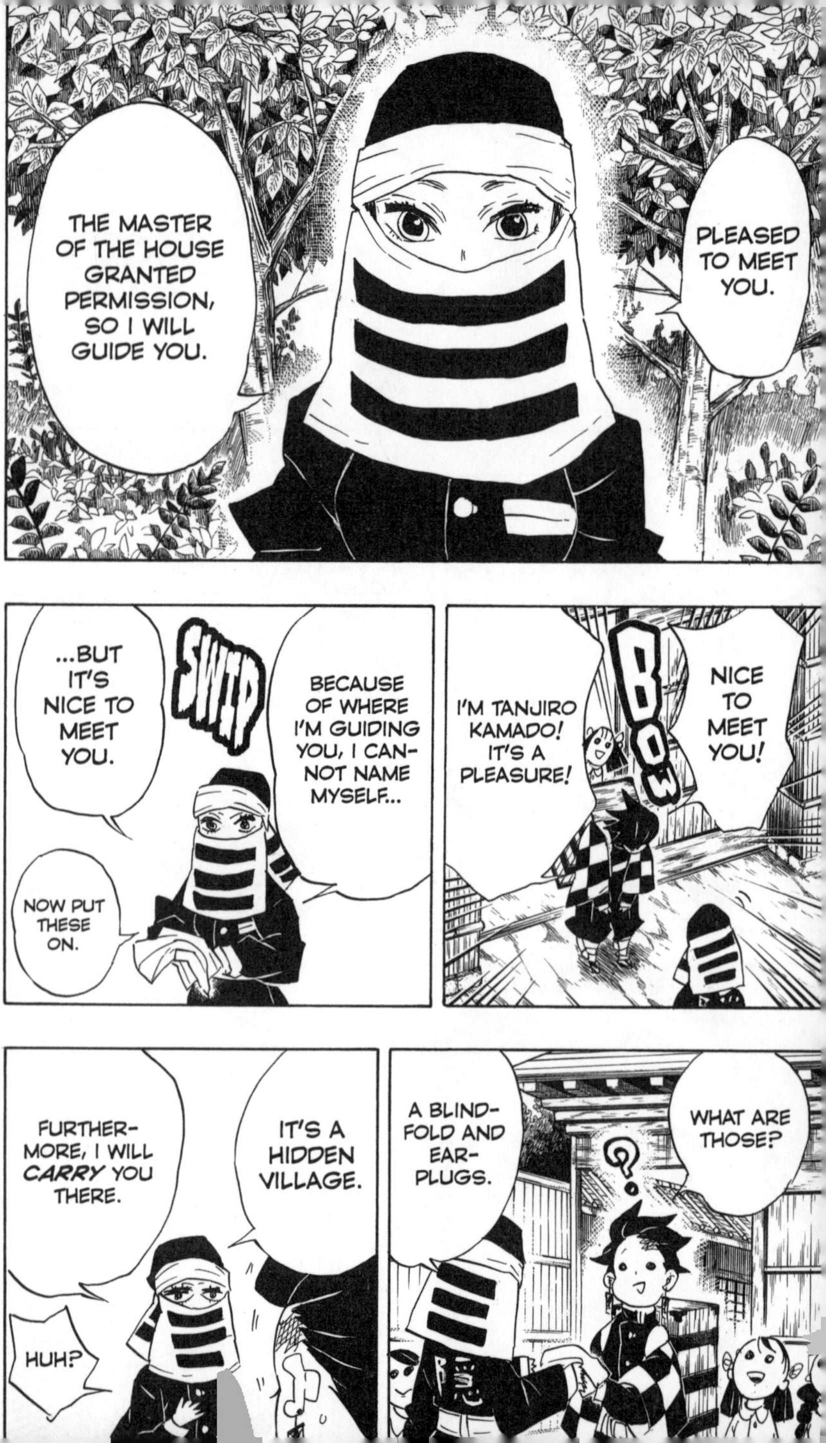
PLEASED TO MEET YOU.
THE MASTER OF THE HOUSE GRANTED PERMISSION, SO I WILL GUIDE YOU.
NICE TO MEET YOU!
BOW
I'M TANJIRO KAMADO! IT'S A PLEASURE!
BECAUSE OF WHERE I'M GUIDING YOU, I CAN-NOT NAME MYSELF...
SWIP
...BUT IT'S NICE TO MEET YOU.
NOW PUT THESE ON.
WHAT ARE THOSE?
A BLIND-FOLD AND EAR-PLUGS.
IT'S A HIDDEN VILLAGE.
FURTHER-MORE, I WILL *CARRY* YOU THERE.
HUH?

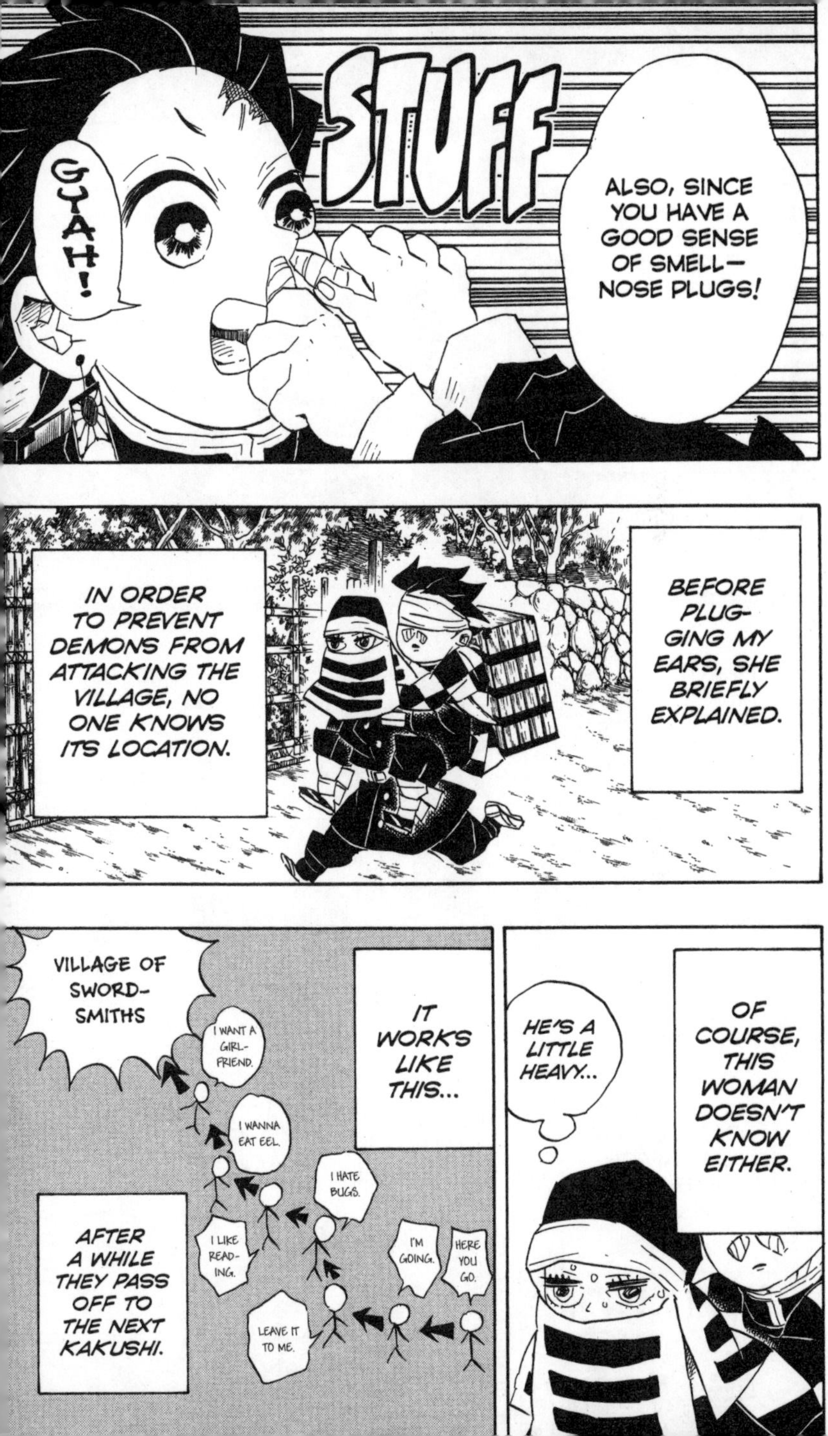
ALSO, SINCE YOU HAVE A GOOD SENSE OF SMELL— NOSE PLUGS!
STUFF
GYAH!
BEFORE PLUG-GING MY EARS, SHE BRIEFLY EXPLAINED.
IN ORDER TO PREVENT DEMONS FROM ATTACKING THE VILLAGE, NO ONE KNOWS ITS LOCATION.
OF COURSE, THIS WOMAN DOESN'T KNOW EITHER.
HE'S A LITTLE HEAVY...
IT WORKS LIKE THIS...
VILLAGE OF SWORD-SMITHS
HERE YOU GO.
I'M GOING.
LEAVE IT TO ME.
I LIKE READ-ING.
I HATE BUGS.
I WANNA EAT EEL.
I WANT A GIRL-FRIEND.
AFTER A WHILE THEY PASS OFF TO THE NEXT KAKUSHI.

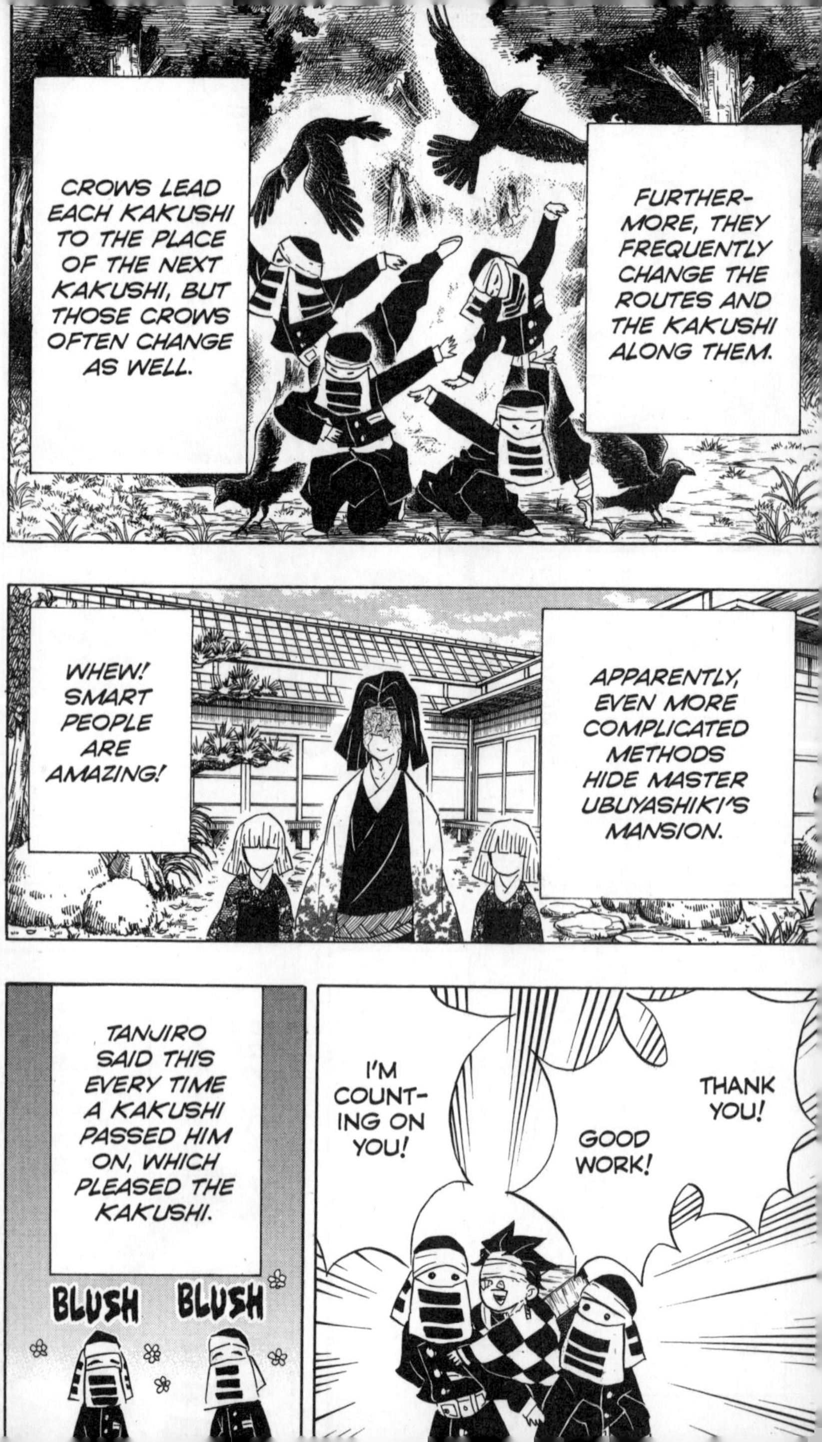
FURTHER-MORE, THEY FREQUENTLY CHANGE THE ROUTES AND THE KAKUSHI ALONG THEM.
CROWS LEAD EACH KAKUSHI TO THE PLACE OF THE NEXT KAKUSHI, BUT THOSE CROWS OFTEN CHANGE AS WELL.
APPARENTLY, EVEN MORE COMPLICATED METHODS HIDE MASTER UBUYASHIKI'S MANSION.
WHEW! SMART PEOPLE ARE AMAZING!
THANK YOU!
I'M COUNT-ING ON YOU!
GOOD WORK!
TANJIRO SAID THIS EVERY TIME A KAKUSHI PASSED HIM ON, WHICH PLEASED THE KAKUSHI.
BLUSH
BLUSH

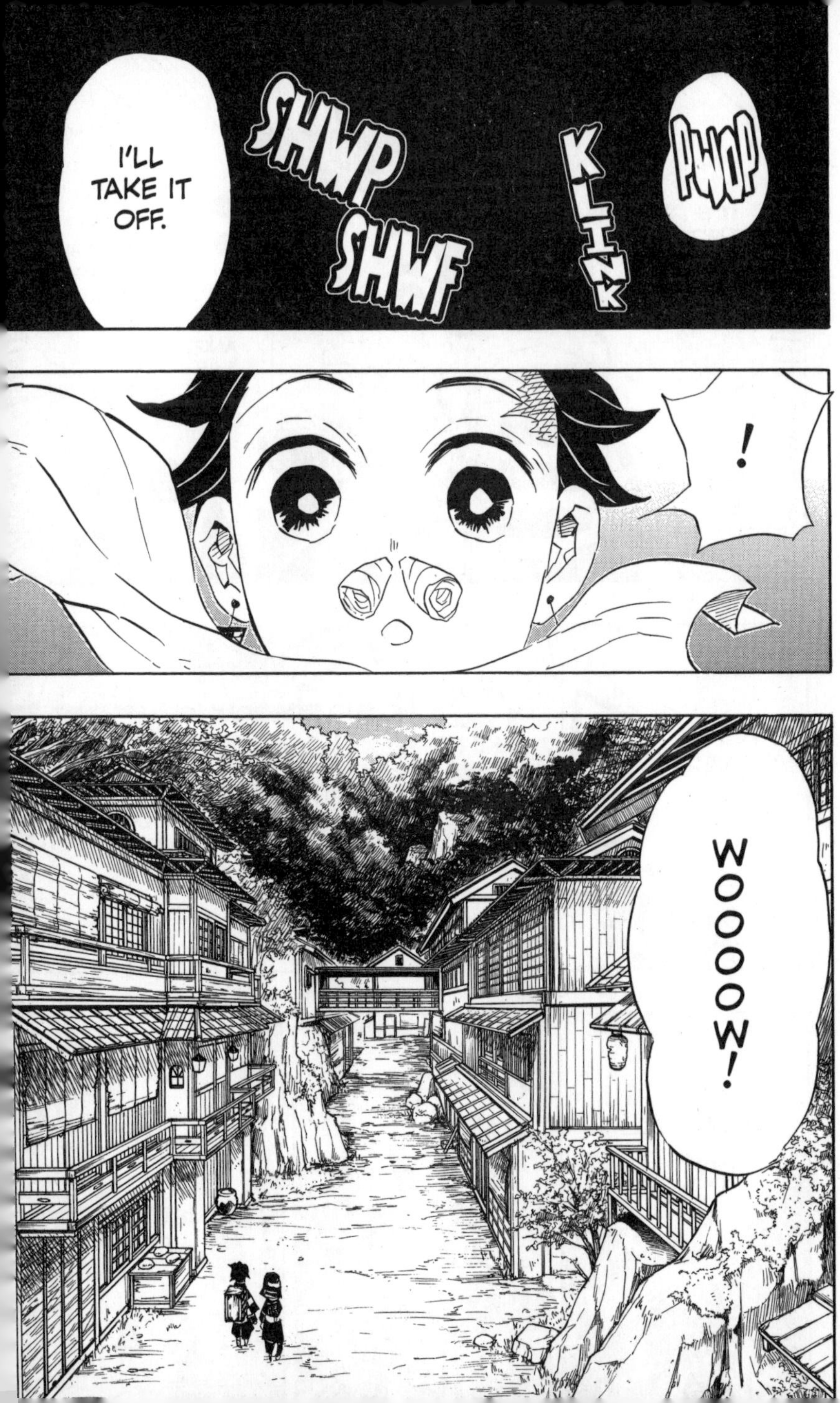
PWOP
KLINK
SHWP
SHWF
I'LL TAKE IT OFF.
!
WOOOOOW!

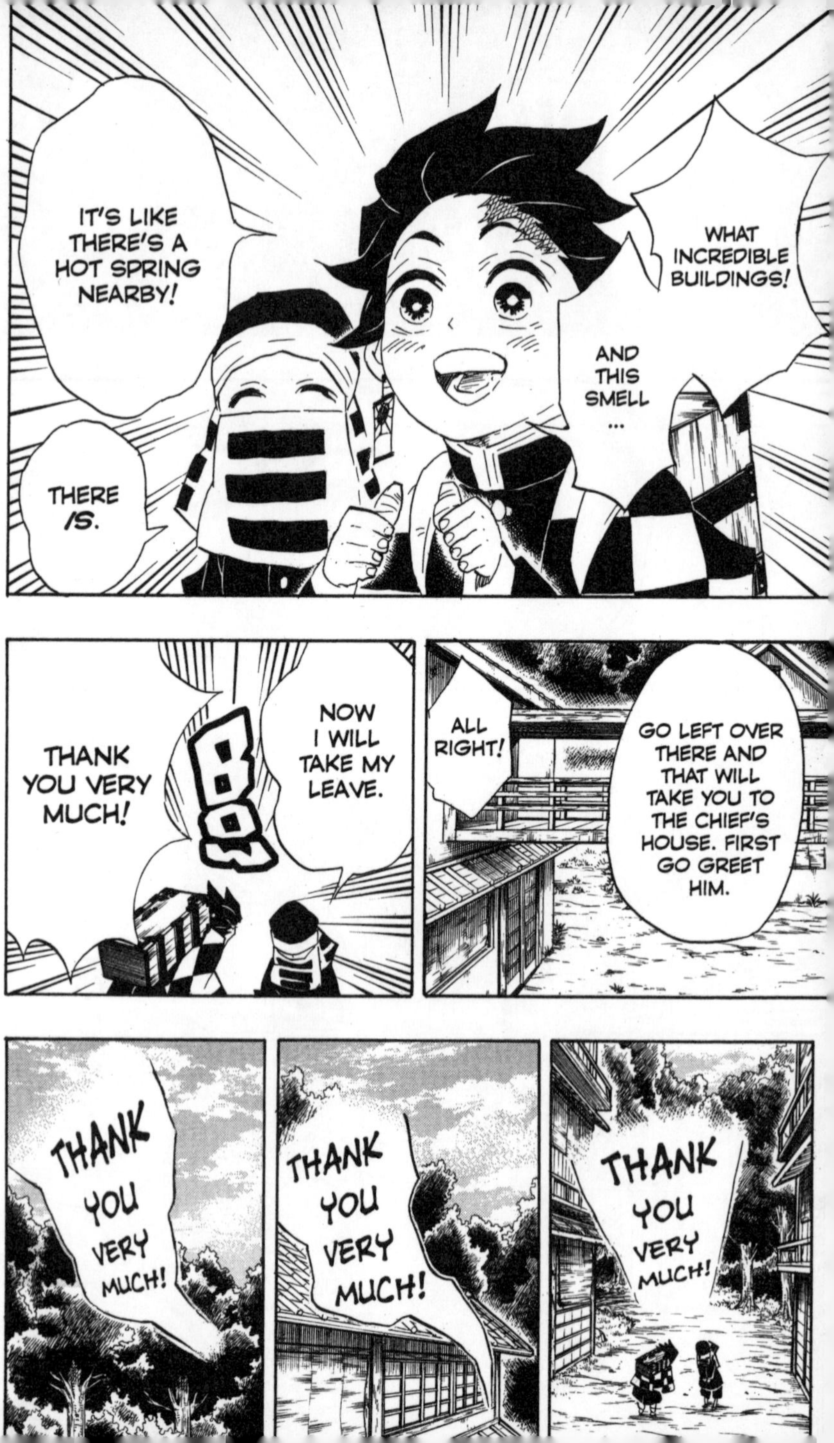
WHAT INCREDIBLE BUILDINGS!
AND THIS SMELL ...
IT'S LIKE THERE'S A HOT SPRING NEARBY!
THERE IS.
GO LEFT OVER THERE AND THAT WILL TAKE YOU TO THE CHIEF'S HOUSE. FIRST GO GREET HIM.
ALL RIGHT!
NOW I WILL TAKE MY LEAVE.
BOW
THANK YOU VERY MUCH!
THANK YOU VERY MUCH!
THANK YOU VERY MUCH!
THANK YOU VERY MUCH!

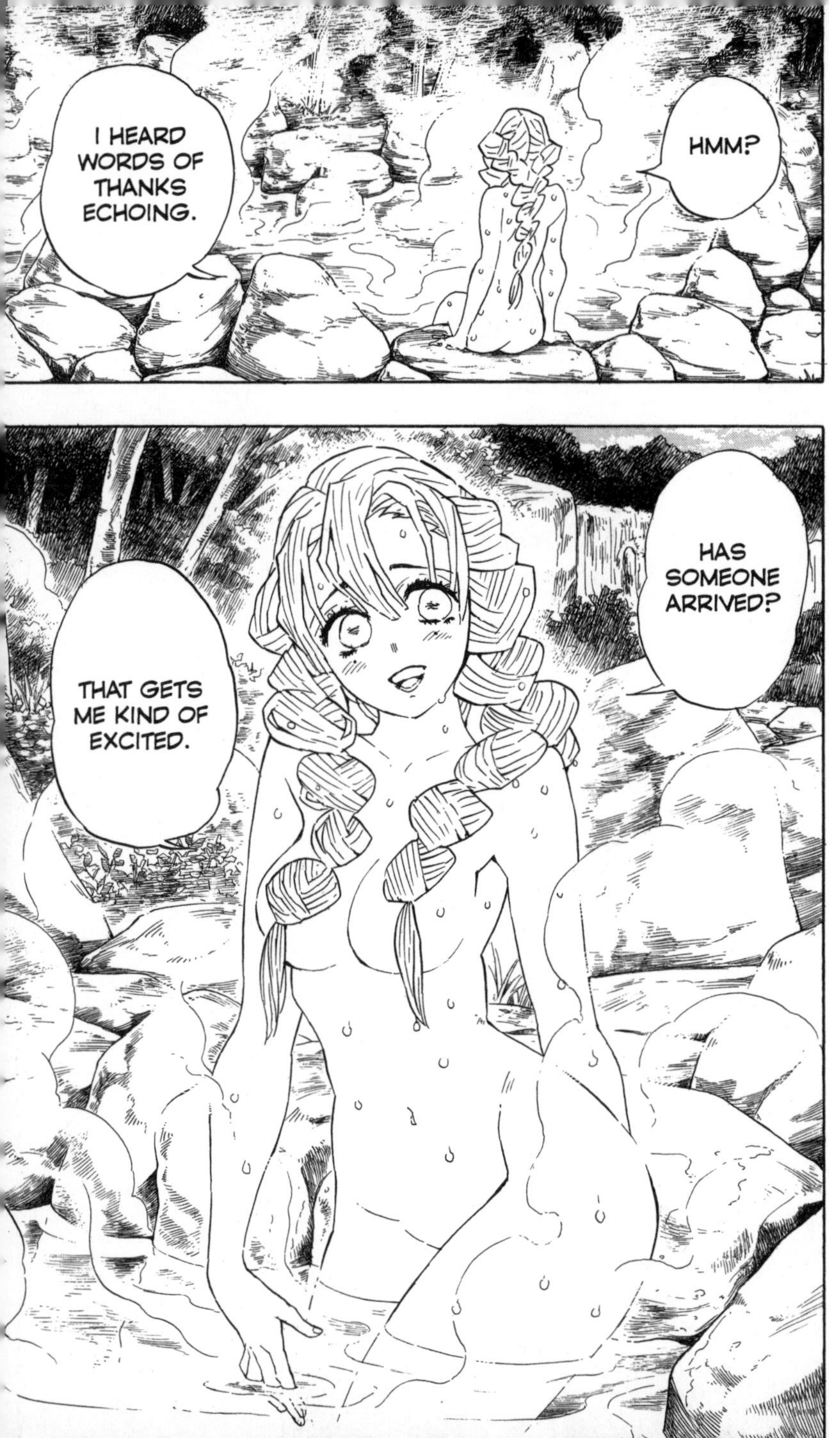
HMM?
I HEARD WORDS OF THANKS ECHOING.
HAS SOMEONE ARRIVED?
THAT GETS ME KIND OF EXCITED.

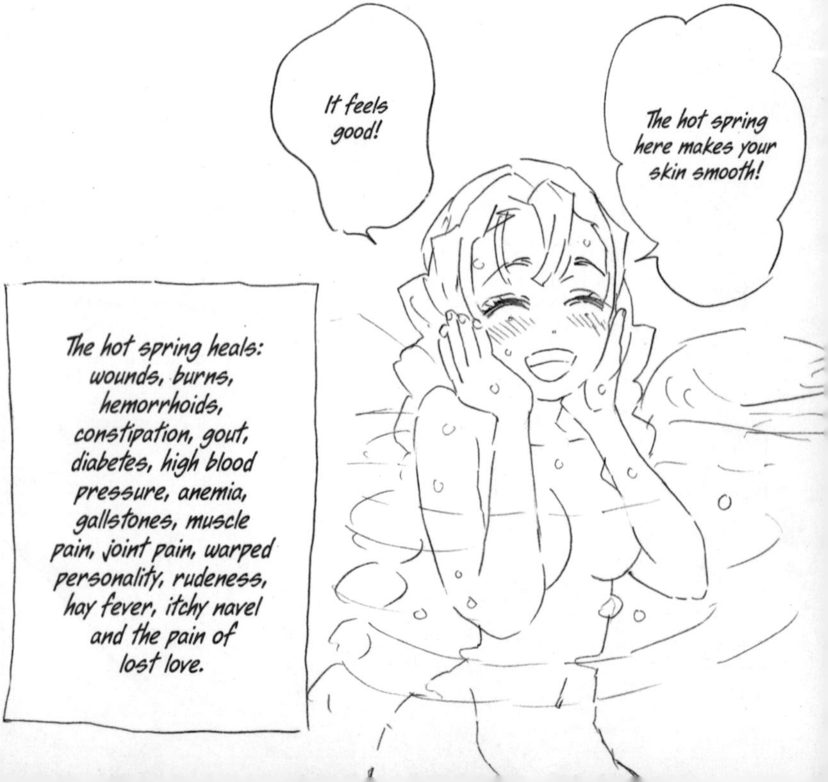
The hot spring here makes your skin smooth!
It feels good!
The hot spring heals: wounds, burns, hemorrhoids, constipation, gout, diabetes, high blood pressure, anemia, gallstones, muscle pain, joint pain, warped personality, rudeness, hay fever, itchy navel and the pain of lost love.

CHAPTER 101: A SECRET

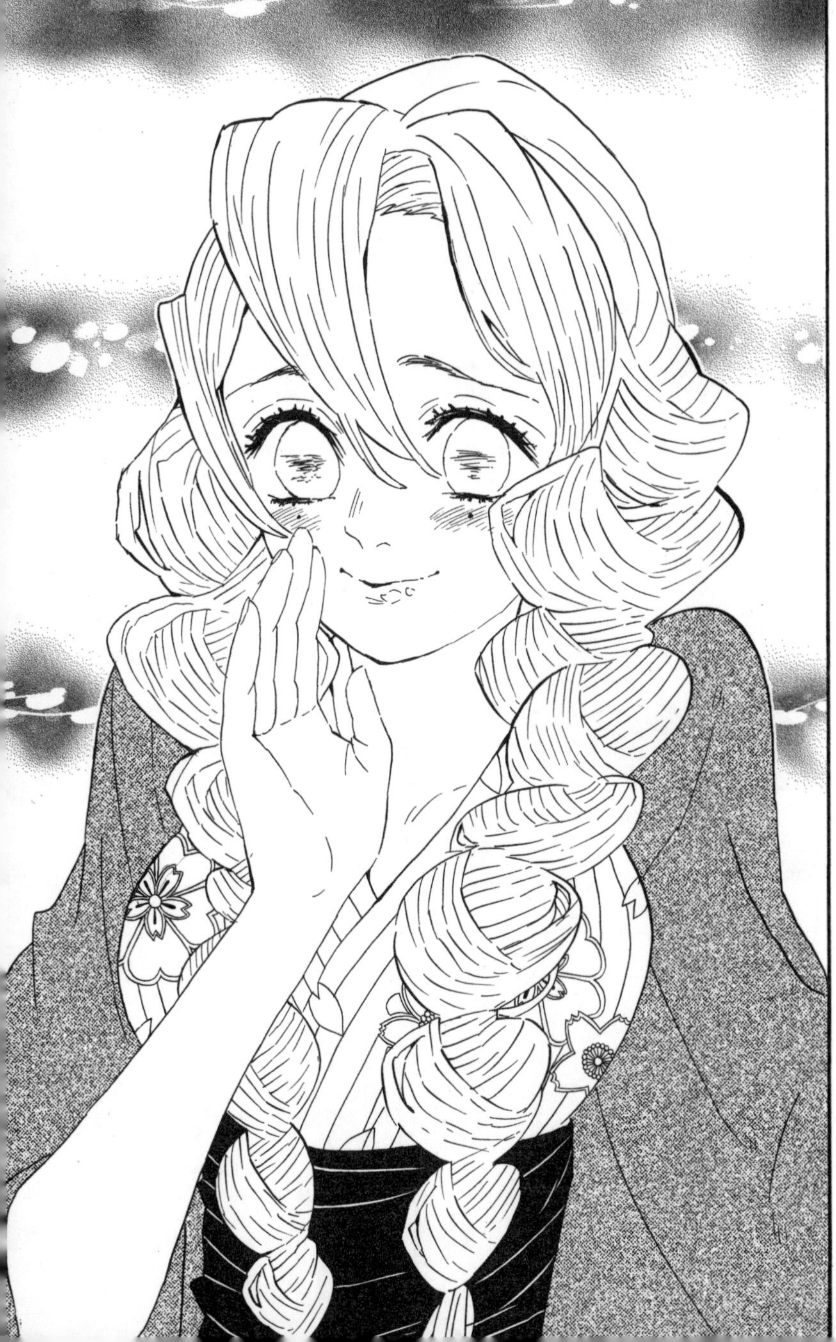

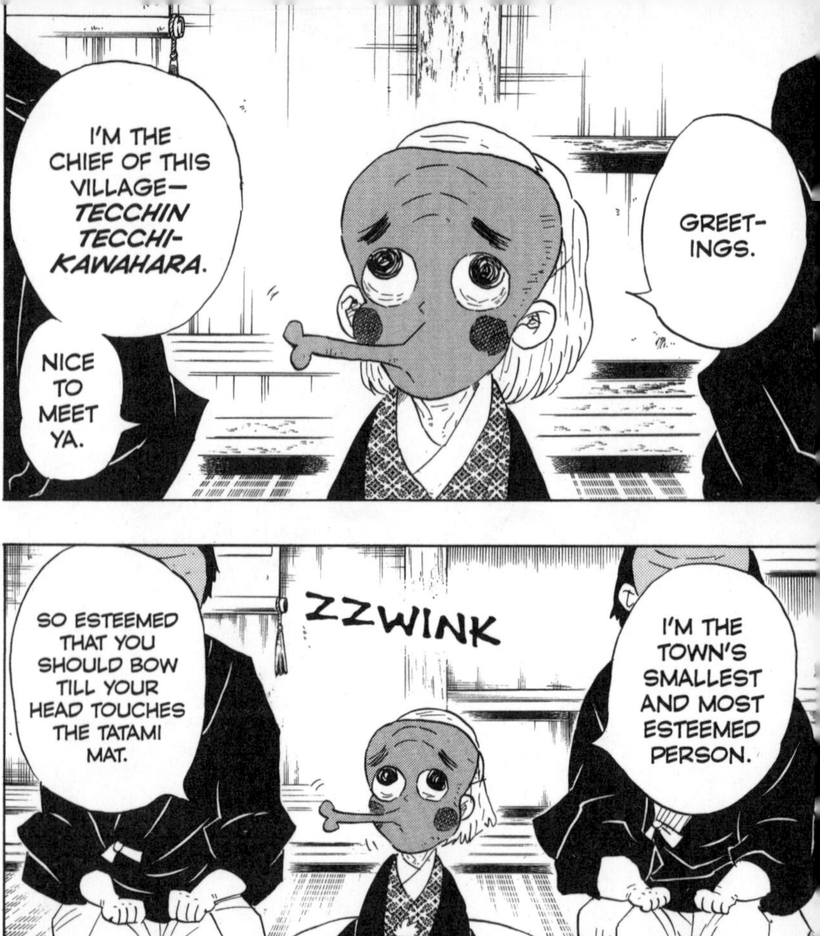
GREET-INGS.
I'M THE CHIEF OF THIS VILLAGE—*TECCHIN TECCHI-KAWAHARA*.
NICE TO MEET YA.
I'M THE TOWN'S SMALLEST AND MOST ESTEEMED PERSON.
ZZWINK
SO ESTEEMED THAT YOU SHOULD BOW TILL YOUR HEAD TOUCHES THE TATAMI MAT.

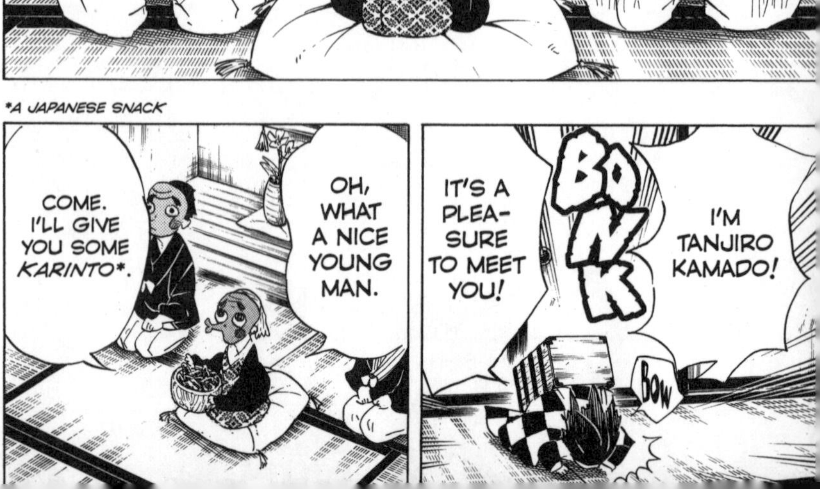
I'M TANJIRO KAMADO!
BONK
BOW
IT'S A PLEA-SURE TO MEET YOU!
OH, WHAT A NICE YOUNG MAN.
COME. I'LL GIVE YOU SOME *KARINTO**.

**A JAPANESE SNACK*

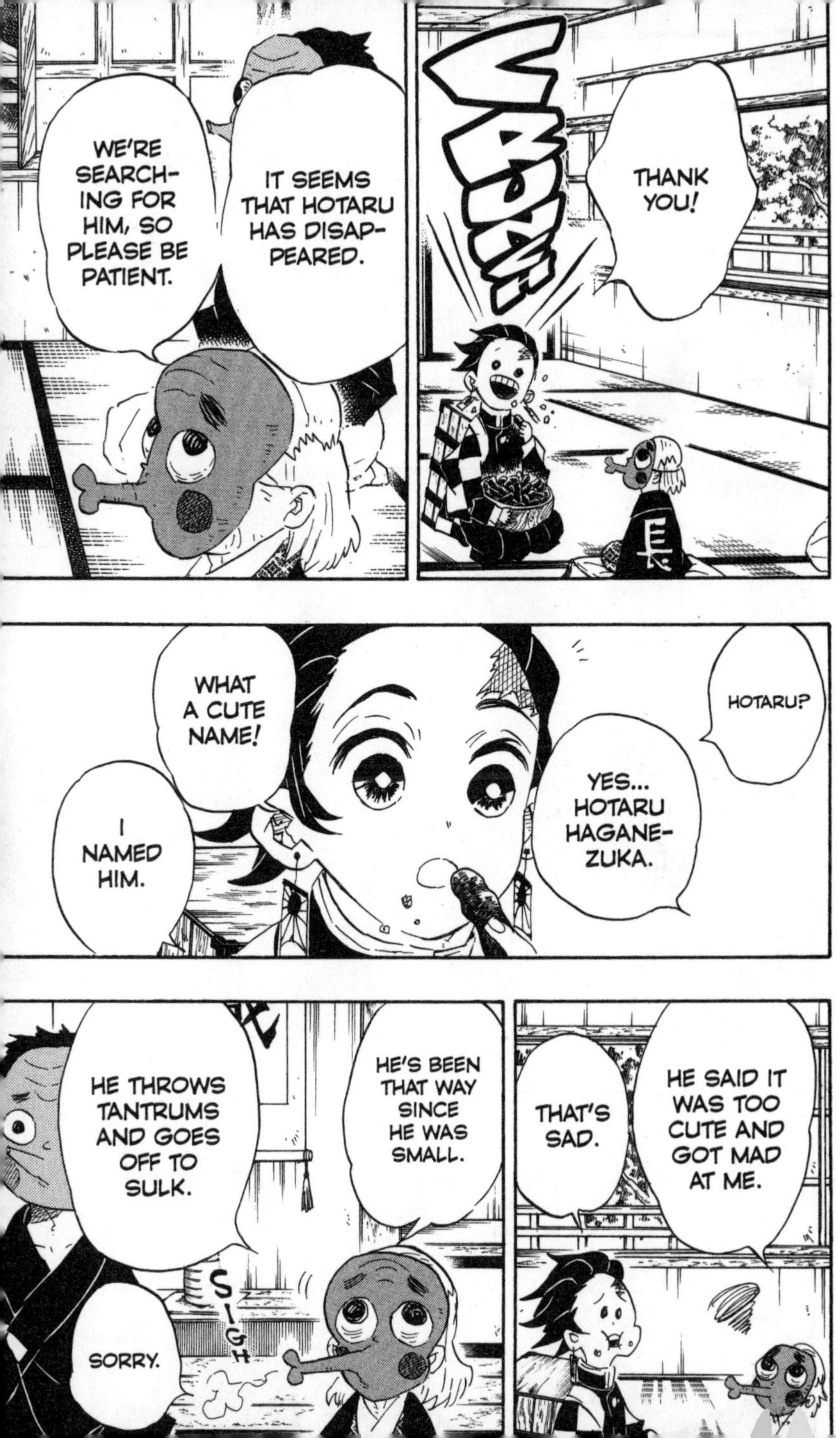
THANK YOU!
IT SEEMS THAT HOTARU HAS DISAPPEARED.
WE'RE SEARCHING FOR HIM, SO PLEASE BE PATIENT.
HOTARU?
YES... HOTARU HAGANEZUKA.
WHAT A CUTE NAME!
I NAMED HIM.
HE SAID IT WAS TOO CUTE AND GOT MAD AT ME.
THAT'S SAD.
HE'S BEEN THAT WAY SINCE HE WAS SMALL.
HE THROWS TANTRUMS AND GOES OFF TO SULK.
SIGH
SORRY.

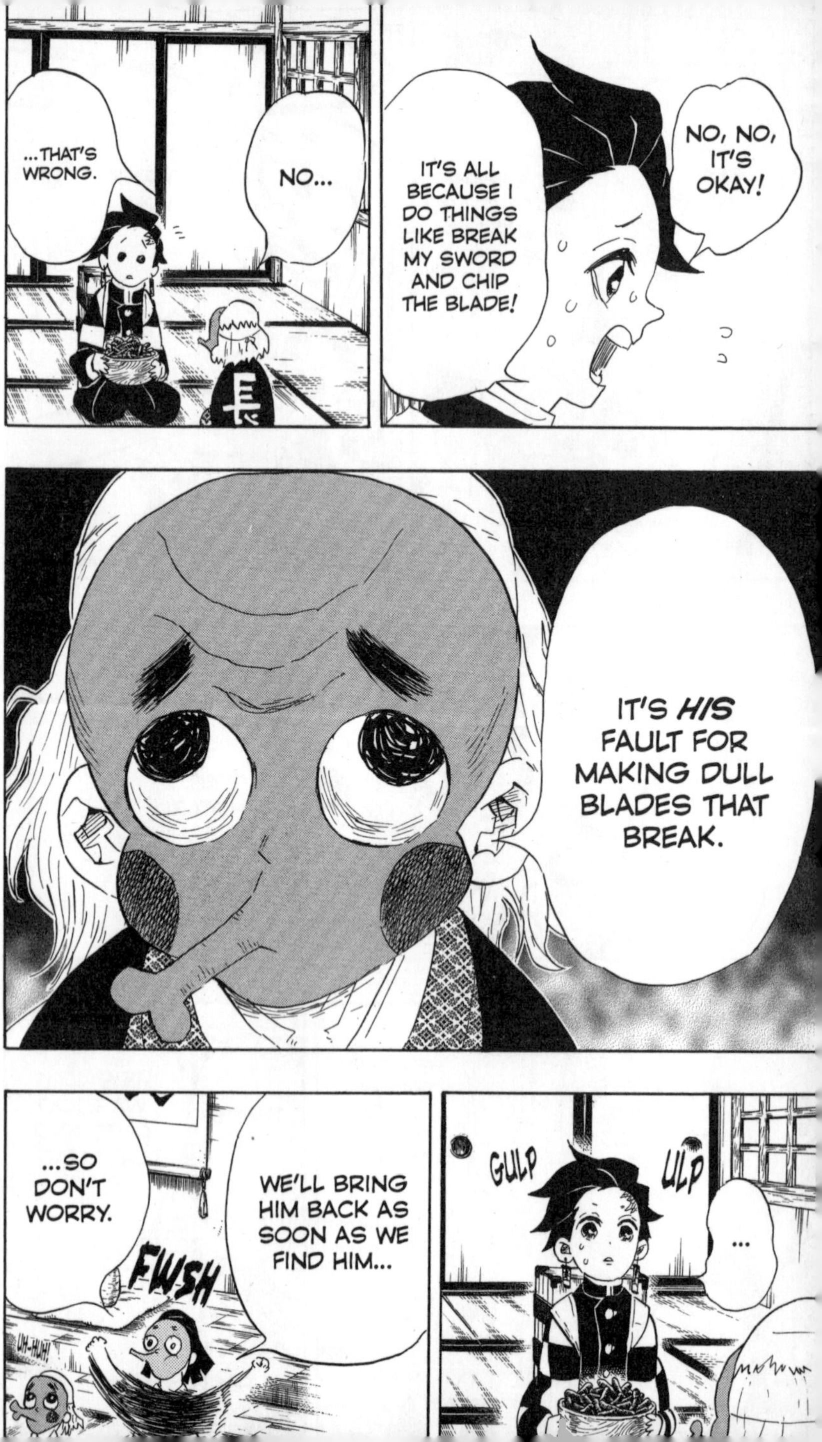
NO, NO, IT'S OKAY!
IT'S ALL BECAUSE I DO THINGS LIKE BREAK MY SWORD AND CHIP THE BLADE!
NO...
...THAT'S WRONG.
IT'S *HIS* FAULT FOR MAKING DULL BLADES THAT BREAK.
...
GULP
ULP
WE'LL BRING HIM BACK AS SOON AS WE FIND HIM...
...SO DON'T WORRY.
FWSH
UH-HUH!

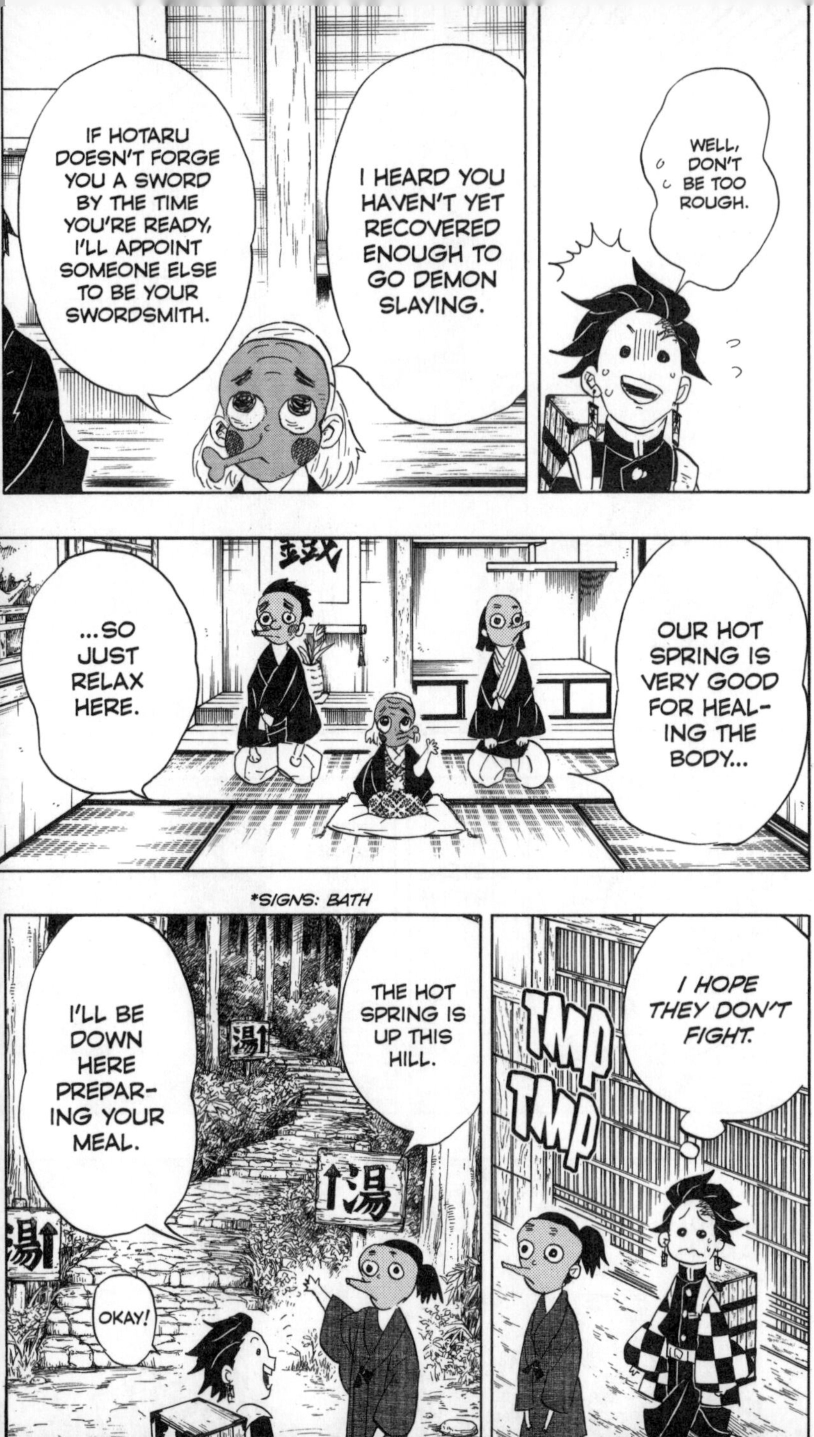
WELL, DON'T BE TOO ROUGH.
I HEARD YOU HAVEN'T YET RECOVERED ENOUGH TO GO DEMON SLAYING.
IF HOTARU DOESN'T FORGE YOU A SWORD BY THE TIME YOU'RE READY, I'LL APPOINT SOMEONE ELSE TO BE YOUR SWORDSMITH.
OUR HOT SPRING IS VERY GOOD FOR HEALING THE BODY...
...SO JUST RELAX HERE.
*SIGNS: BATH
I HOPE THEY DON'T FIGHT.
TMP TMP
THE HOT SPRING IS UP THIS HILL.
湯
I'LL BE DOWN HERE PREPARING YOUR MEAL.
OKAY!

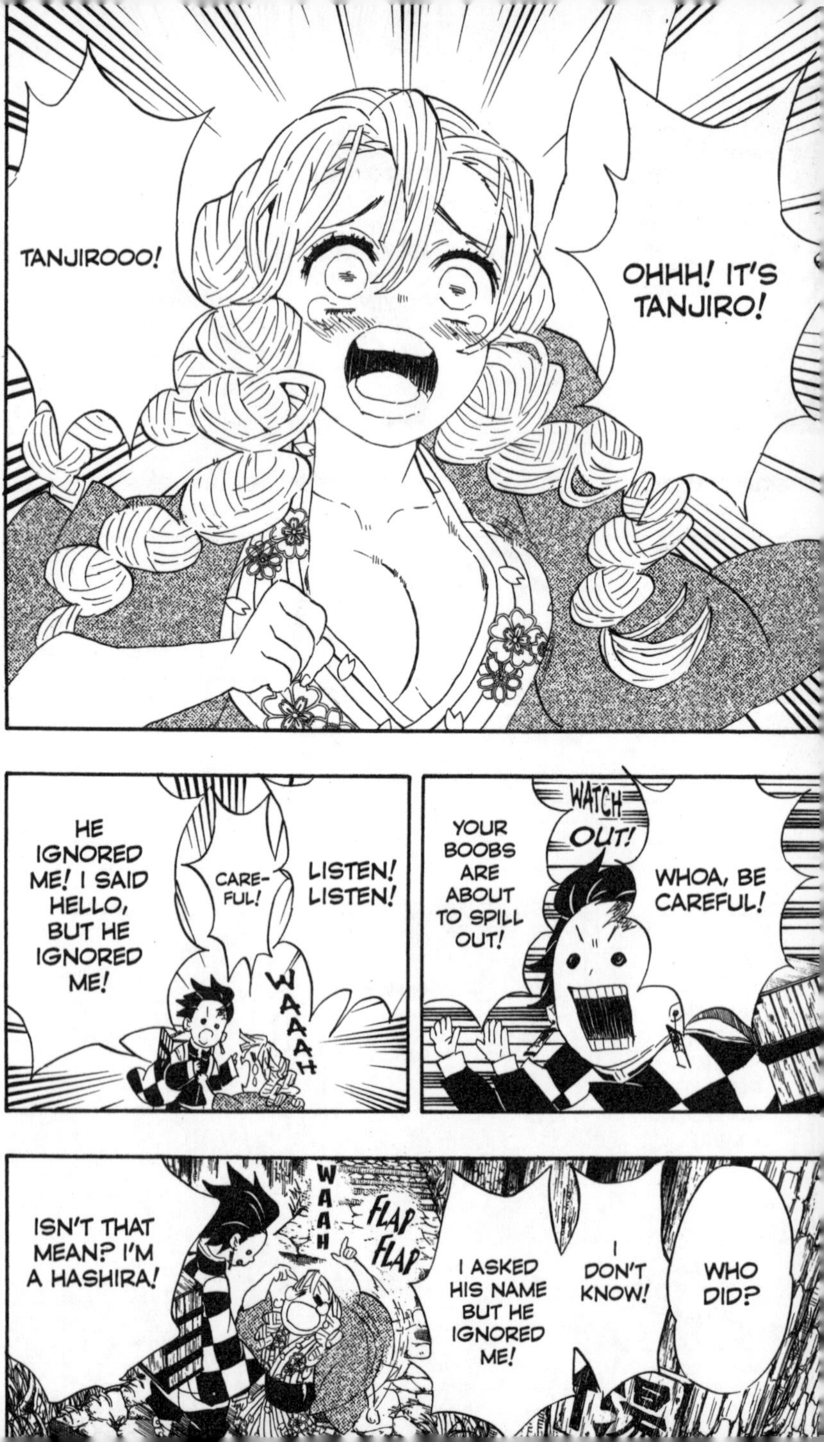
OHHH! IT'S TANJIRO!
TANJIROOO!
WATCH OUT!
WHOA, BE CAREFUL!
YOUR BOOBS ARE ABOUT TO SPILL OUT!
LISTEN! LISTEN!
CARE-FUL!
WAAAAH
HE IGNORED ME! I SAID HELLO, BUT HE IGNORED ME!
WHO DID?
I DON'T KNOW!
I ASKED HIS NAME BUT HE IGNORED ME!
FLAP FLAP
WAAH
ISN'T THAT MEAN? I'M A HASHIRA!

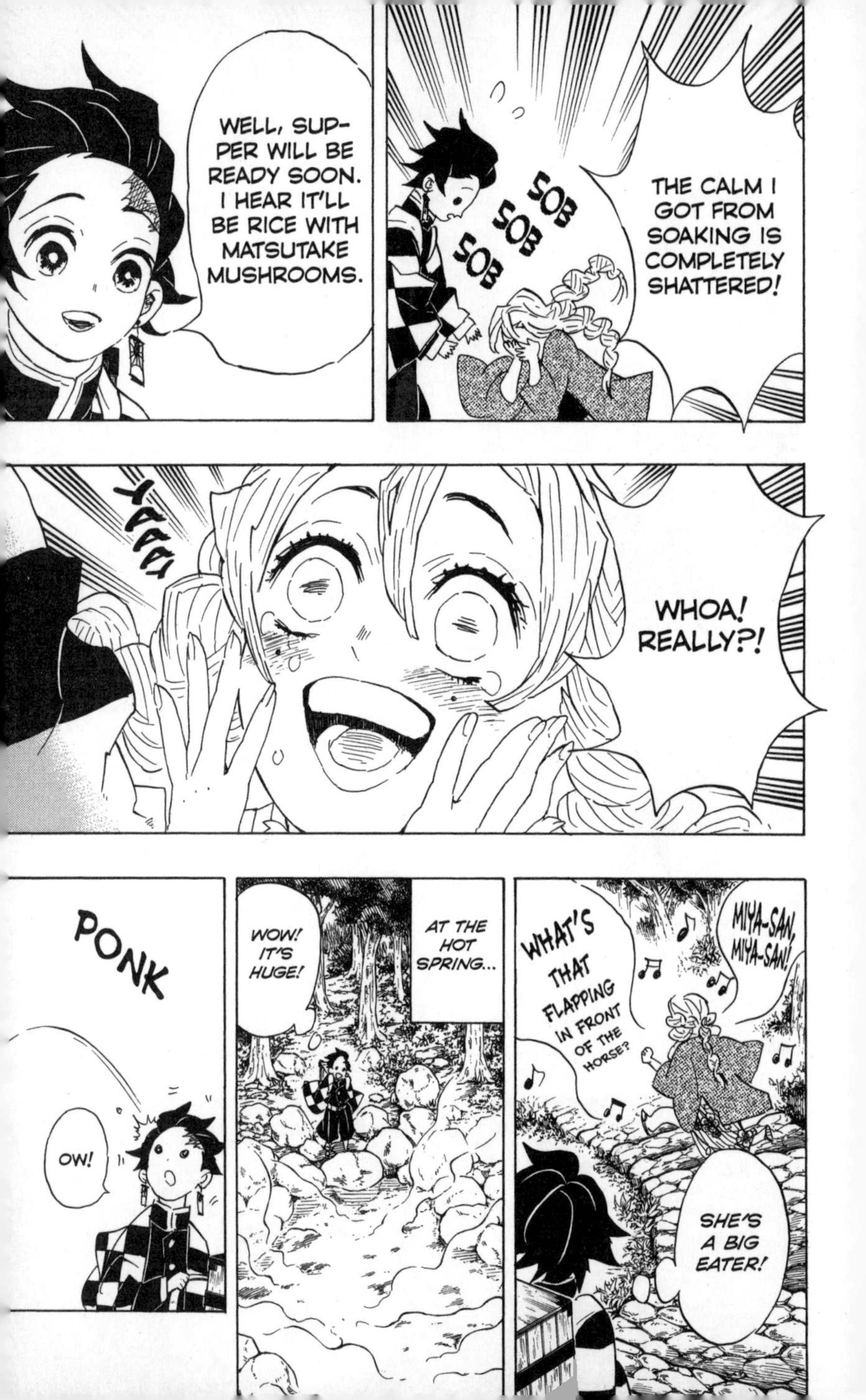
SOB SOB SOB
THE CALM I GOT FROM SOAKING IS COMPLETELY SHATTERED!
WELL, SUPPER WILL BE READY SOON. I HEAR IT'LL BE RICE WITH MATSUTAKE MUSHROOMS.
WHOA! REALLY?!
MIYA-SAN, MIYA-SAN!
WHAT'S THAT FLAPPING IN FRONT OF THE HORSE?
SHE'S A BIG EATER!
AT THE HOT SPRING...
WOW! IT'S HUGE!
PONK
OW!

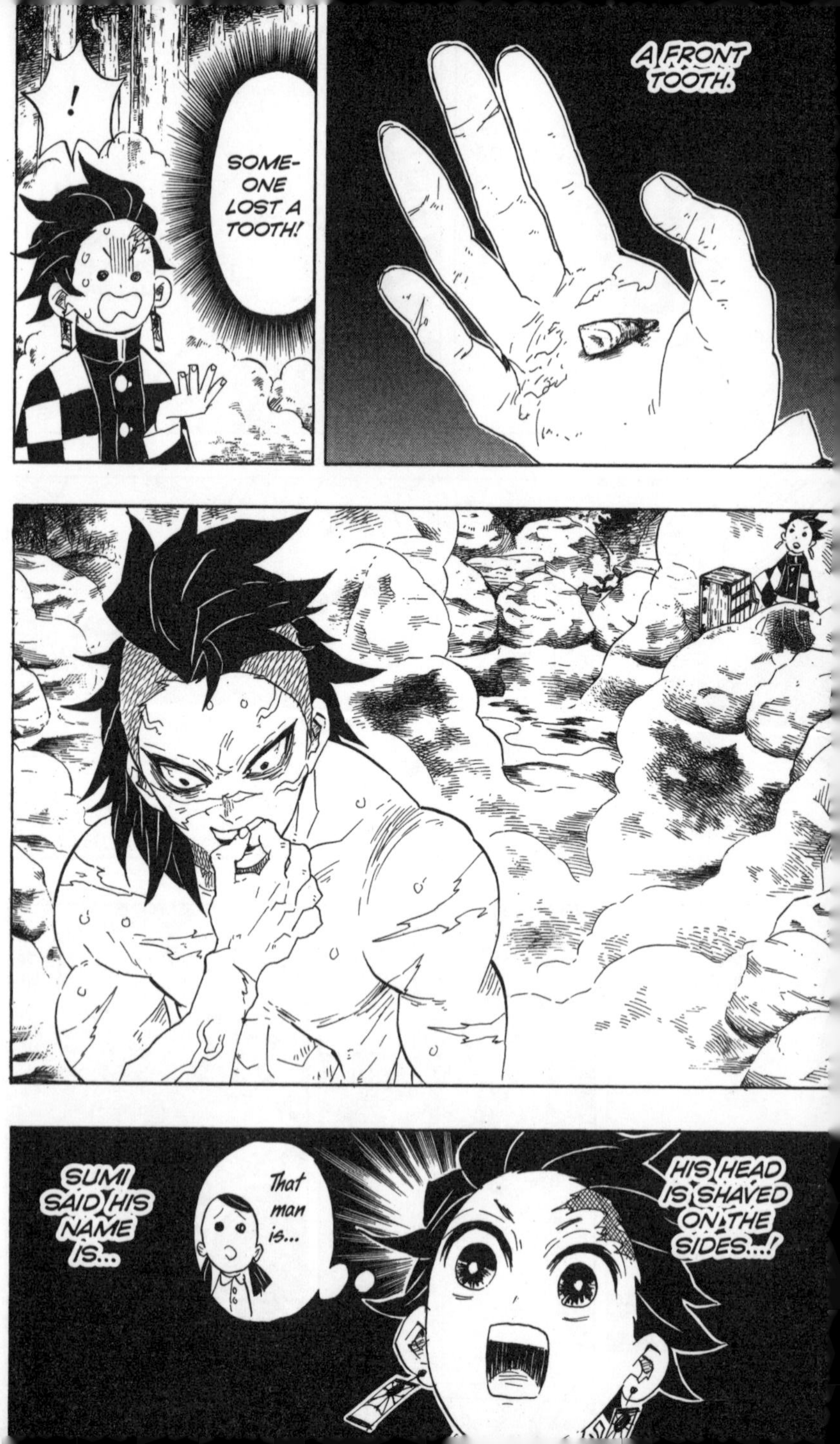
A FRONT TOOTH.
!
SOME-ONE LOST A TOOTH!
HIS HEAD IS SHAVED ON THE SIDES...!
That man is...
SUMI SAID HIS NAME IS...

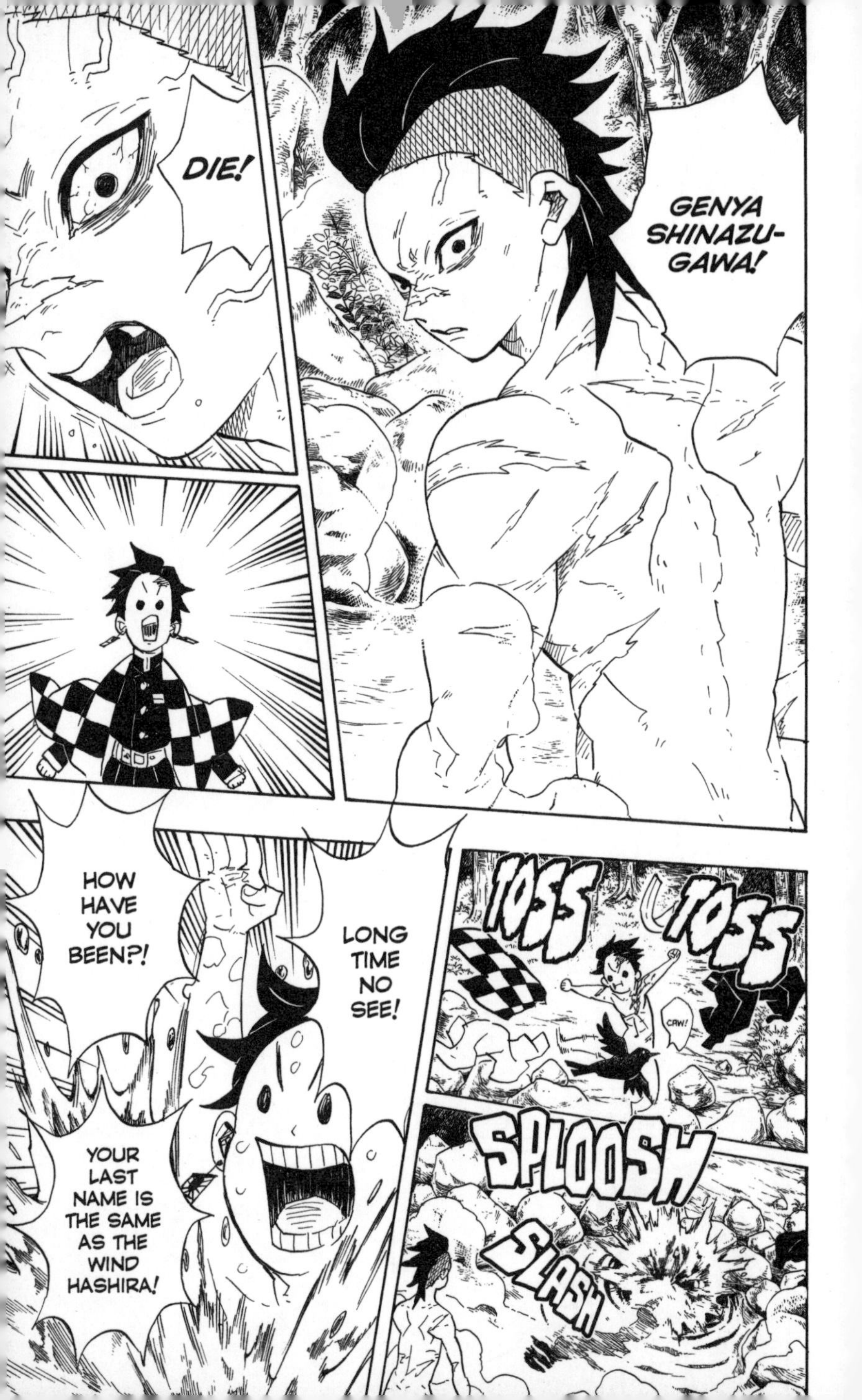
GENYA SHINAZU-GAWA!
DIE!
TOSS
TOSS
CAW!
SPLOOSH
SLASH
LONG TIME NO SEE!
HOW HAVE YOU BEEN?!
YOUR LAST NAME IS THE SAME AS THE WIND HASHIRA!

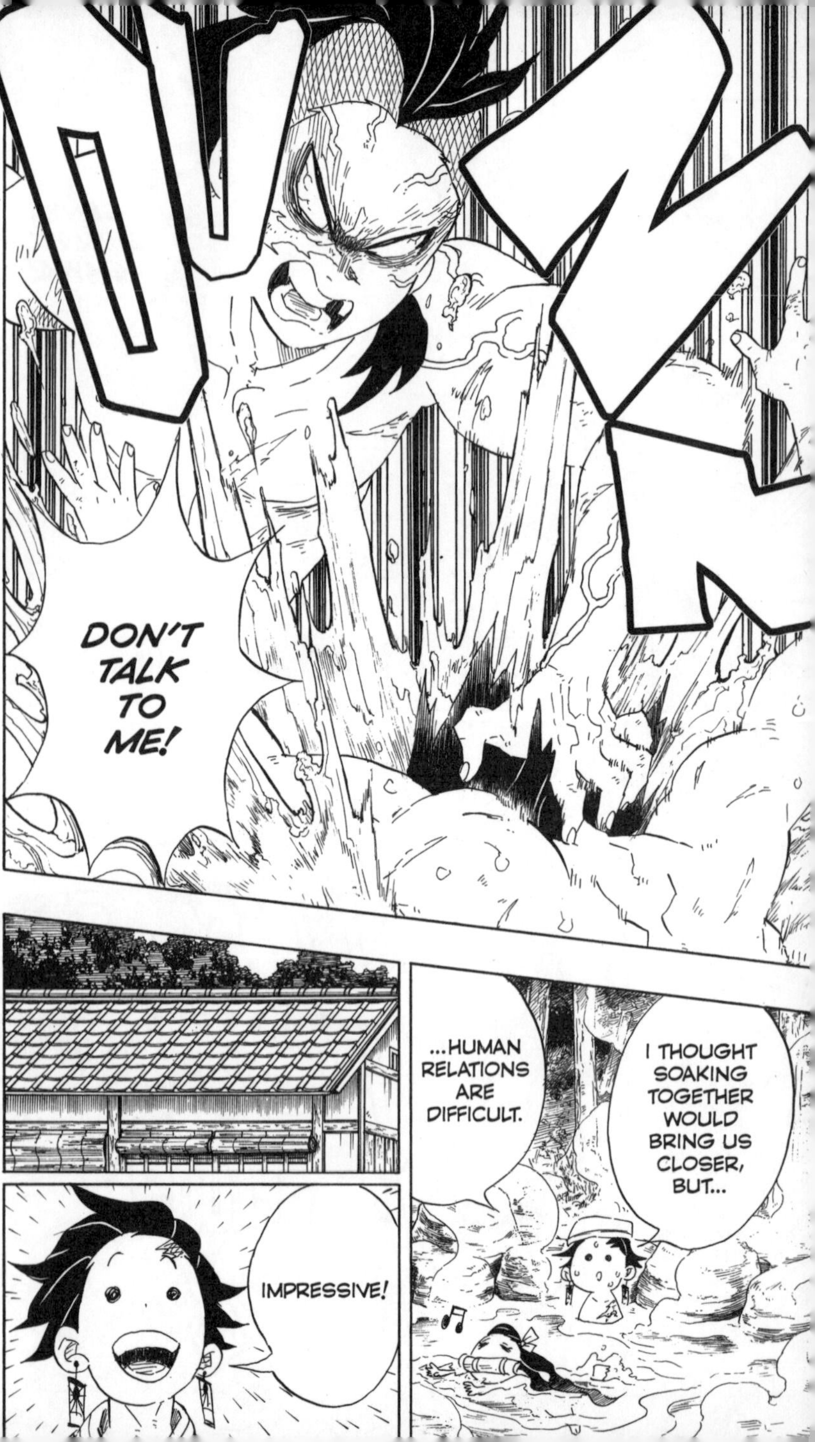
DON'T TALK TO ME!
I THOUGHT SOAKING TOGETHER WOULD BRING US CLOSER, BUT...
...HUMAN RELATIONS ARE DIFFICULT.
IMPRESSIVE!

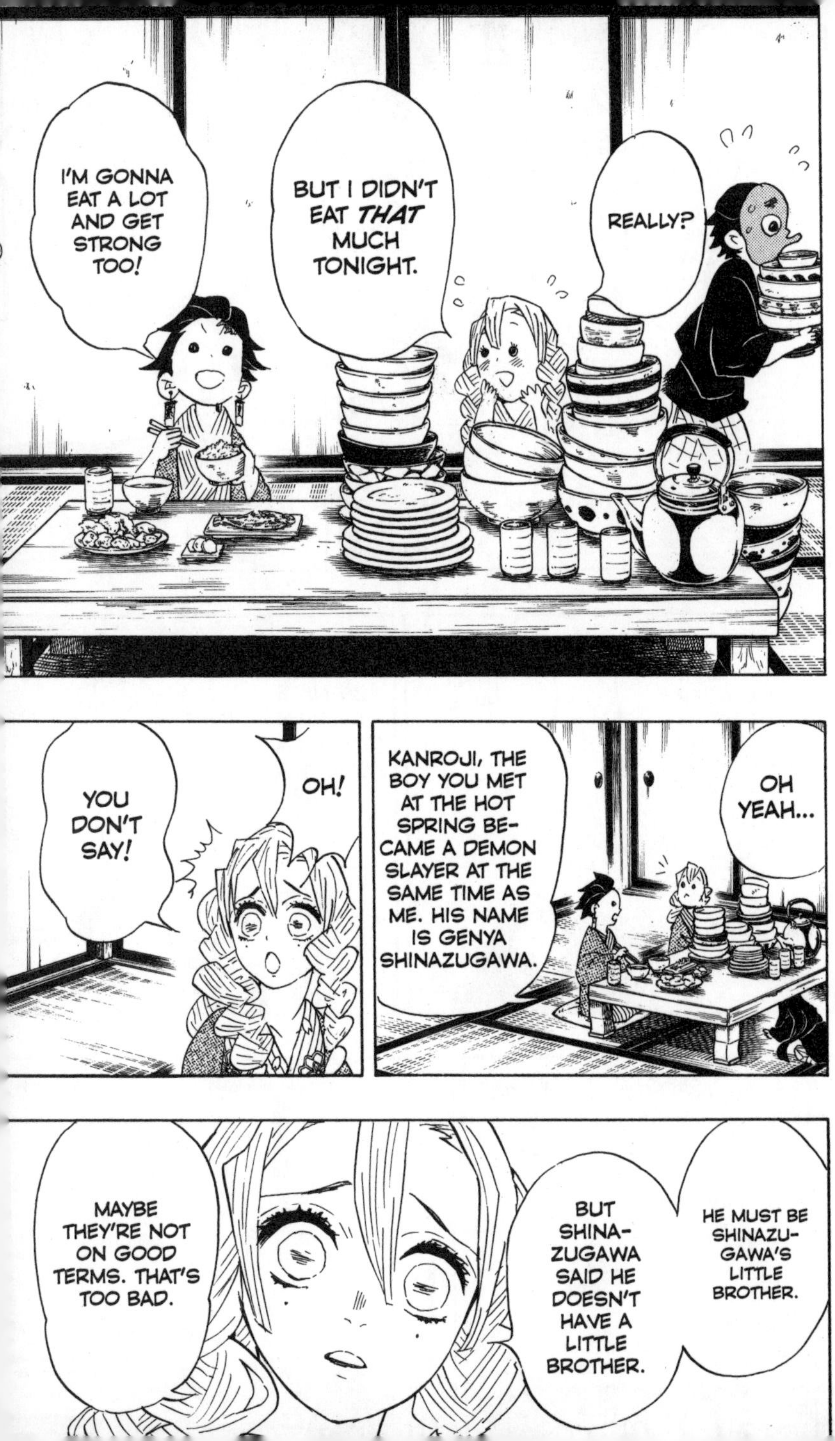
REALLY?
BUT I DIDN'T EAT *THAT* MUCH TONIGHT.
I'M GONNA EAT A LOT AND GET STRONG TOO!
OH YEAH...
KANROJI, THE BOY YOU MET AT THE HOT SPRING BECAME A DEMON SLAYER AT THE SAME TIME AS ME. HIS NAME IS GENYA SHINAZUGAWA.
OH!
YOU DON'T SAY!
HE MUST BE SHINAZUGAWA'S LITTLE BROTHER.
BUT SHINAZUGAWA SAID HE DOESN'T HAVE A LITTLE BROTHER.
MAYBE THEY'RE NOT ON GOOD TERMS. THAT'S TOO BAD.

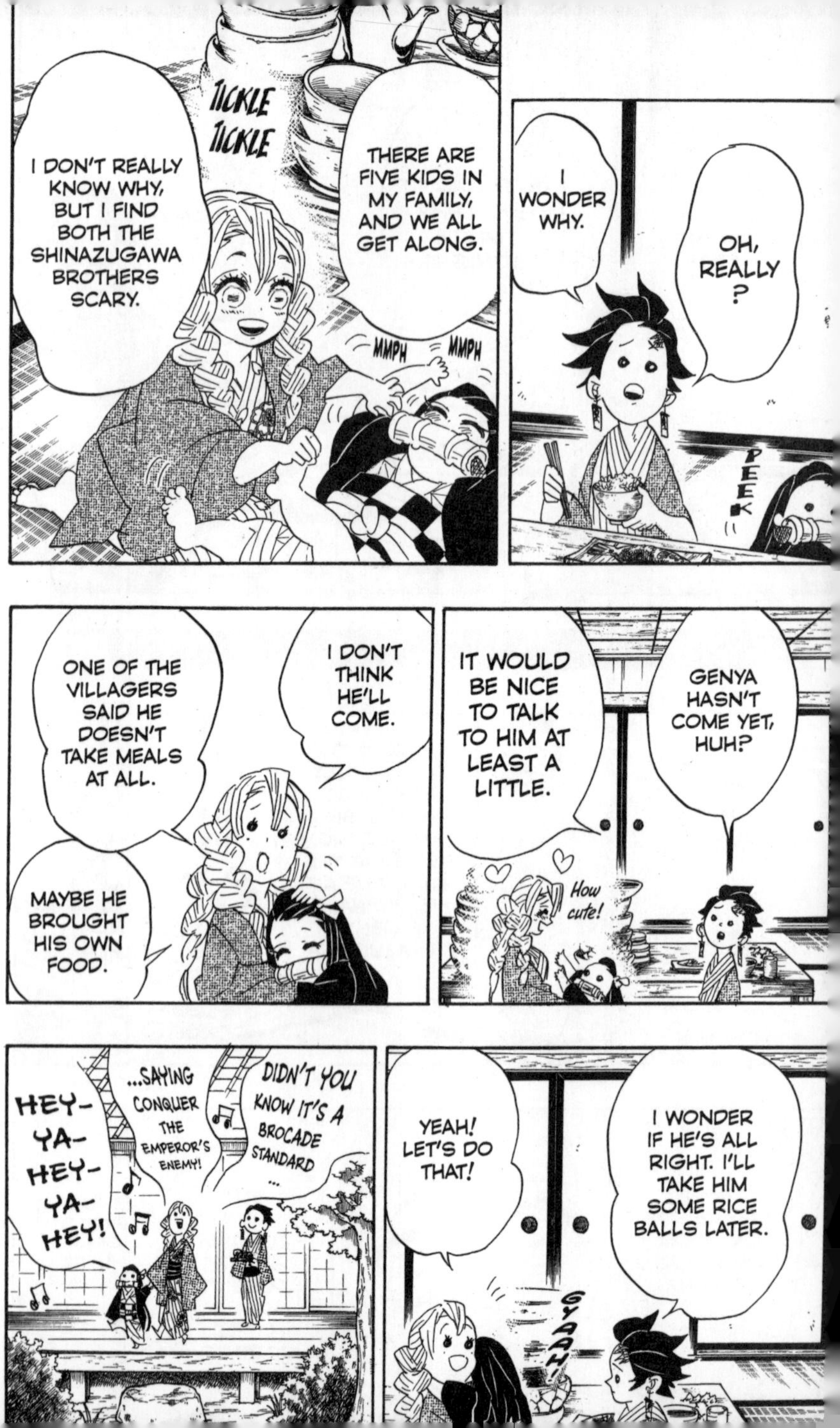
OH, REALLY?
I WONDER WHY.
PEEK
THERE ARE FIVE KIDS IN MY FAMILY, AND WE ALL GET ALONG.
I DON'T REALLY KNOW WHY, BUT I FIND BOTH THE SHINAZUGAWA BROTHERS SCARY.
TICKLE TICKLE
MMPH MMPH
GENYA HASN'T COME YET, HUH?
IT WOULD BE NICE TO TALK TO HIM AT LEAST A LITTLE.
How cute!
I DON'T THINK HE'LL COME.
ONE OF THE VILLAGERS SAID HE DOESN'T TAKE MEALS AT ALL.
MAYBE HE BROUGHT HIS OWN FOOD.
I WONDER IF HE'S ALL RIGHT. I'LL TAKE HIM SOME RICE BALLS LATER.
YEAH! LET'S DO THAT!
GYAAAH!
DIDN'T YOU KNOW IT'S A BROCADE STANDARD ...
...SAYING CONQUER THE EMPEROR'S ENEMY!
HEY-YA-HEY-YA-HEY!

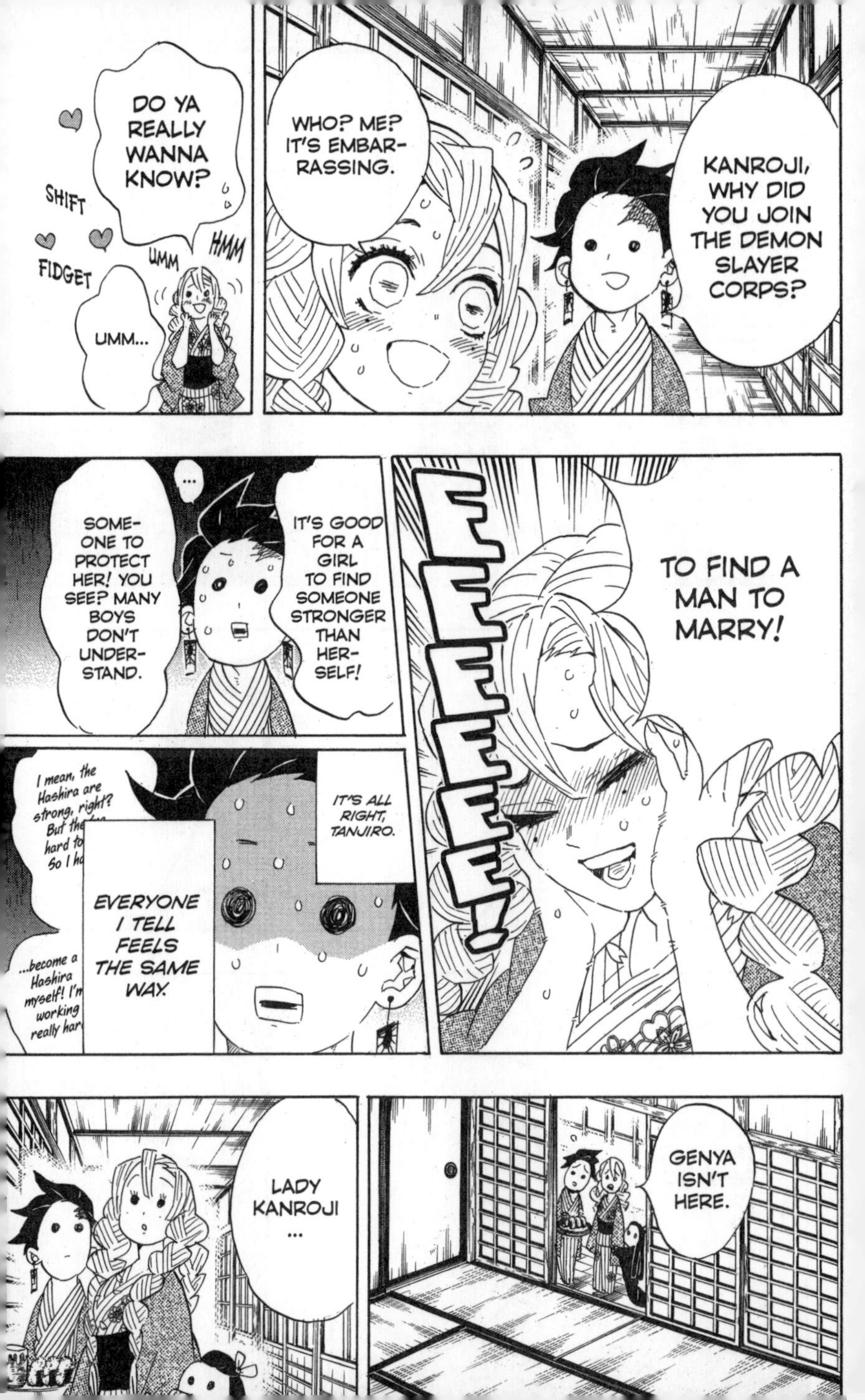
KANROJI, WHY DID YOU JOIN THE DEMON SLAYER CORPS?
WHO? ME? IT'S EMBARRASSING.
DO YA REALLY WANNA KNOW?
SHIFT
FIDGET
HMM
UMM
UMM...
TO FIND A MAN TO MARRY!
IT'S GOOD FOR A GIRL TO FIND SOMEONE STRONGER THAN HERSELF!
SOMEONE TO PROTECT HER! YOU SEE? MANY BOYS DON'T UNDERSTAND.
...
IT'S ALL RIGHT, TANJIRO.
EVERYONE I TELL FEELS THE SAME WAY.
I mean, the Hashira are strong, right?
...become a Hashira
GENYA ISN'T HERE.
LADY KANROJI ...

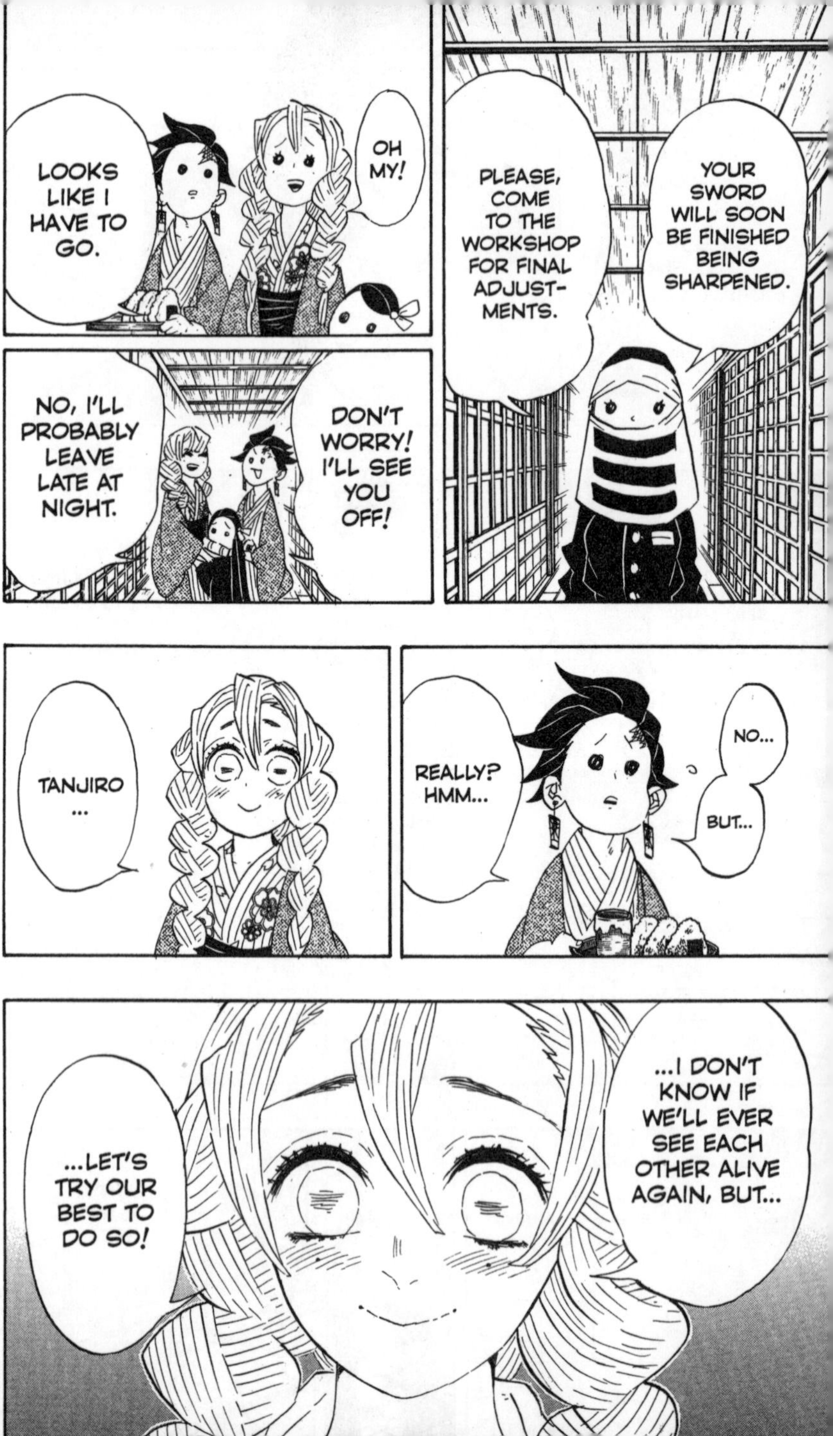
YOUR SWORD WILL SOON BE FINISHED BEING SHARPENED.
PLEASE, COME TO THE WORKSHOP FOR FINAL ADJUSTMENTS.
OH MY!
LOOKS LIKE I HAVE TO GO.
DON'T WORRY! I'LL SEE YOU OFF!
NO, I'LL PROBABLY LEAVE LATE AT NIGHT.
NO...
BUT...
REALLY? HMM...
TANJIRO ...
...I DON'T KNOW IF WE'LL EVER SEE EACH OTHER ALIVE AGAIN, BUT...
...LET'S TRY OUR BEST TO DO SO!

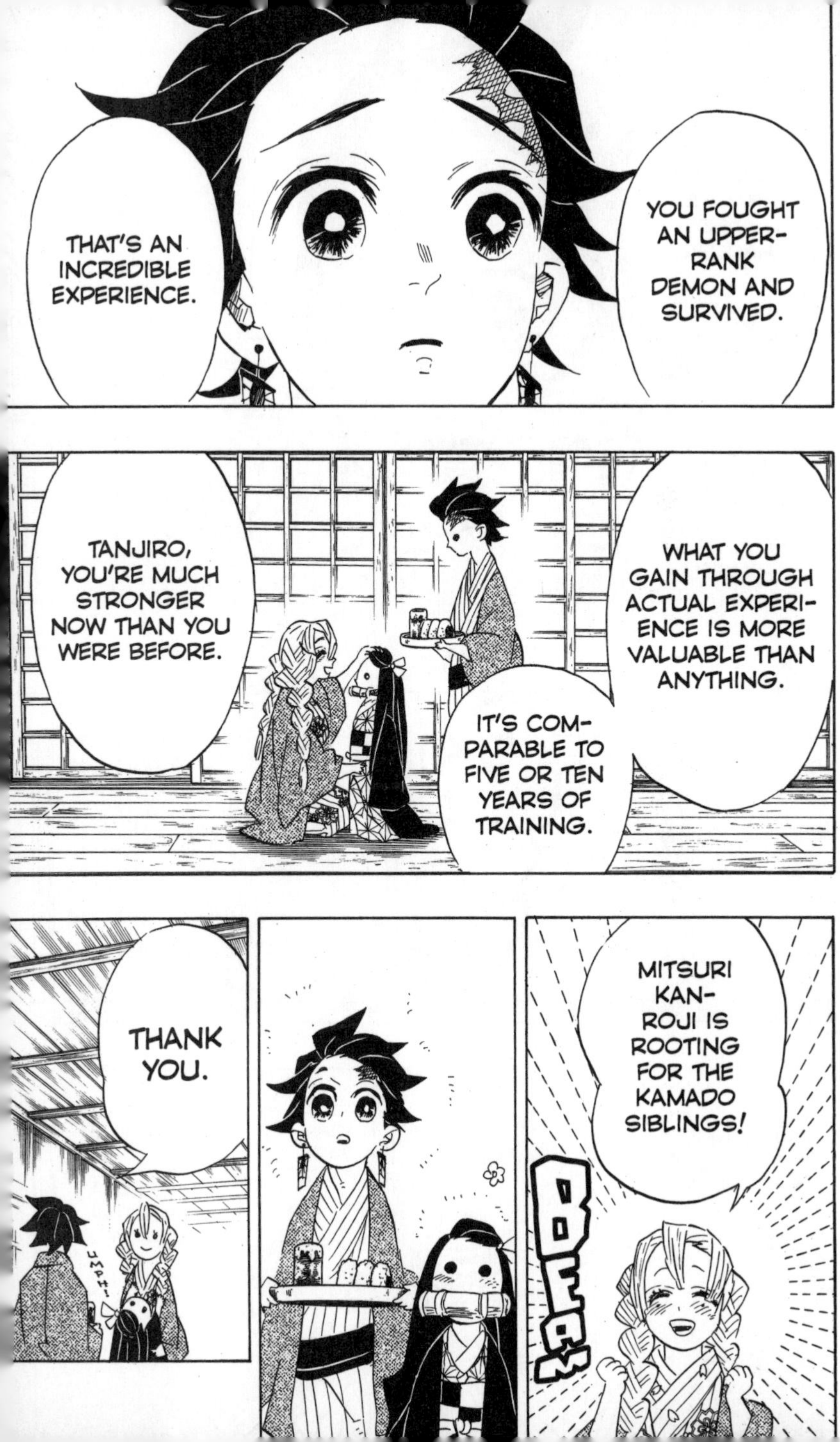
YOU FOUGHT AN UPPER-RANK DEMON AND SURVIVED.
THAT'S AN INCREDIBLE EXPERIENCE.
WHAT YOU GAIN THROUGH ACTUAL EXPERIENCE IS MORE VALUABLE THAN ANYTHING.
IT'S COMPARABLE TO FIVE OR TEN YEARS OF TRAINING.
TANJIRO, YOU'RE MUCH STRONGER NOW THAN YOU WERE BEFORE.
MITSURI KAN-ROJI IS ROOTING FOR THE KAMADO SIBLINGS!
BEAM!
THANK YOU.
UMPH!

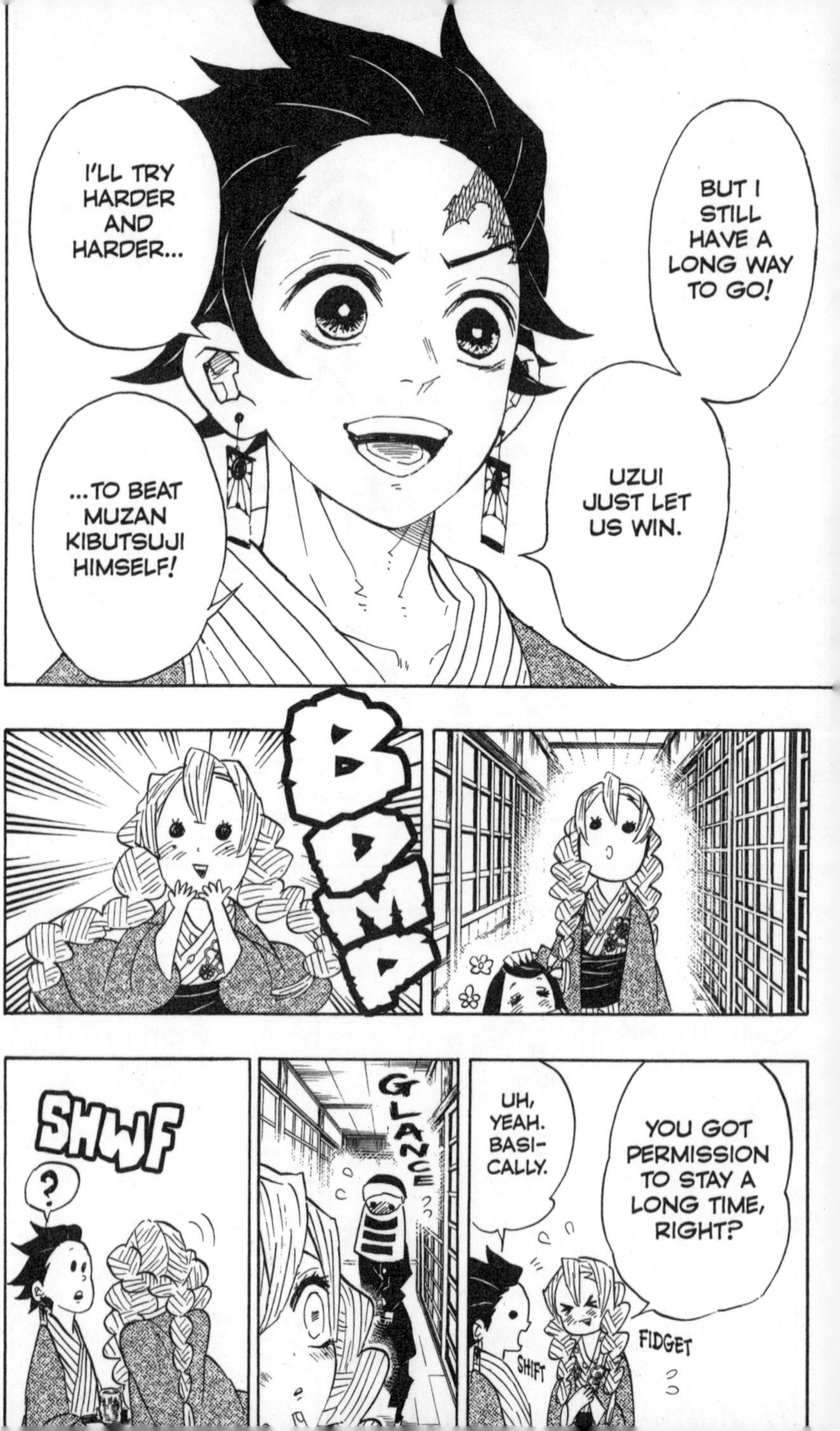
BUT I STILL HAVE A LONG WAY TO GO!
UZUI JUST LET US WIN.
I'LL TRY HARDER AND HARDER...
...TO BEAT MUZAN KIBUTSUJI HIMSELF!
BDMP
YOU GOT PERMISSION TO STAY A LONG TIME, RIGHT?
UH, YEAH. BASI-CALLY.
FIDGET
SHIFT
GLANCE
SHWF
?

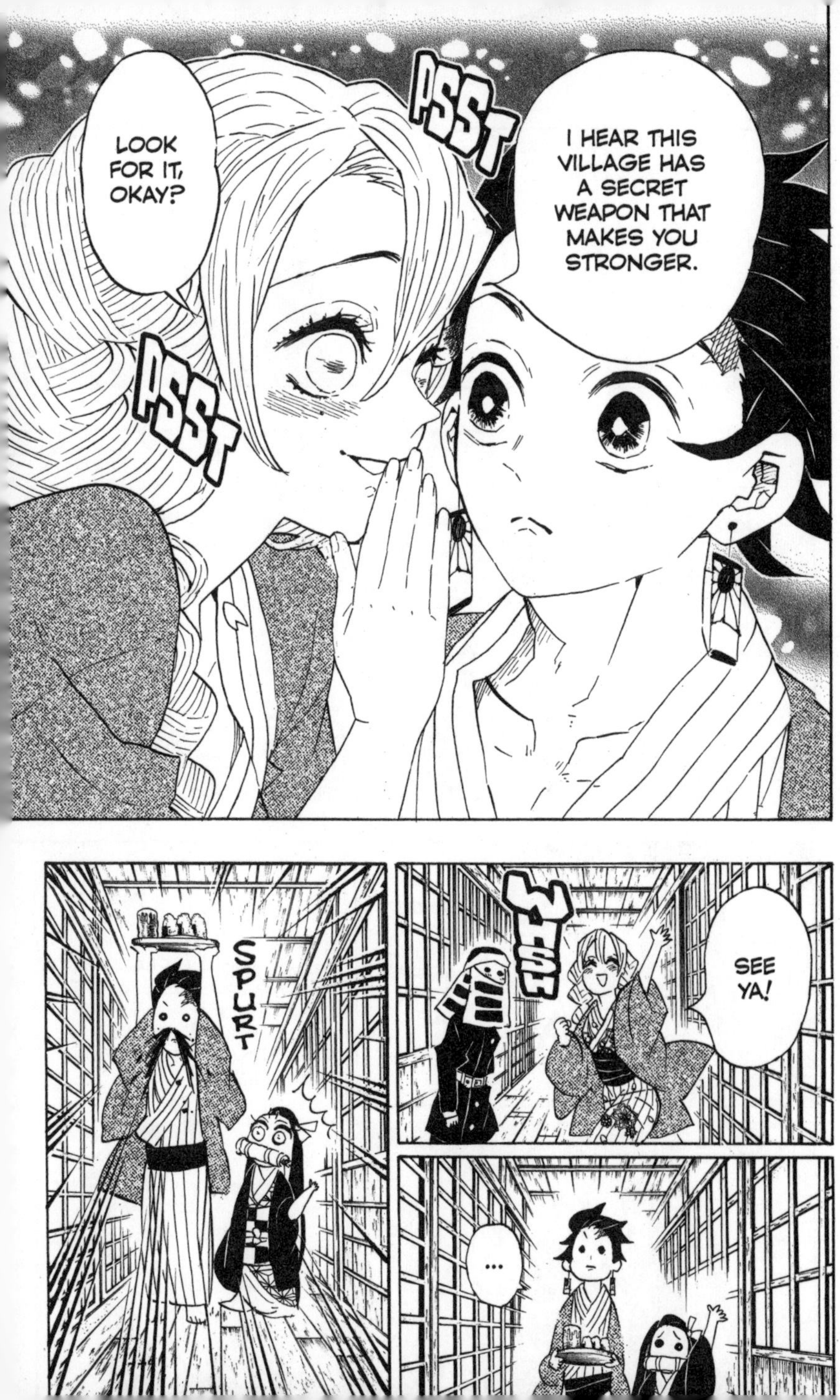
PSST
I HEAR THIS VILLAGE HAS A SECRET WEAPON THAT MAKES YOU STRONGER.
PSST
LOOK FOR IT, OKAY?
WHSH
SEE YA!
...
SPURT

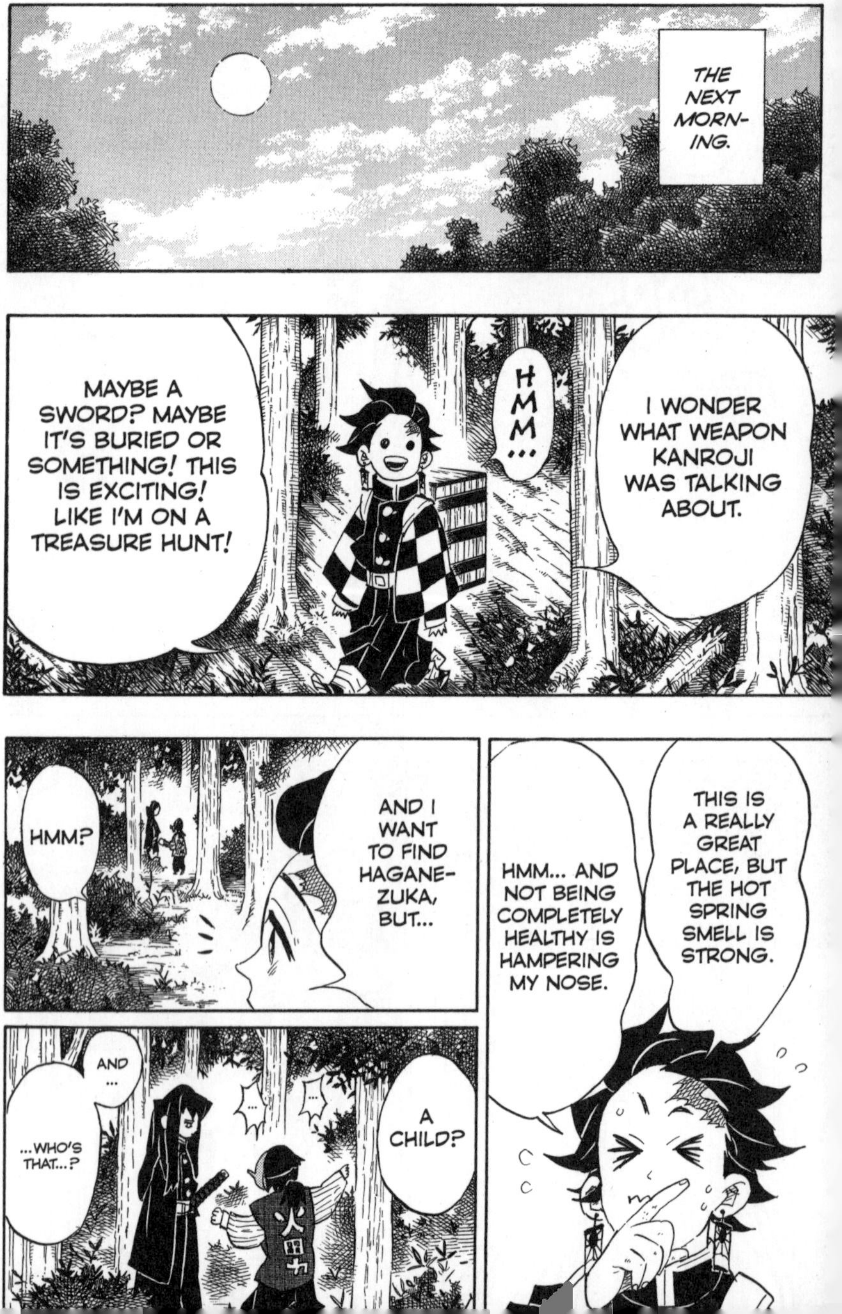
THE NEXT MORNING.
I WONDER WHAT WEAPON KANROJI WAS TALKING ABOUT.
HMM...
MAYBE A SWORD? MAYBE IT'S BURIED OR SOMETHING! THIS IS EXCITING! LIKE I'M ON A TREASURE HUNT!
THIS IS A REALLY GREAT PLACE, BUT THE HOT SPRING SMELL IS STRONG.
HMM... AND NOT BEING COMPLETELY HEALTHY IS HAMPERING MY NOSE.
AND I WANT TO FIND HAGANEZUKA, BUT...
HMM?
A CHILD?
...
...
AND ...
...WHO'S THAT...?

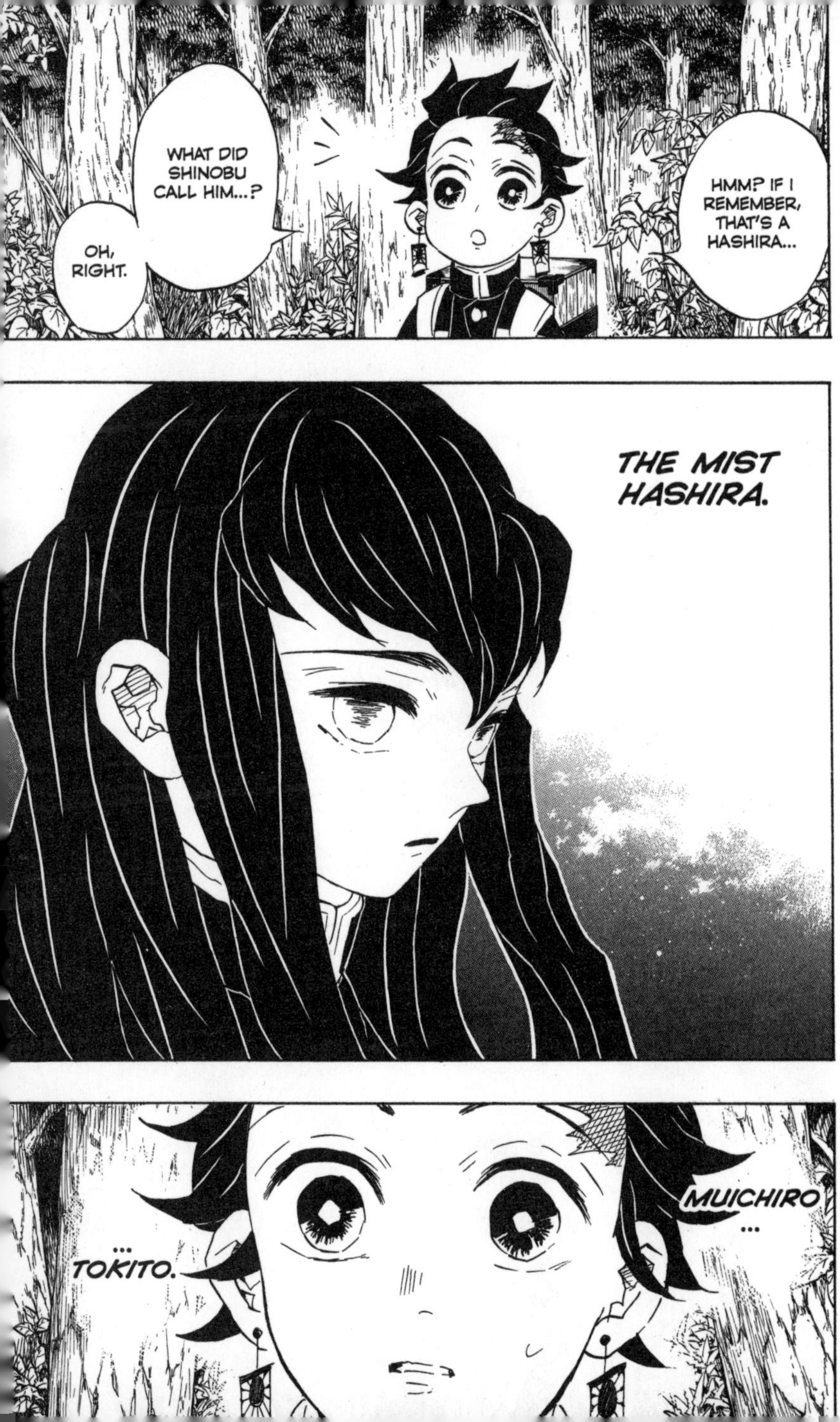
HMM? IF I REMEMBER, THAT'S A HASHIRA...
WHAT DID SHINOBU CALL HIM...?
OH, RIGHT.
THE MIST HASHIRA.
MUICHIRO ...
... TOKITO.

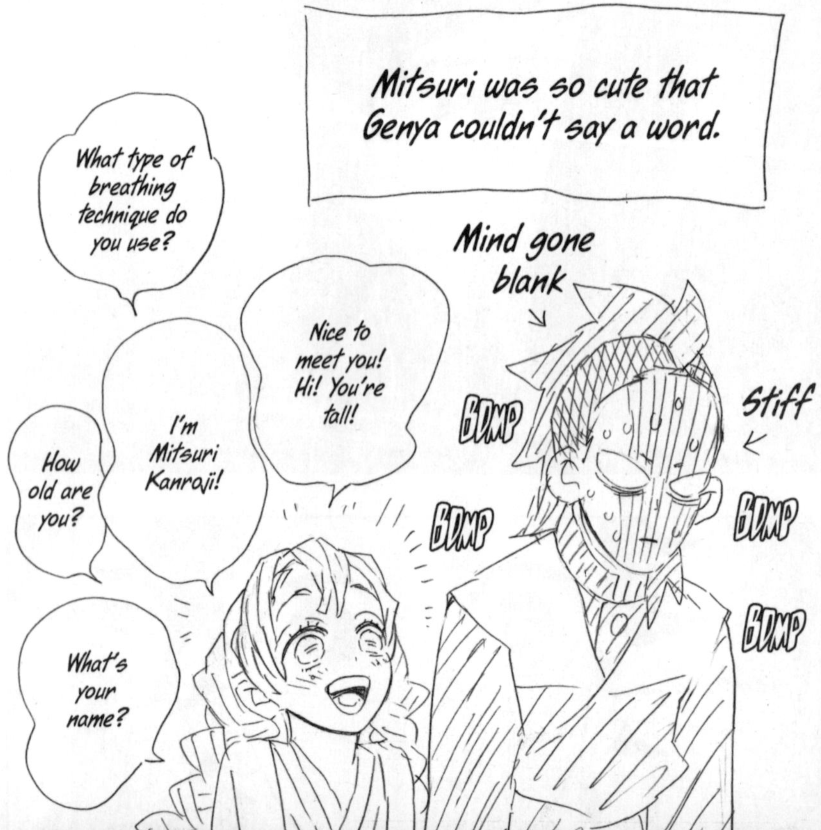

Mitsuri was so cute that Genya couldn't say a word.
Mind gone blank
Stiff
BDMP
BDMP
BDMP
BDMP
Nice to meet you! Hi! You're tall!
What type of breathing technique do you use?
I'm Mitsuri Kanroji!
How old are you?
What's your name?

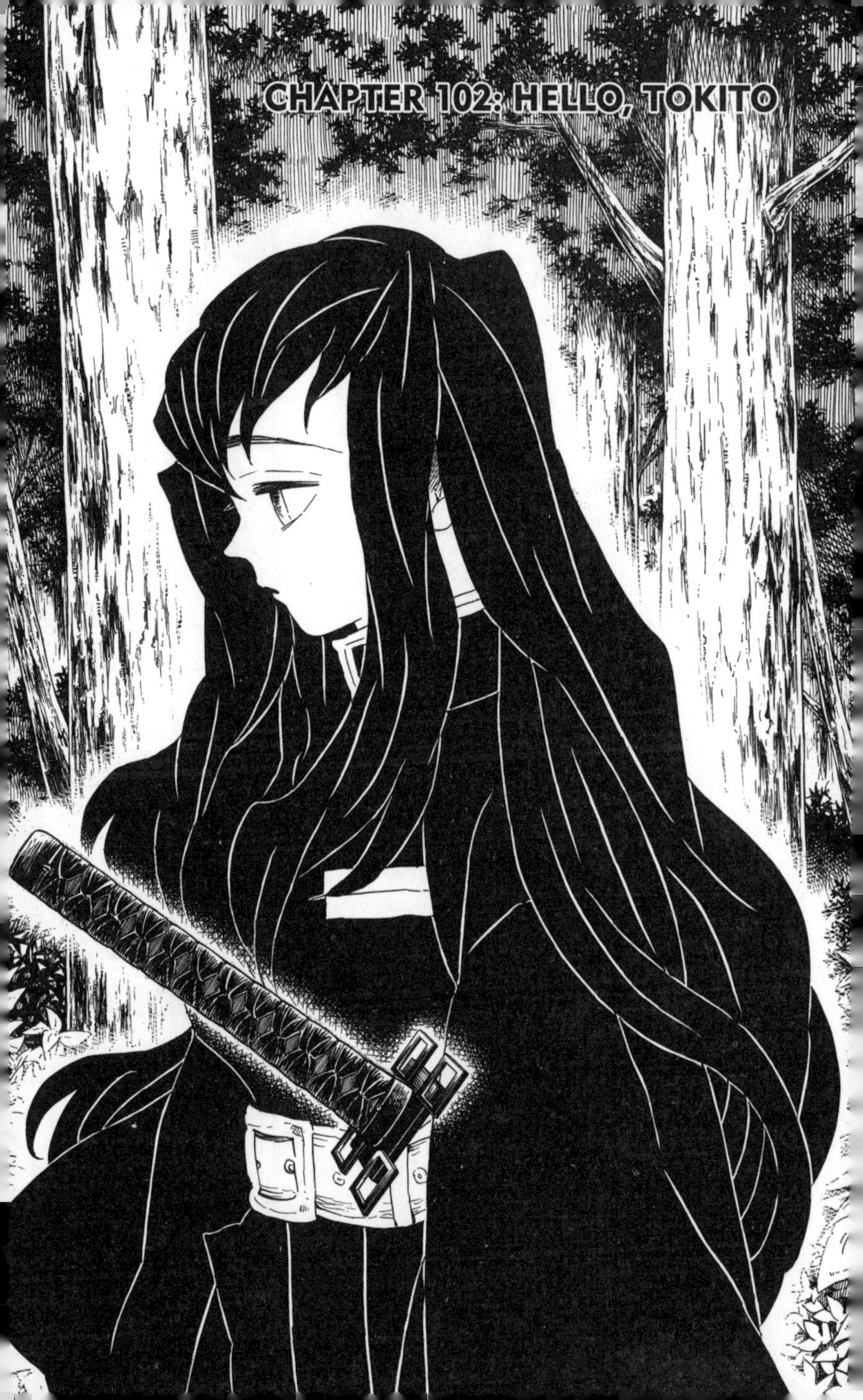
CHAPTER 102: HELLO, TOKITO

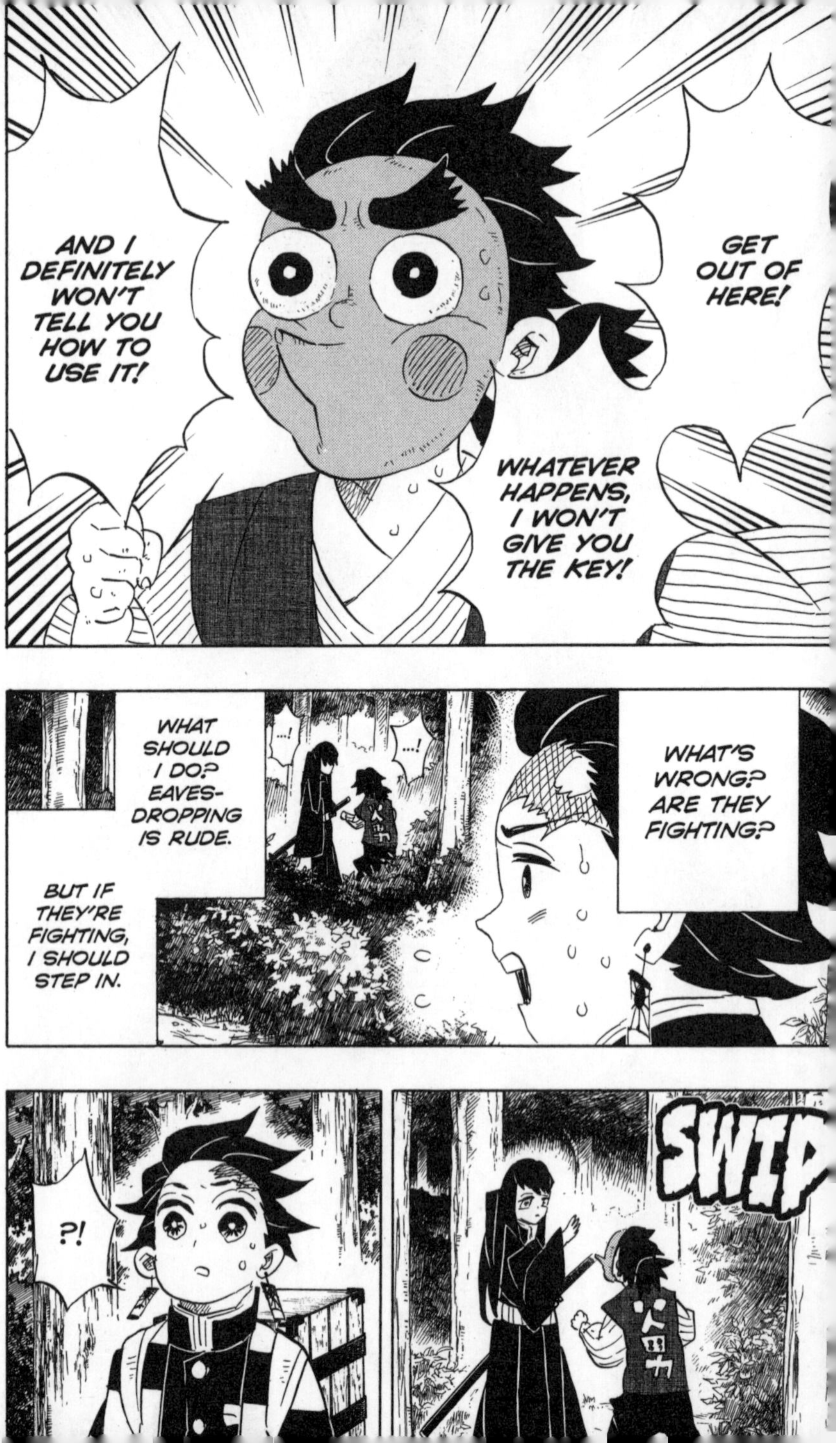
GET OUT OF HERE!
WHATEVER HAPPENS, I WON'T GIVE YOU THE KEY!
AND I DEFINITELY WON'T TELL YOU HOW TO USE IT!
WHAT'S WRONG? ARE THEY FIGHTING?
...!
...!
WHAT SHOULD I DO? EAVES-DROPPING IS RUDE.
BUT IF THEY'RE FIGHTING, I SHOULD STEP IN.
SWIP
?!

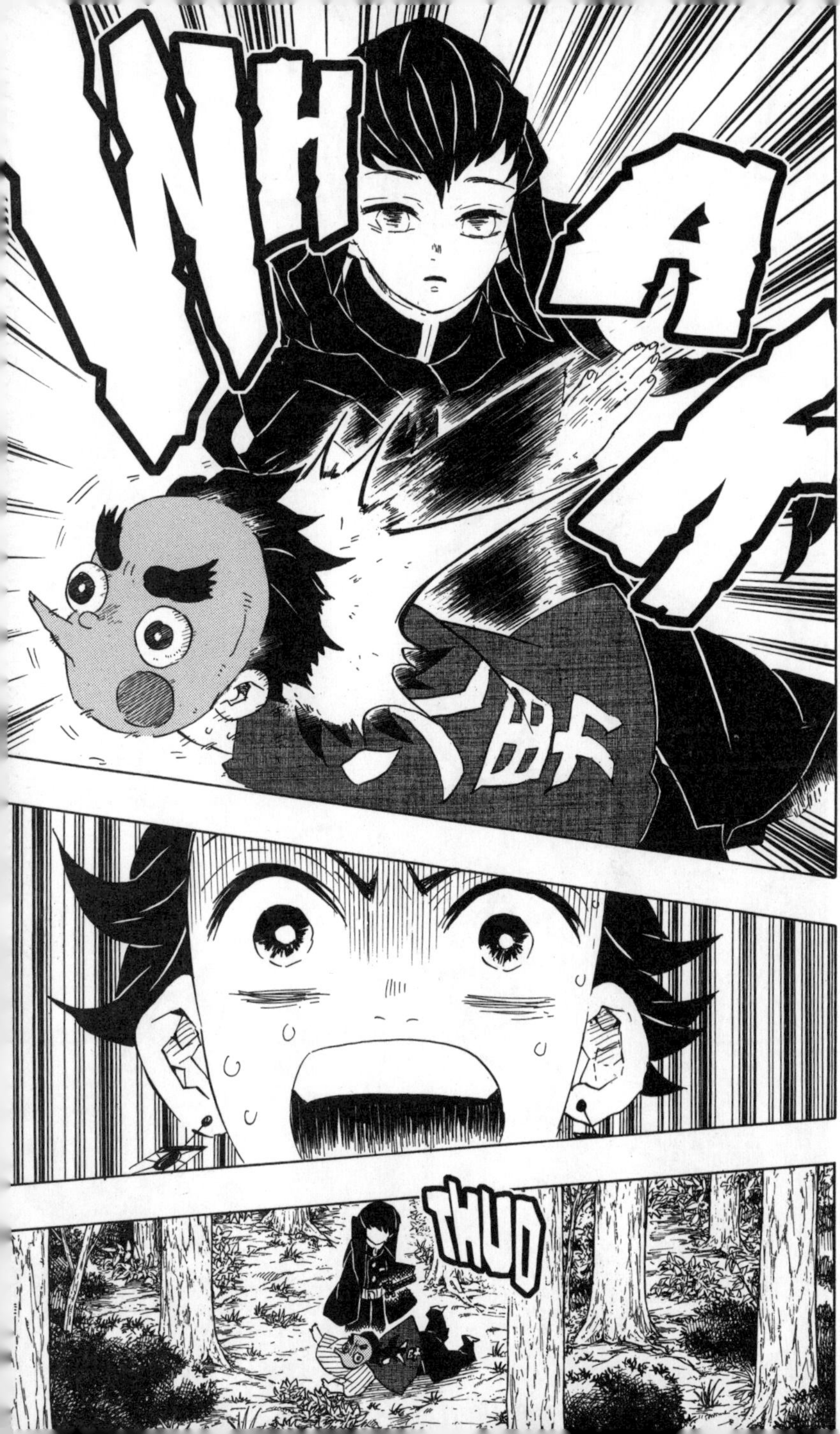
WHAM
THUD

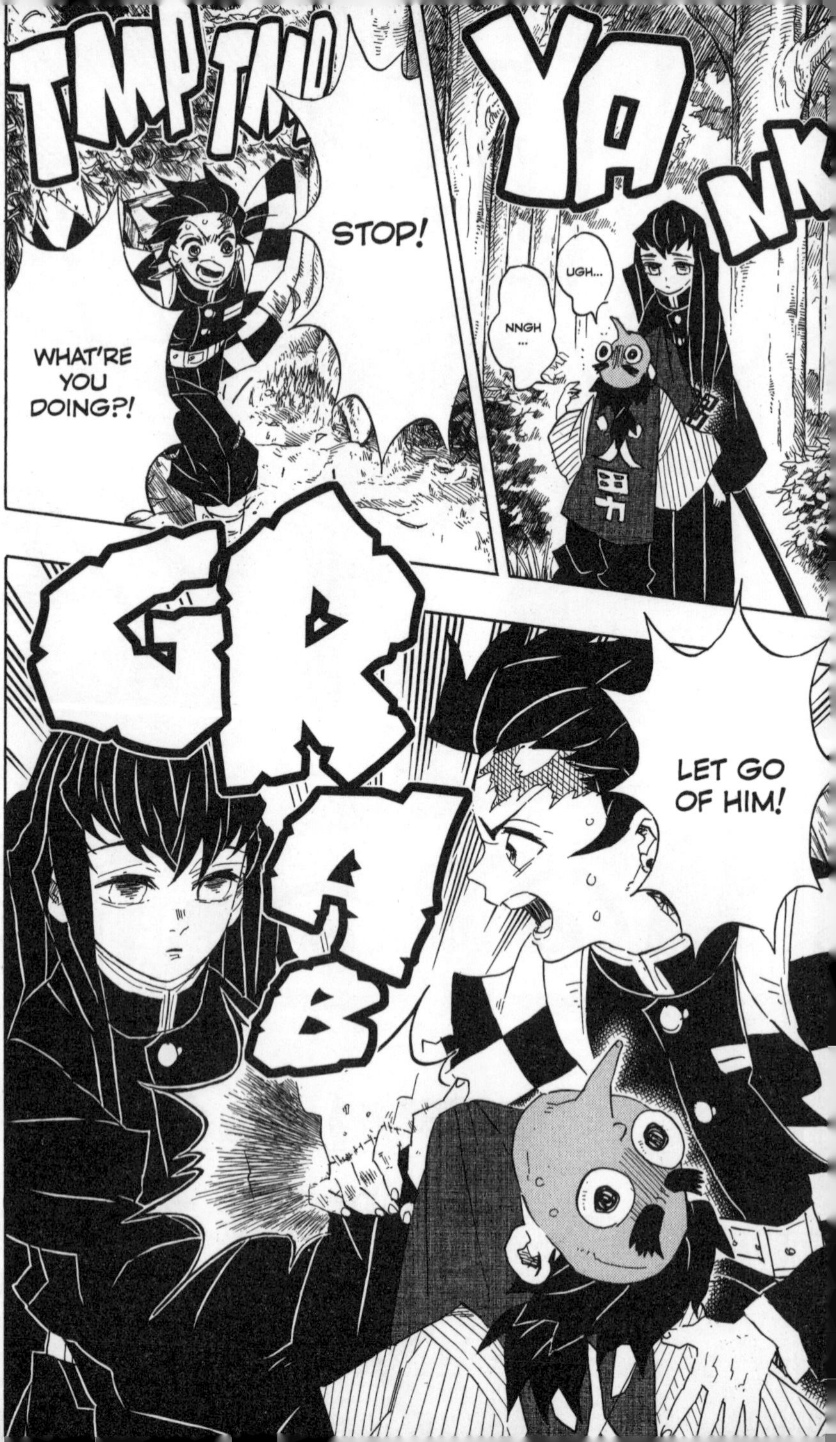
YANK
UGH...
NNGH...
TMP TMP
STOP!
WHAT'RE YOU DOING?!
LET GO OF HIM!
GRAB

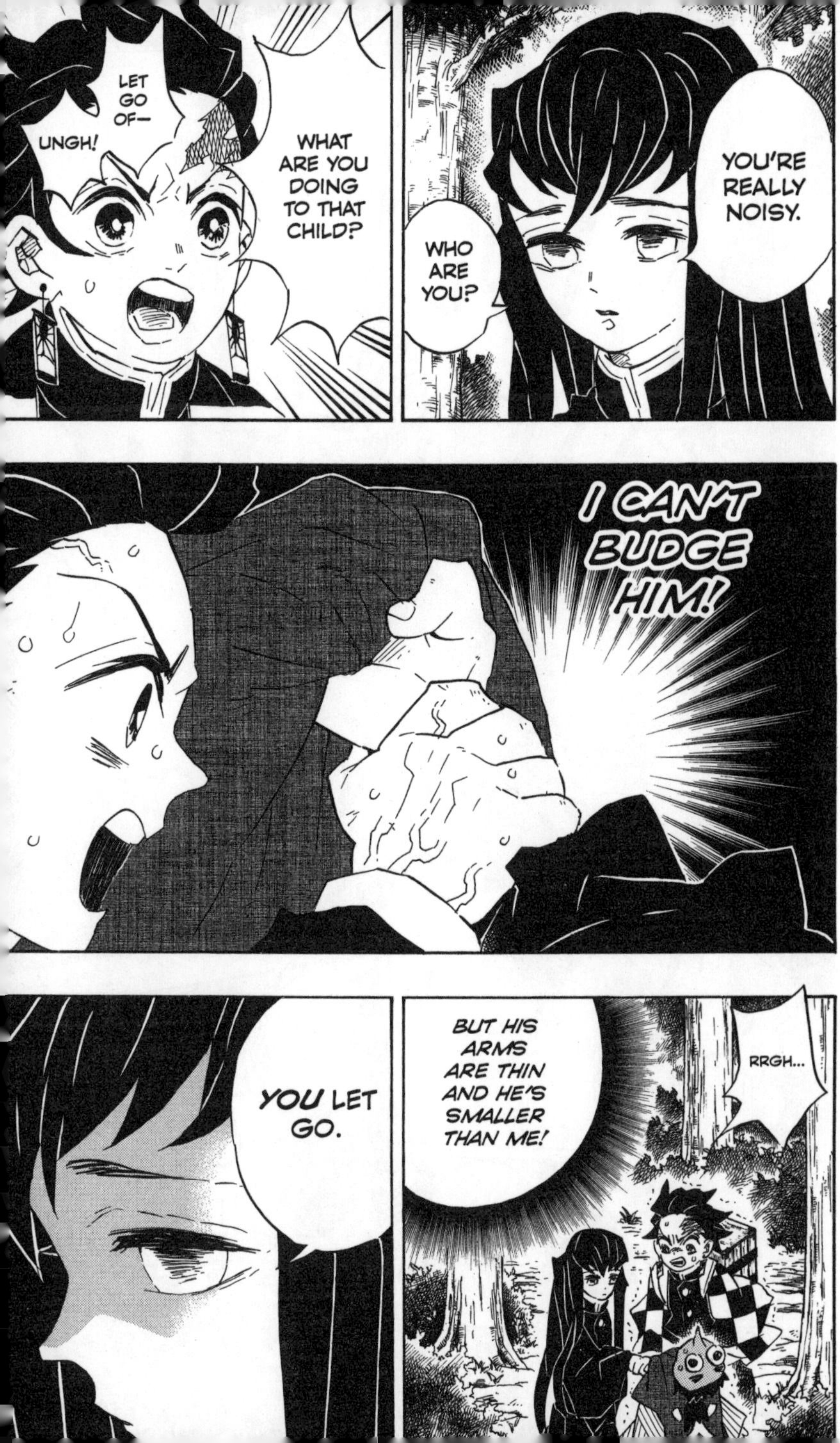
YOU'RE REALLY NOISY.
WHO ARE YOU?
WHAT ARE YOU DOING TO THAT CHILD?
LET GO OF—
UNGH!
I CAN'T BUDGE HIM!
RRGH...
BUT HIS ARMS ARE THIN AND HE'S SMALLER THAN ME!
YOU LET GO.

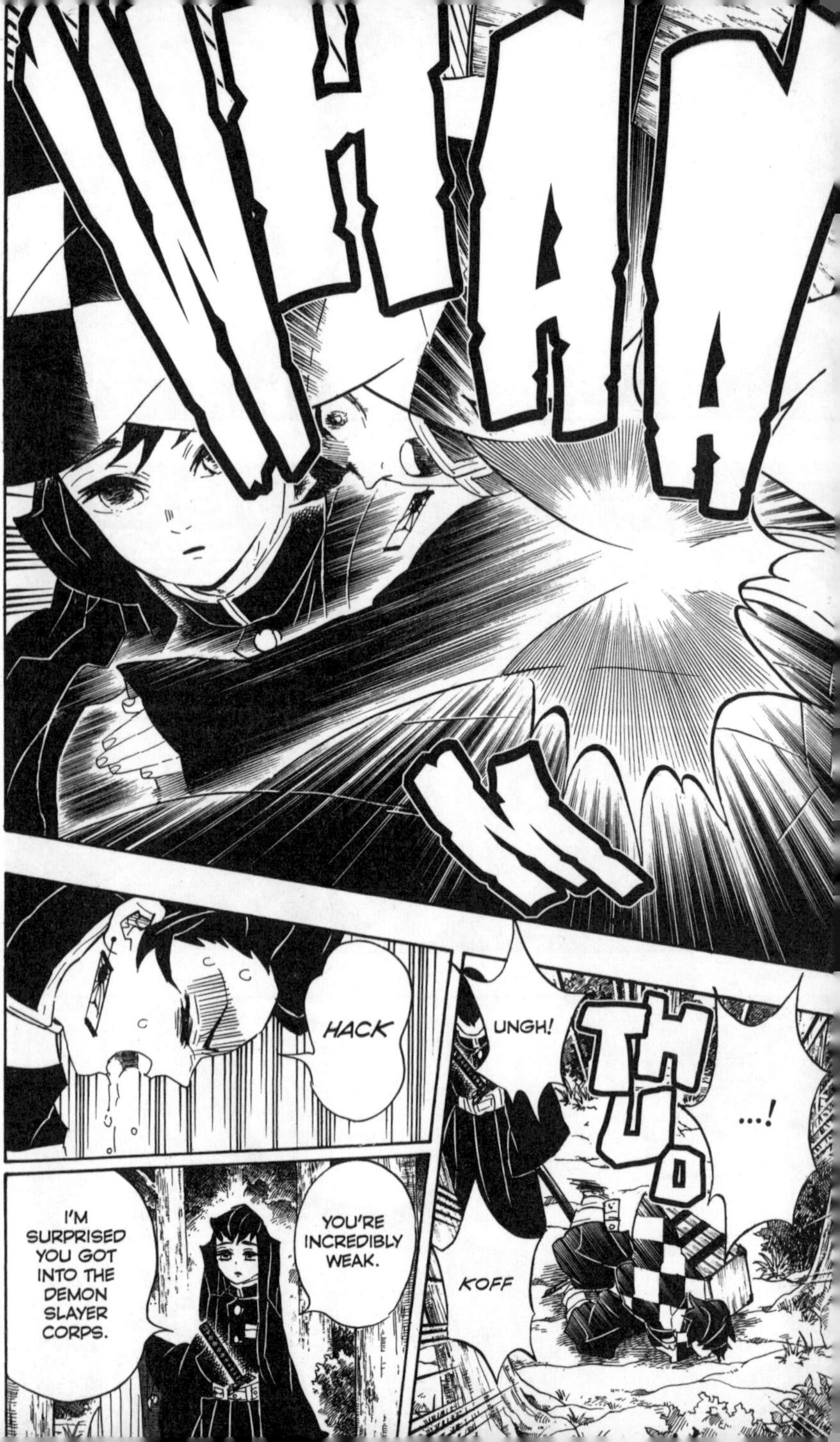

WHAM
UNGH!
THUD
...!
KOFF
HACK
YOU'RE INCREDIBLY WEAK.
I'M SURPRISED YOU GOT INTO THE DEMON SLAYER CORPS.

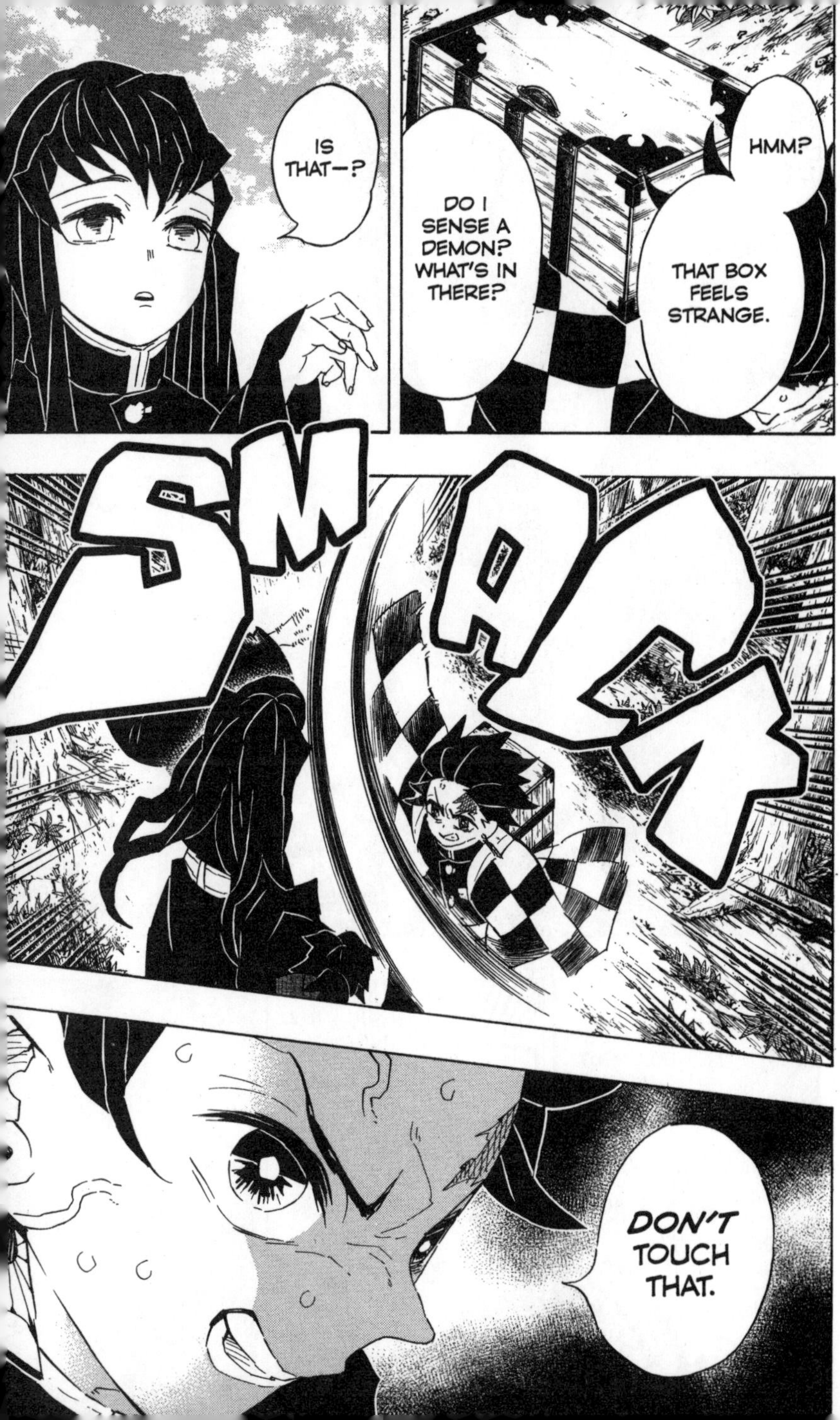
HMM?
THAT BOX FEELS STRANGE.
DO I SENSE A DEMON? WHAT'S IN THERE?
IS THAT—?
SMACK
DON'T TOUCH THAT.

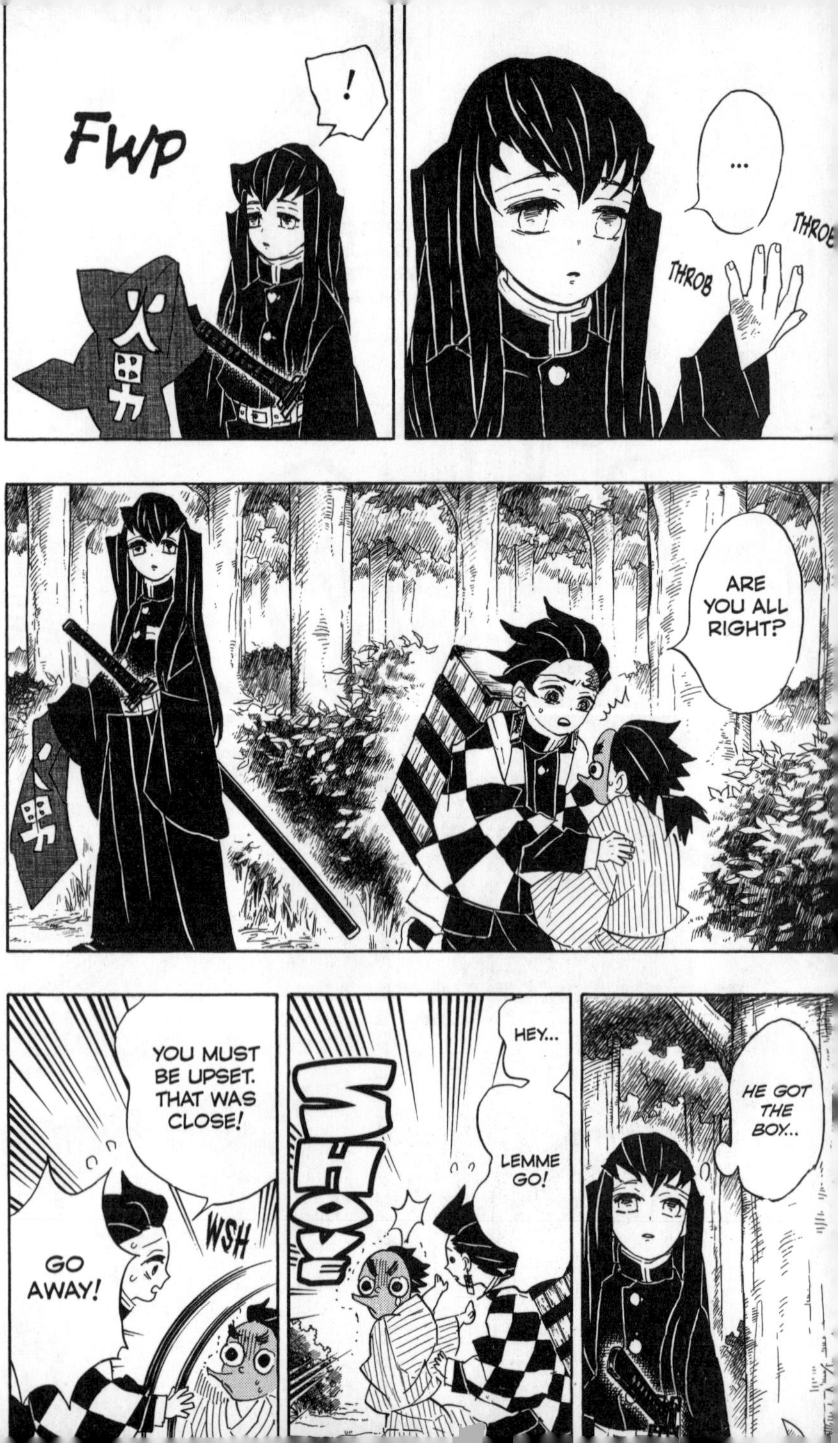
...
THROB
THROB
!
FWP
ARE YOU ALL RIGHT?
HE GOT THE BOY...
HEY...
LEMME GO!
SHOVE
YOU MUST BE UPSET. THAT WAS CLOSE!
WSH
GO AWAY!

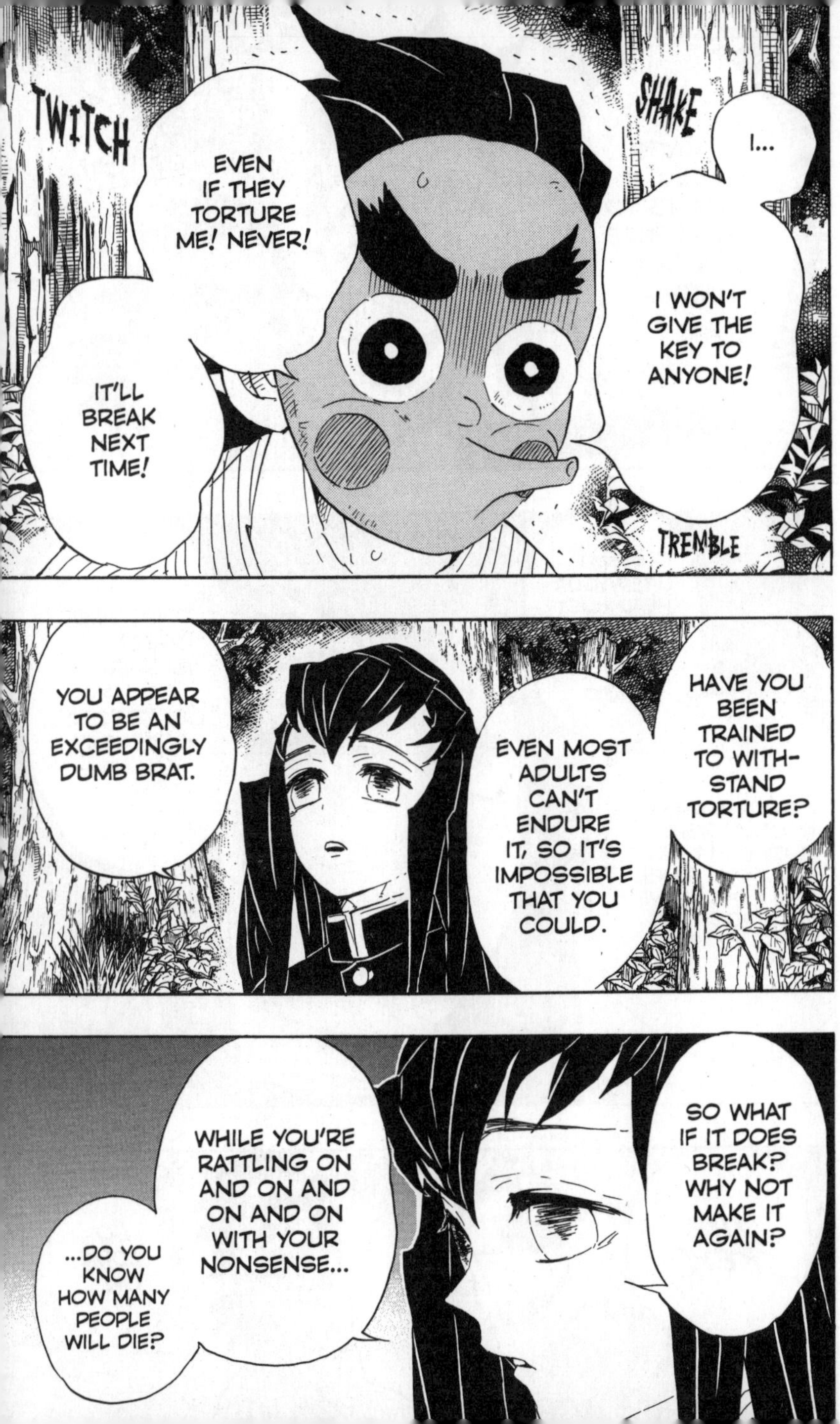
SHAKE
I...
I WON'T GIVE THE KEY TO ANYONE!
TREMBLE
EVEN IF THEY TORTURE ME! NEVER!
TWITCH
IT'LL BREAK NEXT TIME!
HAVE YOU BEEN TRAINED TO WITHSTAND TORTURE?
EVEN MOST ADULTS CAN'T ENDURE IT, SO IT'S IMPOSSIBLE THAT YOU COULD.
YOU APPEAR TO BE AN EXCEEDINGLY DUMB BRAT.
SO WHAT IF IT DOES BREAK? WHY NOT MAKE IT AGAIN?
WHILE YOU'RE RATTLING ON AND ON AND ON AND ON WITH YOUR NONSENSE...
...DO YOU KNOW HOW MANY PEOPLE WILL DIE?

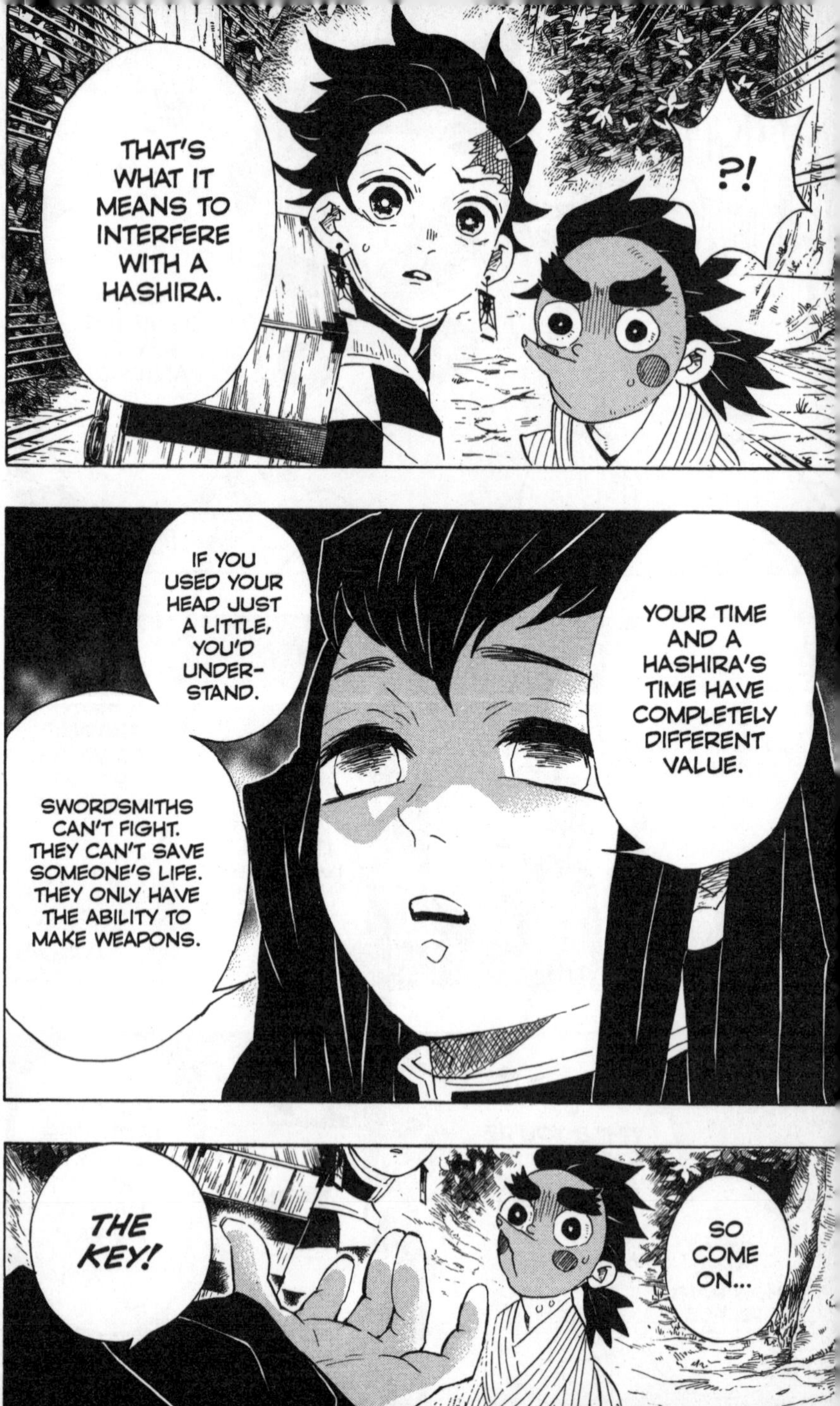
?!
THAT'S WHAT IT MEANS TO INTERFERE WITH A HASHIRA.
YOUR TIME AND A HASHIRA'S TIME HAVE COMPLETELY DIFFERENT VALUE.
IF YOU USED YOUR HEAD JUST A LITTLE, YOU'D UNDER-STAND.
SWORDSMITHS CAN'T FIGHT. THEY CAN'T SAVE SOMEONE'S LIFE. THEY ONLY HAVE THE ABILITY TO MAKE WEAPONS.
SO COME ON...
THE KEY!

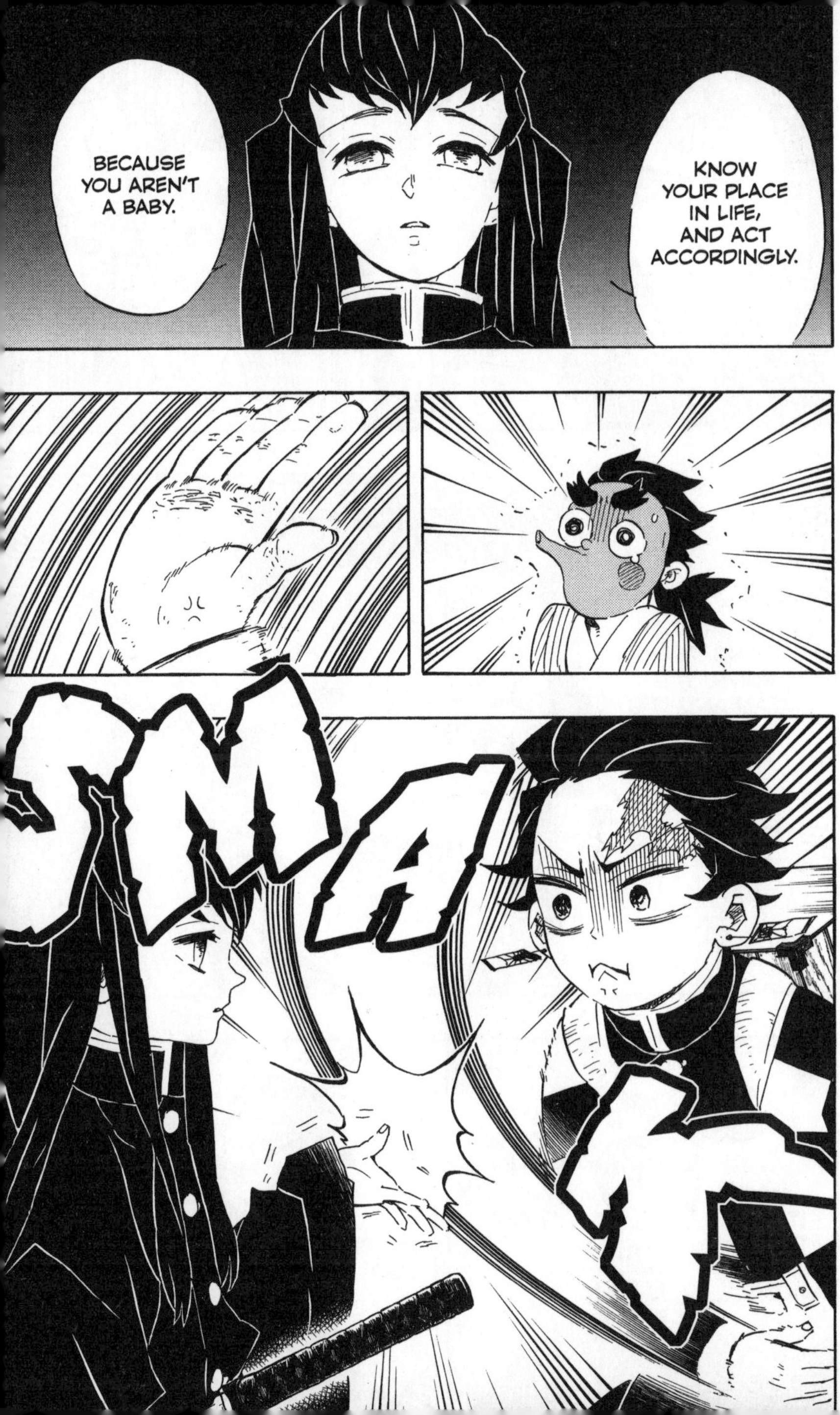
KNOW YOUR PLACE IN LIFE, AND ACT ACCORDINGLY.
BECAUSE YOU AREN'T A BABY.
SMA

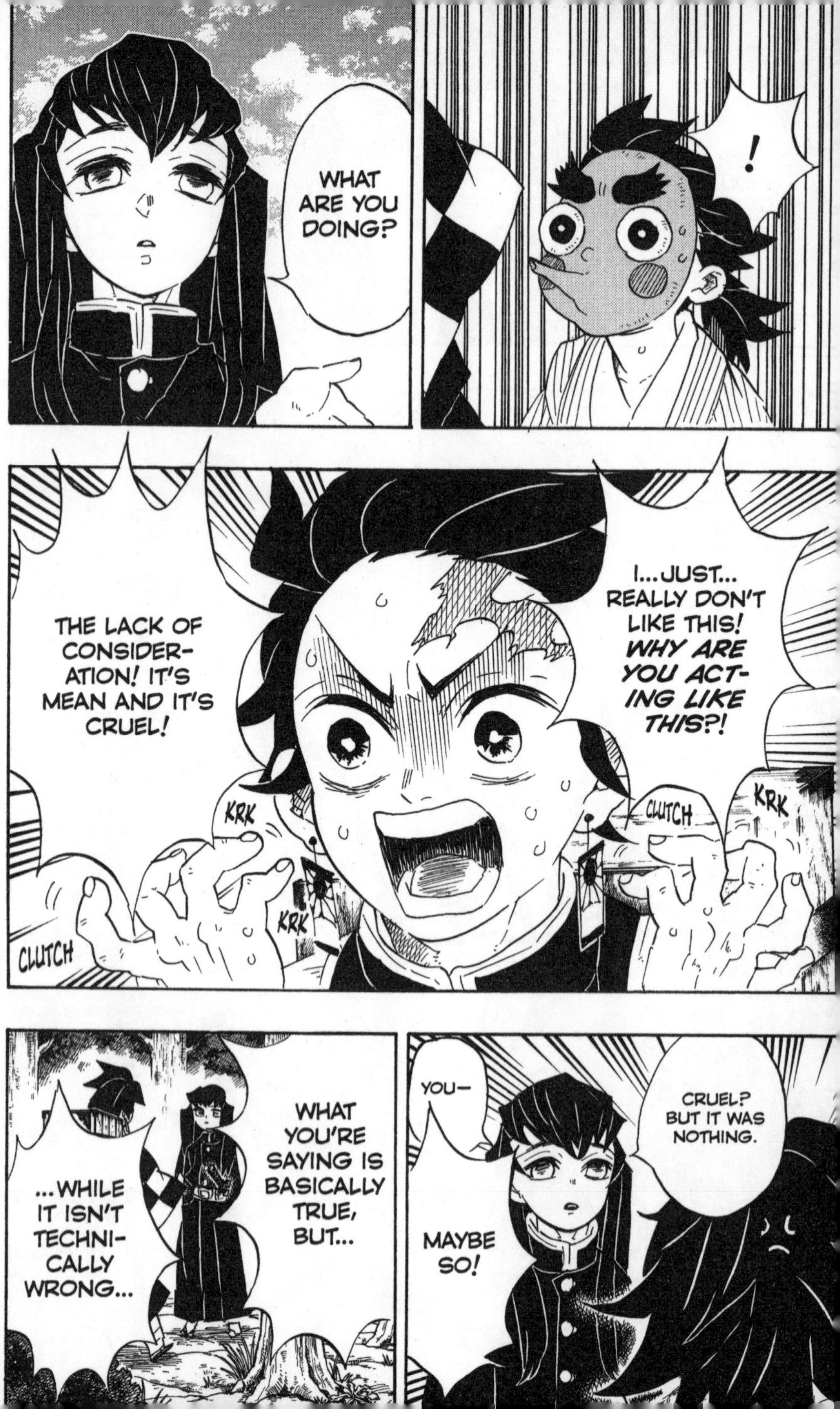
!
WHAT ARE YOU DOING?
I...JUST... REALLY DON'T LIKE THIS! *WHY ARE YOU ACTING LIKE THIS?!*
KRK
CLUTCH
THE LACK OF CONSIDERATION! IT'S MEAN AND IT'S CRUEL!
KRK
KRK
CLUTCH
CRUEL? BUT IT WAS NOTHING.
YOU—
MAYBE SO!
WHAT YOU'RE SAYING IS BASICALLY TRUE, BUT...
...WHILE IT ISN'T TECHNICALLY WRONG...

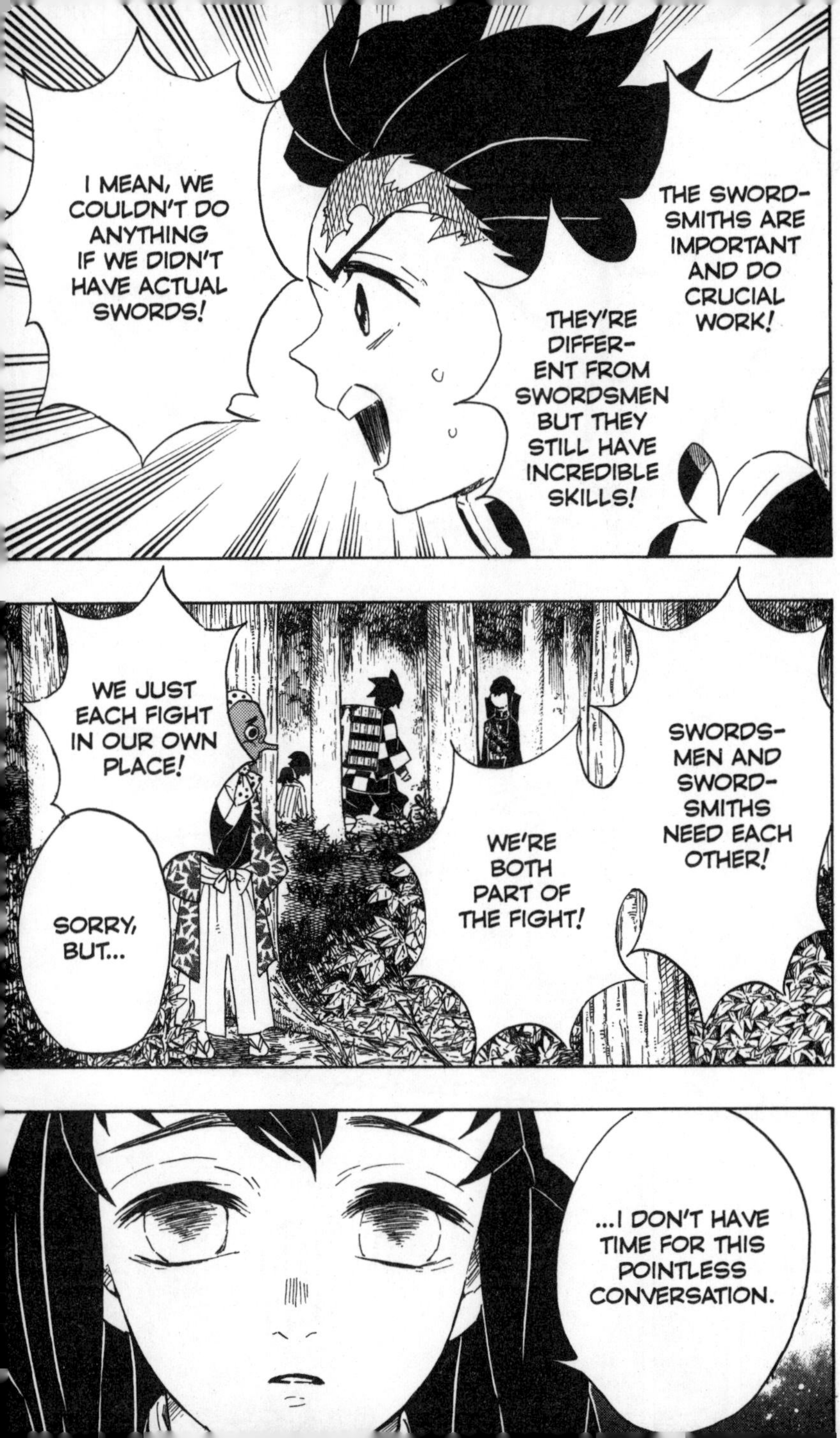
THE SWORDSMITHS ARE IMPORTANT AND DO CRUCIAL WORK!
THEY'RE DIFFERENT FROM SWORDSMEN BUT THEY STILL HAVE INCREDIBLE SKILLS!
I MEAN, WE COULDN'T DO ANYTHING IF WE DIDN'T HAVE ACTUAL SWORDS!
SWORDSMEN AND SWORDSMITHS NEED EACH OTHER!
WE'RE BOTH PART OF THE FIGHT!
WE JUST EACH FIGHT IN OUR OWN PLACE!
SORRY, BUT...
...I DON'T HAVE TIME FOR THIS POINTLESS CONVERSATION.

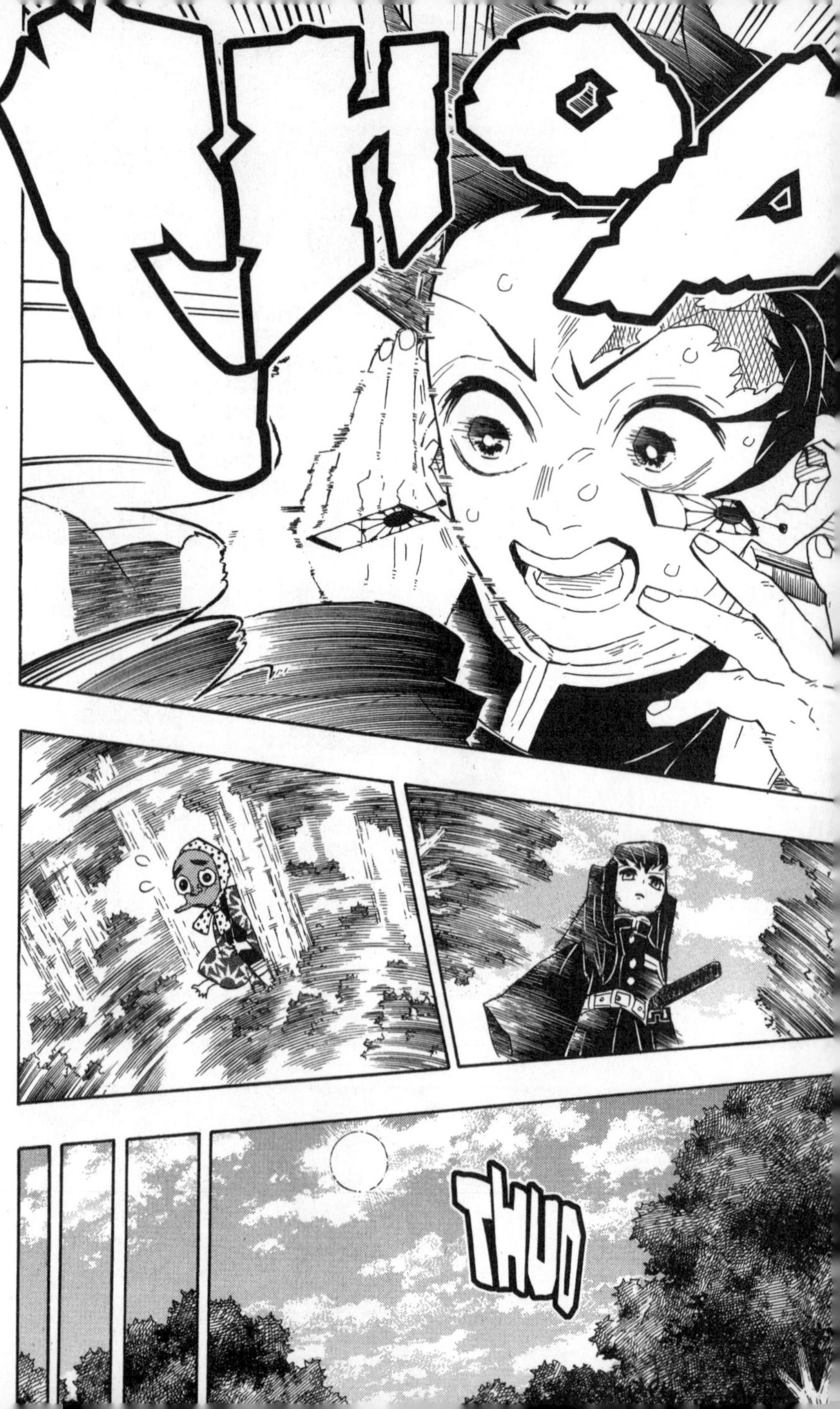
WHOA
THUD

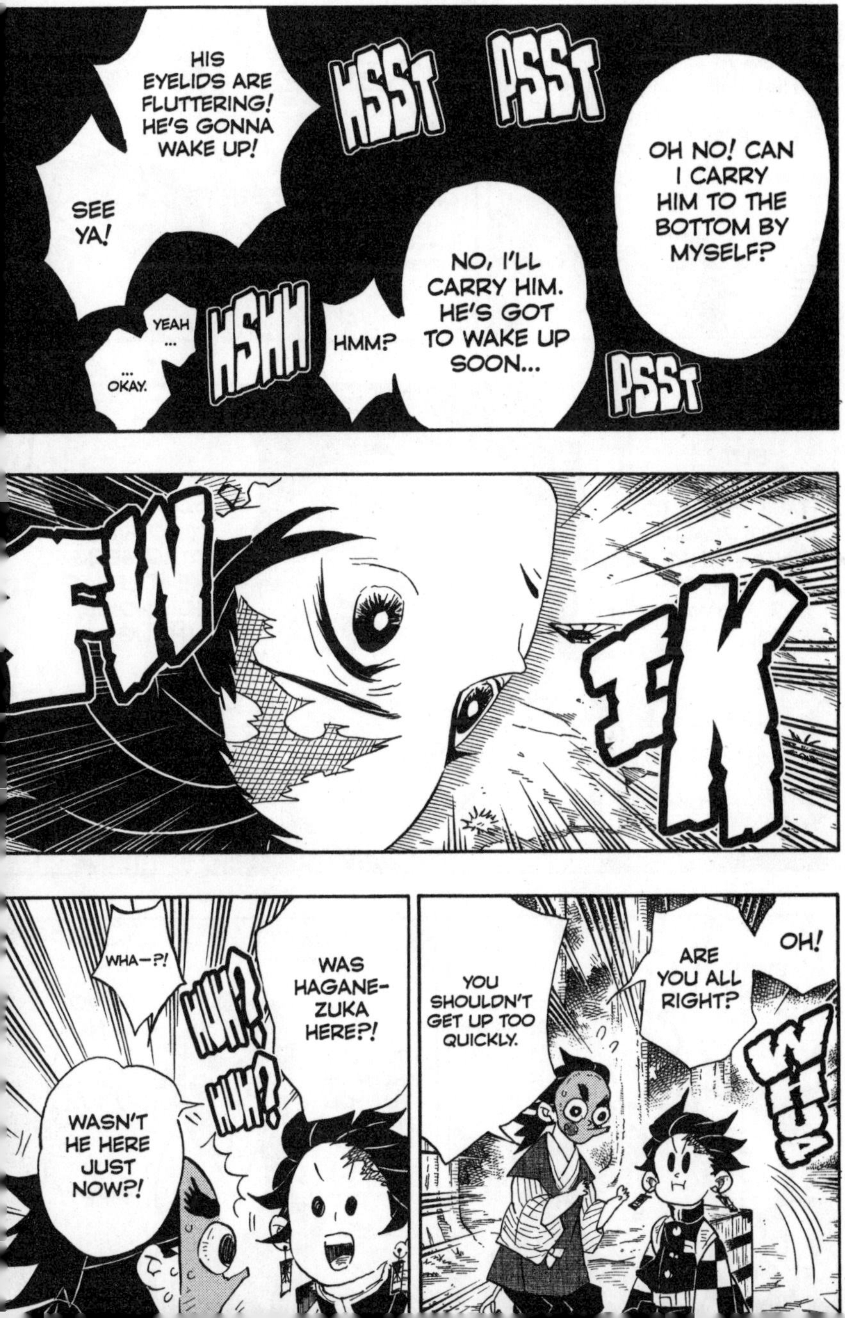
OH NO! CAN I CARRY HIM TO THE BOTTOM BY MYSELF?
PSST
PSST
NO, I'LL CARRY HIM. HE'S GOT TO WAKE UP SOON...
HMM?
HSST
HIS EYELIDS ARE FLUTTERING! HE'S GONNA WAKE UP!
SEE YA!
HSHH
YEAH...
...OKAY.
IK
FW
OH!
ARE YOU ALL RIGHT?
WHUP
YOU SHOULDN'T GET UP TOO QUICKLY.
WAS HAGANE-ZUKA HERE?!
HUH?
HUH?
WHA-?!
WASN'T HE HERE JUST NOW?!

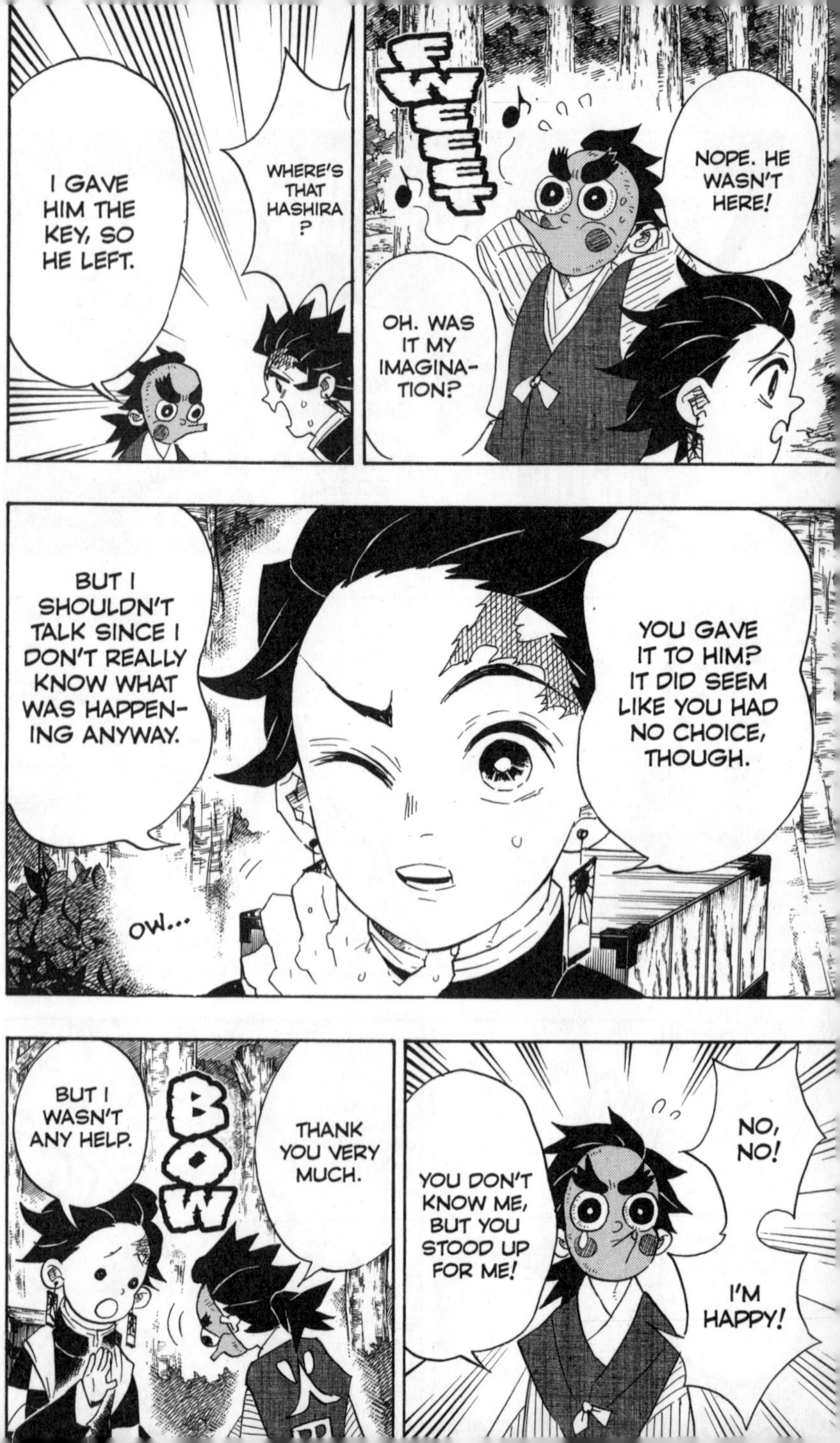
NOPE. HE WASN'T HERE!
FWEET
OH. WAS IT MY IMAGINATION?
WHERE'S THAT HASHIRA?
I GAVE HIM THE KEY, SO HE LEFT.
YOU GAVE IT TO HIM? IT DID SEEM LIKE YOU HAD NO CHOICE, THOUGH.
BUT I SHOULDN'T TALK SINCE I DON'T REALLY KNOW WHAT WAS HAPPENING ANYWAY.
OW...
NO, NO!
I'M HAPPY!
YOU DON'T KNOW ME, BUT YOU STOOD UP FOR ME!
THANK YOU VERY MUCH.
BOW
BUT I WASN'T ANY HELP.

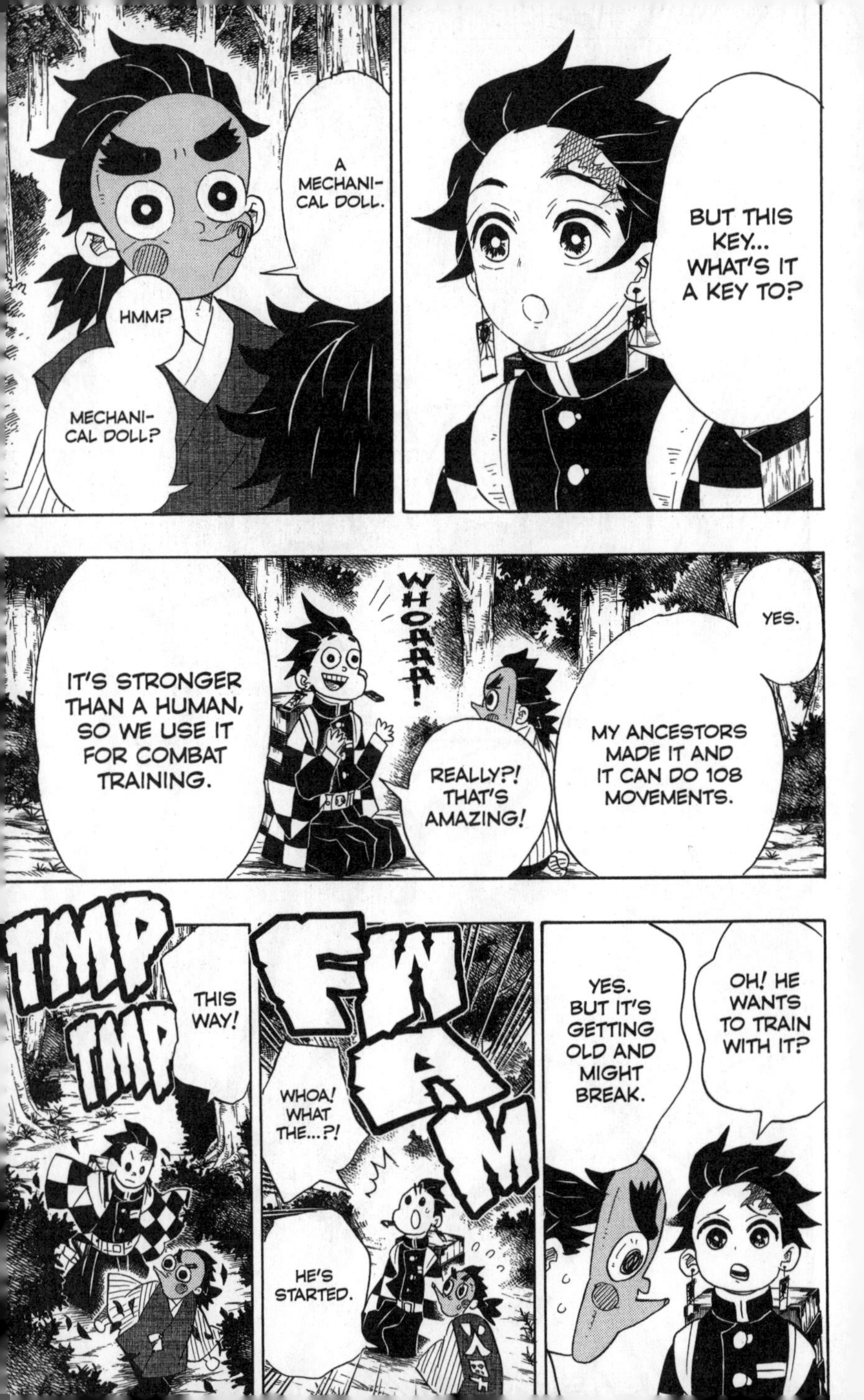
BUT THIS KEY... WHAT'S IT A KEY TO?
A MECHANICAL DOLL.
HMM?
MECHANICAL DOLL?
YES.
MY ANCESTORS MADE IT AND IT CAN DO 108 MOVEMENTS.
REALLY?! THAT'S AMAZING!
WHOAAA!
IT'S STRONGER THAN A HUMAN, SO WE USE IT FOR COMBAT TRAINING.
OH! HE WANTS TO TRAIN WITH IT?
YES. BUT IT'S GETTING OLD AND MIGHT BREAK.
FWAM
WHOA! WHAT THE...?!
HE'S STARTED.
TMP TMP
THIS WAY!

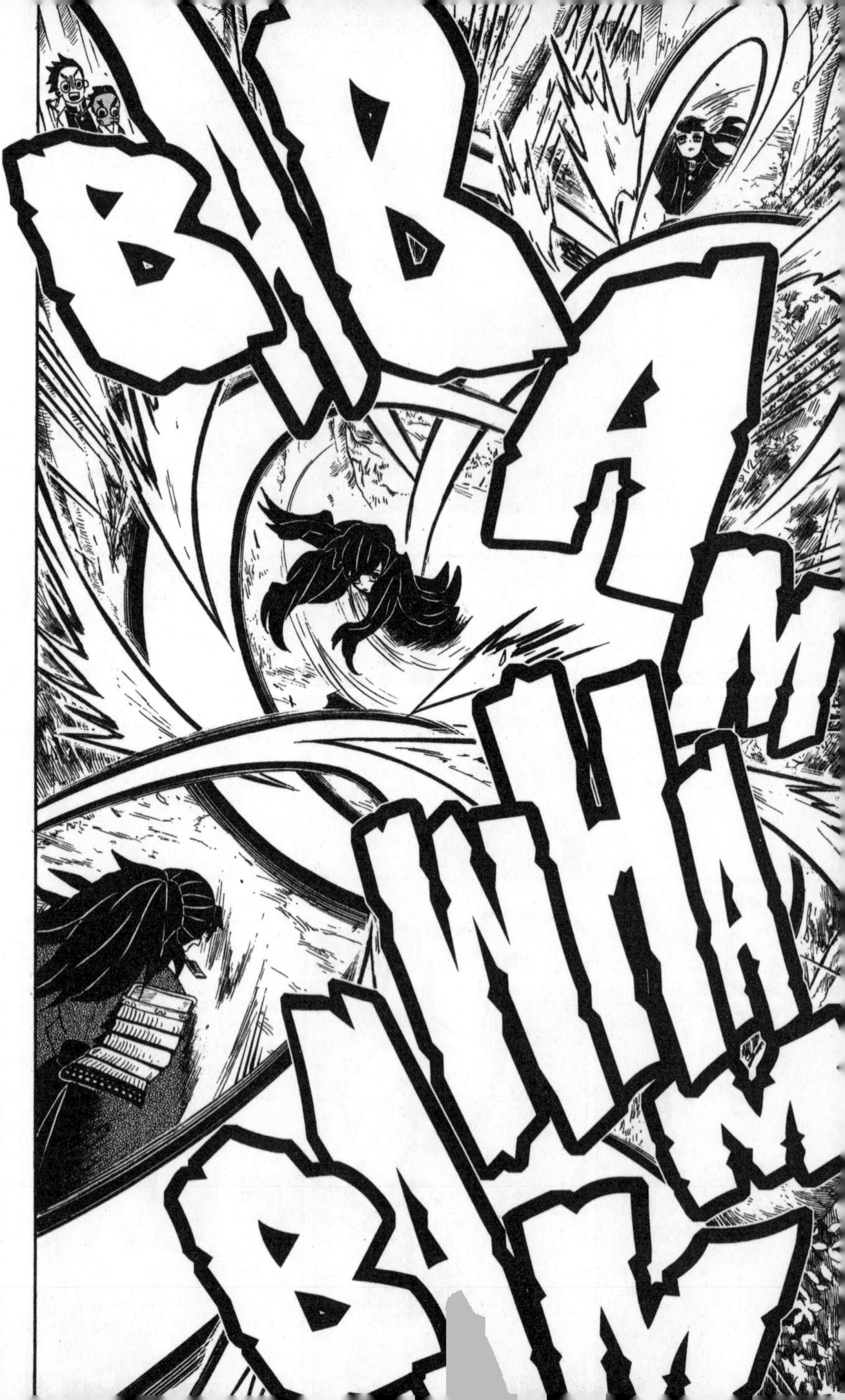

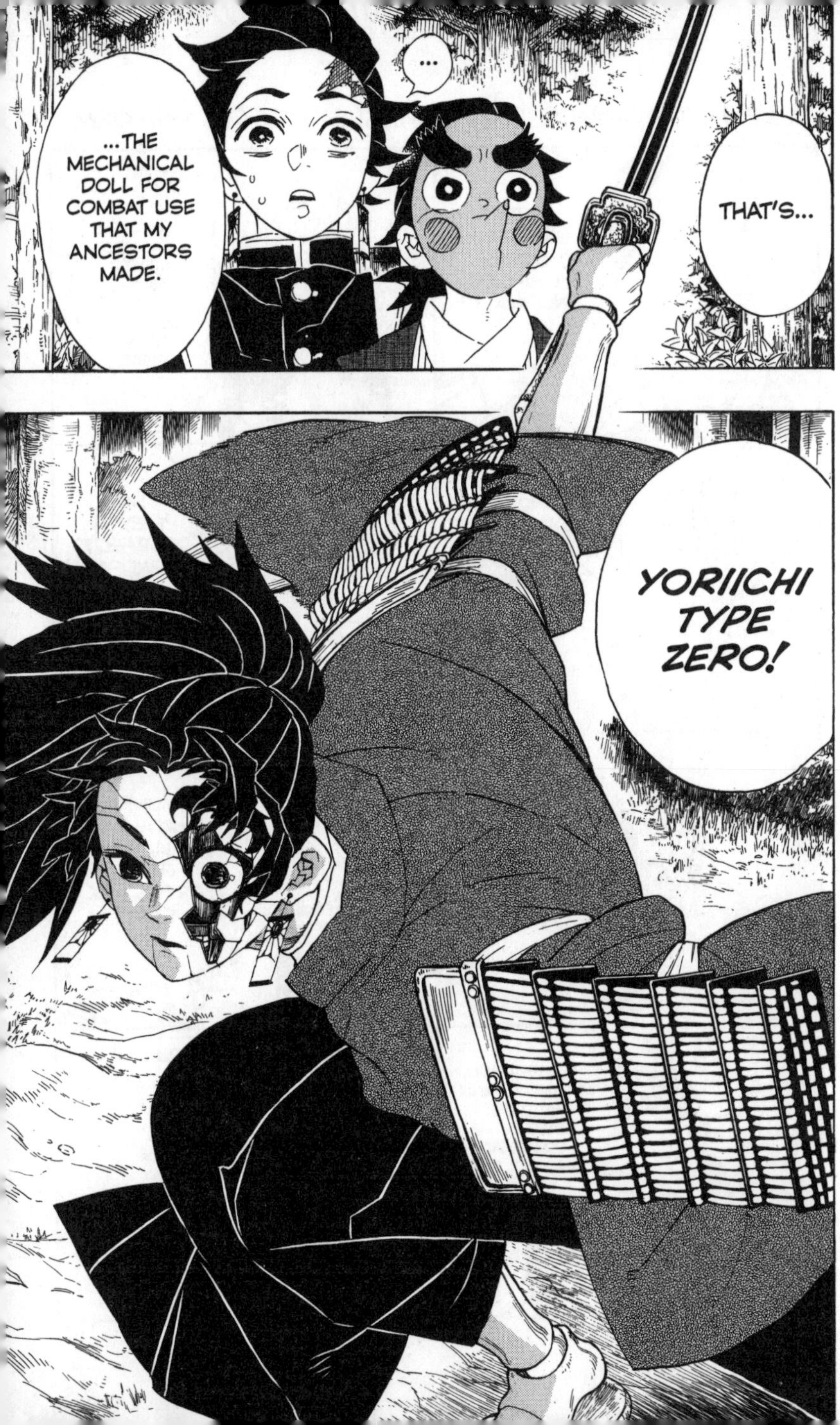
THAT'S...
...
...THE MECHANICAL DOLL FOR COMBAT USE THAT MY ANCESTORS MADE.
YORIICHI TYPE ZERO!

A NEW EIGHT-PANEL COMIC: MITSURI'S CORPS UNIFORM

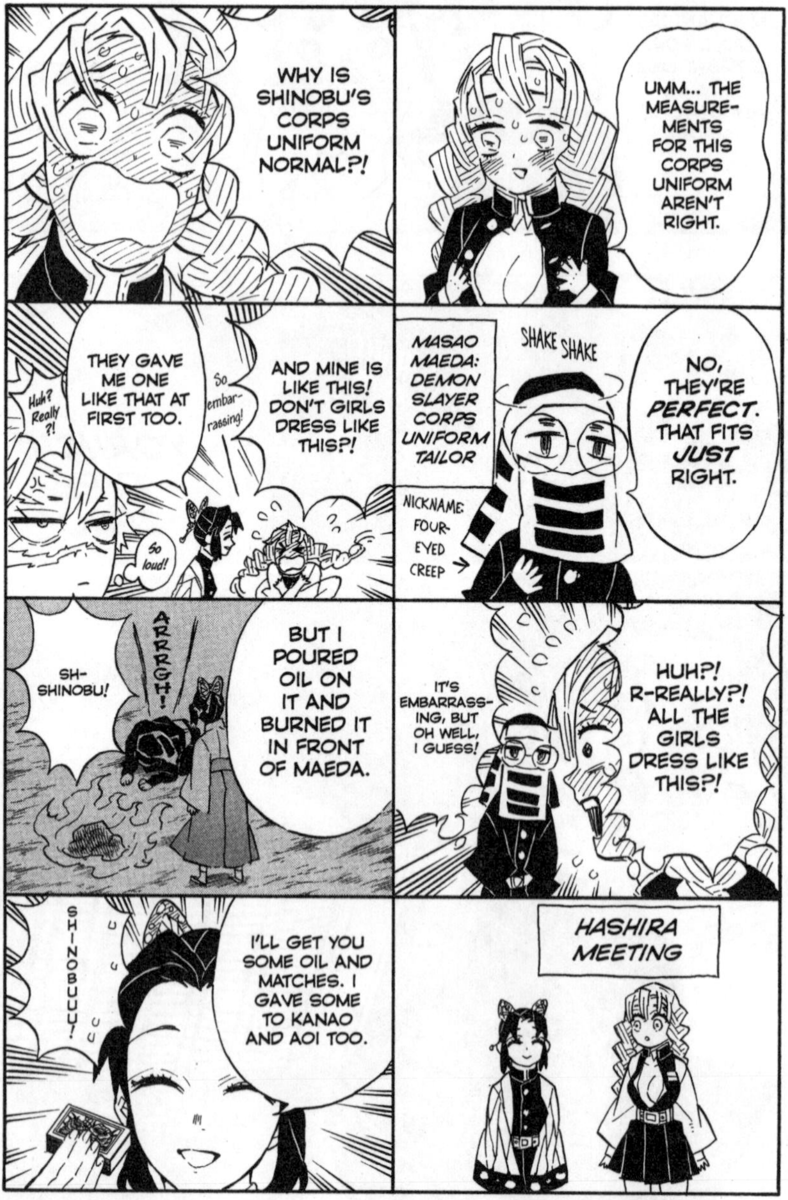
UMM... THE MEASUREMENTS FOR THIS CORPS UNIFORM AREN'T RIGHT.
NO, THEY'RE *PERFECT*. THAT FITS *JUST* RIGHT.
SHAKE SHAKE
MASAO MAEDA: DEMON SLAYER CORPS UNIFORM TAILOR
NICKNAME: FOUR-EYED CREEP
HUH?! R-REALLY?! ALL THE GIRLS DRESS LIKE THIS?!
IT'S EMBARRASSING, BUT OH WELL, I GUESS!
HASHIRA MEETING
WHY IS SHINOBU'S CORPS UNIFORM NORMAL?!
AND MINE IS LIKE THIS! DON'T GIRLS DRESS LIKE THIS?!
So embarrassing!
THEY GAVE ME ONE LIKE THAT AT FIRST TOO.
Huh? Really ?!
So loud!
BUT I POURED OIL ON IT AND BURNED IT IN FRONT OF MAEDA.
ARRRGH!
SH-SHINOBU!
I'LL GET YOU SOME OIL AND MATCHES. I GAVE SOME TO KANAO AND AOI TOO.
SHINOBUUU!

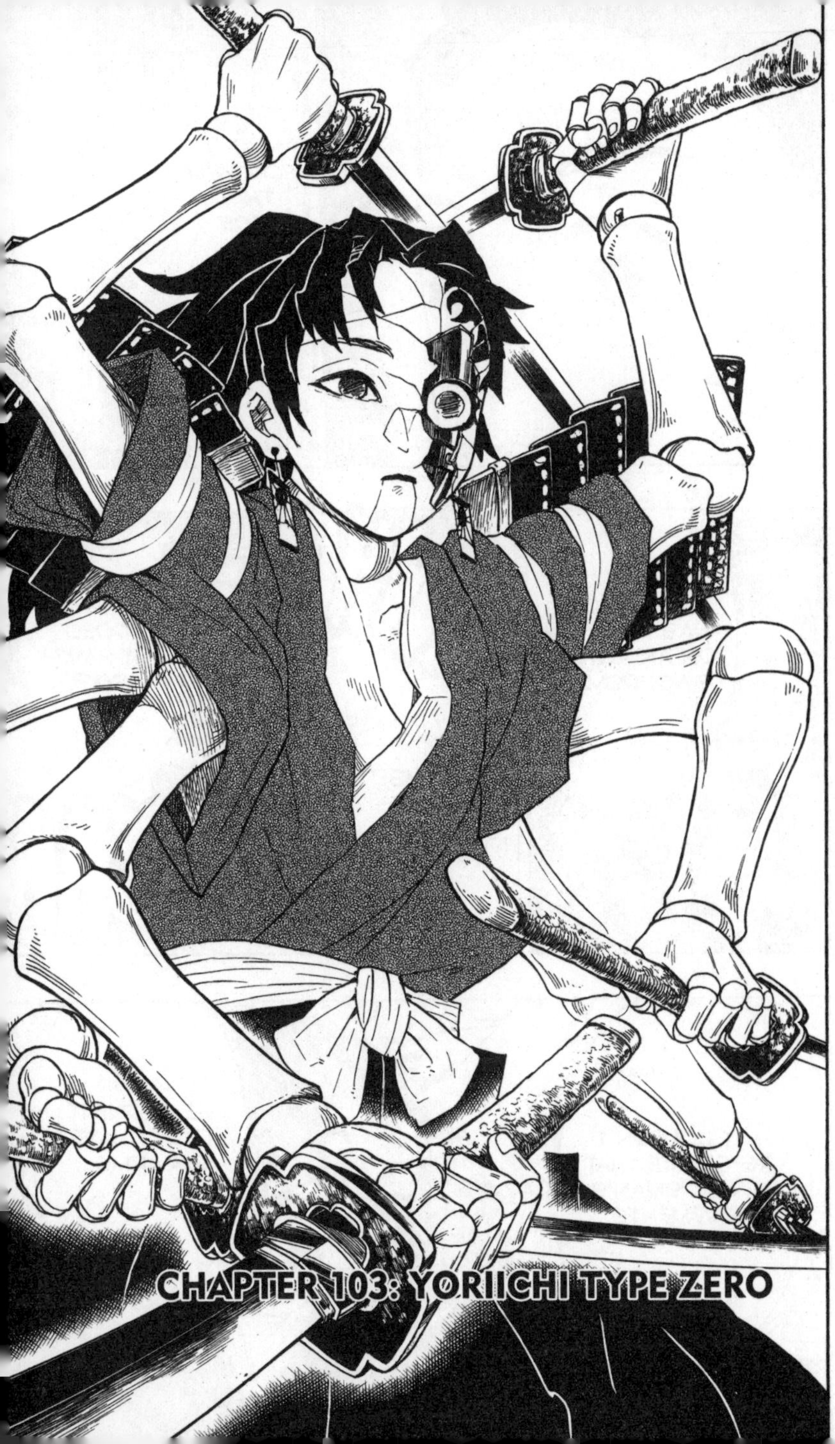
CHAPTER 103: YORIICHI TYPE ZERO

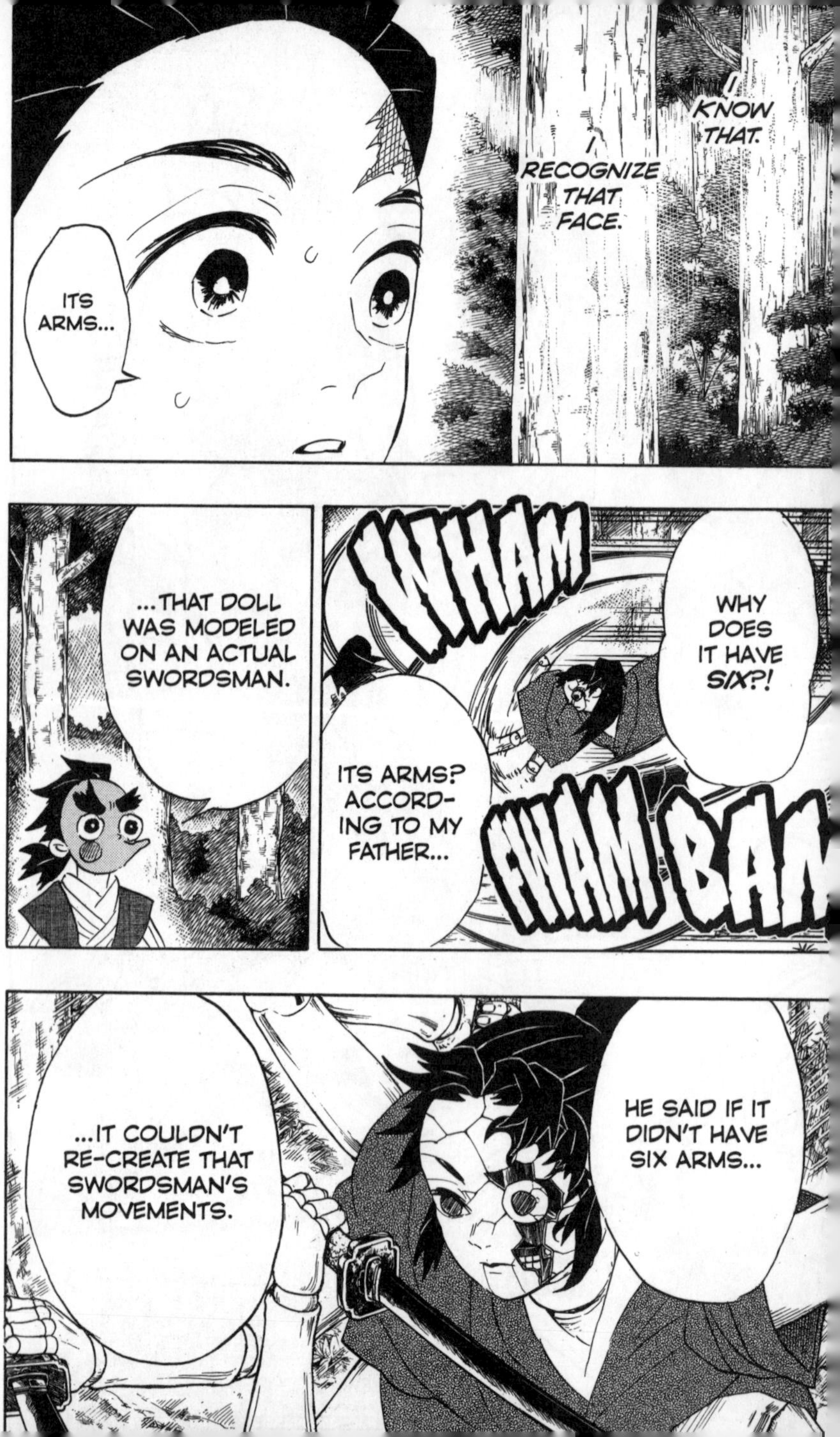
I KNOW THAT.
I RECOGNIZE THAT FACE.
ITS ARMS...
WHAM
WHY DOES IT HAVE SIX?!
ITS ARMS? ACCORD-ING TO MY FATHER...
WHAM
...THAT DOLL WAS MODELED ON AN ACTUAL SWORDSMAN.
HE SAID IF IT DIDN'T HAVE SIX ARMS...
...IT COULDN'T RE-CREATE THAT SWORDSMAN'S MOVEMENTS.

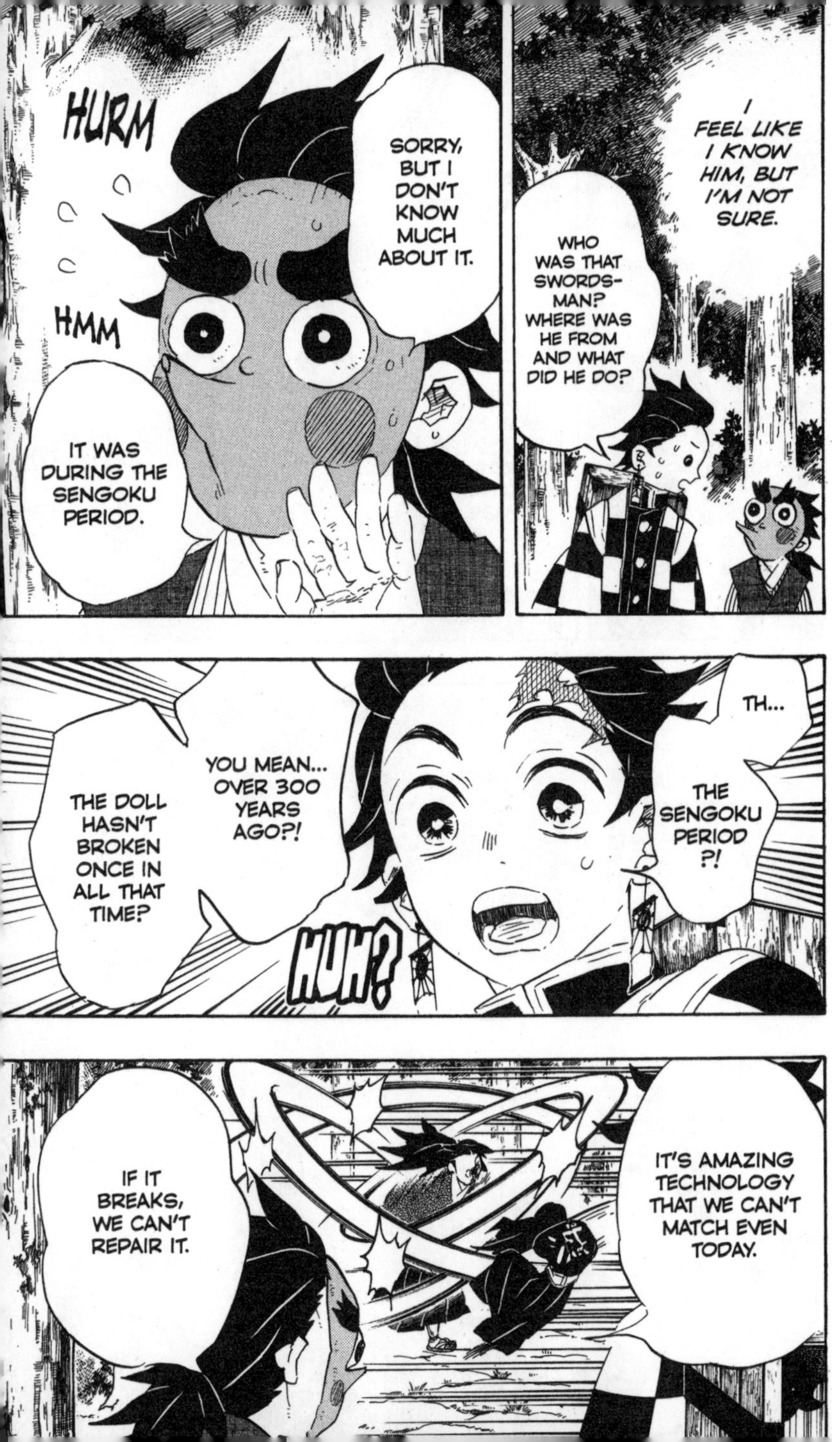
I FEEL LIKE I KNOW HIM, BUT I'M NOT SURE.
WHO WAS THAT SWORDS-MAN? WHERE WAS HE FROM AND WHAT DID HE DO?
SORRY, BUT I DON'T KNOW MUCH ABOUT IT.
HURM
HMM
IT WAS DURING THE SENGOKU PERIOD.
TH...
THE SENGOKU PERIOD ?!
HUH?
YOU MEAN... OVER 300 YEARS AGO?!
THE DOLL HASN'T BROKEN ONCE IN ALL THAT TIME?
IT'S AMAZING TECHNOLOGY THAT WE CAN'T MATCH EVEN TODAY.
IF IT BREAKS, WE CAN'T REPAIR IT.

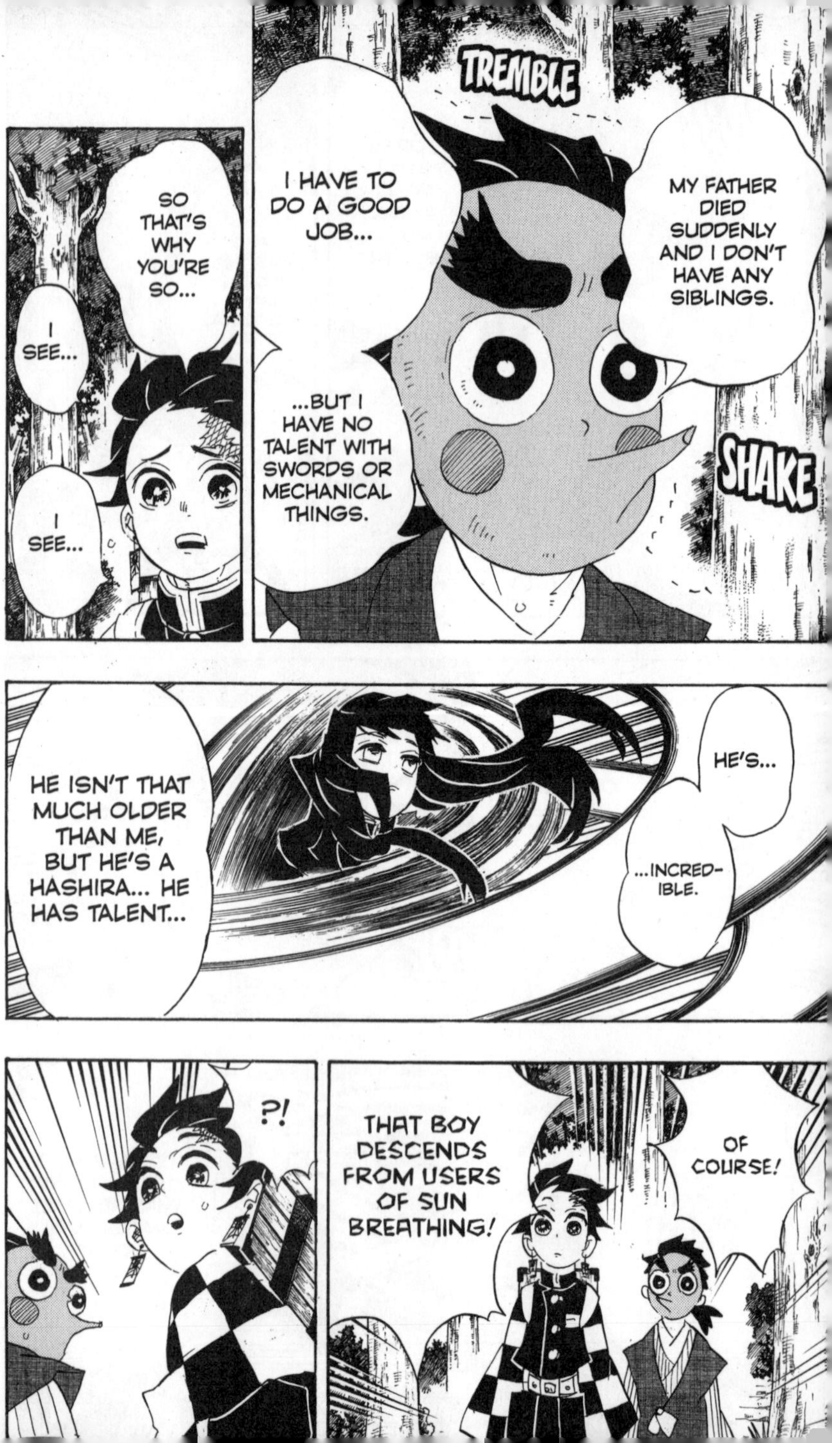
TREMBLE
MY FATHER DIED SUDDENLY AND I DON'T HAVE ANY SIBLINGS.
SHAKE
I HAVE TO DO A GOOD JOB...
...BUT I HAVE NO TALENT WITH SWORDS OR MECHANICAL THINGS.
SO THAT'S WHY YOU'RE SO...
I SEE...
I SEE...
HE'S...
...INCRED-IBLE.
HE ISN'T THAT MUCH OLDER THAN ME, BUT HE'S A HASHIRA... HE HAS TALENT...
OF COURSE!
THAT BOY DESCENDS FROM USERS OF SUN BREATHING!
?!

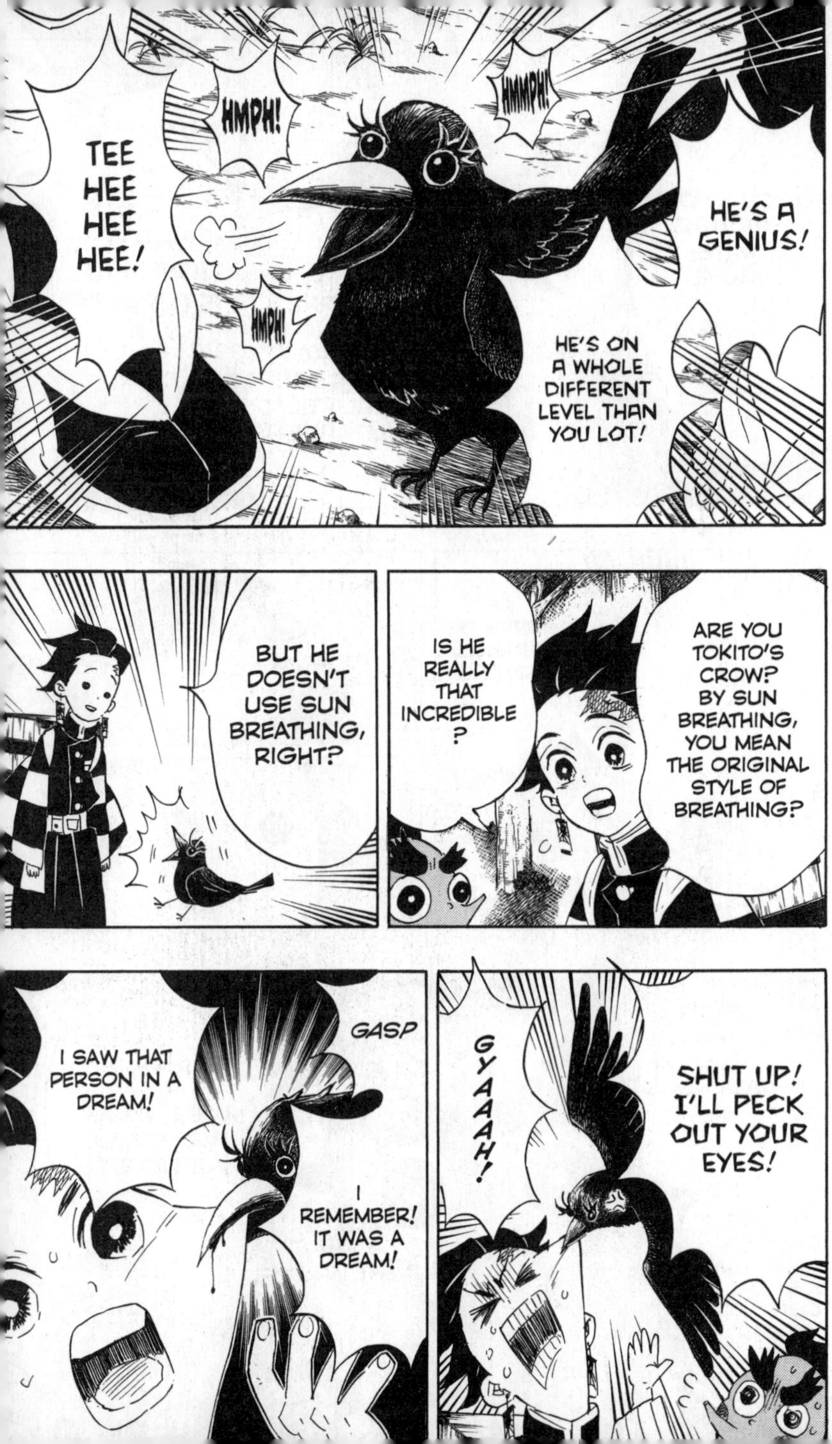
HMMPH!
HE'S A GENIUS!
HE'S ON A WHOLE DIFFERENT LEVEL THAN YOU LOT!
HMPH!
HMPH!
TEE HEE HEE HEE!
ARE YOU TOKITO'S CROW? BY SUN BREATHING, YOU MEAN THE ORIGINAL STYLE OF BREATHING?
IS HE REALLY THAT INCREDIBLE?
BUT HE DOESN'T USE SUN BREATHING, RIGHT?
SHUT UP! I'LL PECK OUT YOUR EYES!
GYAAAH!
GASP
I SAW THAT PERSON IN A DREAM!
I REMEMBER! IT WAS A DREAM!

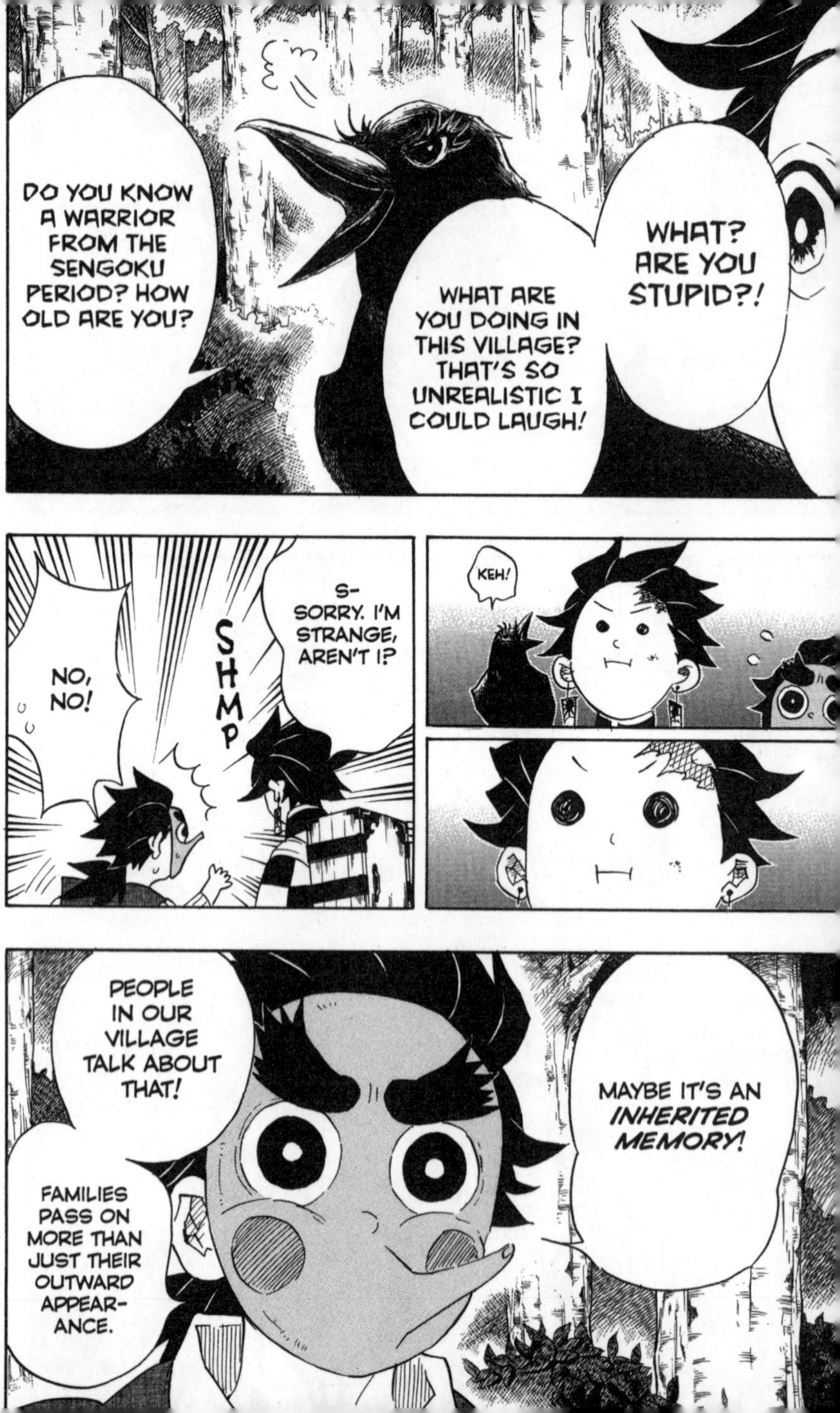
WHAT? ARE YOU STUPID?!
WHAT ARE YOU DOING IN THIS VILLAGE? THAT'S SO UNREALISTIC I COULD LAUGH!
DO YOU KNOW A WARRIOR FROM THE SENGOKU PERIOD? HOW OLD ARE YOU?
KEH!
S- SORRY. I'M STRANGE, AREN'T I?
SHMP
NO, NO!
MAYBE IT'S AN *INHERITED MEMORY*!
PEOPLE IN OUR VILLAGE TALK ABOUT THAT!
FAMILIES PASS ON MORE THAN JUST THEIR OUTWARD APPEAR- ANCE.

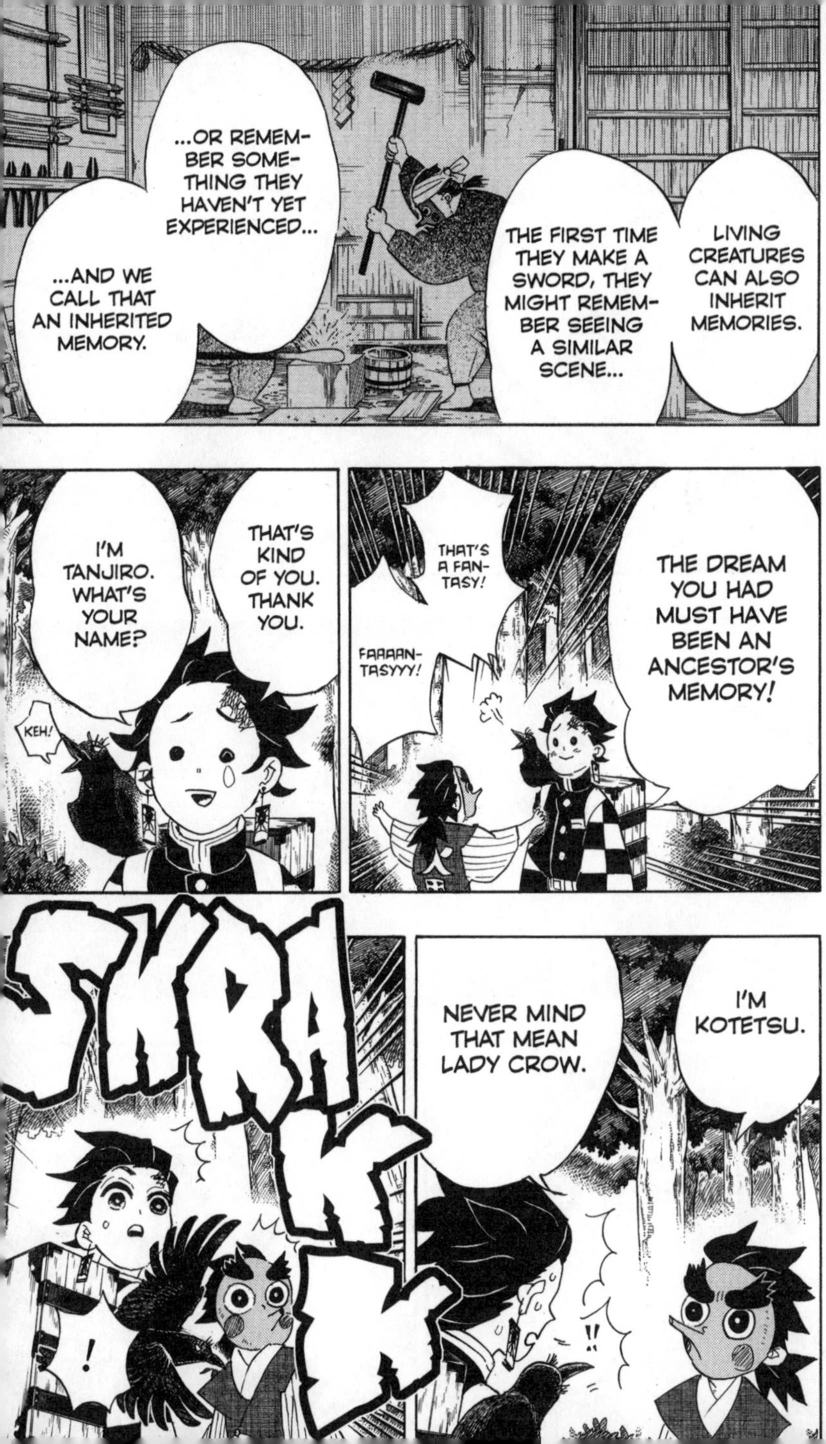
LIVING CREATURES CAN ALSO INHERIT MEMORIES.
THE FIRST TIME THEY MAKE A SWORD, THEY MIGHT REMEMBER SEEING A SIMILAR SCENE...
...OR REMEMBER SOMETHING THEY HAVEN'T YET EXPERIENCED...
...AND WE CALL THAT AN INHERITED MEMORY.
THE DREAM YOU HAD MUST HAVE BEEN AN ANCESTOR'S MEMORY!
THAT'S A FANTASY!
FAAAAN-TASYYY!
THAT'S KIND OF YOU. THANK YOU.
I'M TANJIRO. WHAT'S YOUR NAME?
KEH!
I'M KOTETSU.
NEVER MIND THAT MEAN LADY CROW.
!!
SKRAK
!

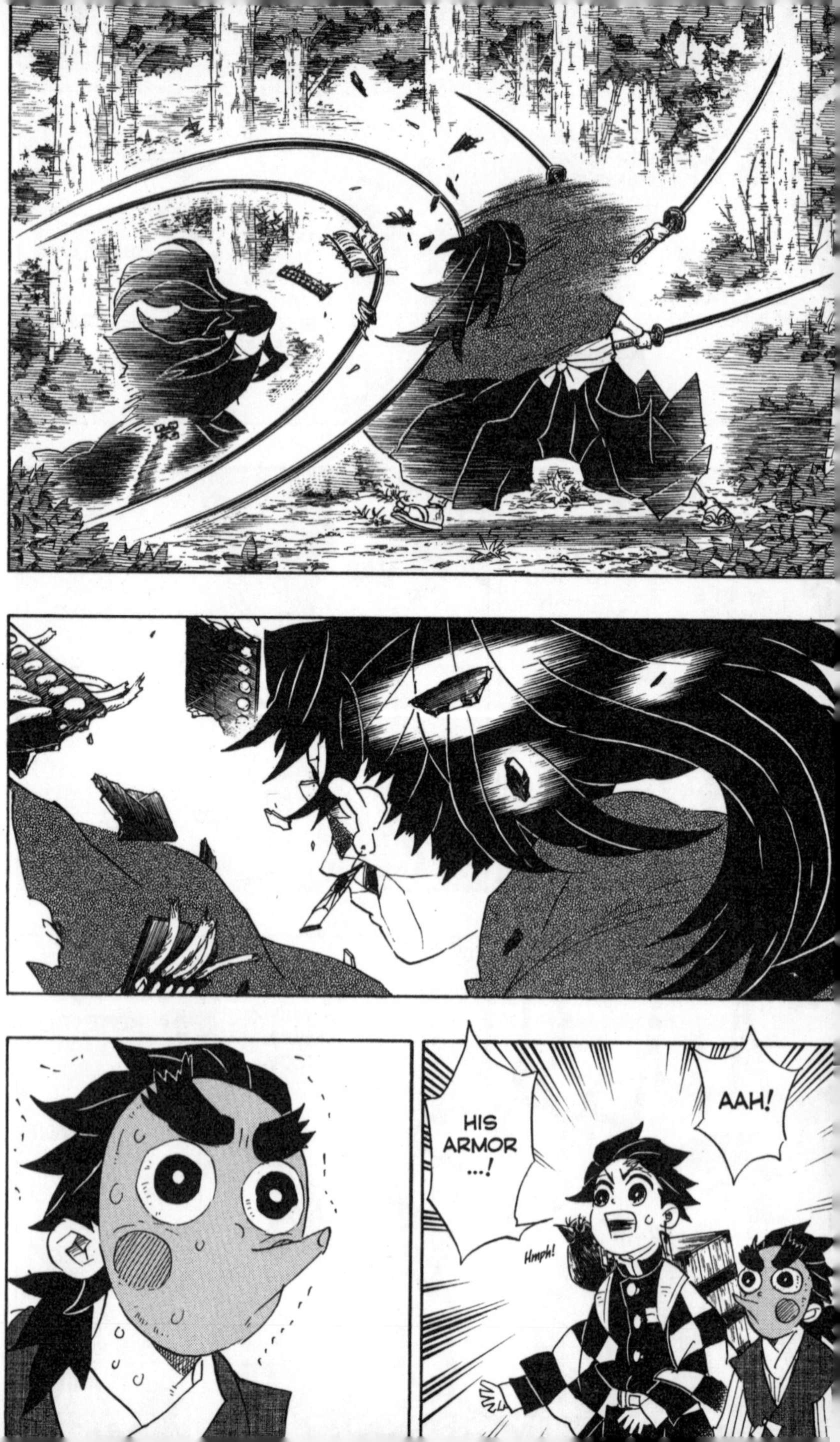
AAH!
HIS ARMOR ...!
Hmph!

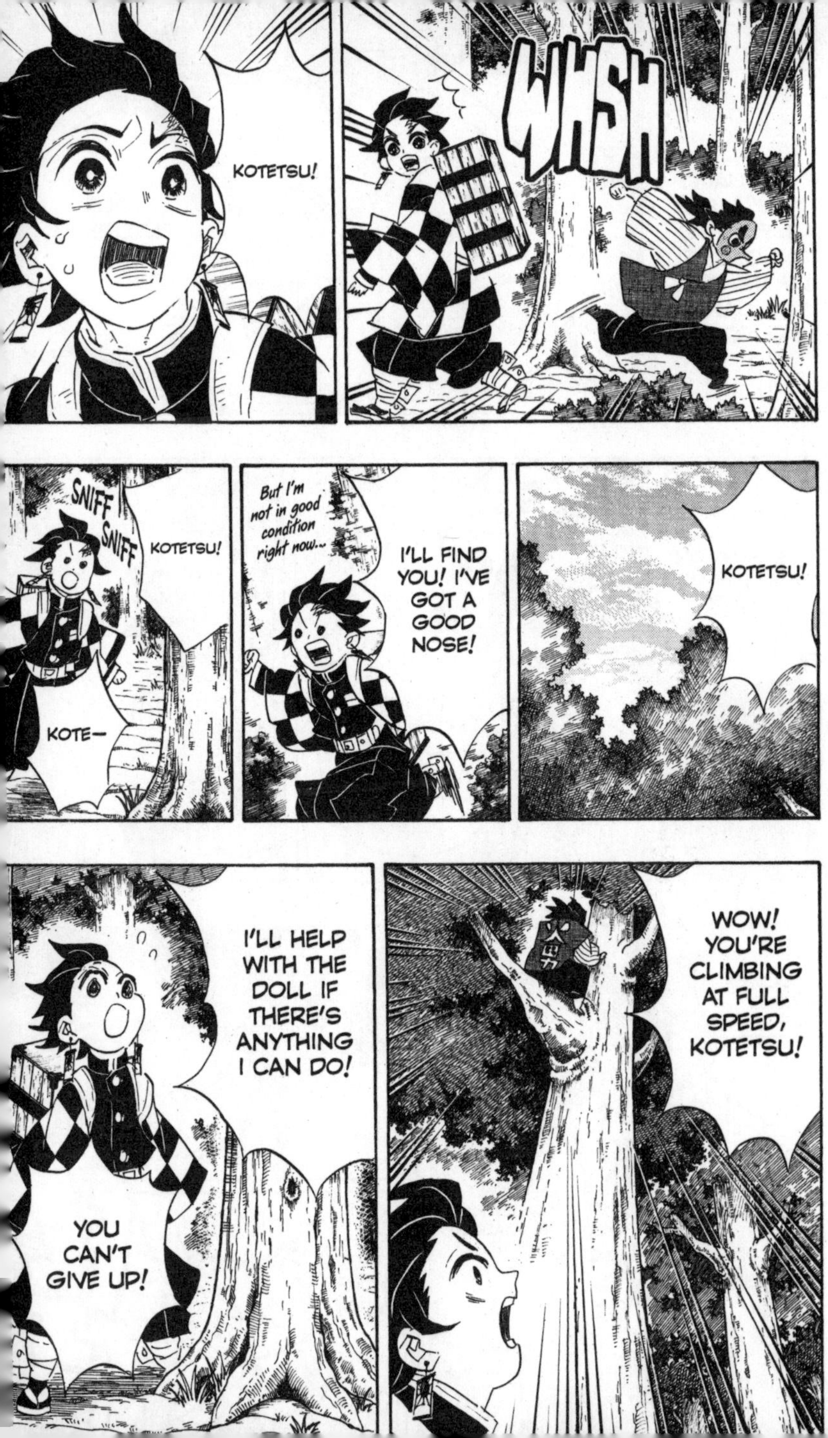
WHSH
KOTETSU!
KOTETSU!
But I'm not in good condition right now...
I'LL FIND YOU! I'VE GOT A GOOD NOSE!
SNIFF SNIFF
KOTETSU!
KOTE—
WOW! YOU'RE CLIMBING AT FULL SPEED, KOTETSU!
I'LL HELP WITH THE DOLL IF THERE'S ANYTHING I CAN DO!
YOU CAN'T GIVE UP!

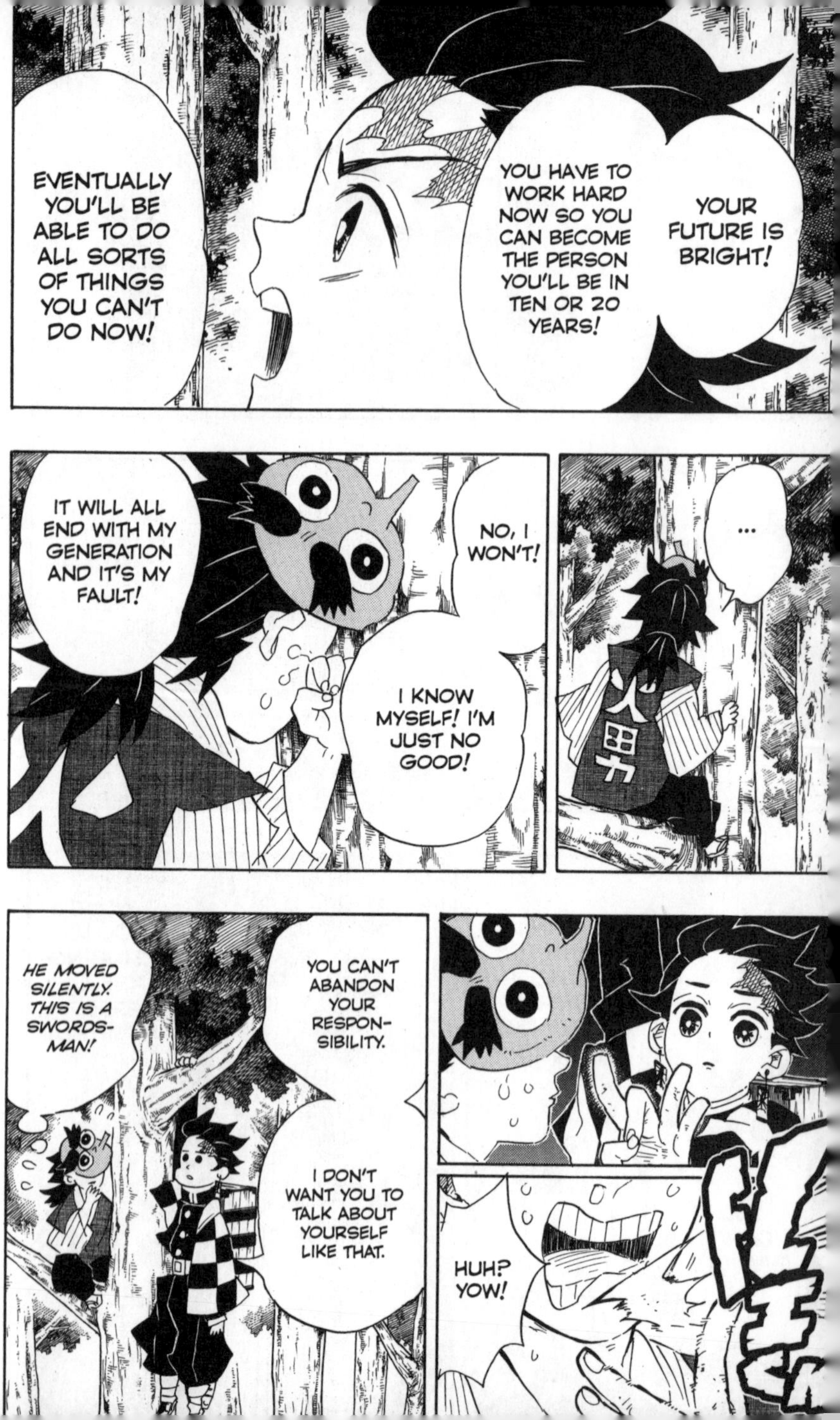
YOUR FUTURE IS BRIGHT!
YOU HAVE TO WORK HARD NOW SO YOU CAN BECOME THE PERSON YOU'LL BE IN TEN OR 20 YEARS!
EVENTUALLY YOU'LL BE ABLE TO DO ALL SORTS OF THINGS YOU CAN'T DO NOW!
...
NO, I WON'T!
IT WILL ALL END WITH MY GENERATION AND IT'S MY FAULT!
I KNOW MYSELF! I'M JUST NO GOOD!
HUH? YOW!
YOU CAN'T ABANDON YOUR RESPON-SIBILITY.
I DON'T WANT YOU TO TALK ABOUT YOURSELF LIKE THAT.
HE MOVED SILENTLY. THIS IS A SWORDS-MAN!

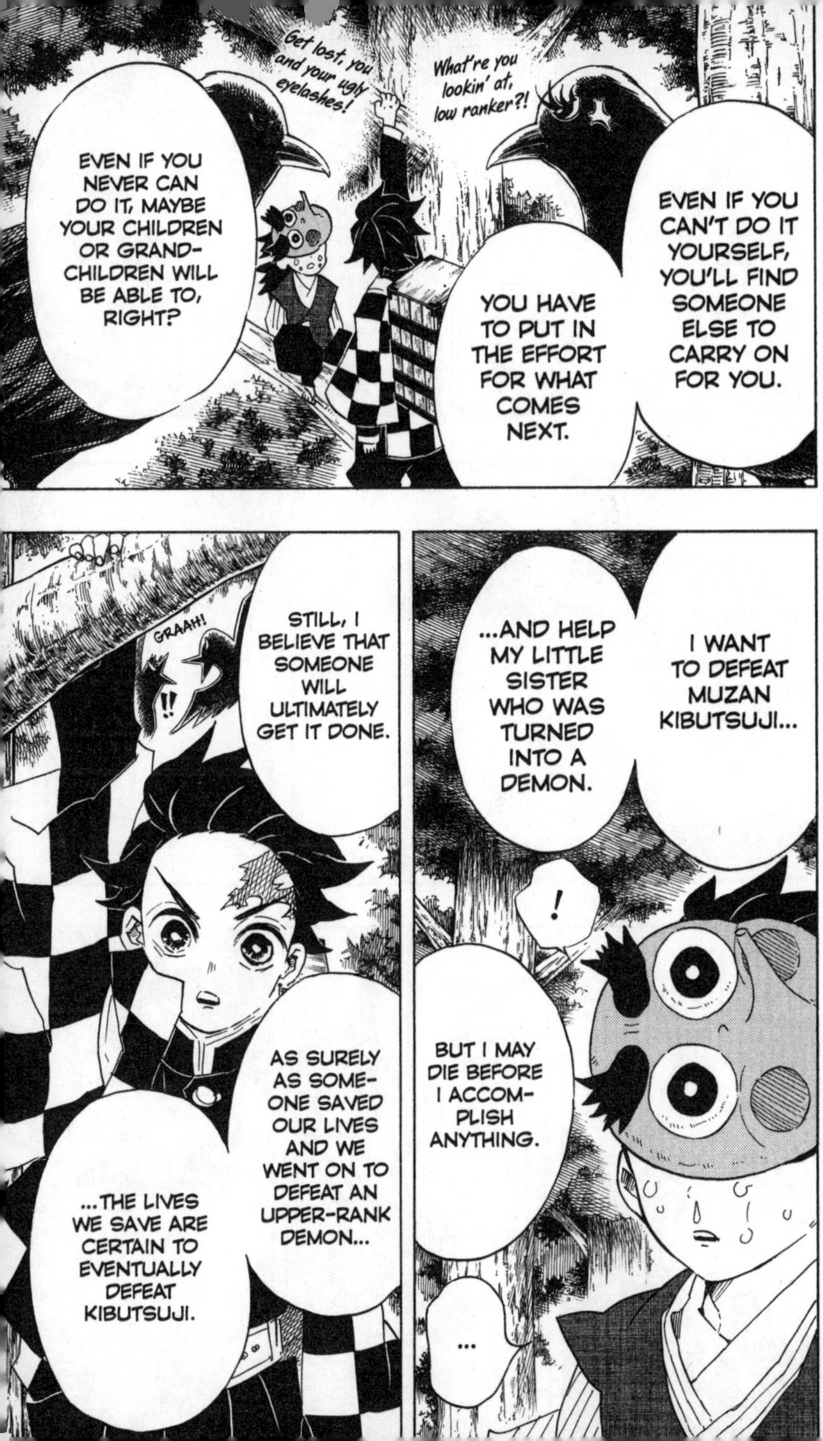
What're you lookin' at, low ranker?!
Get lost, you and your ugly eyelashes!
EVEN IF YOU CAN'T DO IT YOURSELF, YOU'LL FIND SOMEONE ELSE TO CARRY ON FOR YOU.
YOU HAVE TO PUT IN THE EFFORT FOR WHAT COMES NEXT.
EVEN IF YOU NEVER CAN DO IT, MAYBE YOUR CHILDREN OR GRAND-CHILDREN WILL BE ABLE TO, RIGHT?
I WANT TO DEFEAT MUZAN KIBUTSUJI...
...AND HELP MY LITTLE SISTER WHO WAS TURNED INTO A DEMON.
!
BUT I MAY DIE BEFORE I ACCOM-PLISH ANYTHING.
...
STILL, I BELIEVE THAT SOMEONE WILL ULTIMATELY GET IT DONE.
GRAAH!
!!
AS SURELY AS SOME-ONE SAVED OUR LIVES AND WE WENT ON TO DEFEAT AN UPPER-RANK DEMON...
...THE LIVES WE SAVE ARE CERTAIN TO EVENTUALLY DEFEAT KIBUTSUJI.

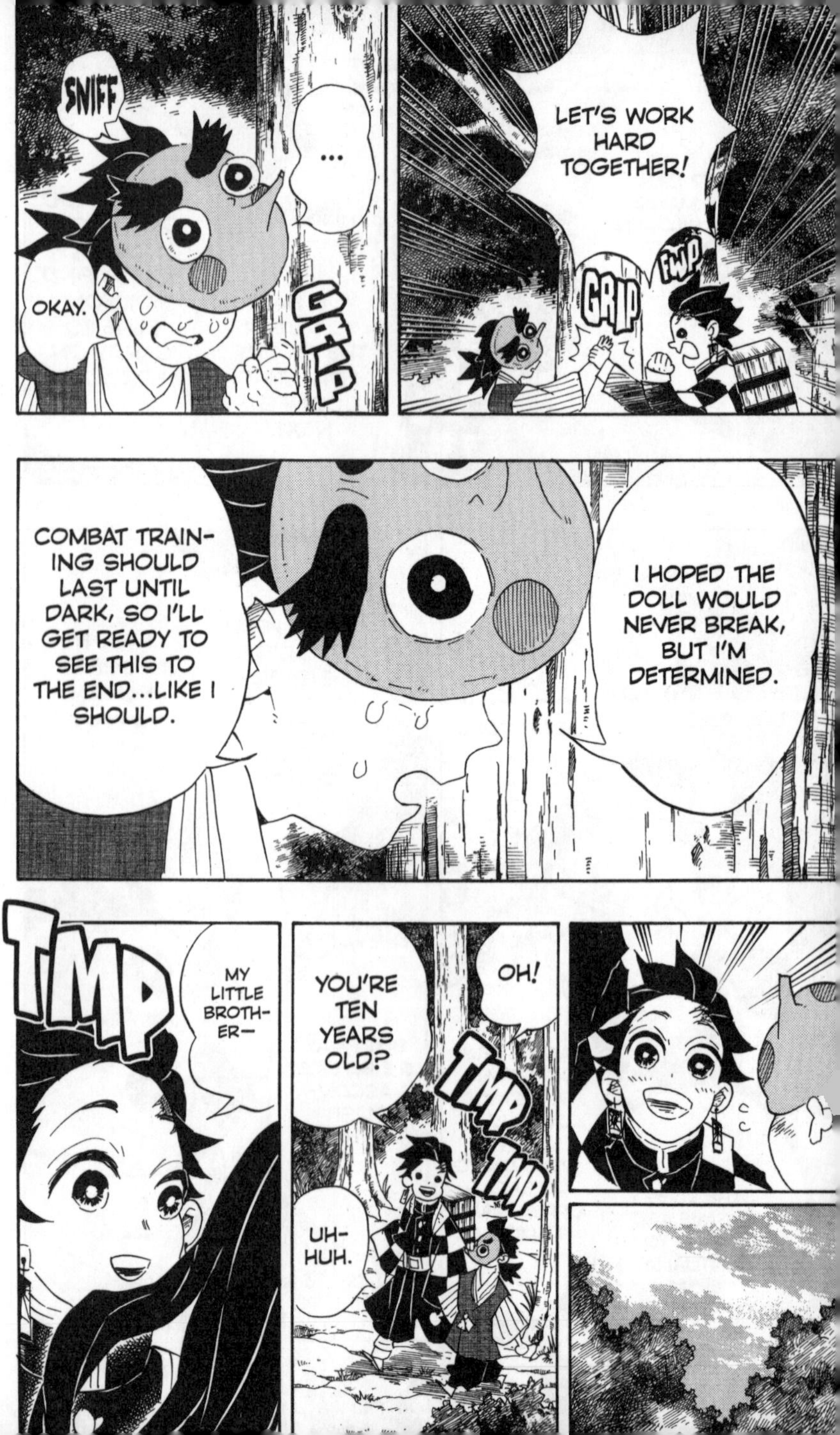
LET'S WORK HARD TOGETHER!
FWP
GRIP
SNIFF
...
GRIP
OKAY.
I HOPED THE DOLL WOULD NEVER BREAK, BUT I'M DETERMINED.
COMBAT TRAINING SHOULD LAST UNTIL DARK, SO I'LL GET READY TO SEE THIS TO THE END...LIKE I SHOULD.
OH!
YOU'RE TEN YEARS OLD?
TMP
TMP
UH-HUH.
MY LITTLE BROTHER—
TMP

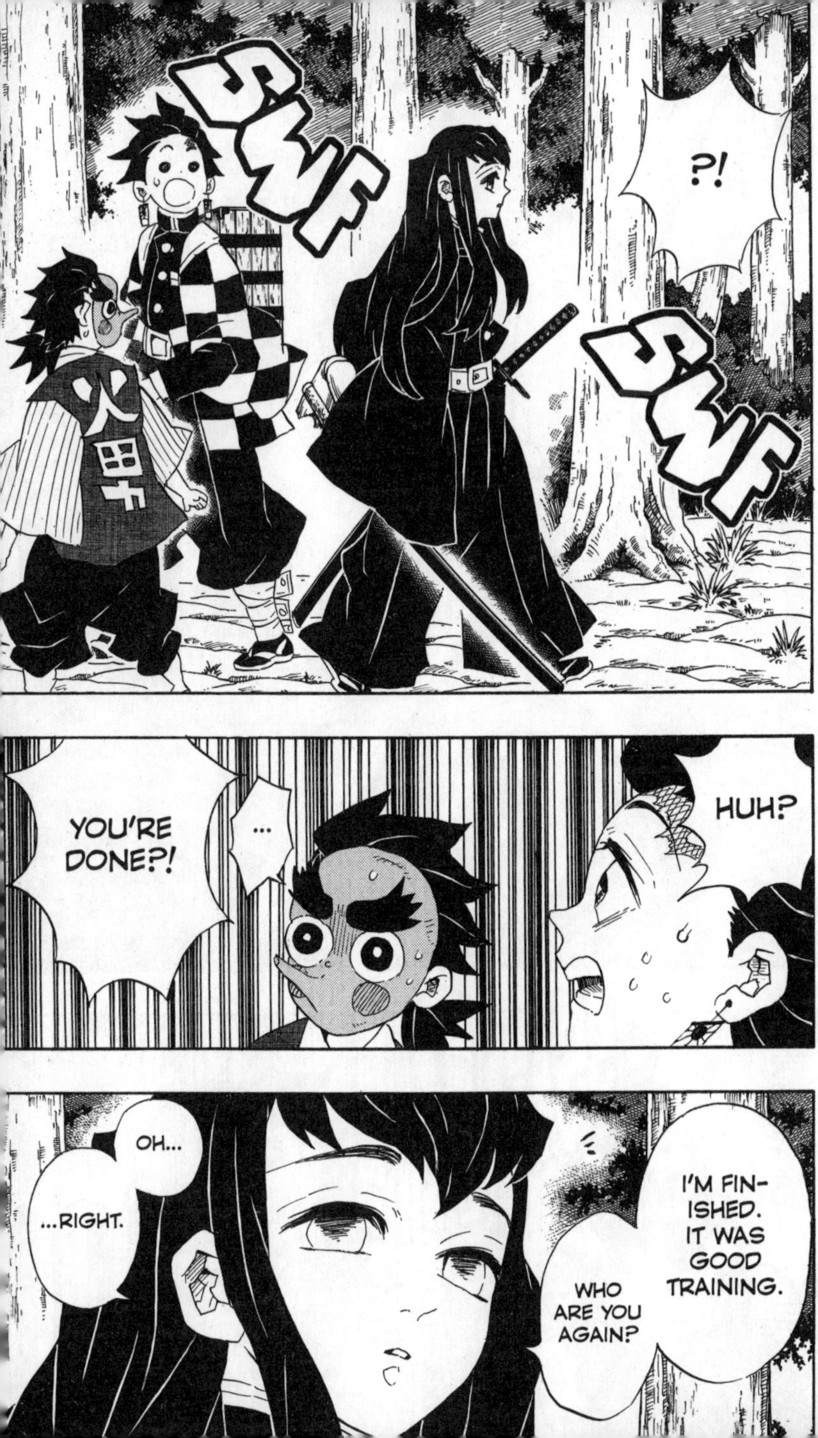
?!
SWF
SWF
HUH?
...
YOU'RE DONE?!
I'M FIN-ISHED. IT WAS GOOD TRAINING.
WHO ARE YOU AGAIN?
OH...
...RIGHT.

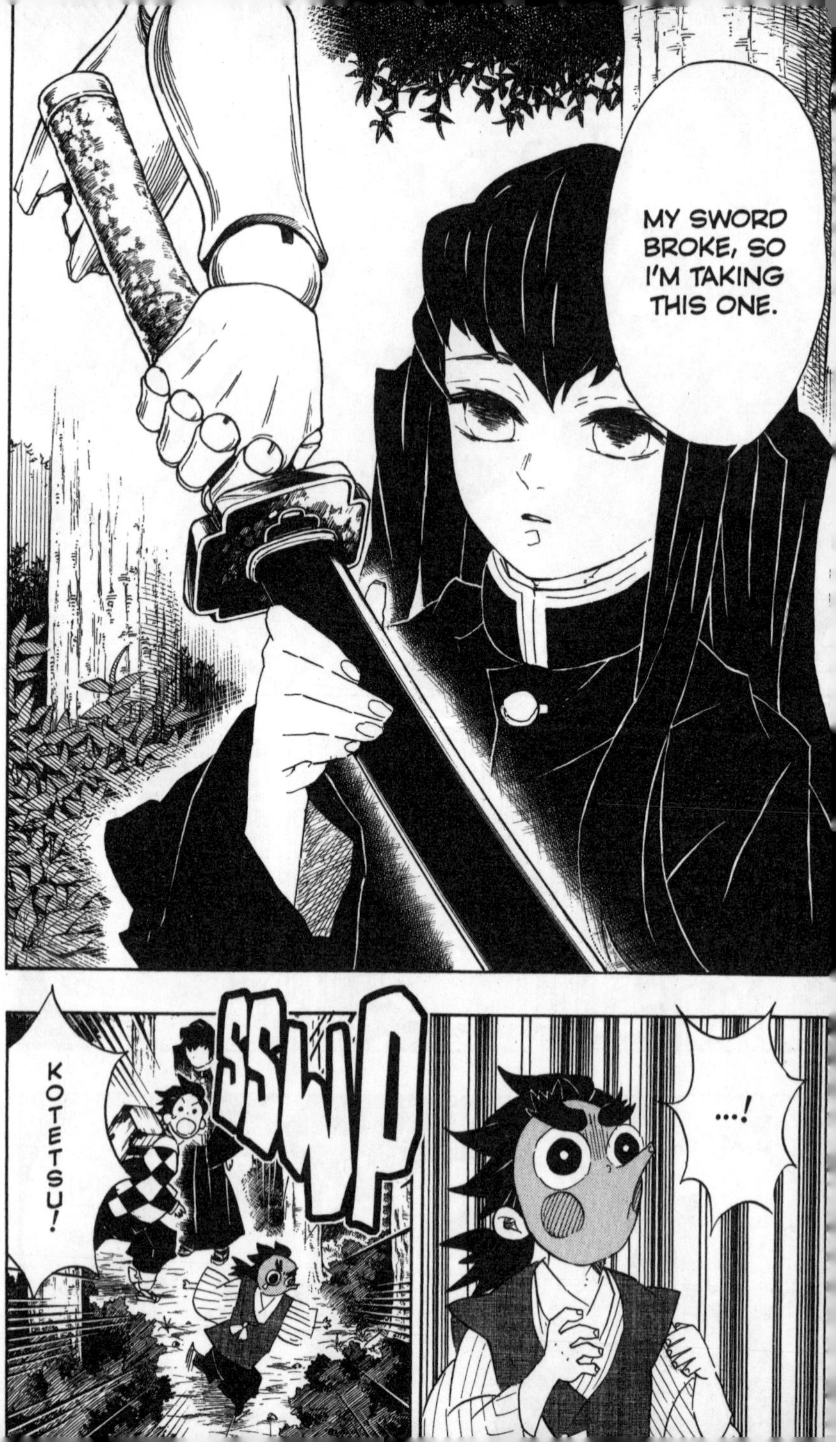
MY SWORD BROKE, SO I'M TAKING THIS ONE.
...!
SSWP
KOTETSU!

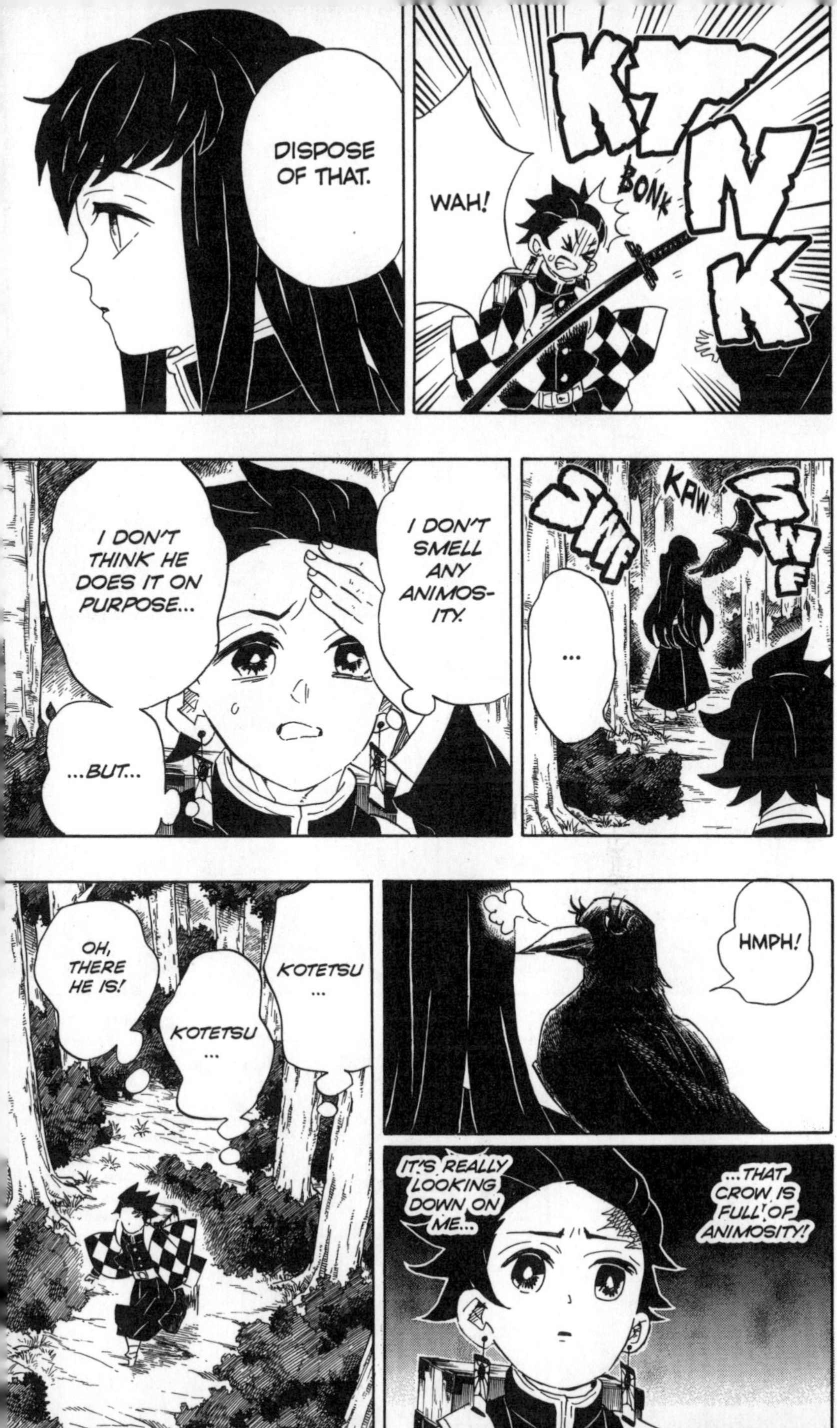
KTNK
BONK
WAH!
DISPOSE OF THAT.
KAW
SWF
SWF
...
I DON'T SMELL ANY ANIMOSITY.
I DON'T THINK HE DOES IT ON PURPOSE...
...BUT...
HMPH!
...THAT CROW IS FULL OF ANIMOSITY!
IT'S REALLY LOOKING DOWN ON ME...
KOTETSU ...
KOTETSU ...
OH, THERE HE IS!

RMBL

RMM

...

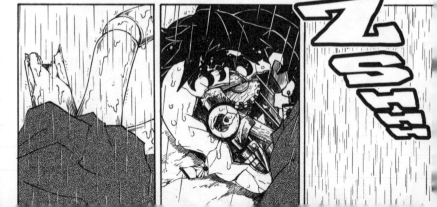

ZSHH

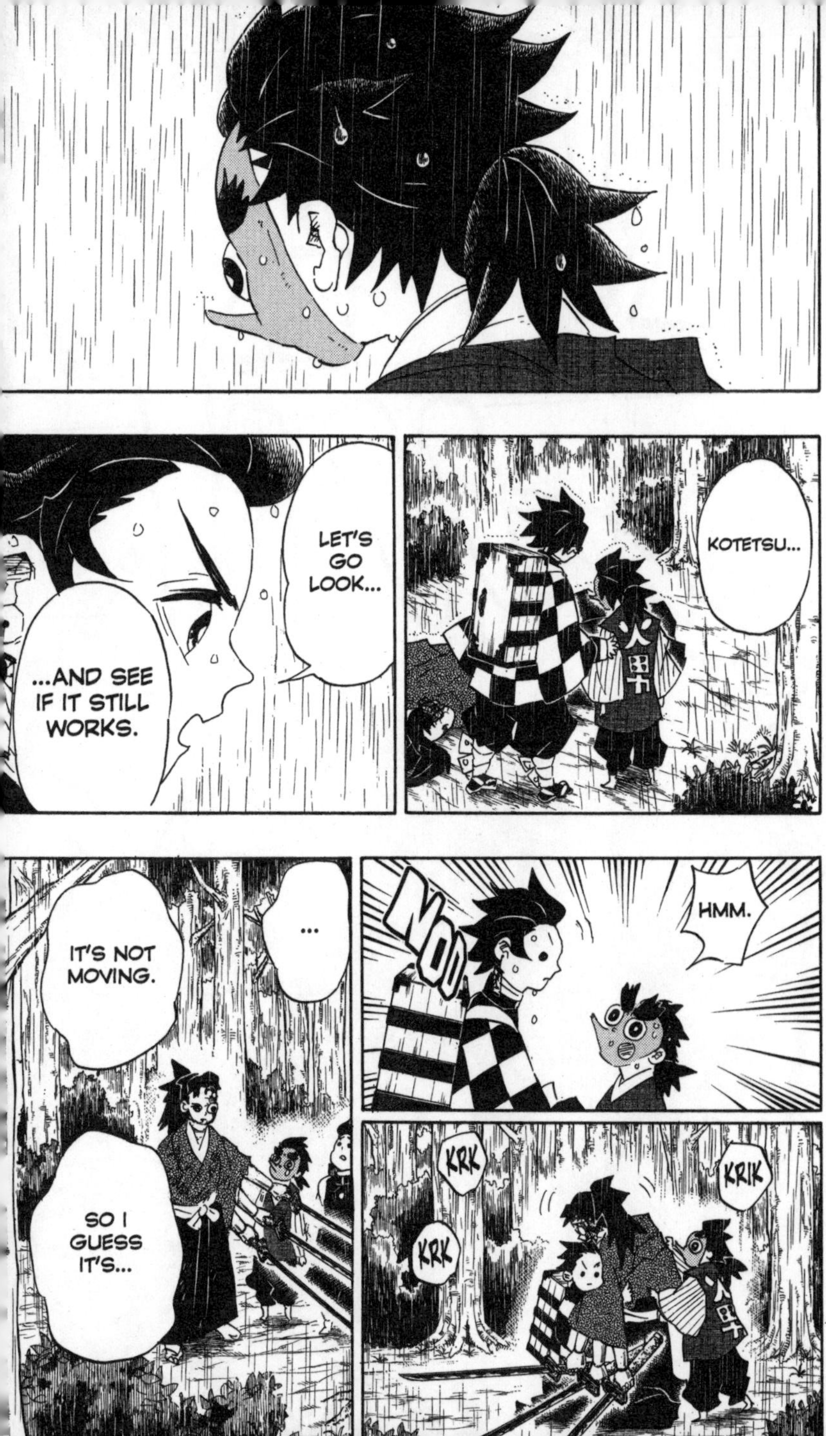
KOTETSU...
LET'S GO LOOK...
...AND SEE IF IT STILL WORKS.
HMM.
NOD
KRIK
KRK
KRK
...
IT'S NOT MOVING.
SO I GUESS IT'S...

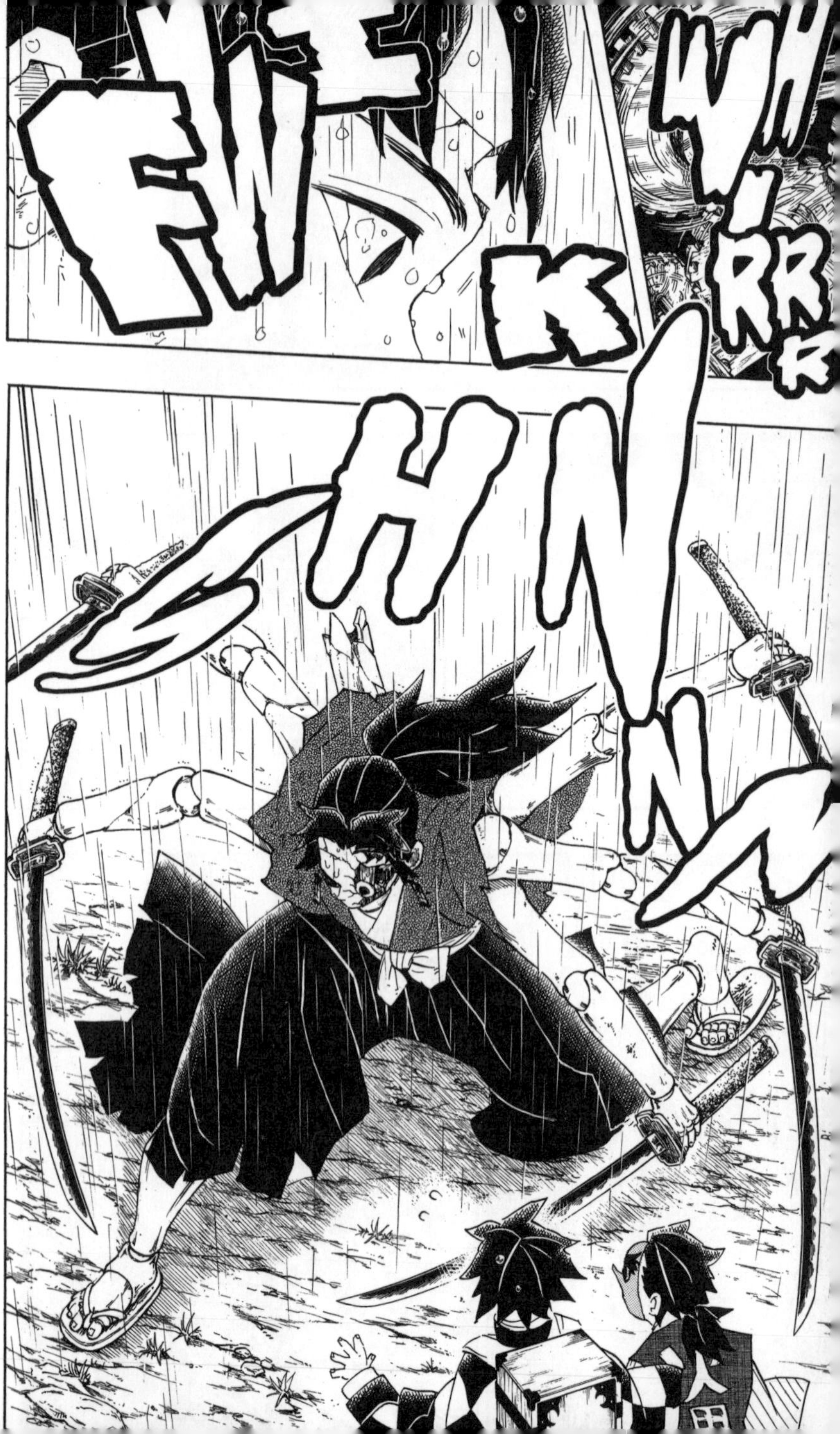
WHIRR
FWIK
SHNNN

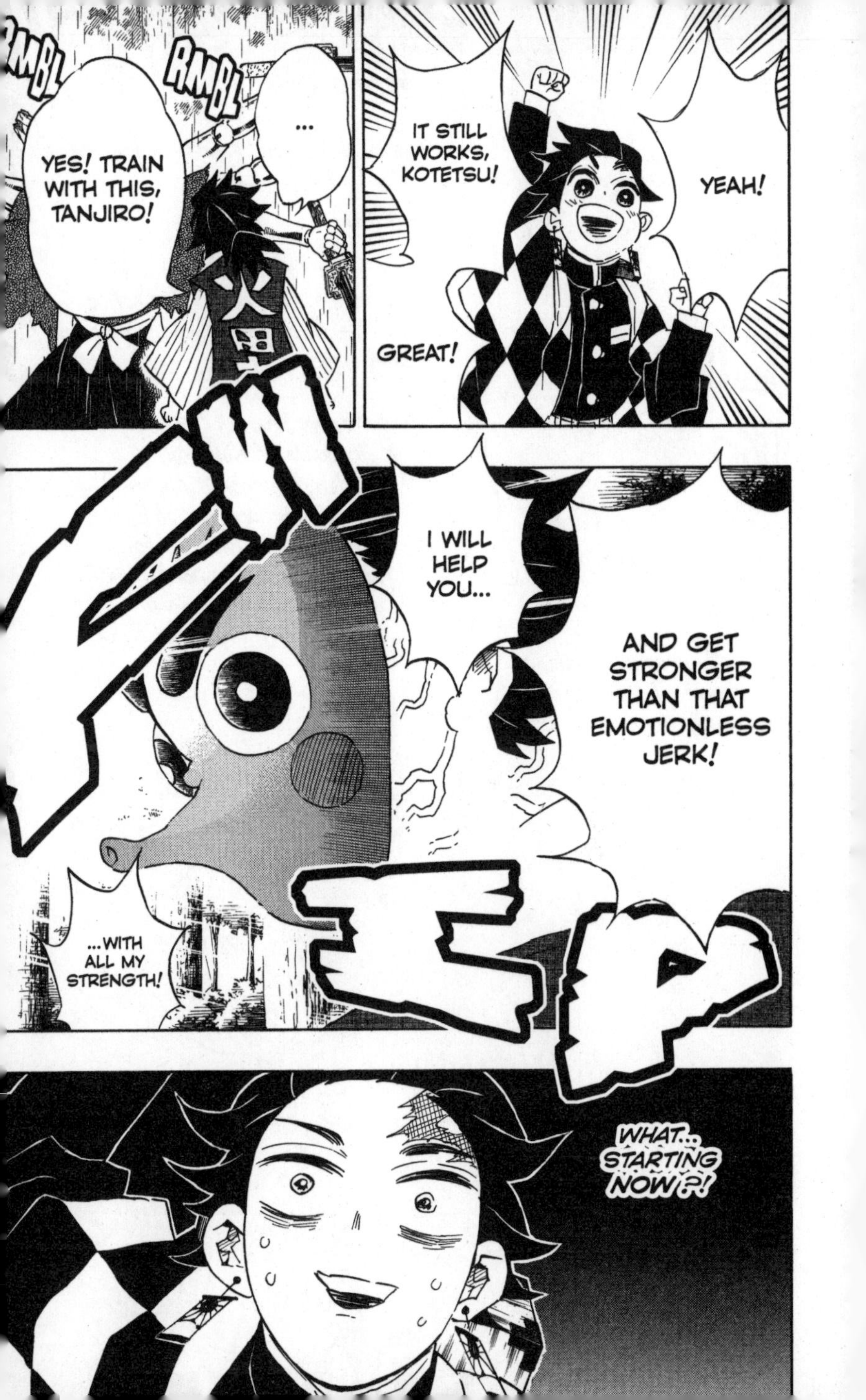
IT STILL WORKS, KOTETSU!
YEAH!
GREAT!
RMBL
RMBL
...
YES! TRAIN WITH THIS, TANJIRO!
I WILL HELP YOU...
AND GET STRONGER THAN THAT EMOTIONLESS JERK!
...WITH ALL MY STRENGTH!
WHAT... STARTING NOW?!

It's been a while!

Junior High and High School ♡ Kimetsu Academy Story!

By Mitsuri

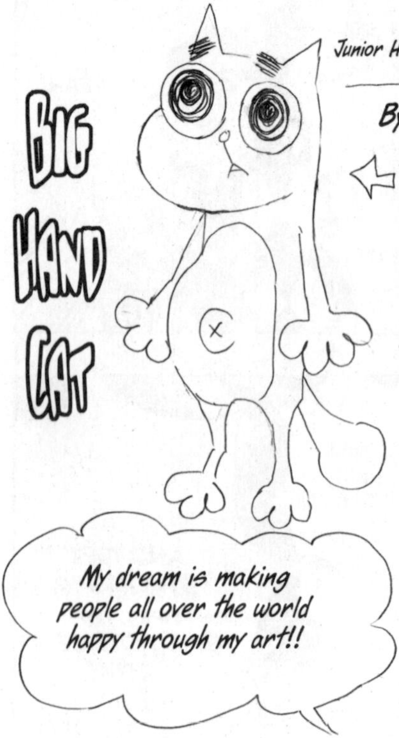
BIG HAND CAT
My dream is making people all over the world happy through my art!!

Big Hand Cat. In addition to its big hands, this cat is distinctive for its fuzzy eyebrows and outie belly button.

Mitsuri Kanroji (19). Graduate of Kimetsu Academy. Currently she is attending a local art college. She's popular with the boys, but she hasn't noticed it, so she thinks she needs to search for a boyfriend.

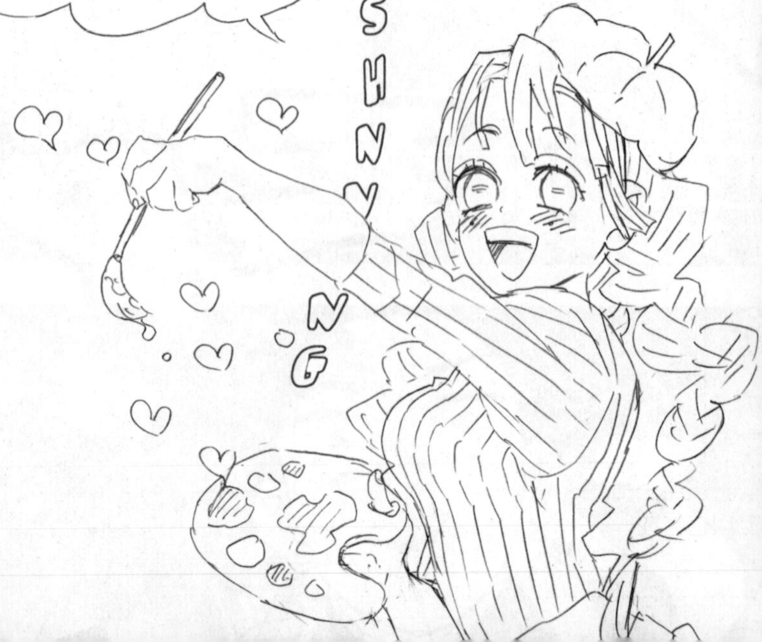
SHINING

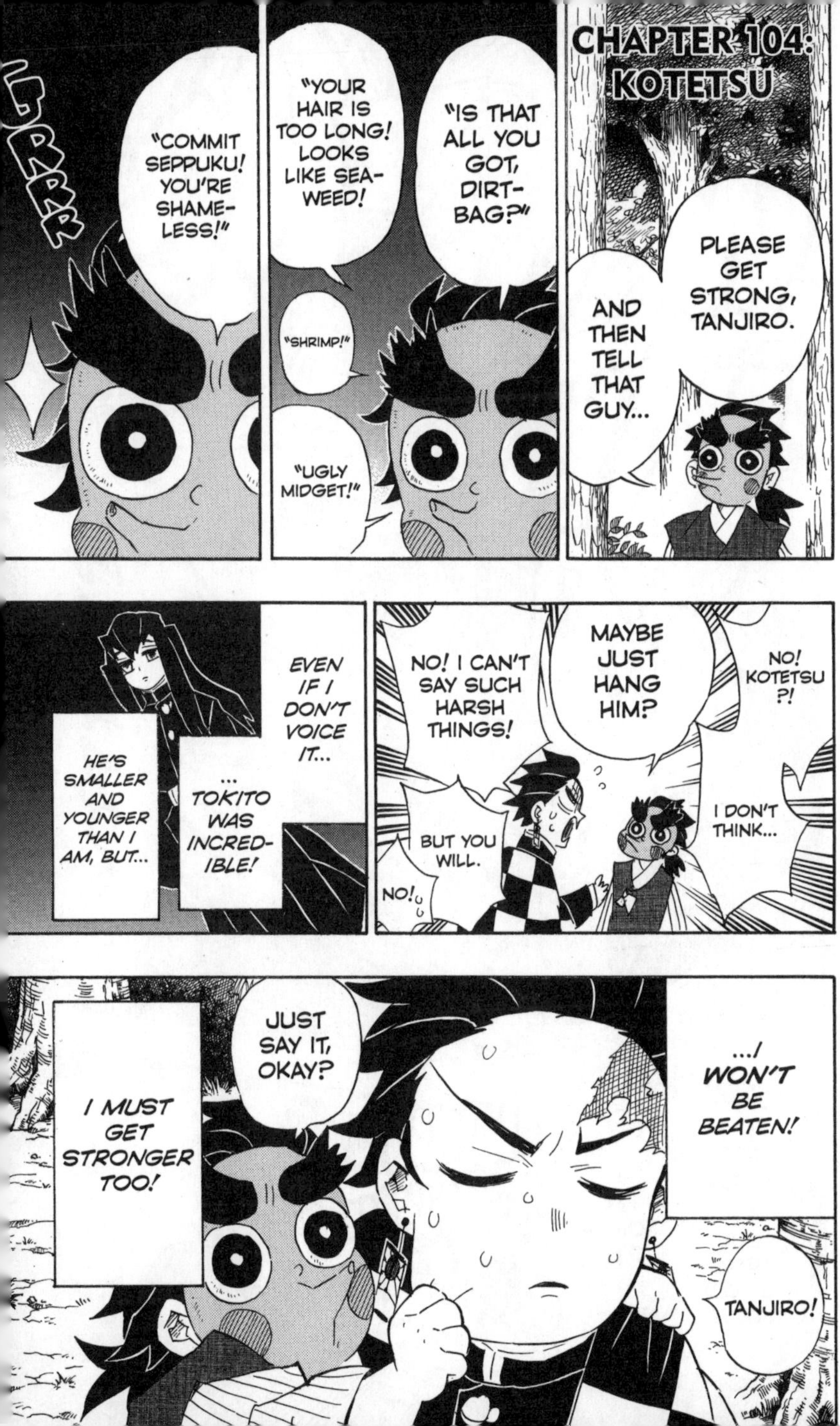
CHAPTER 104: KOTETSU
PLEASE GET STRONG, TANJIRO.
AND THEN TELL THAT GUY...
"IS THAT ALL YOU GOT, DIRT-BAG?"
"YOUR HAIR IS TOO LONG! LOOKS LIKE SEA-WEED!"
"SHRIMP!"
"UGLY MIDGET!"
GRRRR
"COMMIT SEPPUKU! YOU'RE SHAME-LESS!"
NO! KOTETSU?!
MAYBE JUST HANG HIM?
NO! I CAN'T SAY SUCH HARSH THINGS!
I DON'T THINK...
BUT YOU WILL.
NO!
EVEN IF I DON'T VOICE IT...
...TOKITO WAS INCRED-IBLE!
HE'S SMALLER AND YOUNGER THAN I AM, BUT...
...I WON'T BE BEATEN!
TANJIRO!
JUST SAY IT, OKAY?
I MUST GET STRONGER TOO!

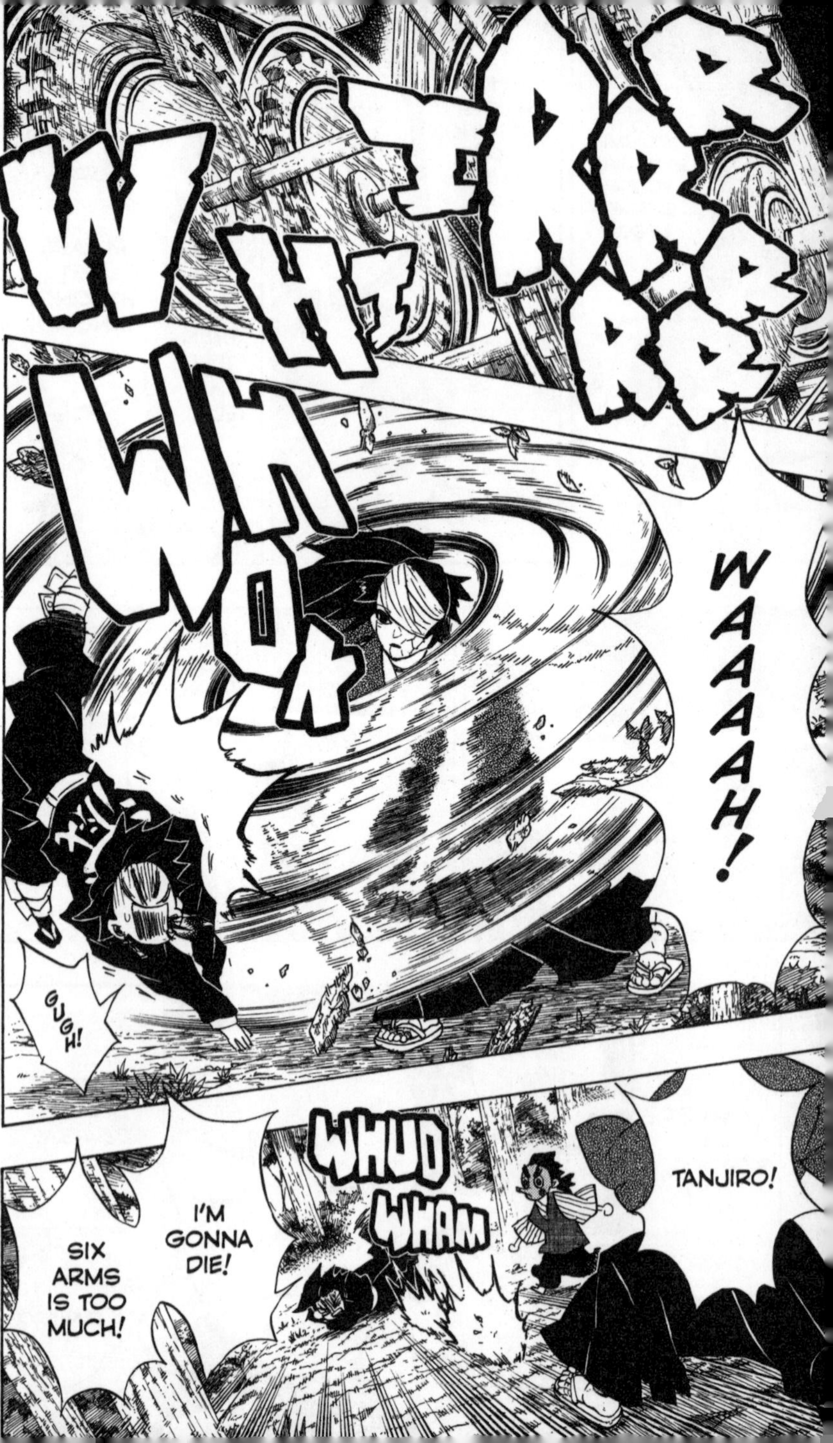
WHIRRRRRR
WAAAAAH!
GUGH!
TANJIRO!
WHUD
WHAM
I'M GONNA DIE!
SIX ARMS IS TOO MUCH!

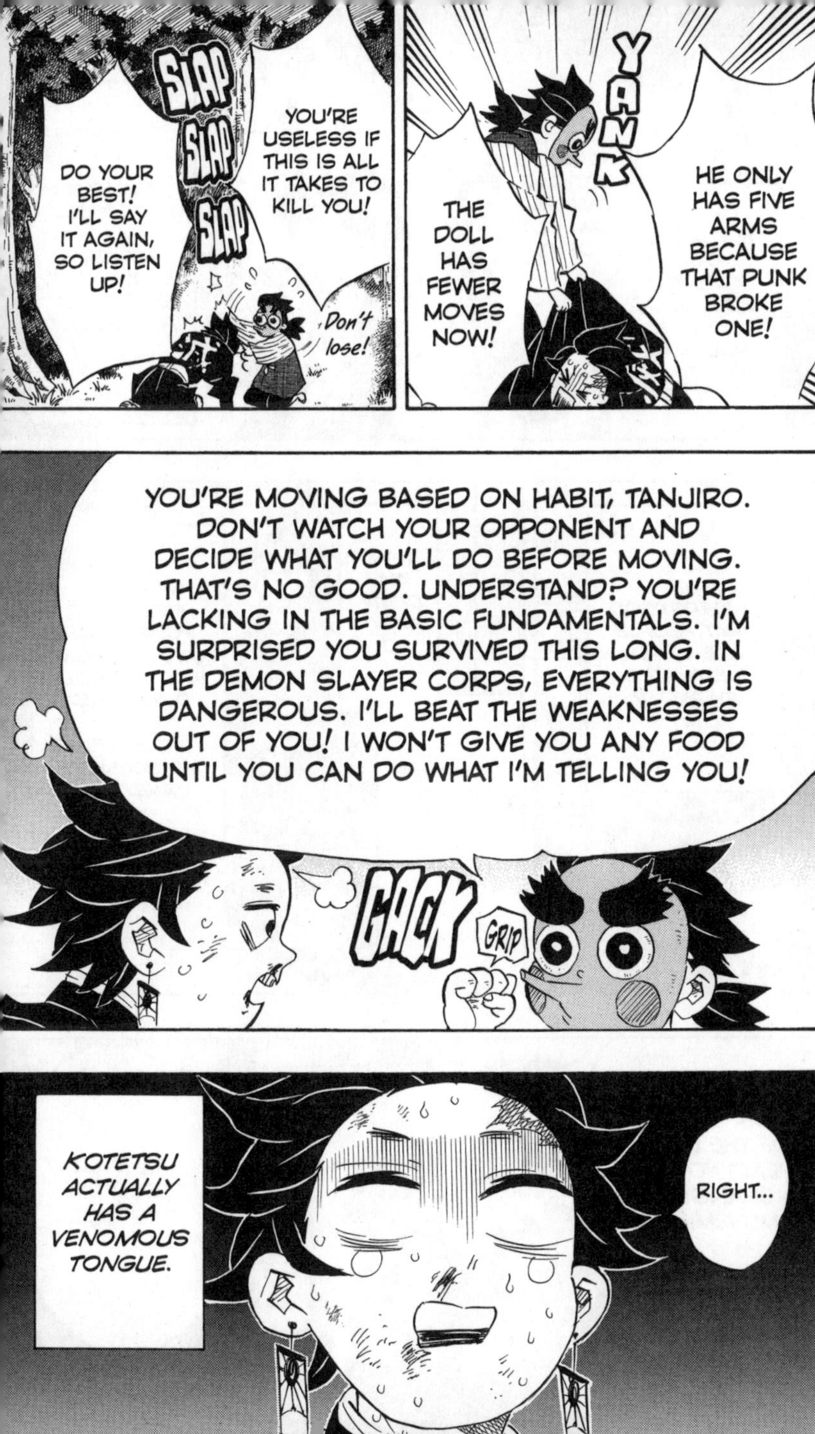
YANK
HE ONLY HAS FIVE ARMS BECAUSE THAT PUNK BROKE ONE!
THE DOLL HAS FEWER MOVES NOW!
YOU'RE USELESS IF THIS IS ALL IT TAKES TO KILL YOU!
SLAP SLAP SLAP
DO YOUR BEST! I'LL SAY IT AGAIN, SO LISTEN UP!
Don't lose!
YOU'RE MOVING BASED ON HABIT, TANJIRO. DON'T WATCH YOUR OPPONENT AND DECIDE WHAT YOU'LL DO BEFORE MOVING. THAT'S NO GOOD. UNDERSTAND? YOU'RE LACKING IN THE BASIC FUNDAMENTALS. I'M SURPRISED YOU SURVIVED THIS LONG. IN THE DEMON SLAYER CORPS, EVERYTHING IS DANGEROUS. I'LL BEAT THE WEAKNESSES OUT OF YOU! I WON'T GIVE YOU ANY FOOD UNTIL YOU CAN DO WHAT I'M TELLING YOU!
GRIP
GACK
RIGHT...
KOTETSU ACTUALLY HAS A VENOMOUS TONGUE.

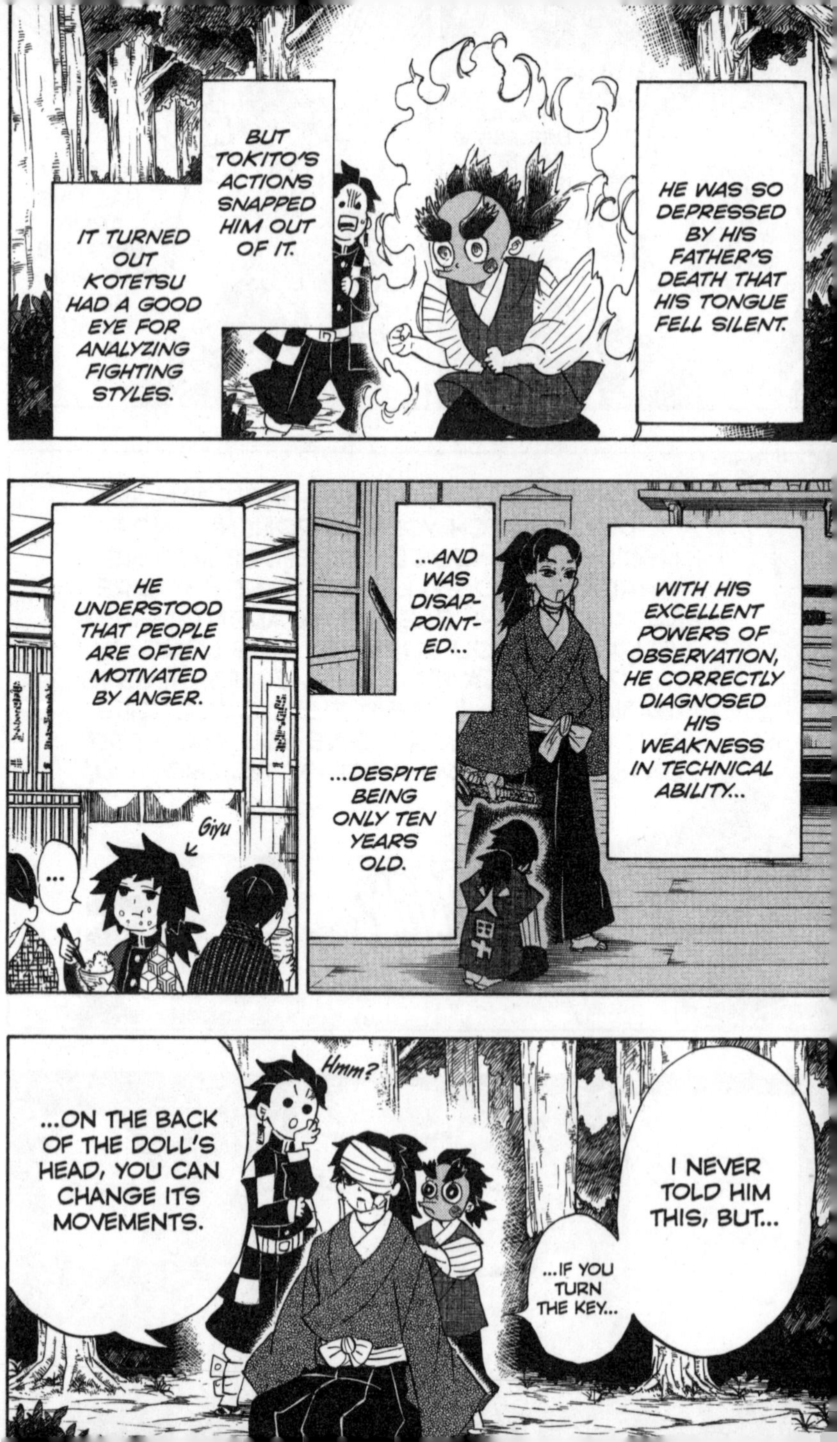
HE WAS SO DEPRESSED BY HIS FATHER'S DEATH THAT HIS TONGUE FELL SILENT.
BUT TOKITO'S ACTIONS SNAPPED HIM OUT OF IT.
IT TURNED OUT KOTETSU HAD A GOOD EYE FOR ANALYZING FIGHTING STYLES.
WITH HIS EXCELLENT POWERS OF OBSERVATION, HE CORRECTLY DIAGNOSED HIS WEAKNESS IN TECHNICAL ABILITY...
...AND WAS DISAPPOINTED...
...DESPITE BEING ONLY TEN YEARS OLD.
HE UNDERSTOOD THAT PEOPLE ARE OFTEN MOTIVATED BY ANGER.
Giyu
...
I NEVER TOLD HIM THIS, BUT...
...IF YOU TURN THE KEY...
Hmm?
...ON THE BACK OF THE DOLL'S HEAD, YOU CAN CHANGE ITS MOVEMENTS.

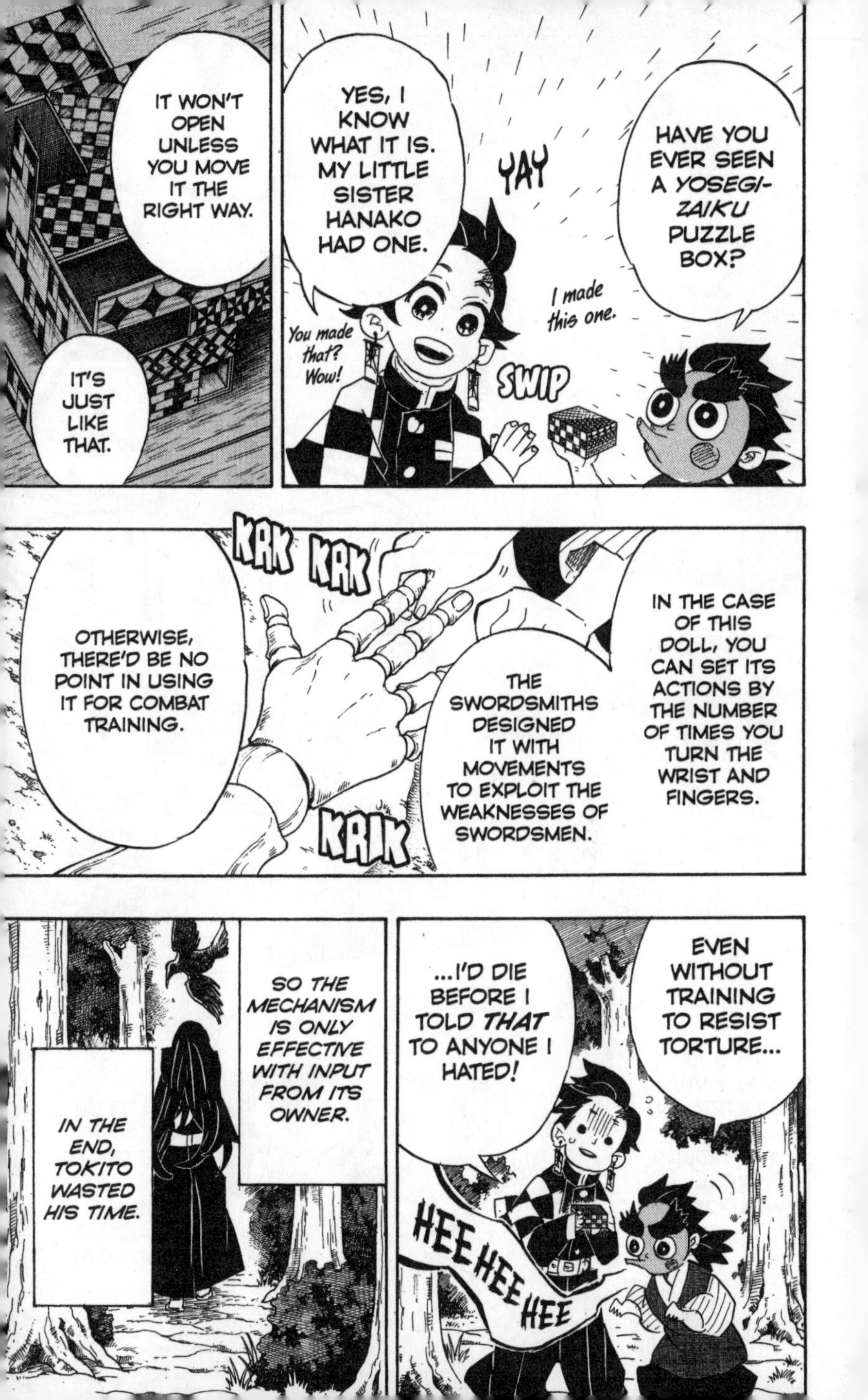
HAVE YOU EVER SEEN A *YOSEGI-ZAIKU* PUZZLE BOX?
I made this one.
SWIP
YAY
You made that? Wow!
YES, I KNOW WHAT IT IS. MY LITTLE SISTER HANAKO HAD ONE.
IT WON'T OPEN UNLESS YOU MOVE IT THE RIGHT WAY.
IT'S JUST LIKE THAT.
IN THE CASE OF THIS DOLL, YOU CAN SET ITS ACTIONS BY THE NUMBER OF TIMES YOU TURN THE WRIST AND FINGERS.
THE SWORDSMITHS DESIGNED IT WITH MOVEMENTS TO EXPLOIT THE WEAKNESSES OF SWORDSMEN.
KRK KRK
KRIK
OTHERWISE, THERE'D BE NO POINT IN USING IT FOR COMBAT TRAINING.
EVEN WITHOUT TRAINING TO RESIST TORTURE...
...I'D DIE BEFORE I TOLD *THAT* TO ANYONE I HATED!
HEE HEE HEE
SO THE MECHANISM IS ONLY EFFECTIVE WITH INPUT FROM ITS OWNER.
IN THE END, TOKITO WASTED HIS TIME.

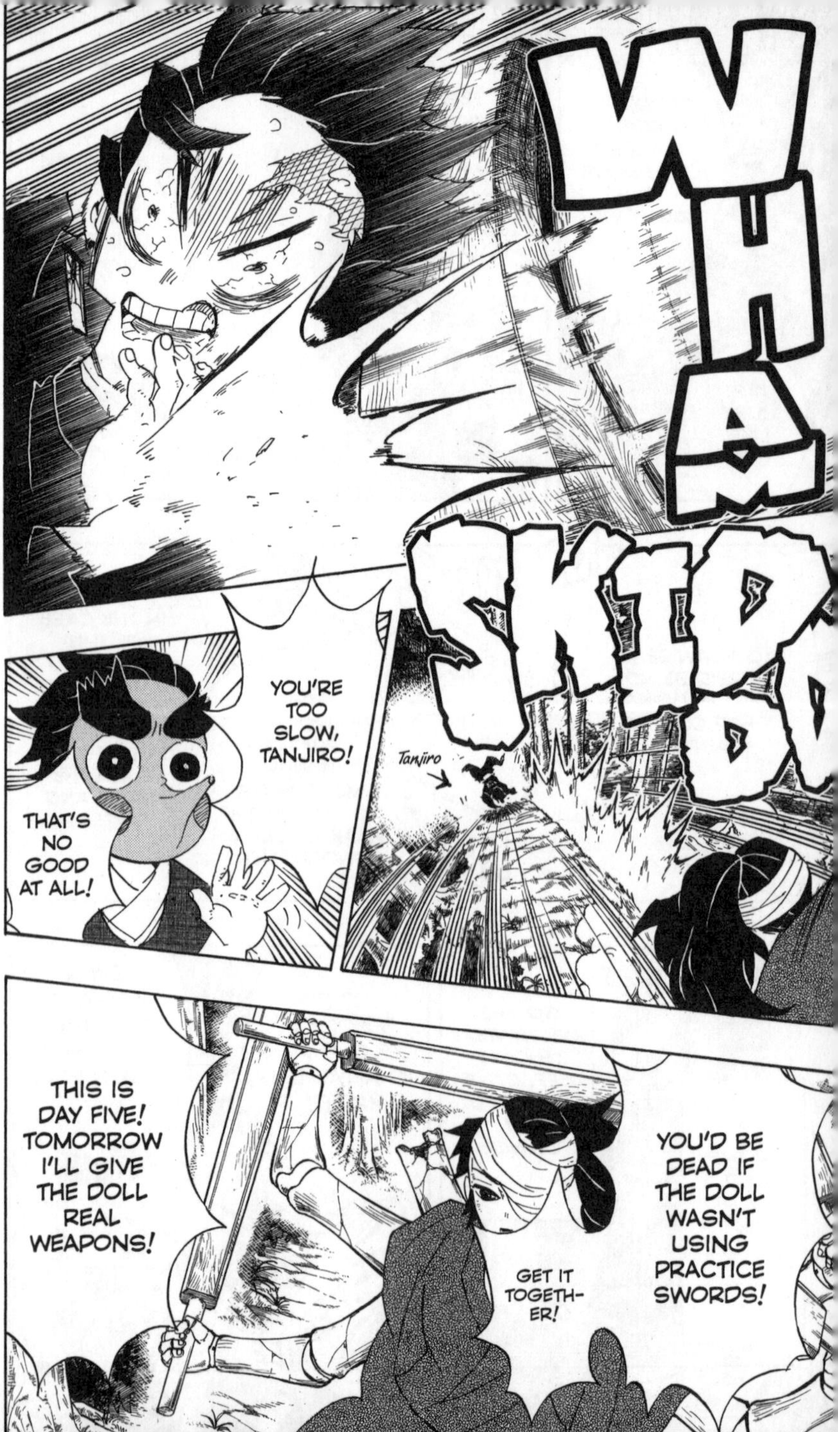
WHAM
SKID
Tanjiro
YOU'RE TOO SLOW, TANJIRO!
THAT'S NO GOOD AT ALL!
YOU'D BE DEAD IF THE DOLL WASN'T USING PRACTICE SWORDS!
GET IT TOGETH-ER!
THIS IS DAY FIVE! TOMORROW I'LL GIVE THE DOLL REAL WEAPONS!

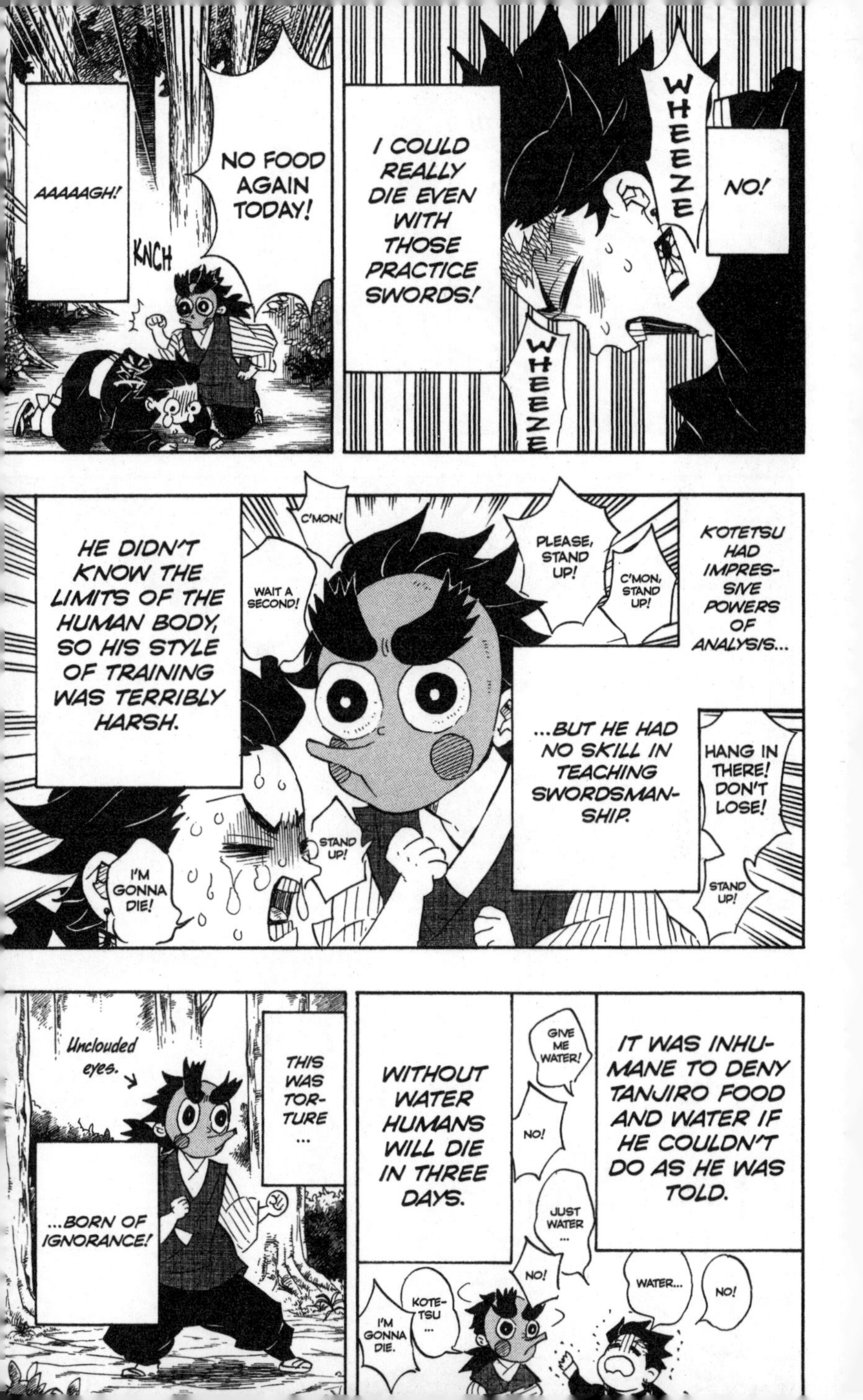
NO!
WHEEZE
WHEEZE
I COULD REALLY DIE EVEN WITH THOSE PRACTICE SWORDS!
NO FOOD AGAIN TODAY!
AAAAAGH!
KNCH
KOTETSU HAD IMPRESSIVE POWERS OF ANALYSIS...
C'MON, STAND UP!
PLEASE, STAND UP!
...BUT HE HAD NO SKILL IN TEACHING SWORDSMANSHIP.
HANG IN THERE! DON'T LOSE!
STAND UP!
C'MON!
WAIT A SECOND!
HE DIDN'T KNOW THE LIMITS OF THE HUMAN BODY, SO HIS STYLE OF TRAINING WAS TERRIBLY HARSH.
STAND UP!
I'M GONNA DIE!
IT WAS INHUMANE TO DENY TANJIRO FOOD AND WATER IF HE COULDN'T DO AS HE WAS TOLD.
GIVE ME WATER!
NO!
WITHOUT WATER HUMANS WILL DIE IN THREE DAYS.
JUST WATER ...
NO!
WATER...
NO!
KOTETSU ...
I'M GONNA DIE.
THIS WAS TORTURE ...
Unclouded eyes.
...BORN OF IGNORANCE!

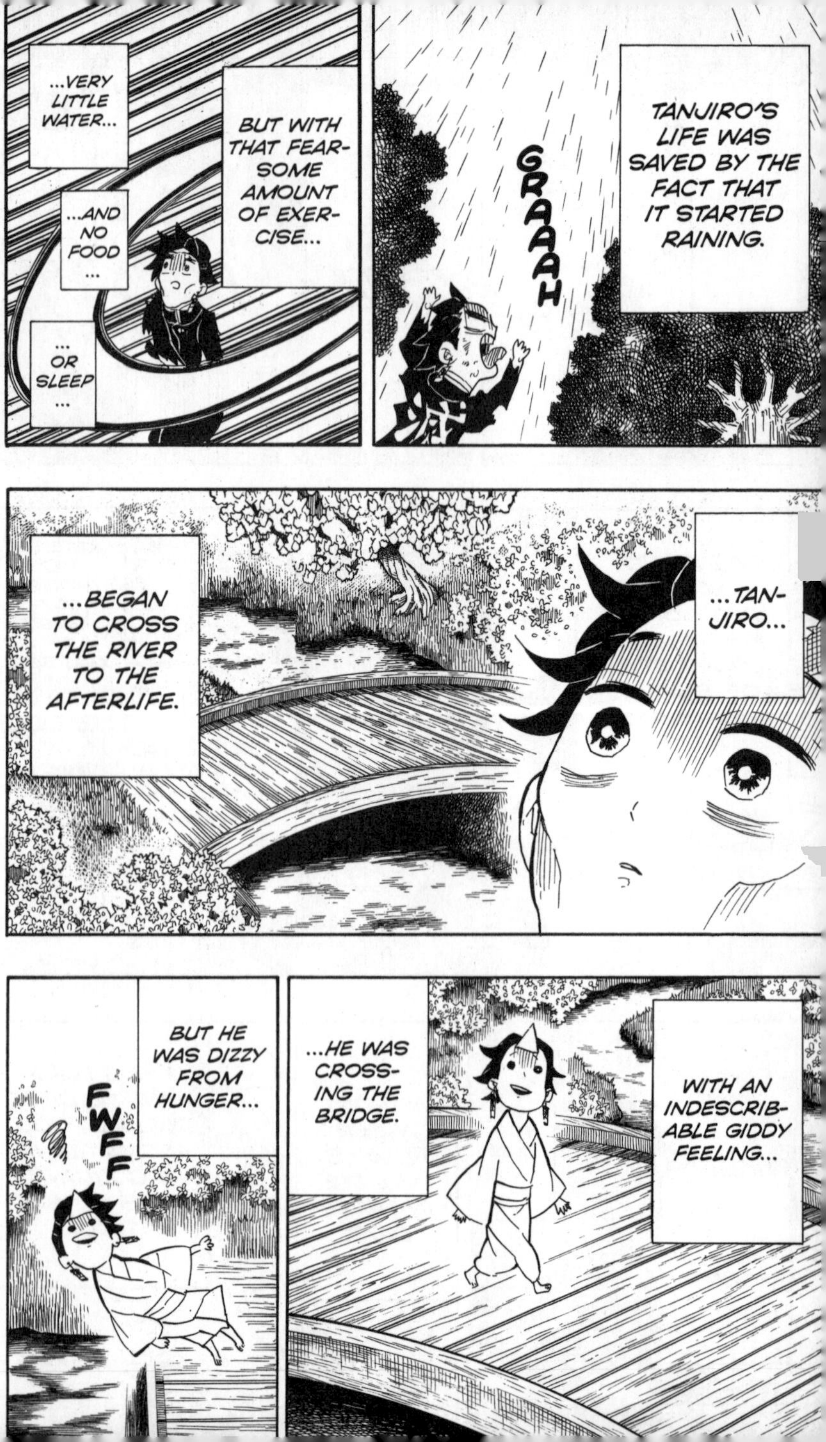
TANJIRO'S LIFE WAS SAVED BY THE FACT THAT IT STARTED RAINING.
GRAAAAH
BUT WITH THAT FEAR-SOME AMOUNT OF EXER-CISE...
...VERY LITTLE WATER...
...AND NO FOOD...
...OR SLEEP...
...TAN-JIRO...
...BEGAN TO CROSS THE RIVER TO THE AFTERLIFE.
WITH AN INDESCRIB-ABLE GIDDY FEELING...
...HE WAS CROSS-ING THE BRIDGE.
BUT HE WAS DIZZY FROM HUNGER...
FWFF

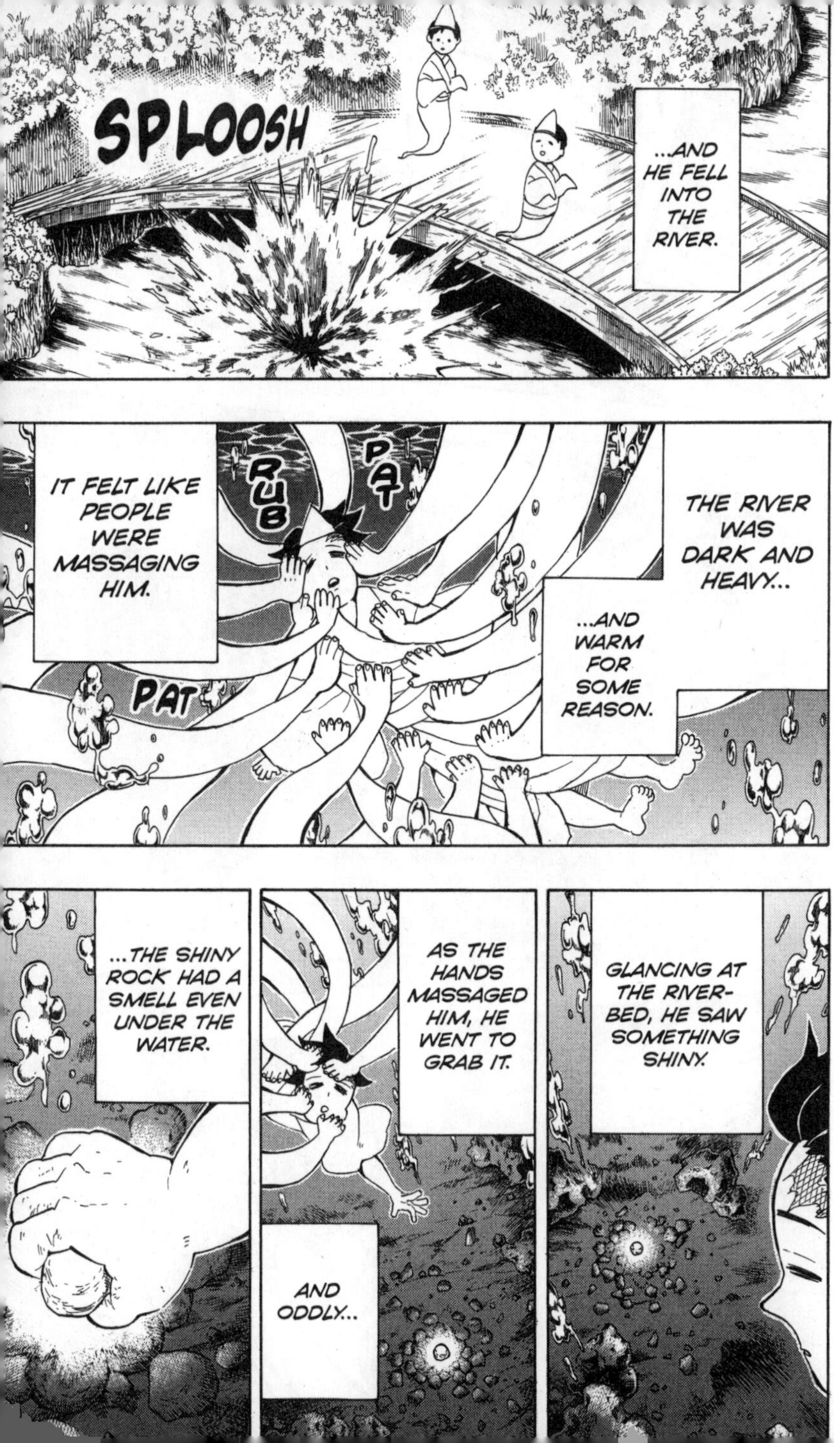
...AND HE FELL INTO THE RIVER.
SPLOOSH
THE RIVER WAS DARK AND HEAVY...
...AND WARM FOR SOME REASON.
PAT
RUB
IT FELT LIKE PEOPLE WERE MASSAGING HIM.
PAT
GLANCING AT THE RIVER-BED, HE SAW SOMETHING SHINY.
AS THE HANDS MASSAGED HIM, HE WENT TO GRAB IT.
AND ODDLY...
...THE SHINY ROCK HAD A SMELL EVEN UNDER THE WATER.

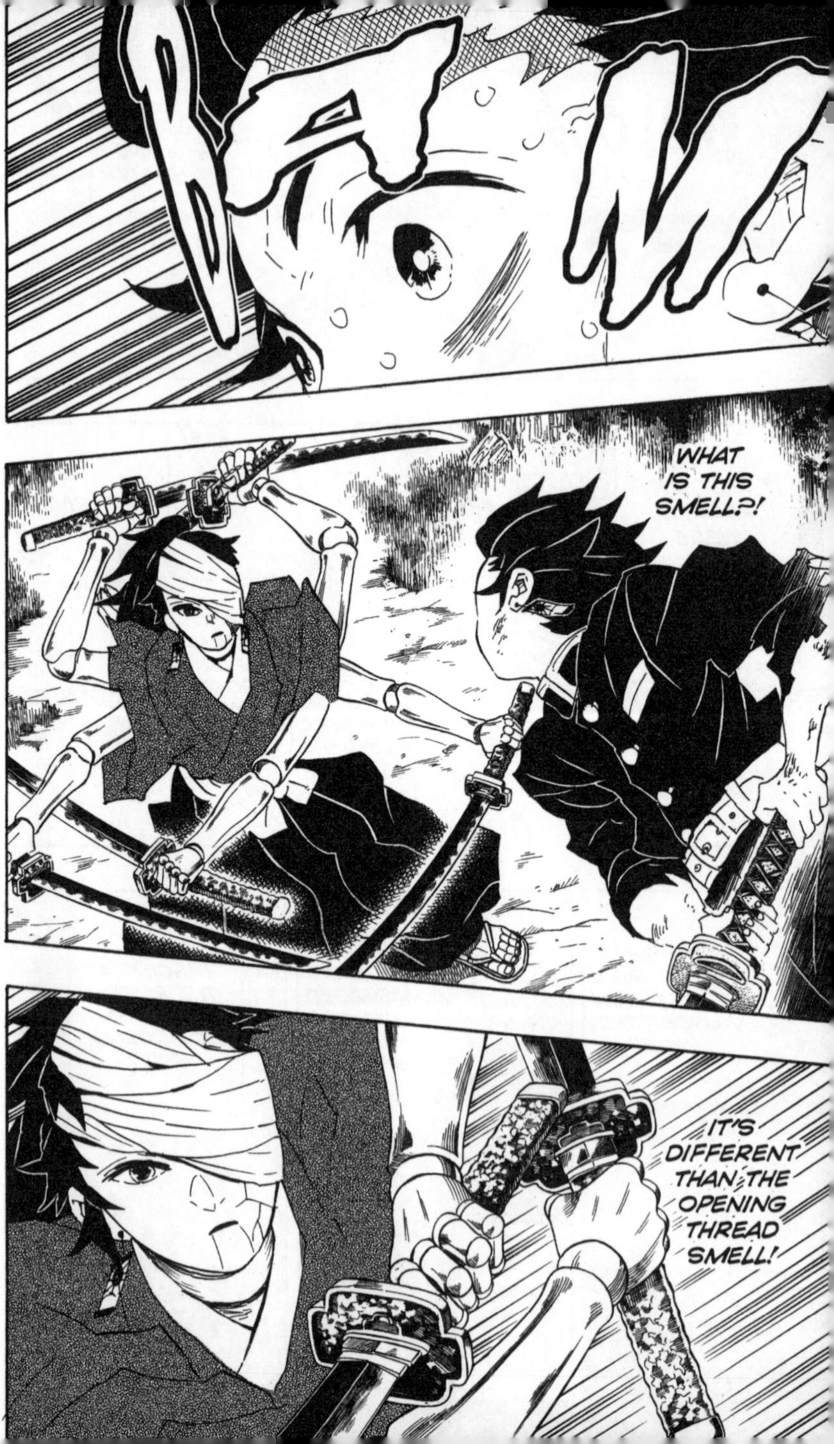
WHAT IS THIS SMELL?!
IT'S DIFFERENT THAN THE OPENING THREAD SMELL!

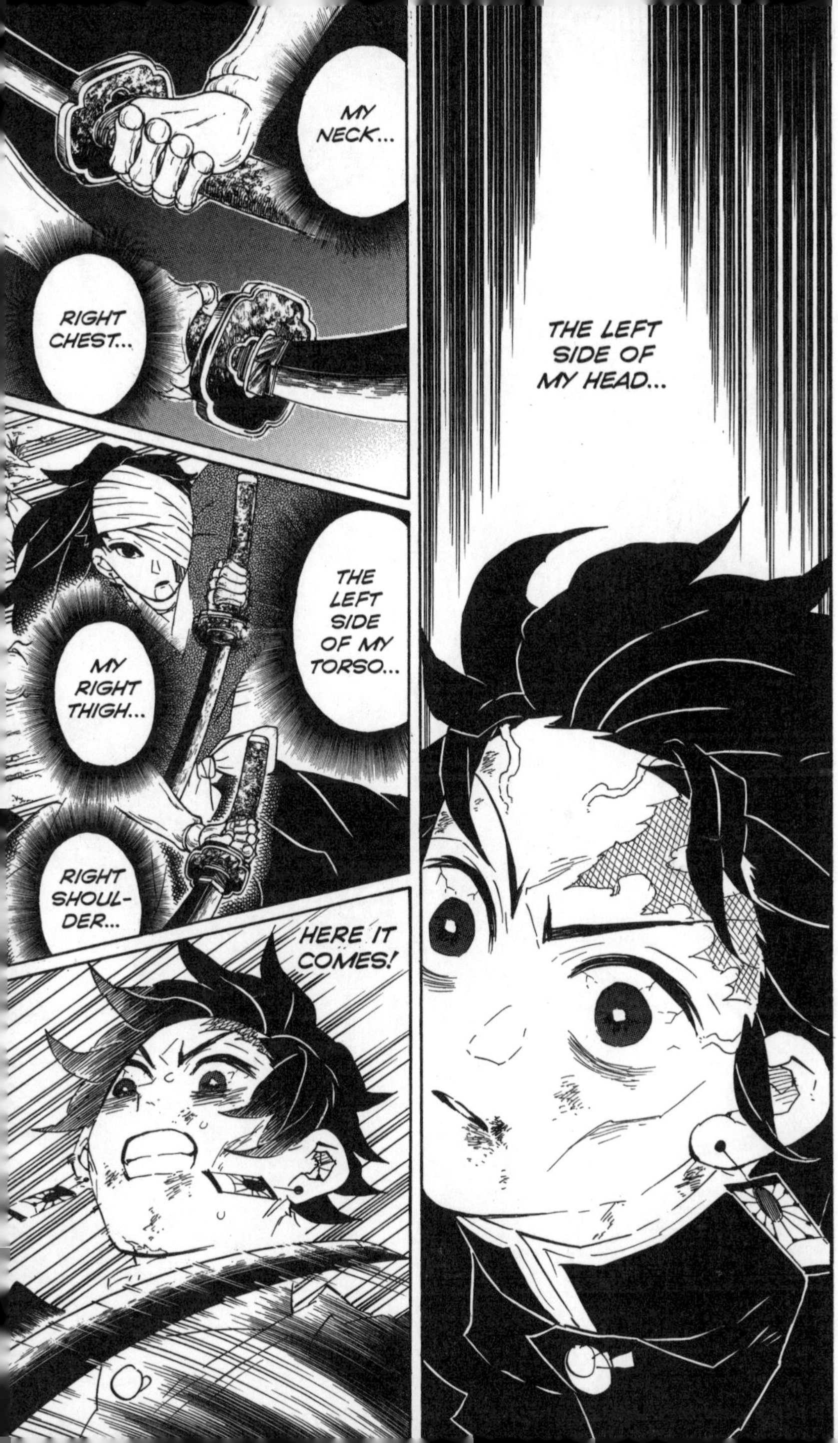
THE LEFT SIDE OF MY HEAD...
MY NECK...
RIGHT CHEST...
THE LEFT SIDE OF MY TORSO...
MY RIGHT THIGH...
RIGHT SHOULDER...
HERE IT COMES!

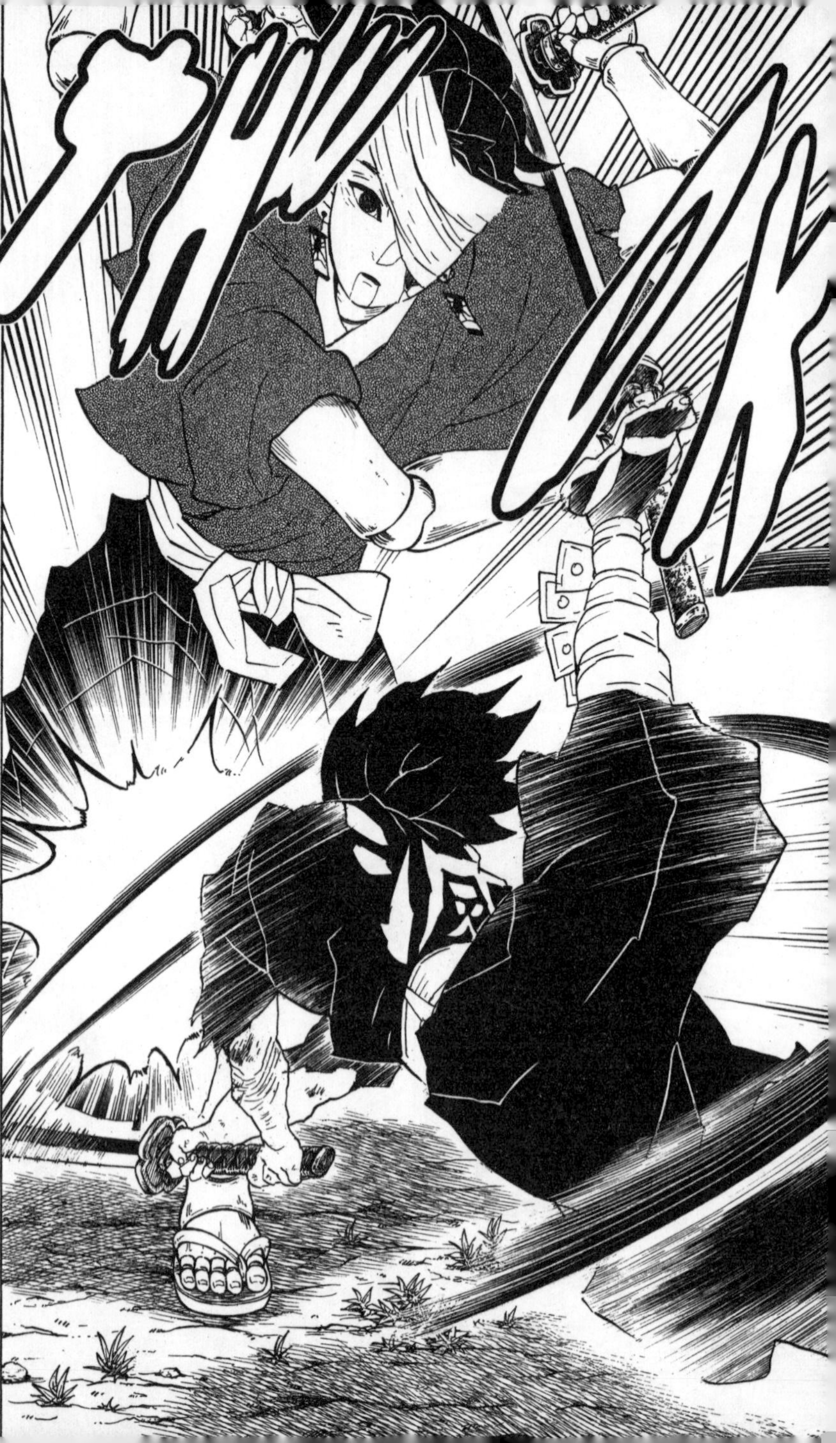

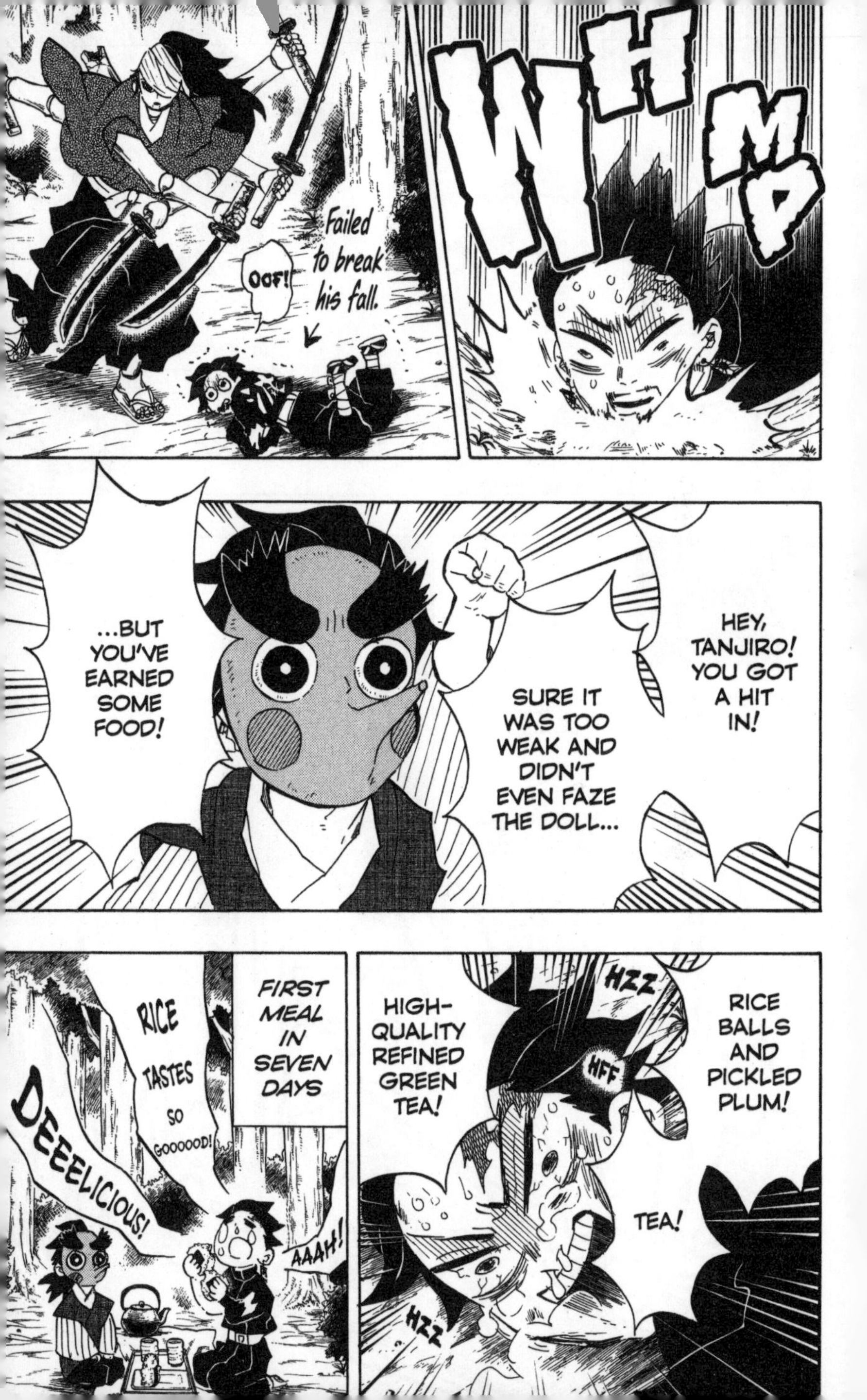
WHMP
Failed to break his fall.
OOF!
HEY, TANJIRO! YOU GOT A HIT IN!
SURE IT WAS TOO WEAK AND DIDN'T EVEN FAZE THE DOLL...
...BUT YOU'VE EARNED SOME FOOD!
RICE BALLS AND PICKLED PLUM!
HZZ
HFF
HIGH-QUALITY REFINED GREEN TEA!
TEA!
HZZ
FIRST MEAL IN SEVEN DAYS
RICE TASTES SO GOOOOOD!
AAAH!
DEEELICIOUS!

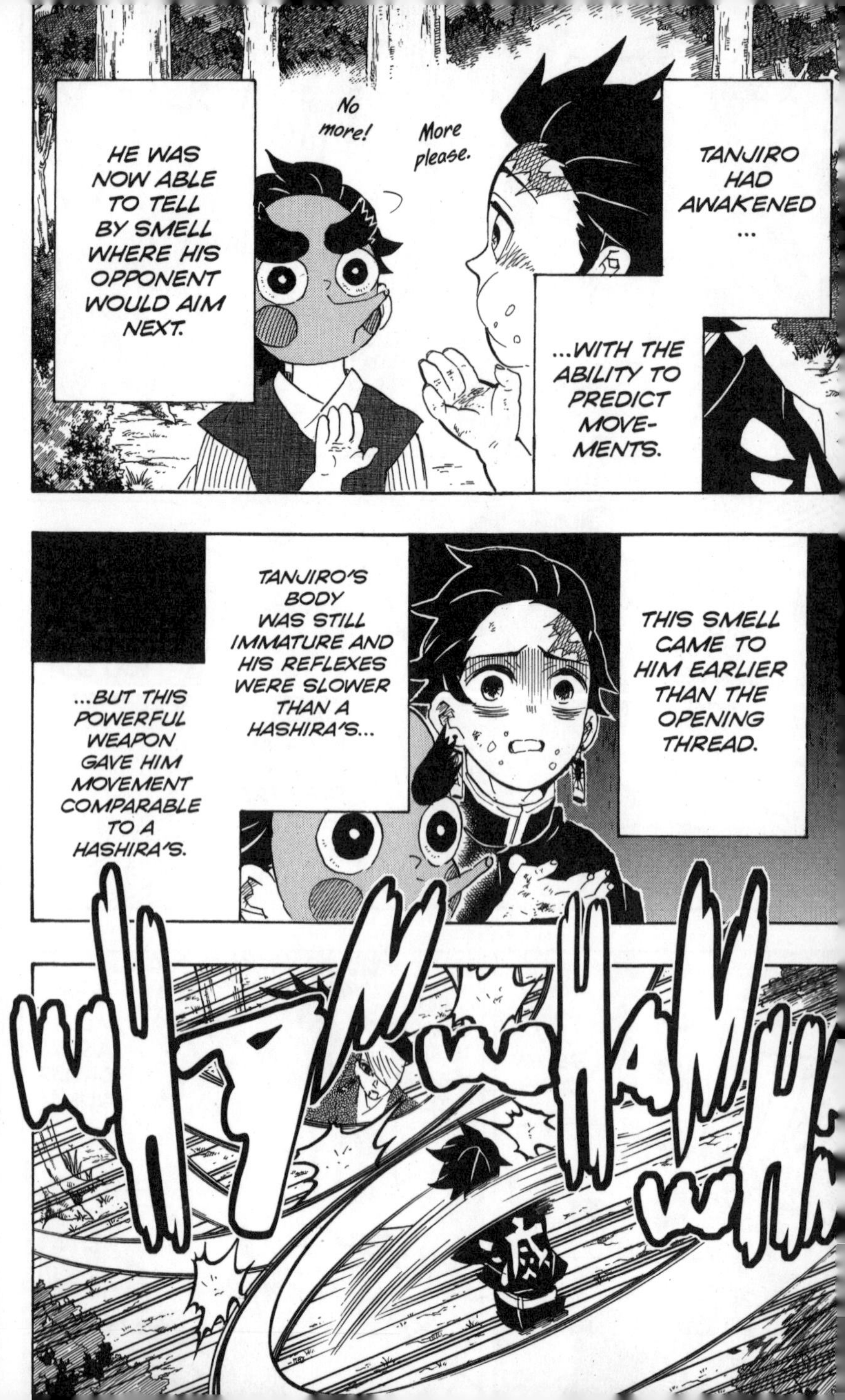
TANJIRO HAD AWAKENED ...
...WITH THE ABILITY TO PREDICT MOVE-MENTS.
More please.
No more!
HE WAS NOW ABLE TO TELL BY SMELL WHERE HIS OPPONENT WOULD AIM NEXT.
THIS SMELL CAME TO HIM EARLIER THAN THE OPENING THREAD.
TANJIRO'S BODY WAS STILL IMMATURE AND HIS REFLEXES WERE SLOWER THAN A HASHIRA'S...
...BUT THIS POWERFUL WEAPON GAVE HIM MOVEMENT COMPARABLE TO A HASHIRA'S.

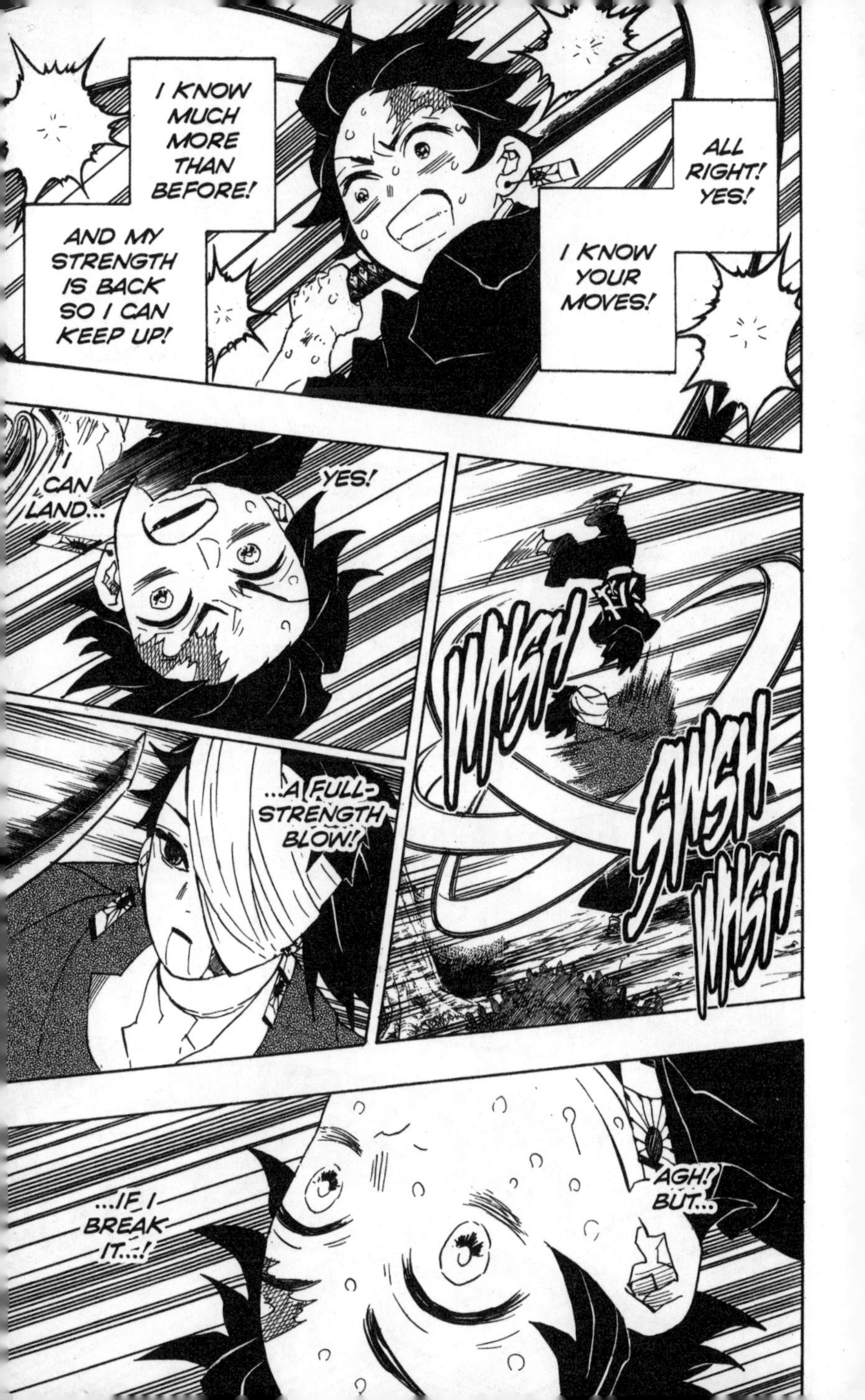
ALL RIGHT! YES!
I KNOW YOUR MOVES!
I KNOW MUCH MORE THAN BEFORE!
AND MY STRENGTH IS BACK SO I CAN KEEP UP!
WHSH
SWSH
WHSH
YES!
I CAN LAND...
...A FULL-STRENGTH BLOW!
AGH! BUT...
...IF I BREAK IT...!

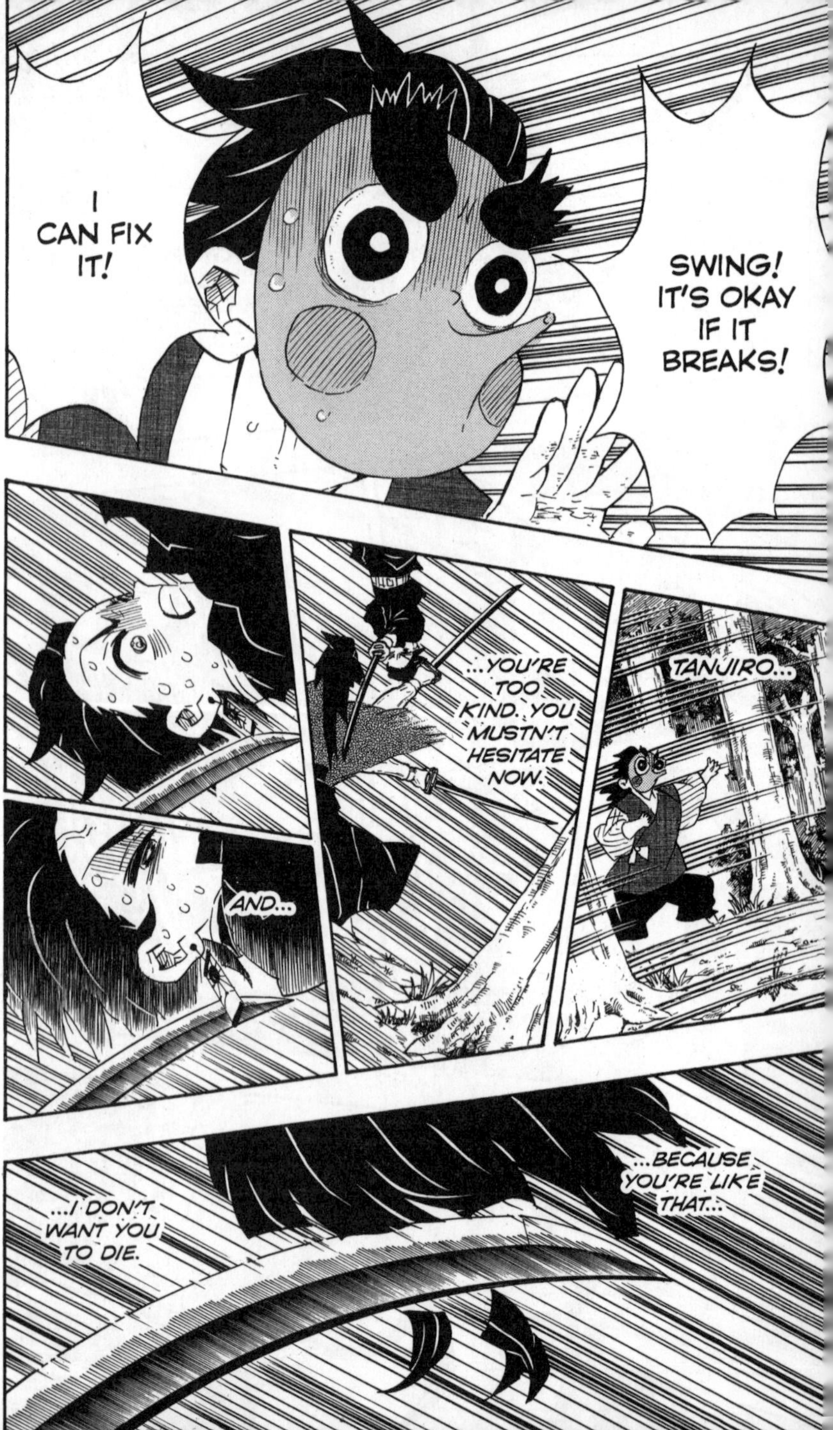
SWING! IT'S OKAY IF IT BREAKS!
I CAN FIX IT!
TANJIRO...
...YOU'RE TOO KIND. YOU MUSTN'T HESITATE NOW.
AND...
...BECAUSE YOU'RE LIKE THAT...
...I DON'T WANT YOU TO DIE.

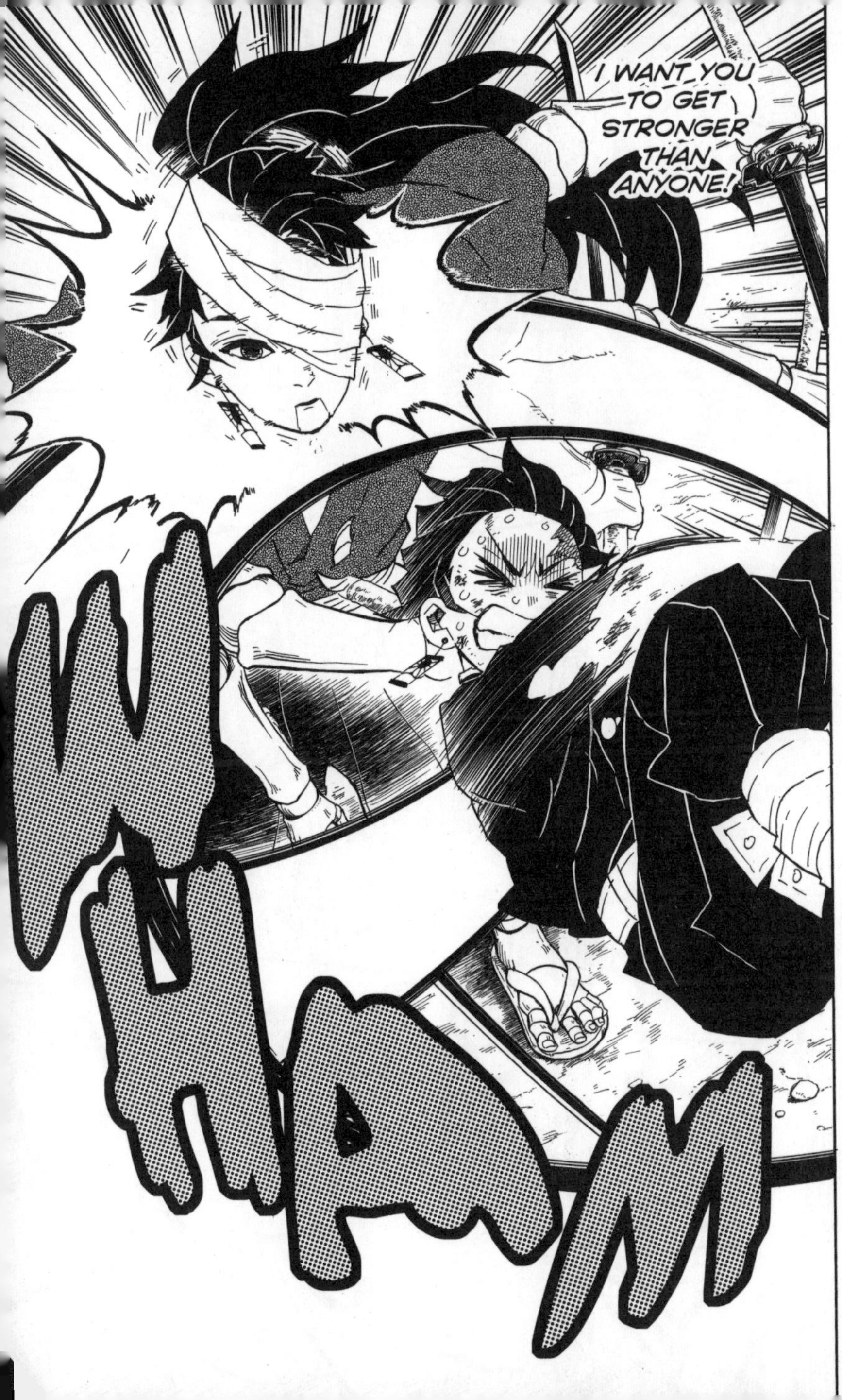
I WANT YOU TO GET STRONGER THAN ANYONE!
WHAM

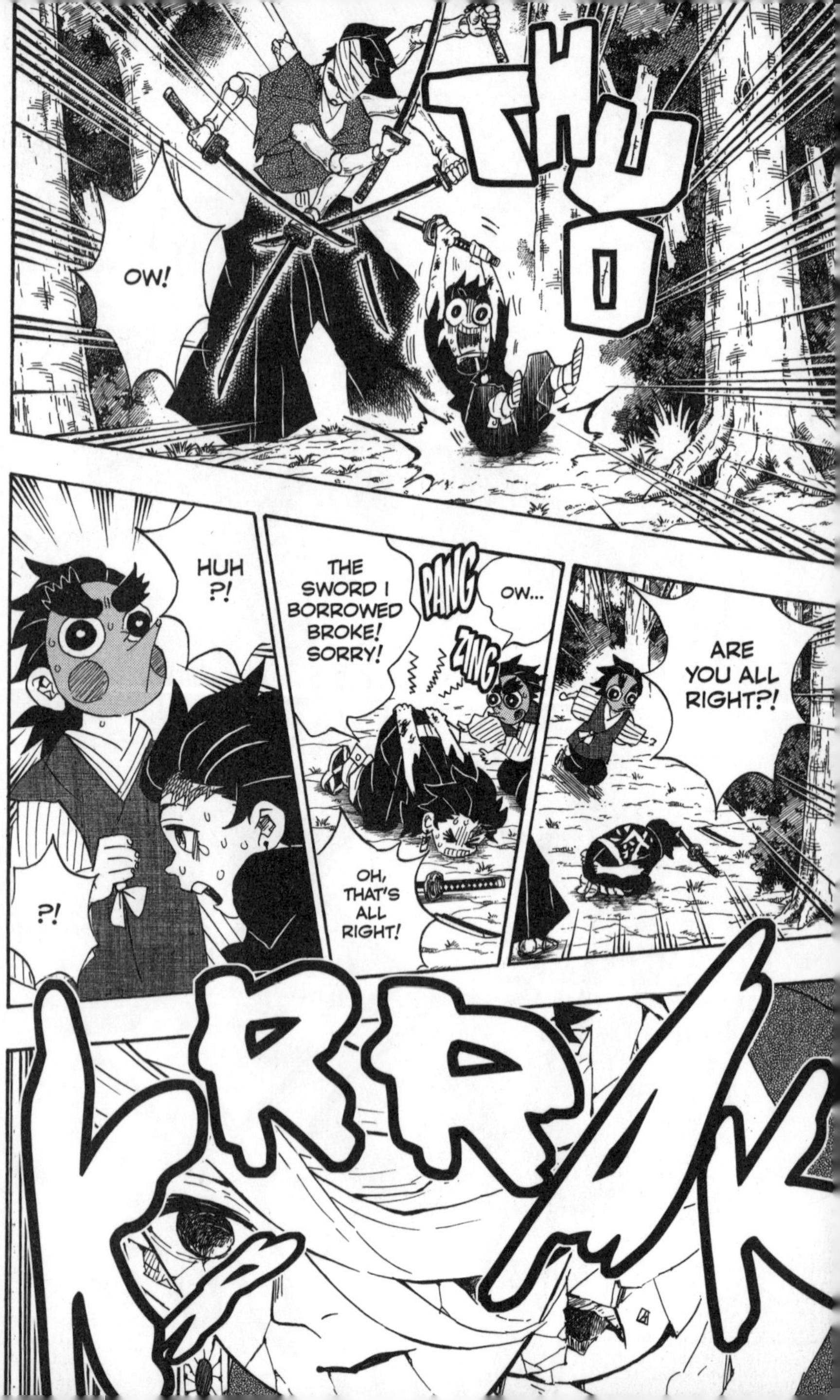
THUD
OW!
ARE YOU ALL RIGHT?!
OW...
PANG
ZING
THE SWORD I BORROWED BROKE! SORRY!
OH, THAT'S ALL RIGHT!
HUH?!
?!
KRAK

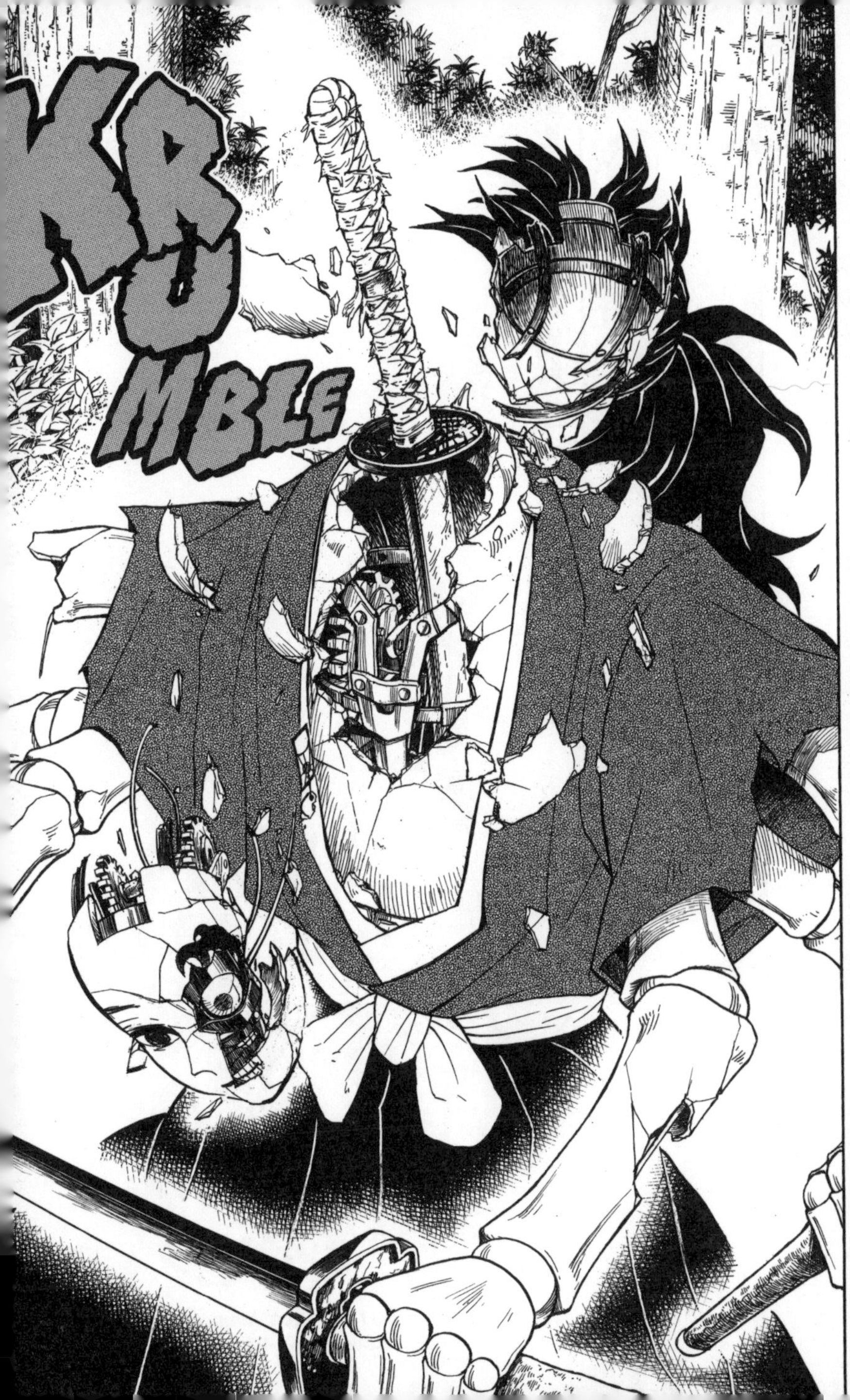
KRUMBLE

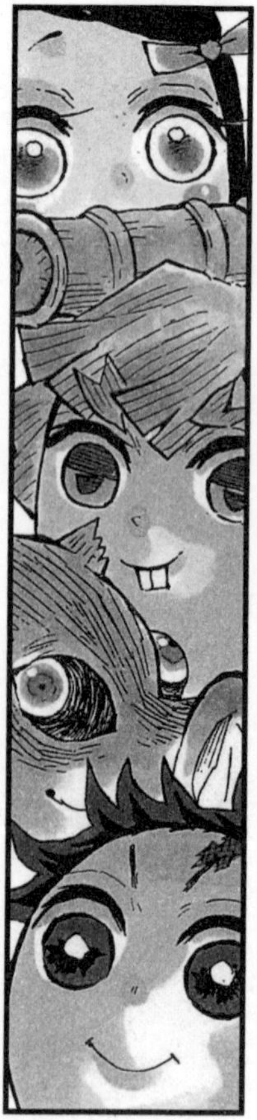

From *Shonen Jump GIGA*, Winter Vol. 2, 2018

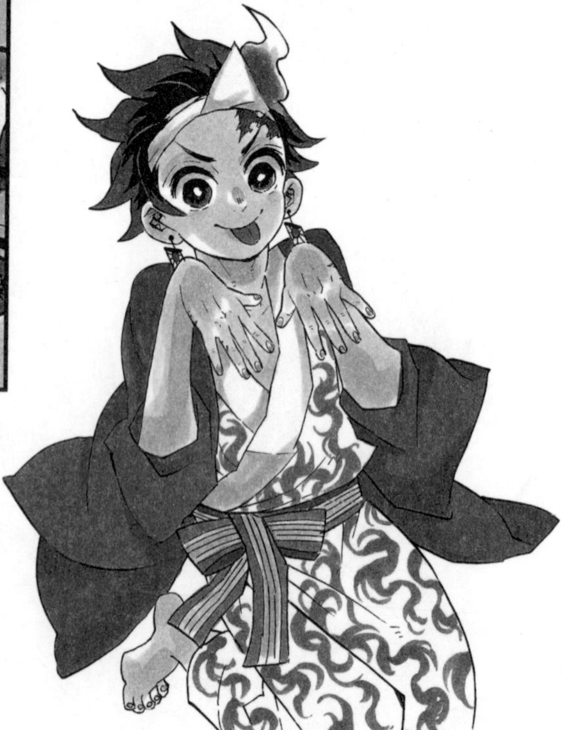

From *Weekly Shonen Jump*, combined issue No. 21-22, 2018

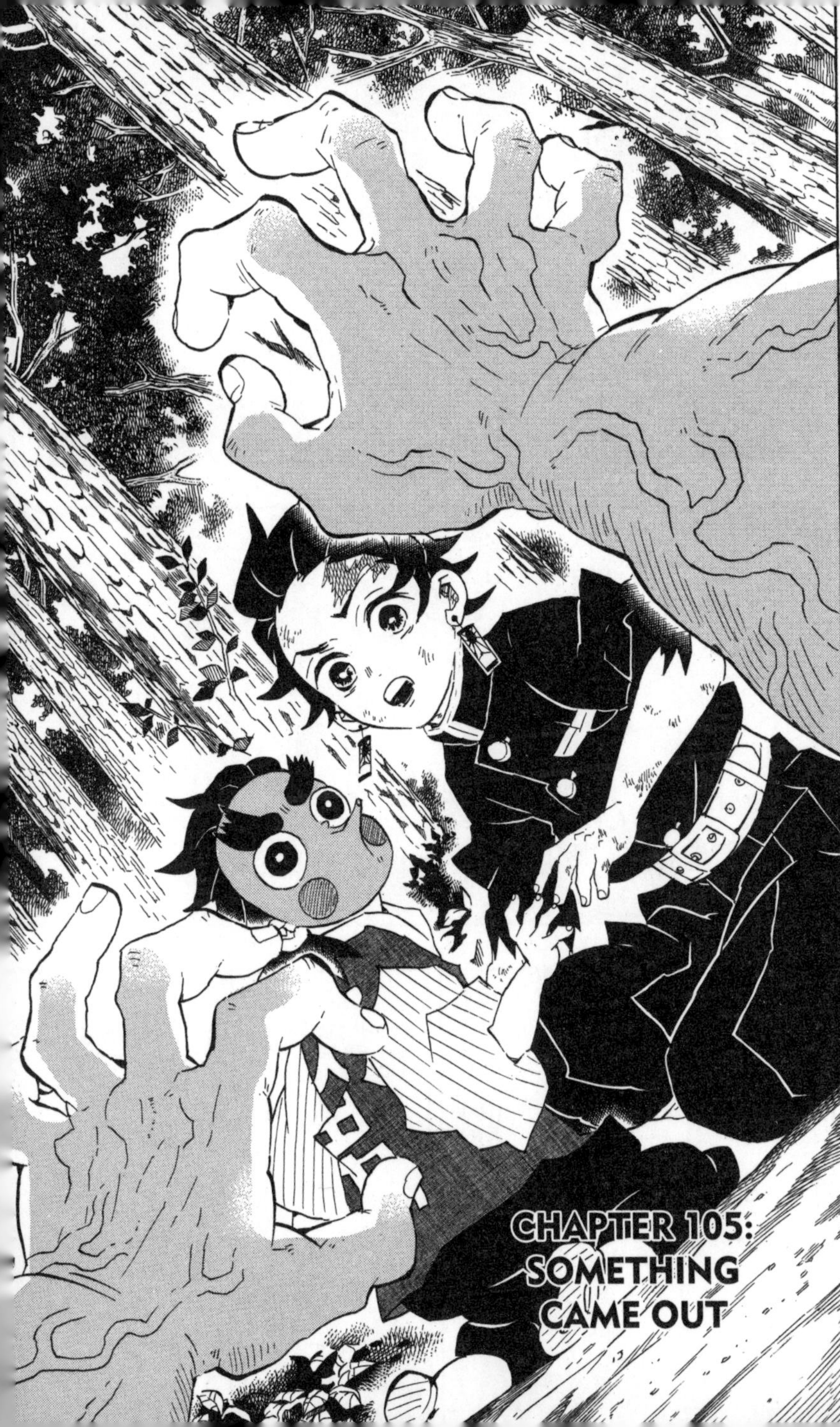
CHAPTER 105:
SOMETHING
CAME OUT

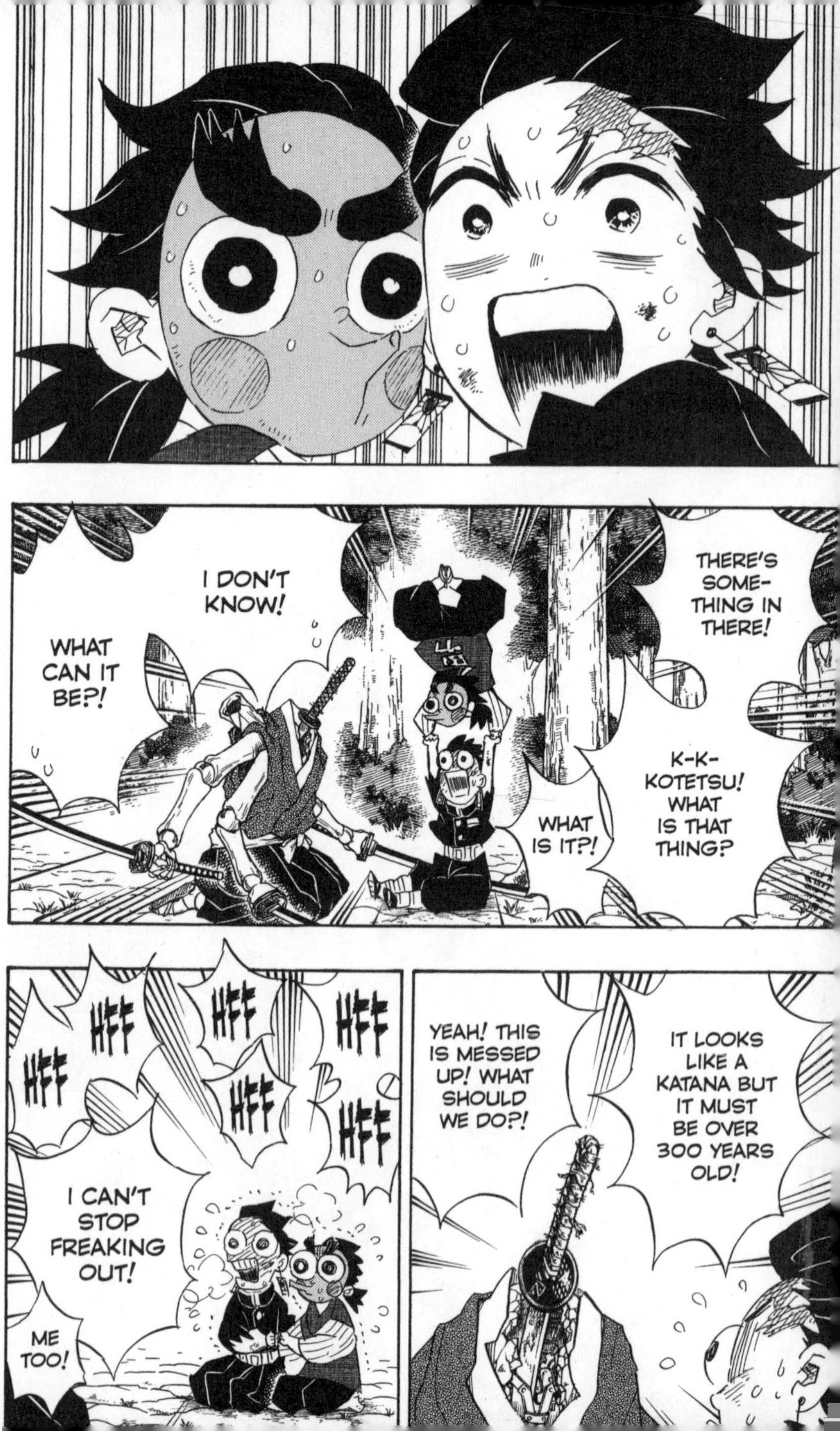
THERE'S SOME-THING IN THERE!
K-K-KOTETSU! WHAT IS THAT THING?
WHAT IS IT?!
I DON'T KNOW!
WHAT CAN IT BE?!
IT LOOKS LIKE A KATANA BUT IT MUST BE OVER 300 YEARS OLD!
YEAH! THIS IS MESSED UP! WHAT SHOULD WE DO?!
HFF
HFF
HFF
HFF
HFF
HFF
I CAN'T STOP FREAKING OUT!
ME TOO!

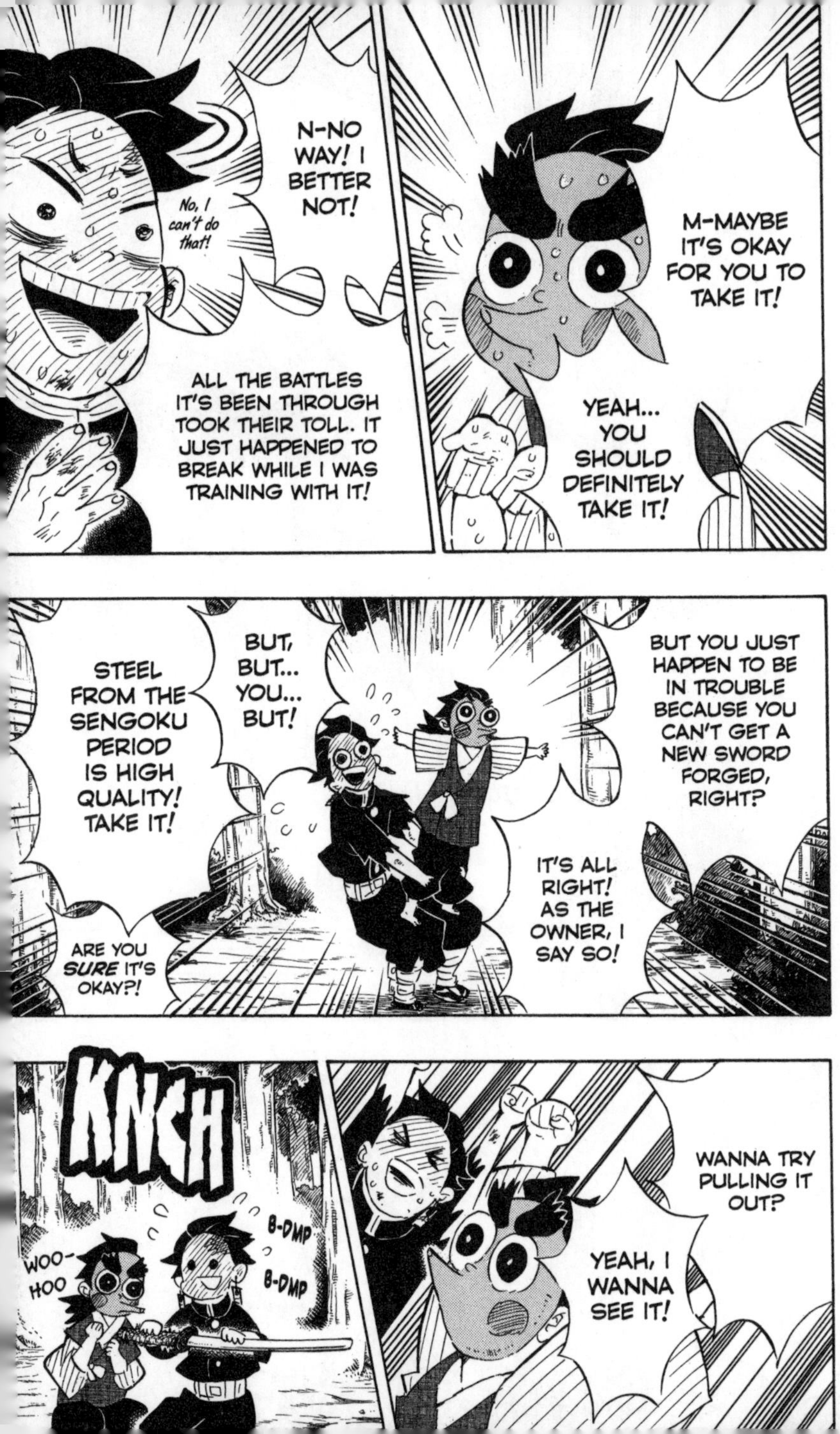
M-MAYBE IT'S OKAY FOR YOU TO TAKE IT!
YEAH... YOU SHOULD DEFINITELY TAKE IT!
N-NO WAY! I BETTER NOT!
No, I can't do that!
ALL THE BATTLES IT'S BEEN THROUGH TOOK THEIR TOLL. IT JUST HAPPENED TO BREAK WHILE I WAS TRAINING WITH IT!
BUT YOU JUST HAPPEN TO BE IN TROUBLE BECAUSE YOU CAN'T GET A NEW SWORD FORGED, RIGHT?
IT'S ALL RIGHT! AS THE OWNER, I SAY SO!
BUT, BUT... YOU... BUT!
STEEL FROM THE SENGOKU PERIOD IS HIGH QUALITY! TAKE IT!
ARE YOU *SURE* IT'S OKAY?!
WANNA TRY PULLING IT OUT?
YEAH, I WANNA SEE IT!
KNCH
B-DMP
B-DMP
WOO-HOO

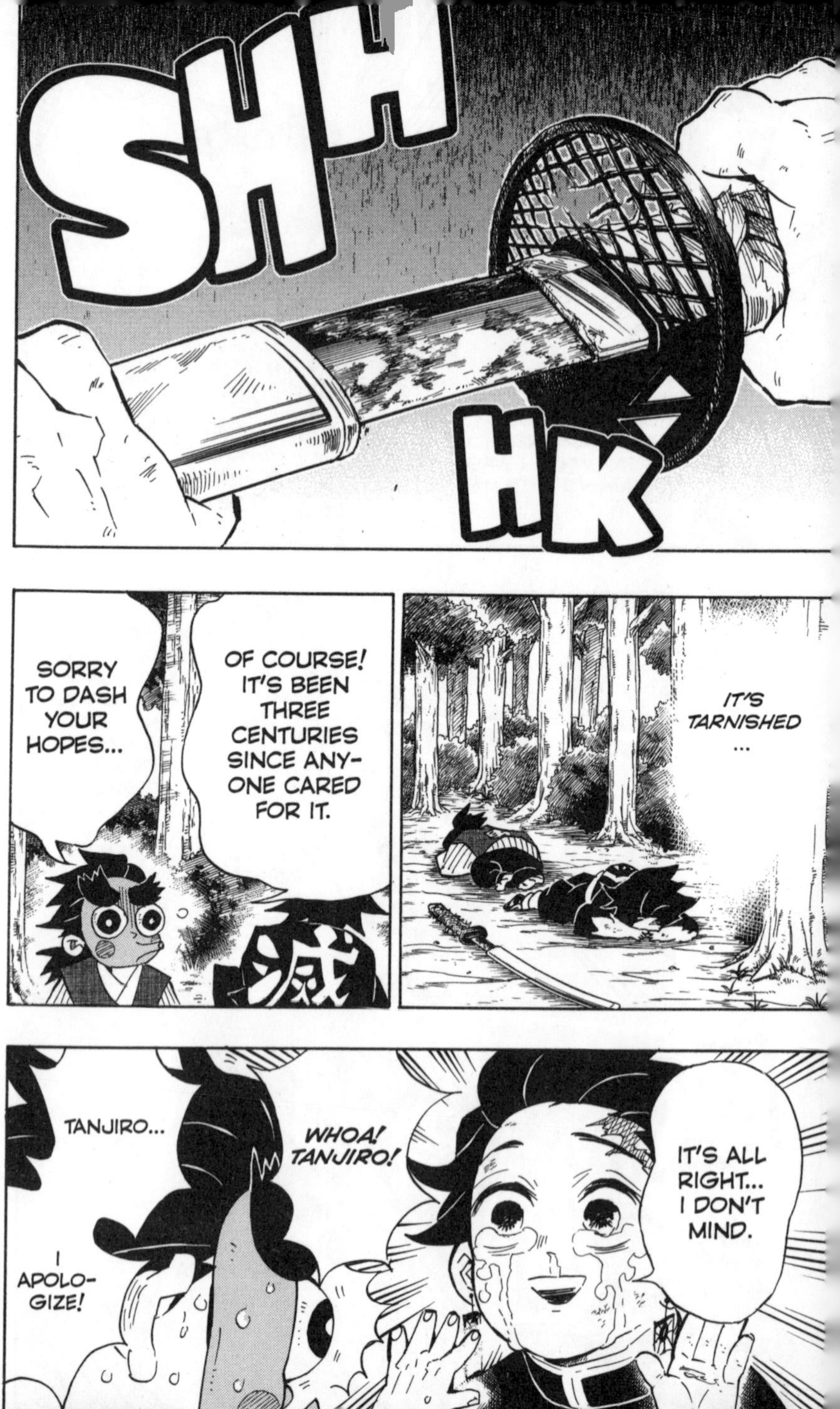
SHH
HK
IT'S TARNISHED ...
OF COURSE! IT'S BEEN THREE CENTURIES SINCE ANY-ONE CARED FOR IT.
SORRY TO DASH YOUR HOPES...
IT'S ALL RIGHT... I DON'T MIND.
WHOA! TANJIRO!
TANJIRO...
I APOLO-GIZE!

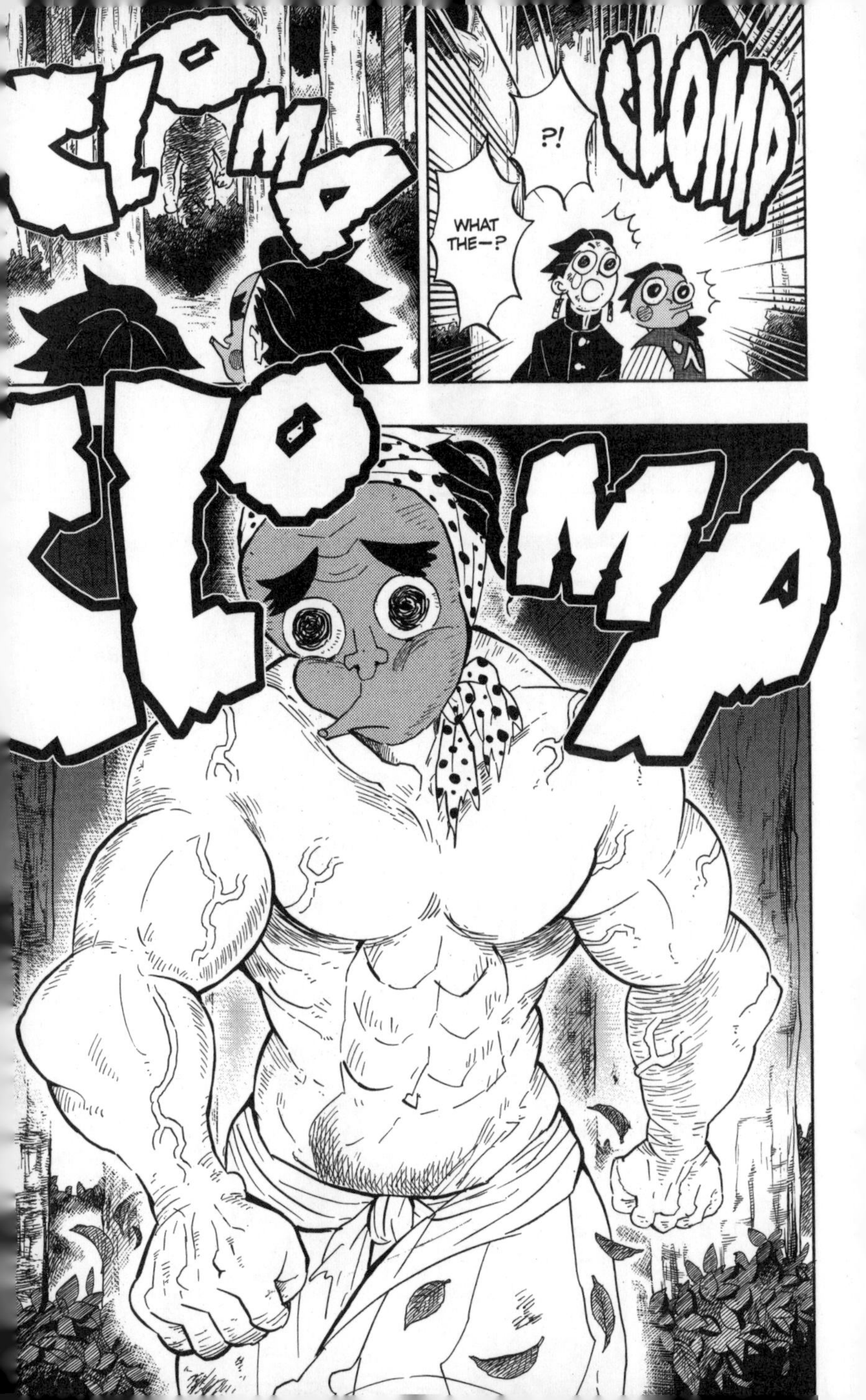
CLOMP
?!
WHAT THE—?
CLOMP
CLOMP

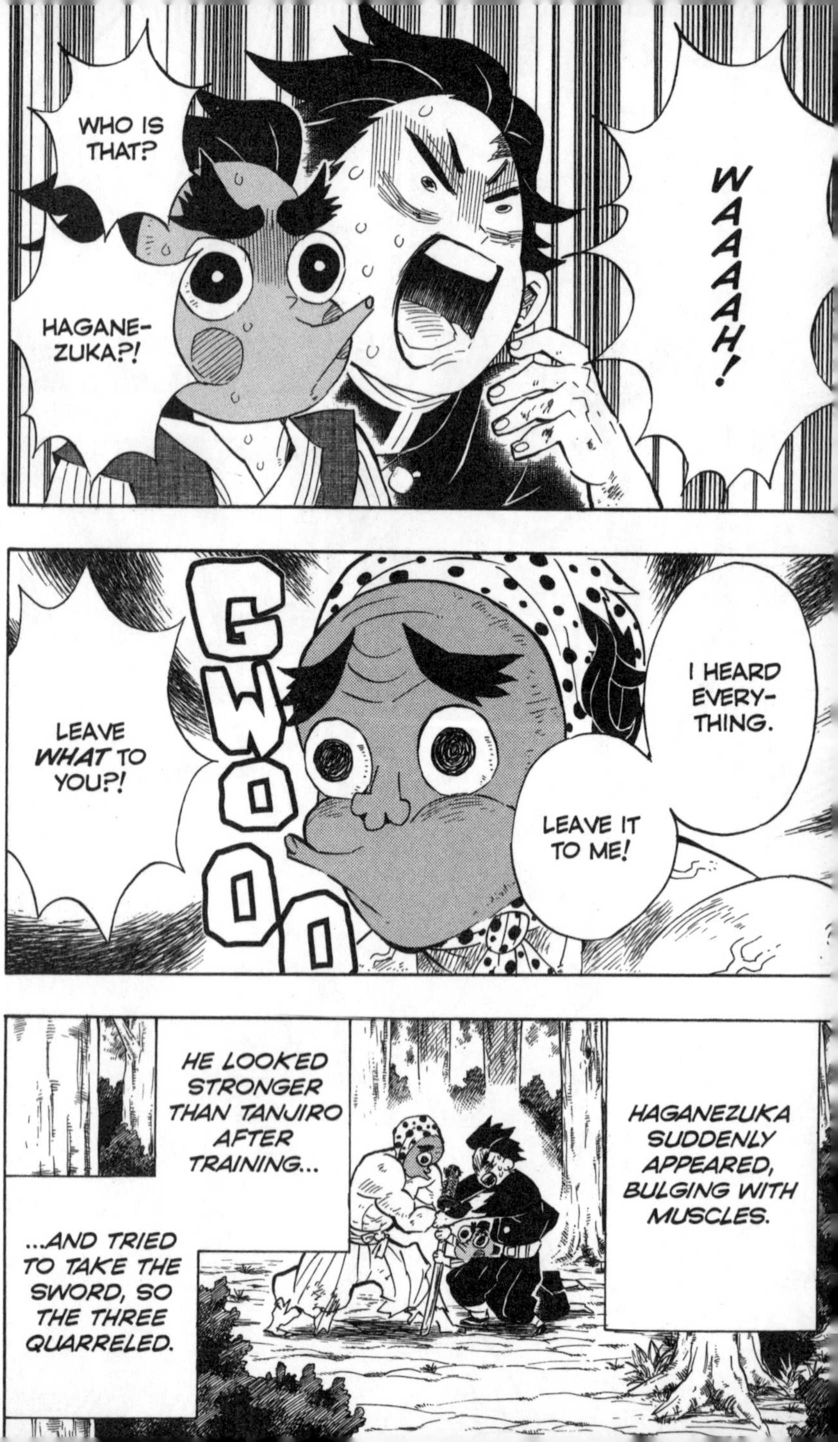
WAAAAAH!
WHO IS THAT?
HAGANE-ZUKA?!
I HEARD EVERY-THING.
LEAVE IT TO ME!
GWOOO
LEAVE *WHAT* TO YOU?!
HAGANEZUKA SUDDENLY APPEARED, BULGING WITH MUSCLES.
HE LOOKED STRONGER THAN TANJIRO AFTER TRAINING...
...AND TRIED TO TAKE THE SWORD, SO THE THREE QUARRELED.

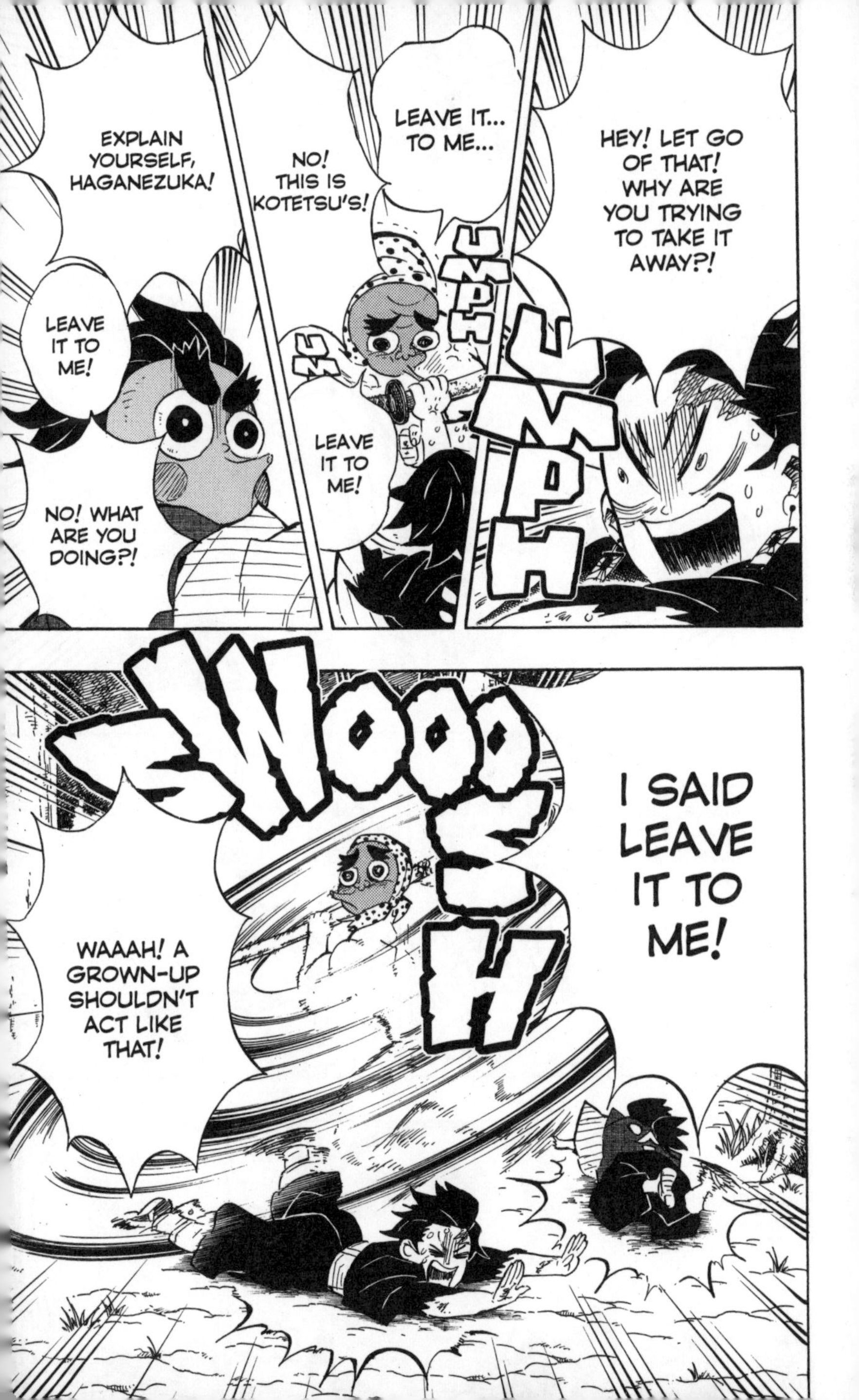
HEY! LET GO OF THAT! WHY ARE YOU TRYING TO TAKE IT AWAY?!
UMPH
UMPH
LEAVE IT... TO ME...
NO! THIS IS KOTETSU'S!
UM
LEAVE IT TO ME!
EXPLAIN YOURSELF, HAGANEZUKA!
LEAVE IT TO ME!
NO! WHAT ARE YOU DOING?!
I SAID LEAVE IT TO ME!
SWOOSH
WAAAH! A GROWN-UP SHOULDN'T ACT LIKE THAT!

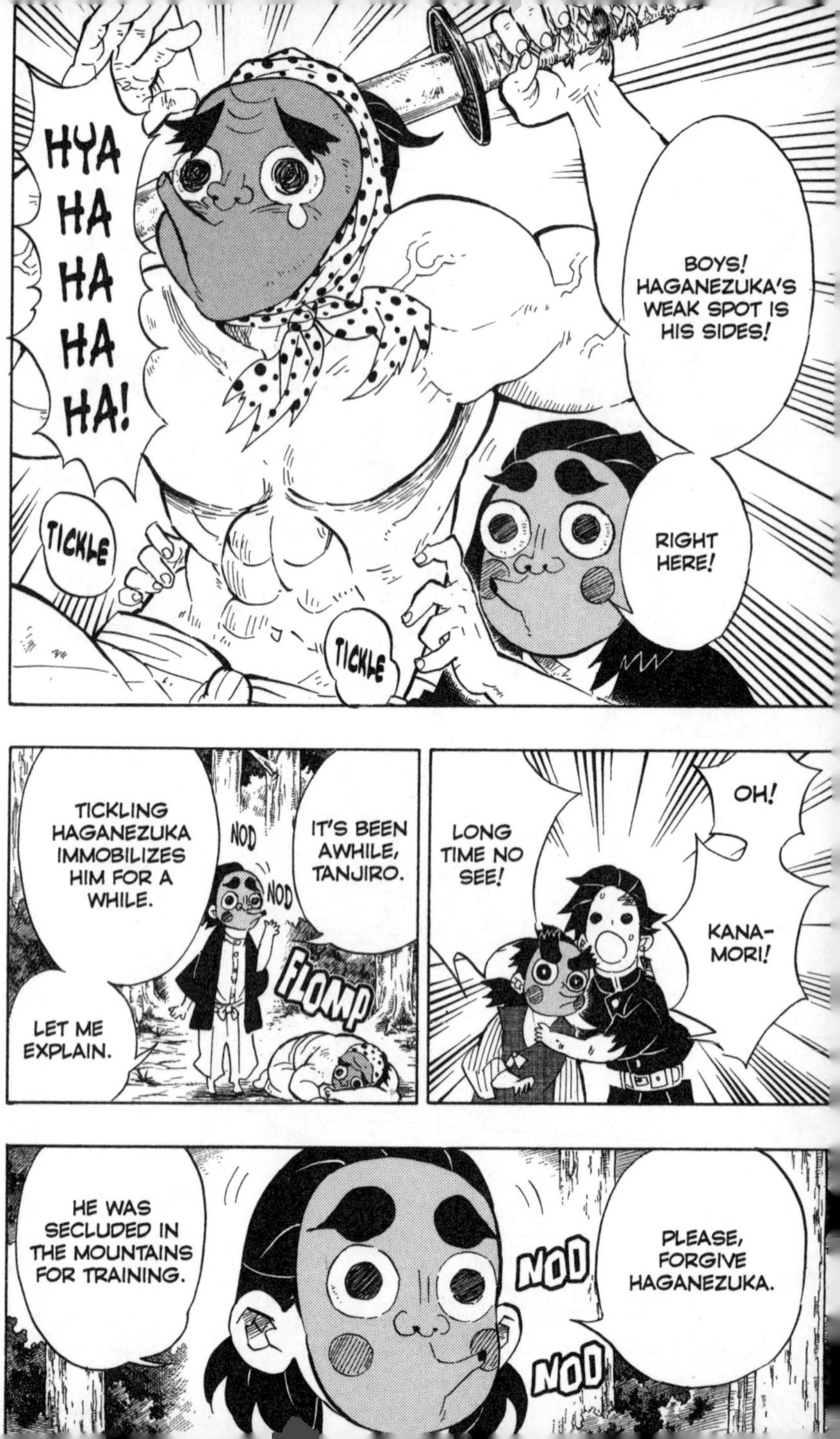
BOYS! HAGANEZUKA'S WEAK SPOT IS HIS SIDES!
RIGHT HERE!
HYA HA HA HA HA HA!
TICKLE
TICKLE
OH!
KANA-MORI!
LONG TIME NO SEE!
IT'S BEEN AWHILE, TANJIRO.
NOD
NOD
FLOMP
TICKLING HAGANEZUKA IMMOBILIZES HIM FOR A WHILE.
LET ME EXPLAIN.
PLEASE, FORGIVE HAGANEZUKA.
NOD
NOD
HE WAS SECLUDED IN THE MOUNTAINS FOR TRAINING.

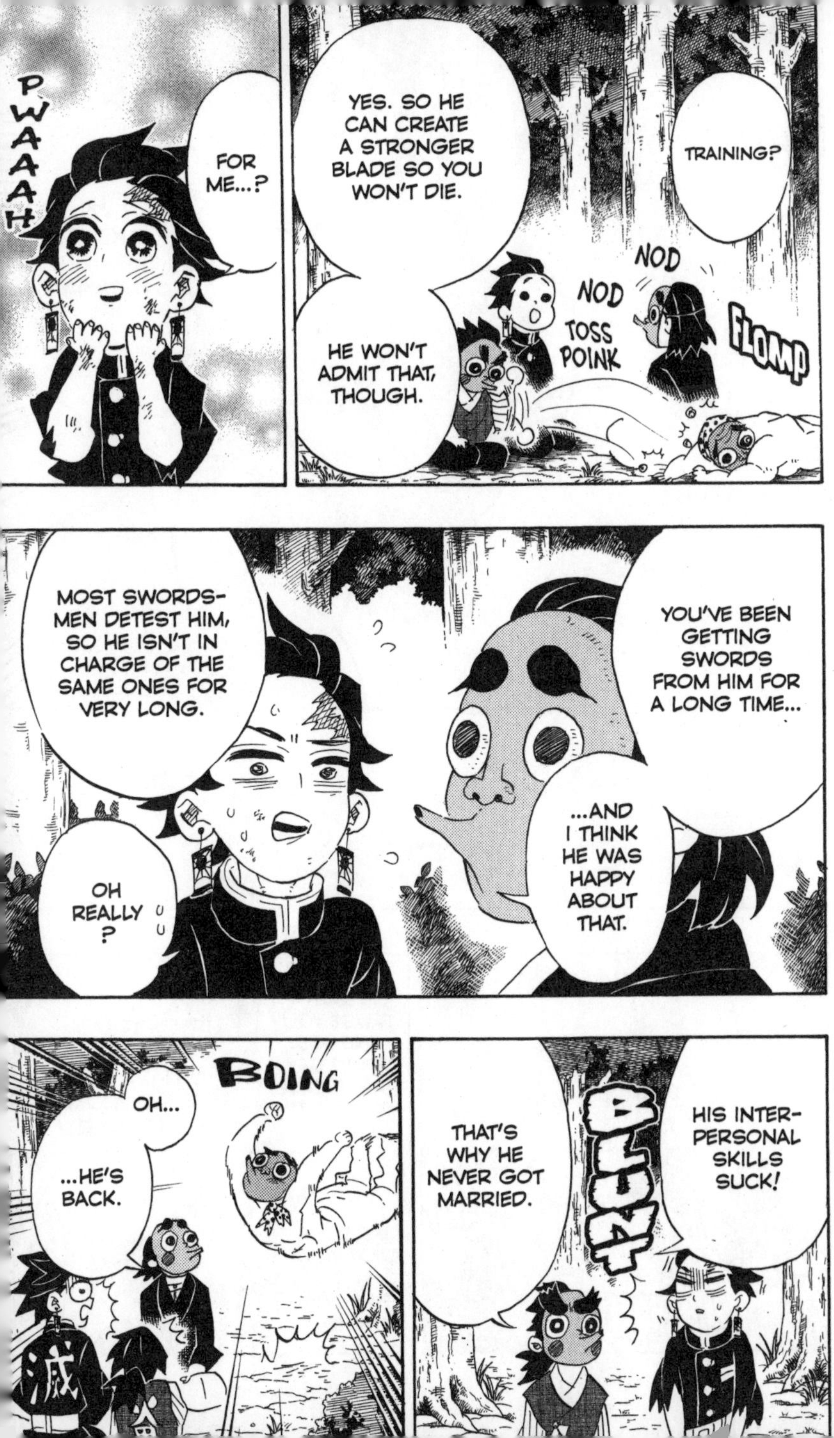
TRAINING?
NOD
NOD
FLOMP
YES. SO HE CAN CREATE A STRONGER BLADE SO YOU WON'T DIE.
HE WON'T ADMIT THAT, THOUGH.
TOSS POINK
PWAAAAH
FOR ME...?
YOU'VE BEEN GETTING SWORDS FROM HIM FOR A LONG TIME...
...AND I THINK HE WAS HAPPY ABOUT THAT.
MOST SWORDS-MEN DETEST HIM, SO HE ISN'T IN CHARGE OF THE SAME ONES FOR VERY LONG.
OH REALLY?
HIS INTER-PERSONAL SKILLS SUCK!
BLUNT
THAT'S WHY HE NEVER GOT MARRIED.
BOING
OH...
...HE'S BACK.

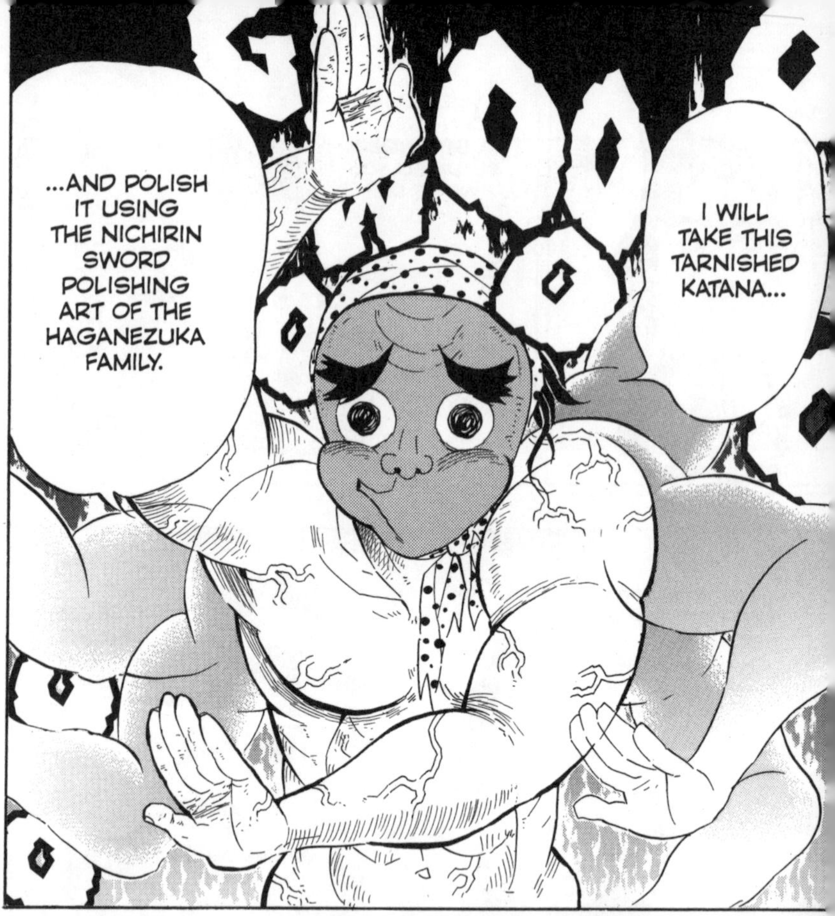
I WILL TAKE THIS TARNISHED KATANA...
...AND POLISH IT USING THE NICHIRIN SWORD POLISHING ART OF THE HAGANEZUKA FAMILY.
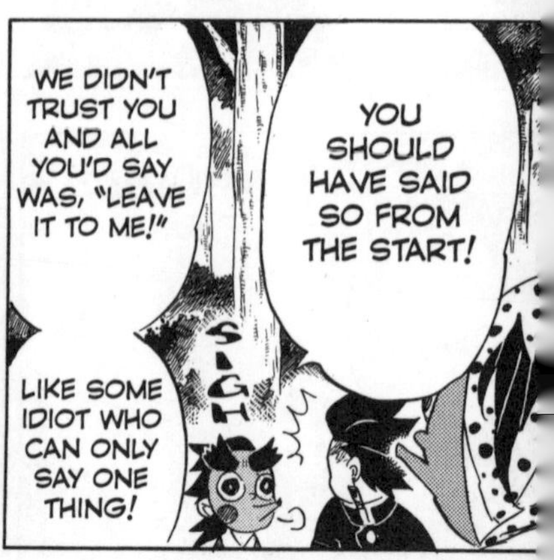
YOU SHOULD HAVE SAID SO FROM THE START!
WE DIDN'T TRUST YOU AND ALL YOU'D SAY WAS, "LEAVE IT TO ME!"
SIGH
LIKE SOME IDIOT WHO CAN ONLY SAY ONE THING!
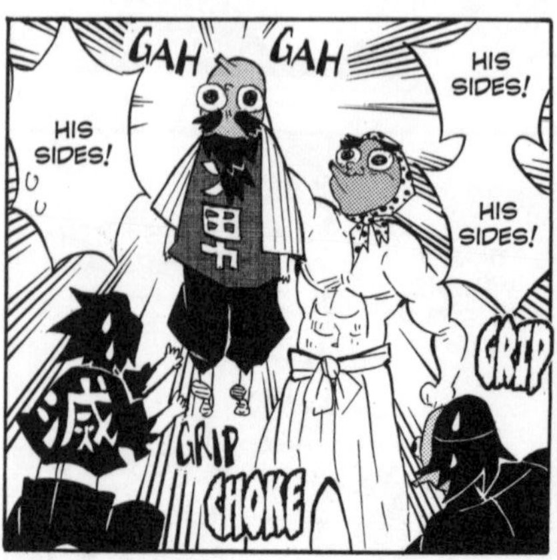
HIS SIDES!
HIS SIDES!
GAH
GAH
HIS SIDES!
GRIP
GRIP
CHOKE
滅

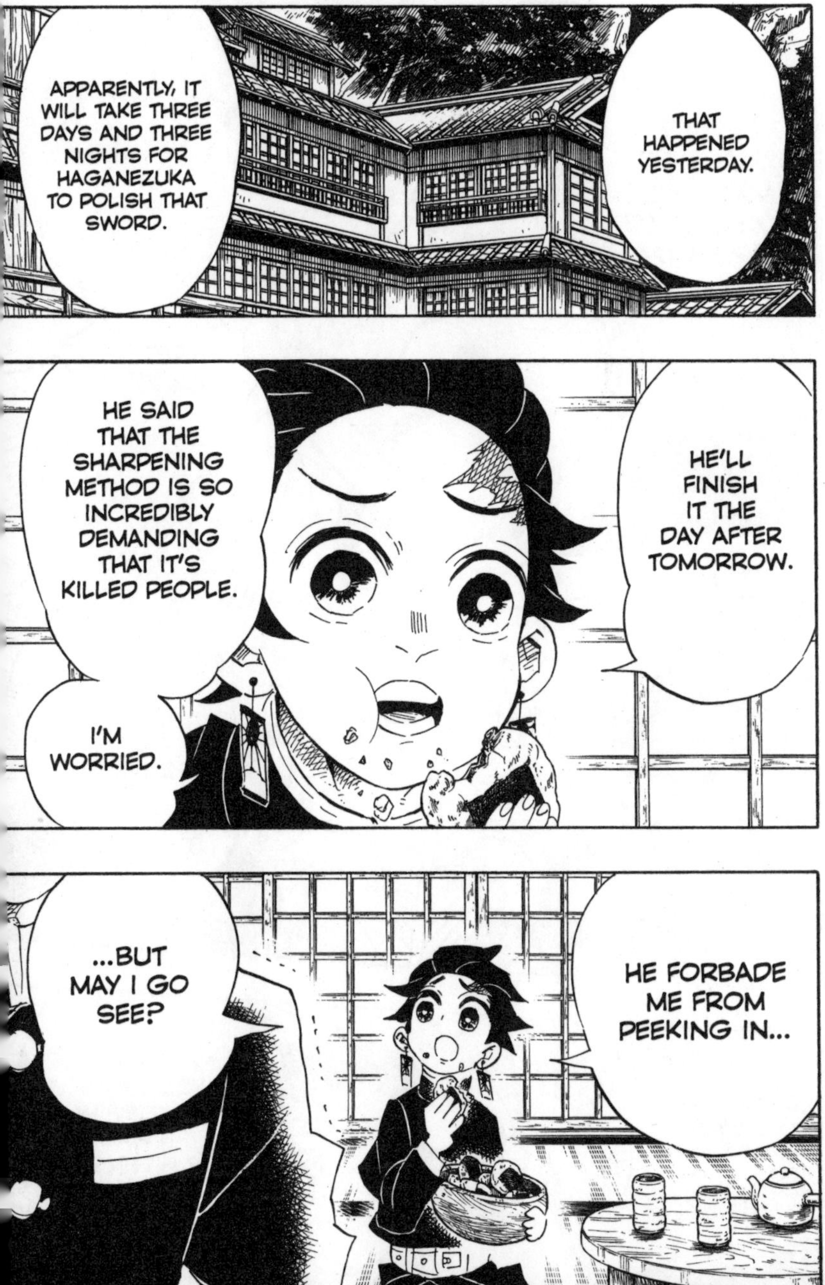
THAT HAPPENED YESTERDAY.
APPARENTLY, IT WILL TAKE THREE DAYS AND THREE NIGHTS FOR HAGANEZUKA TO POLISH THAT SWORD.
HE'LL FINISH IT THE DAY AFTER TOMORROW.
HE SAID THAT THE SHARPENING METHOD IS SO INCREDIBLY DEMANDING THAT IT'S KILLED PEOPLE.
I'M WORRIED.
HE FORBADE ME FROM PEEKING IN...
...BUT MAY I GO SEE?

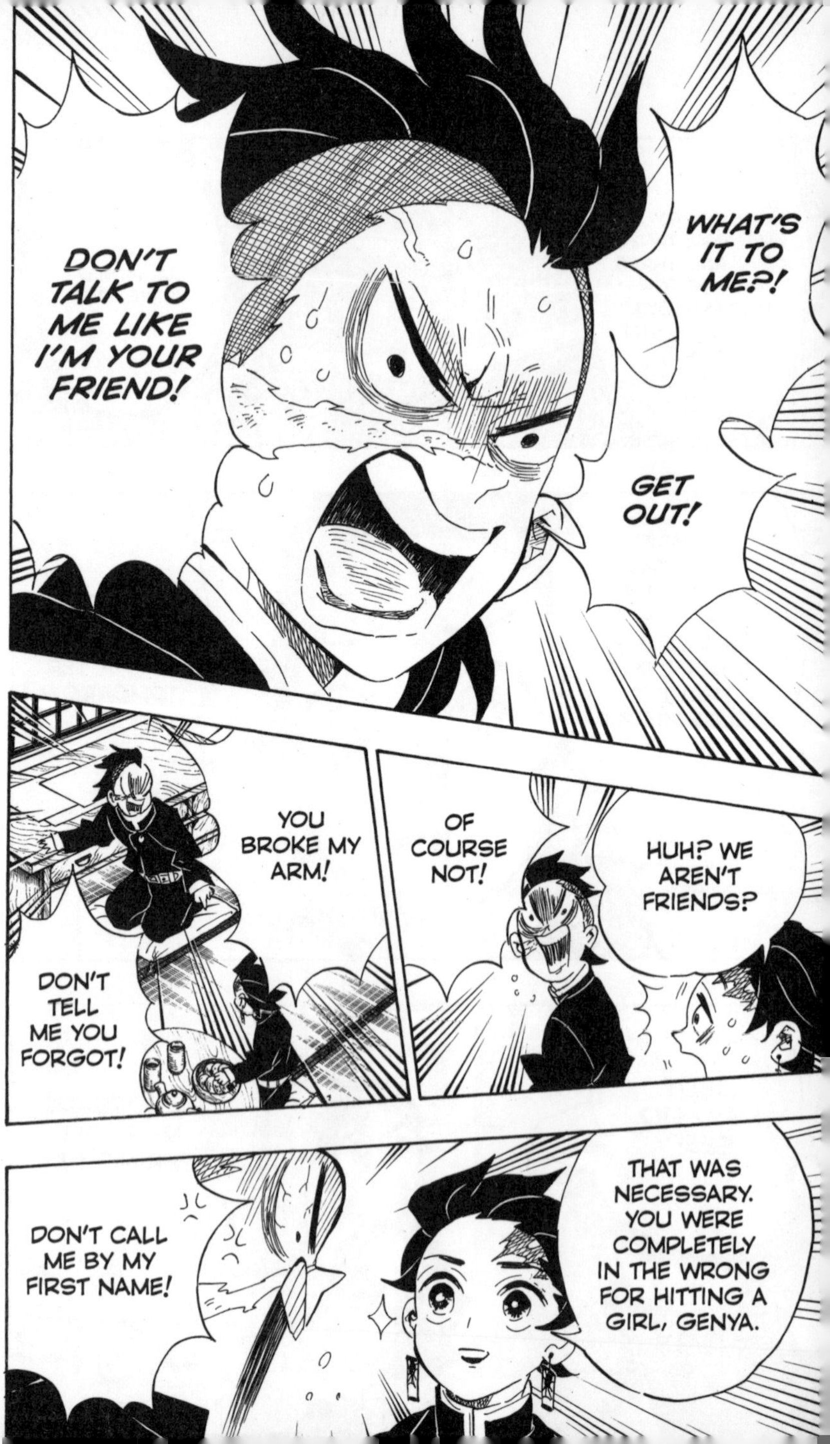
WHAT'S IT TO ME?!
GET OUT!
DON'T TALK TO ME LIKE I'M YOUR FRIEND!
HUH? WE AREN'T FRIENDS?
OF COURSE NOT!
YOU BROKE MY ARM!
DON'T TELL ME YOU FORGOT!
THAT WAS NECESSARY. YOU WERE COMPLETELY IN THE WRONG FOR HITTING A GIRL, GENYA.
DON'T CALL ME BY MY FIRST NAME!

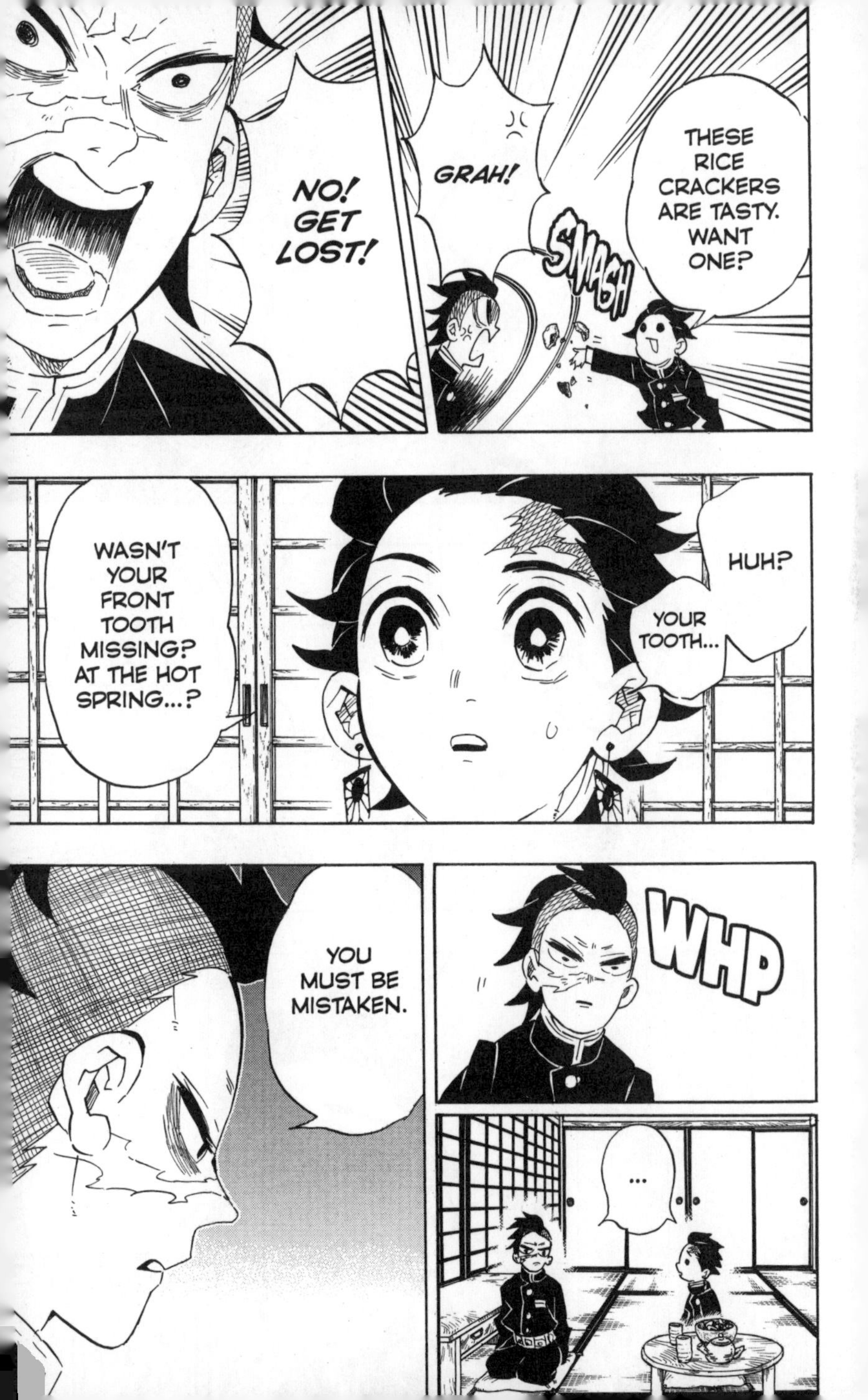
THESE RICE CRACKERS ARE TASTY. WANT ONE?
SMASH
GRAH!
NO! GET LOST!
HUH?
YOUR TOOTH...
WASN'T YOUR FRONT TOOTH MISSING? AT THE HOT SPRING...?
WHP
...
YOU MUST BE MISTAKEN.

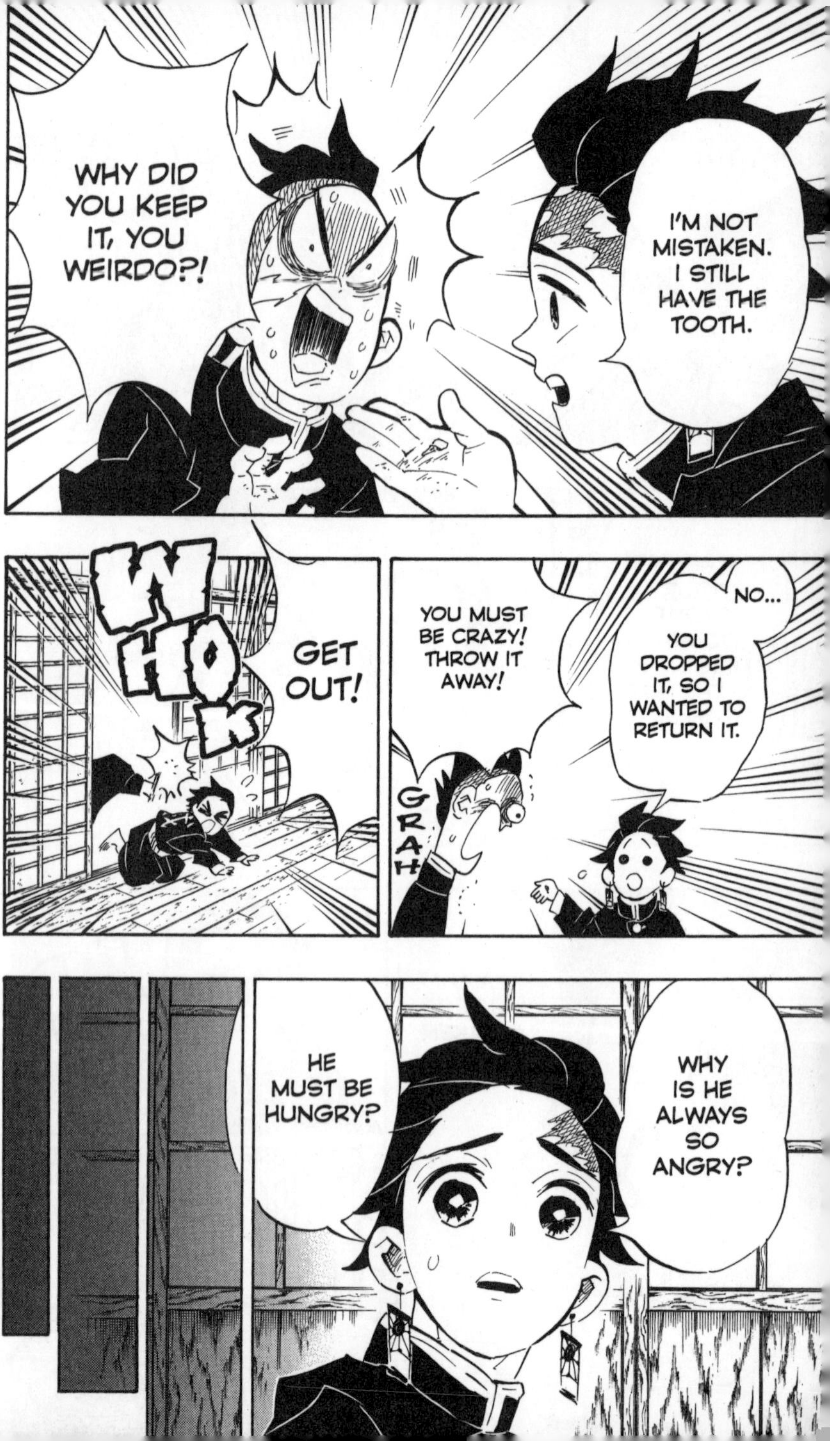
I'M NOT MISTAKEN. I STILL HAVE THE TOOTH.
WHY DID YOU KEEP IT, YOU WEIRDO?!
NO...
YOU DROPPED IT, SO I WANTED TO RETURN IT.
YOU MUST BE CRAZY! THROW IT AWAY!
GRAH
GET OUT!
WHOK
WHY IS HE ALWAYS SO ANGRY?
HE MUST BE HUNGRY?

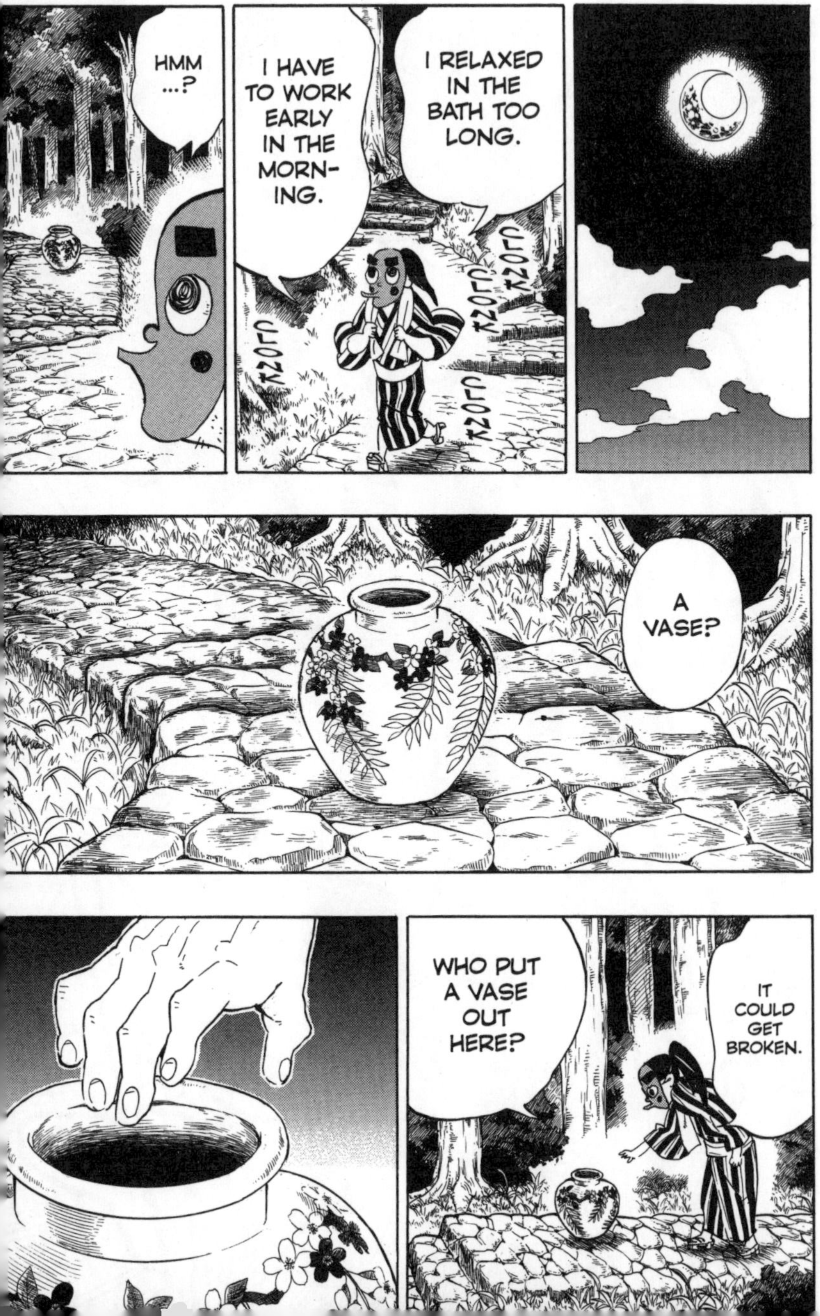
I RELAXED IN THE BATH TOO LONG.
I HAVE TO WORK EARLY IN THE MORN-ING.
CLONK
CLONK
CLONK
CLONK
HMM ...?
A VASE?
IT COULD GET BROKEN.
WHO PUT A VASE OUT HERE?

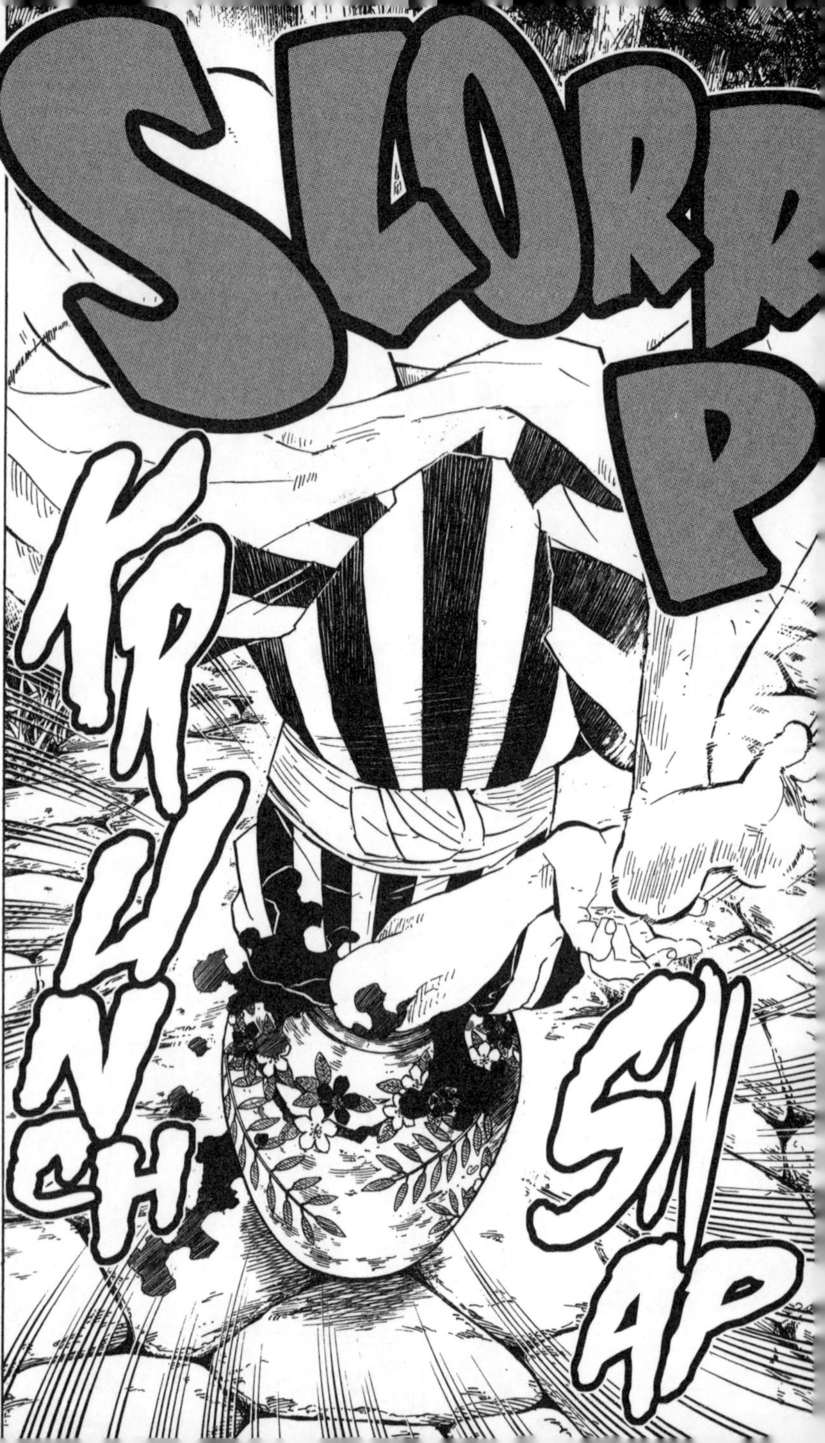
SLORRP
KRUNCH
SNAP

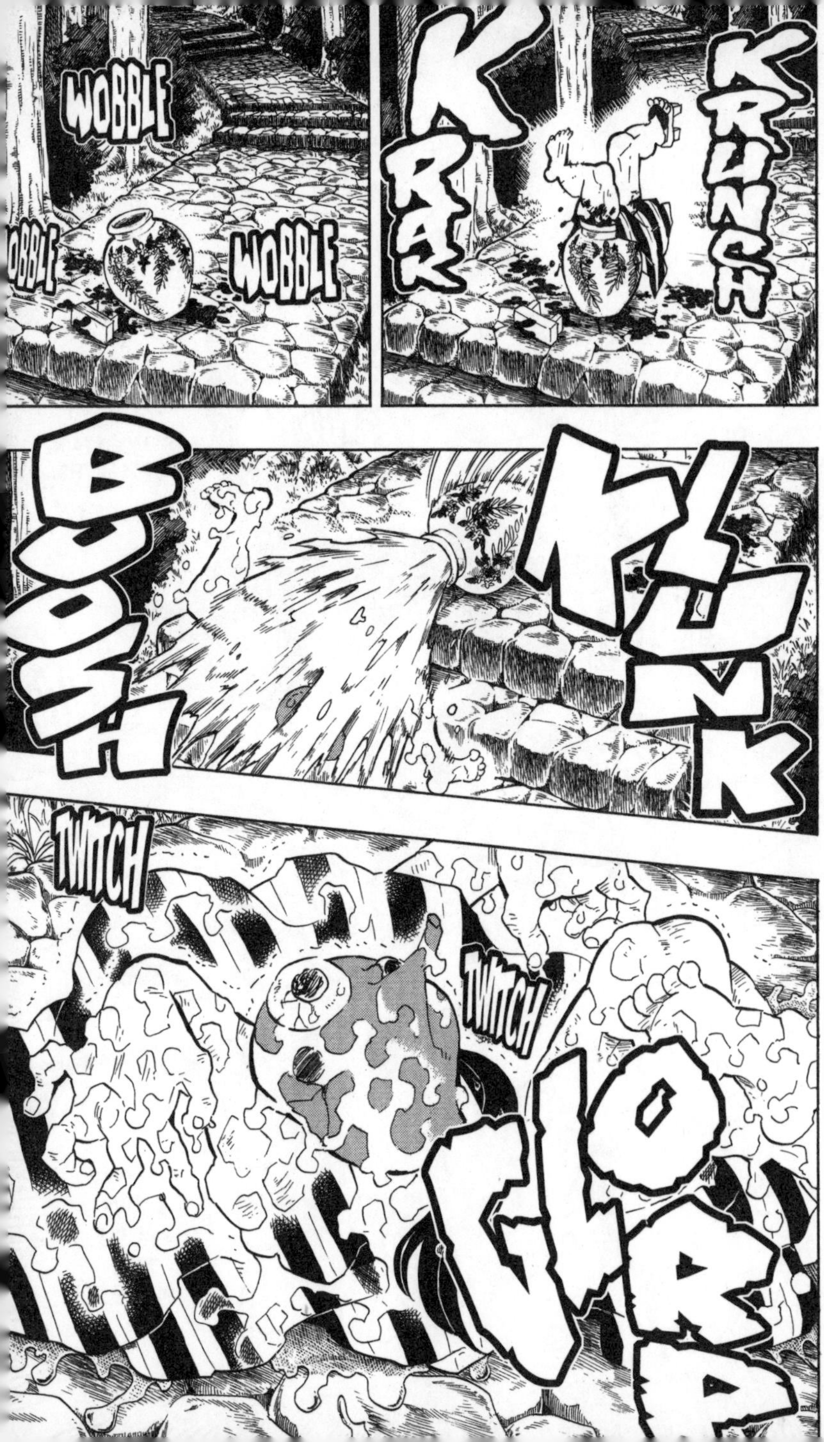
KRUNCH
KRAK
WOBBLE
WOBBLE
WOBBLE
KLUNK
BOOSH
TWITCH
TWITCH
GLORP!

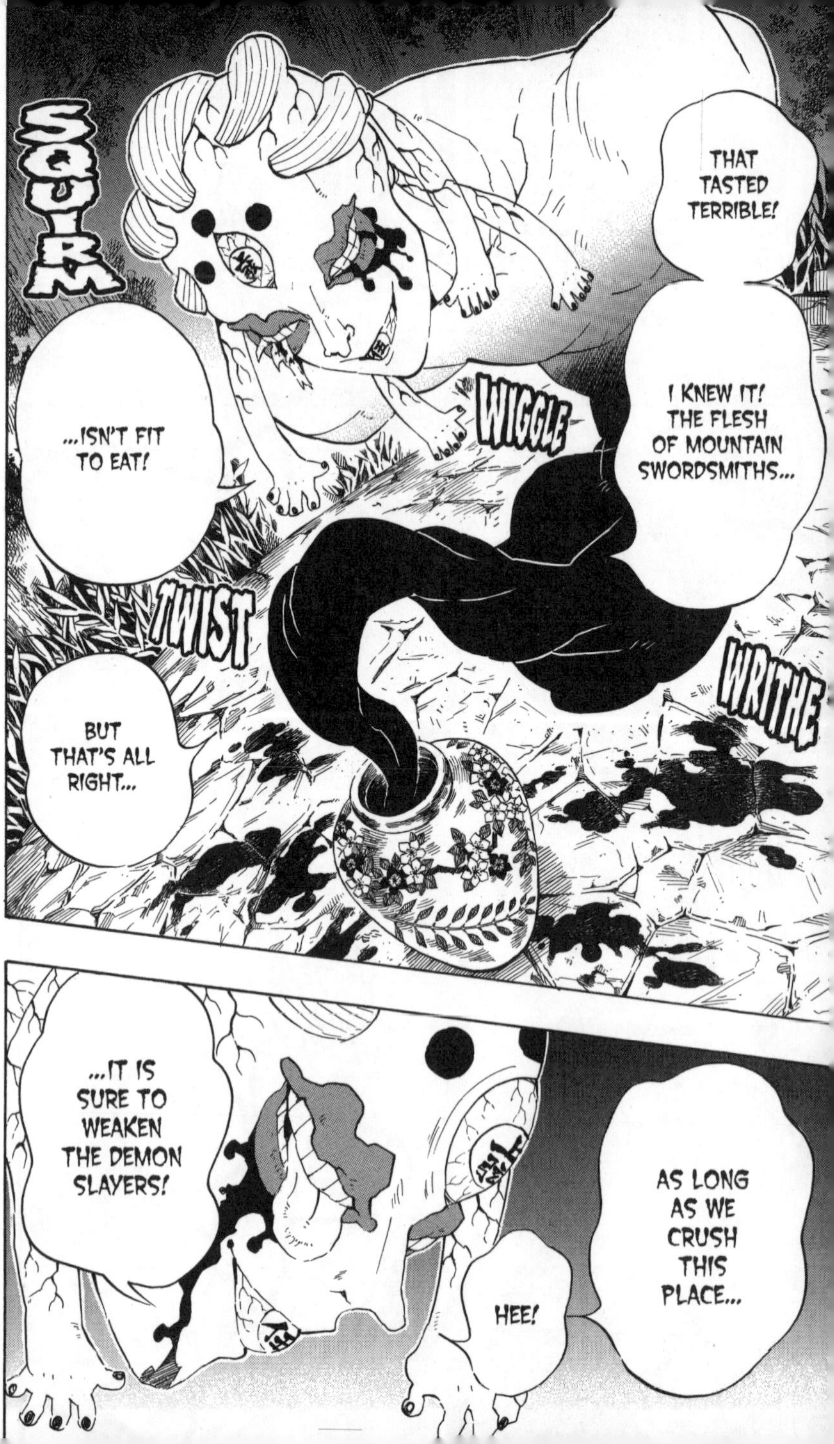
THAT TASTED TERRIBLE!
I KNEW IT! THE FLESH OF MOUNTAIN SWORDSMITHS...
SQUIRM
WIGGLE
...ISN'T FIT TO EAT!
WRITHE
TWIST
BUT THAT'S ALL RIGHT...
AS LONG AS WE CRUSH THIS PLACE...
HEE!
...IT IS SURE TO WEAKEN THE DEMON SLAYERS!

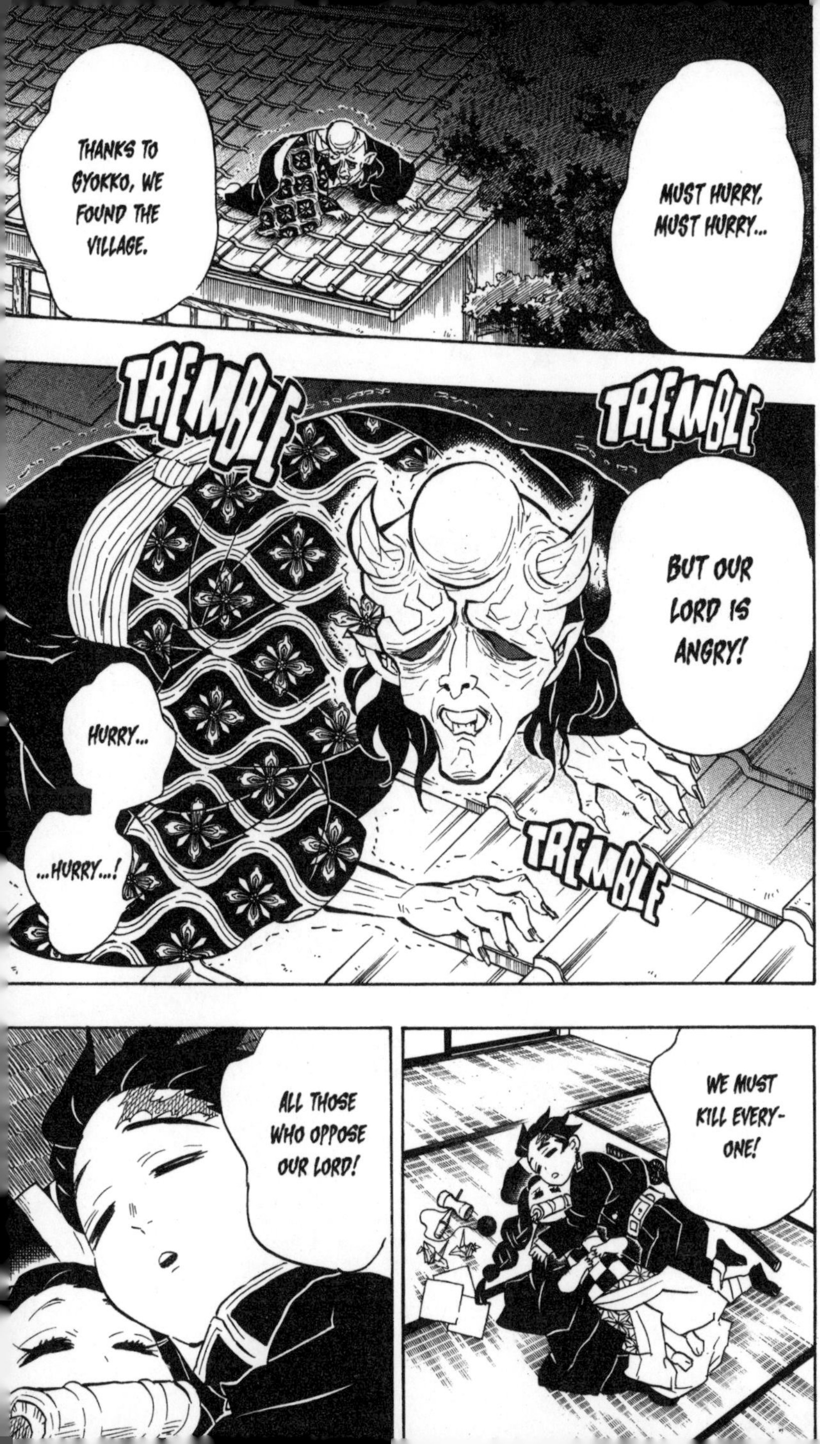
MUST HURRY, MUST HURRY...
THANKS TO GYOKKO, WE FOUND THE VILLAGE.
TREMBLE
TREMBLE
BUT OUR LORD IS ANGRY!
HURRY...
TREMBLE
...HURRY...!
WE MUST KILL EVERY-ONE!
ALL THOSE WHO OPPOSE OUR LORD!

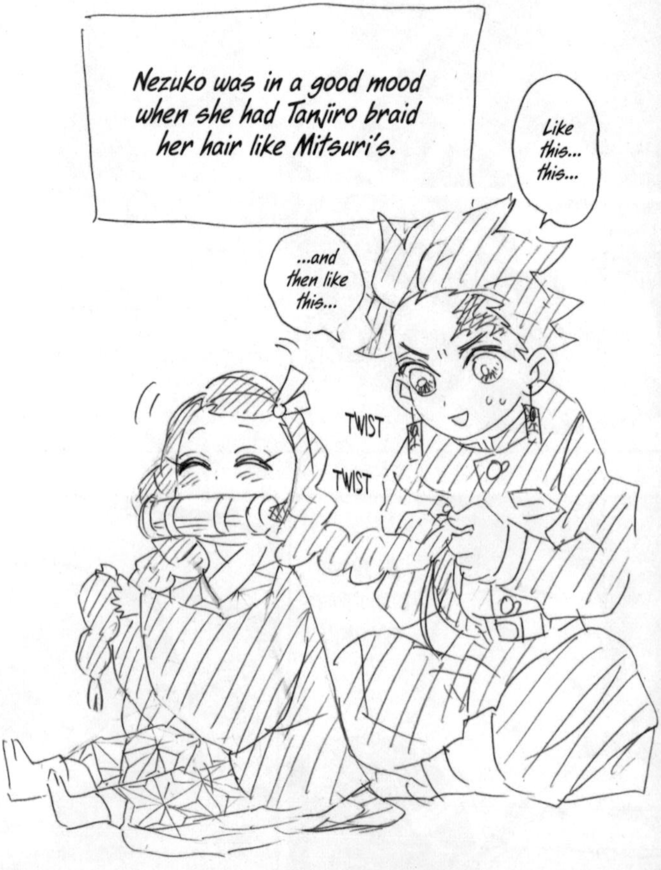
Nezuko was in a good mood when she had Tanjiro braid her hair like Mitsuri's.
Like this... this...
...and then like this...
TWIST
TWIST

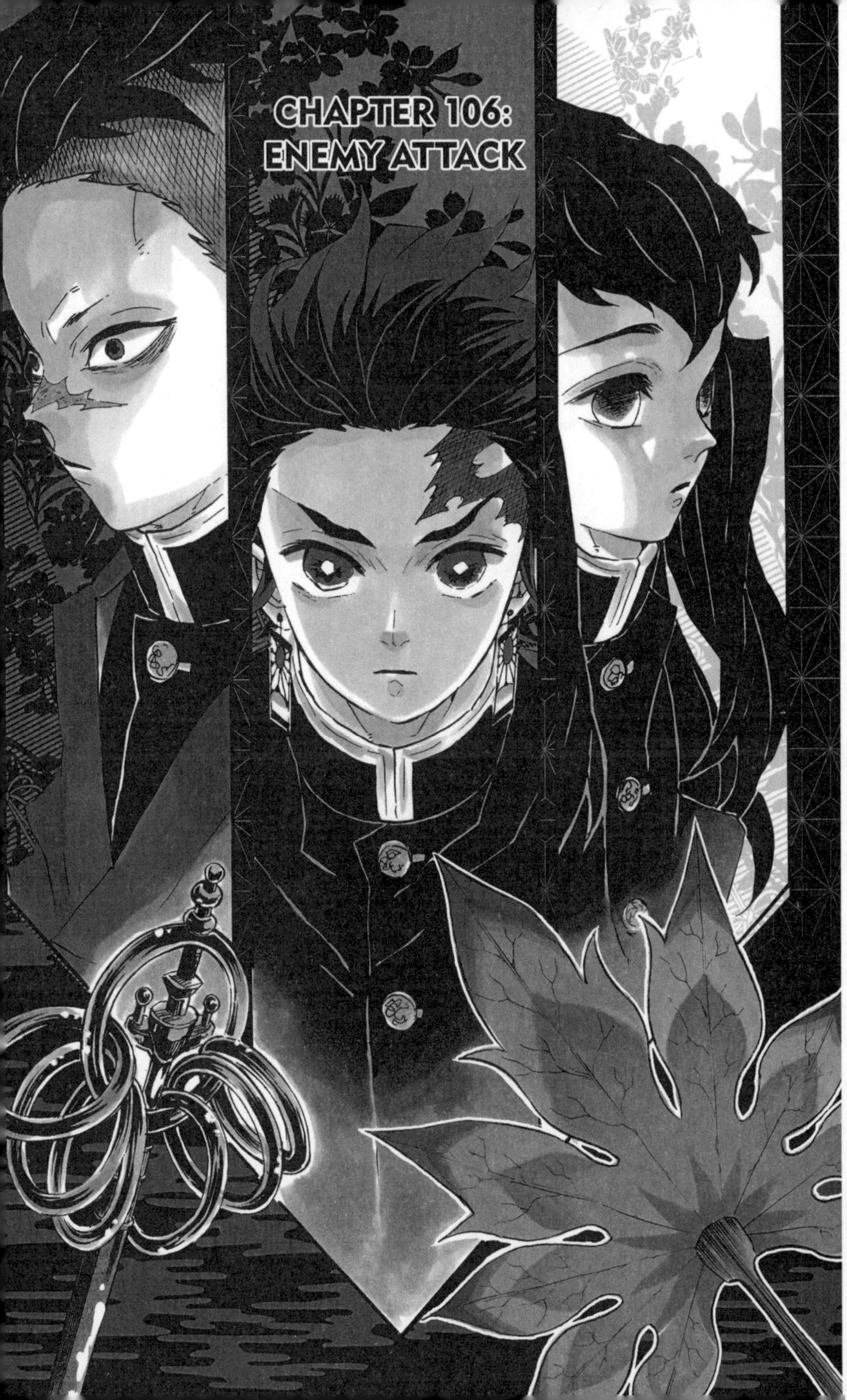
CHAPTER 106:
ENEMY ATTACK

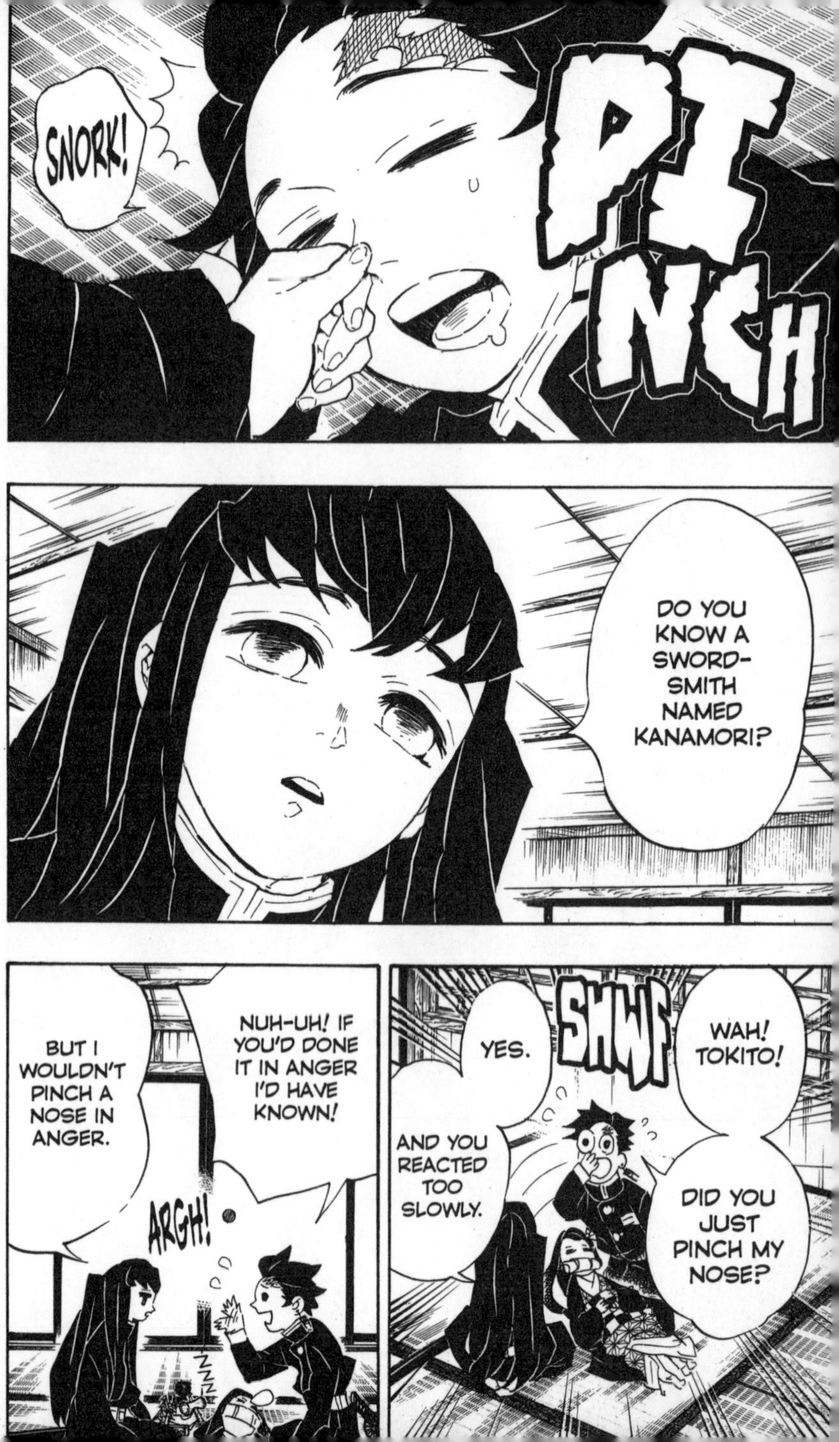
PINCH
SNORK!
DO YOU KNOW A SWORD-SMITH NAMED KANAMORI?
WAH! TOKITO!
SHWF
DID YOU JUST PINCH MY NOSE?
YES.
AND YOU REACTED TOO SLOWLY.
NUH-UH! IF YOU'D DONE IT IN ANGER I'D HAVE KNOWN!
BUT I WOULDN'T PINCH A NOSE IN ANGER.
ARGH!

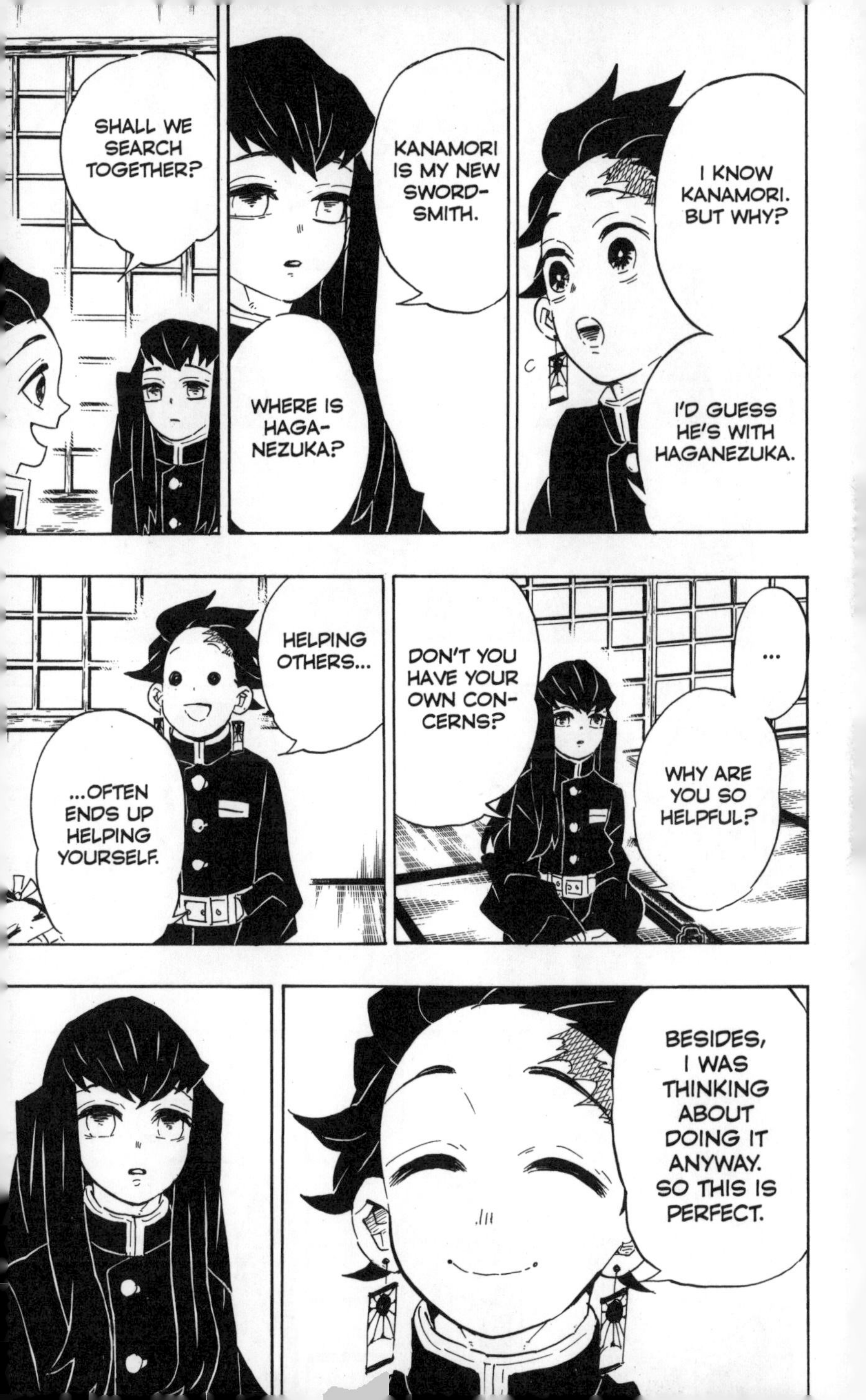
I KNOW KANAMORI. BUT WHY?
I'D GUESS HE'S WITH HAGANEZUKA.
KANAMORI IS MY NEW SWORD-SMITH.
WHERE IS HAGA-NEZUKA?
SHALL WE SEARCH TOGETHER?
...
DON'T YOU HAVE YOUR OWN CON-CERNS?
WHY ARE YOU SO HELPFUL?
HELPING OTHERS...
...OFTEN ENDS UP HELPING YOURSELF.
BESIDES, I WAS THINKING ABOUT DOING IT ANYWAY. SO THIS IS PERFECT.

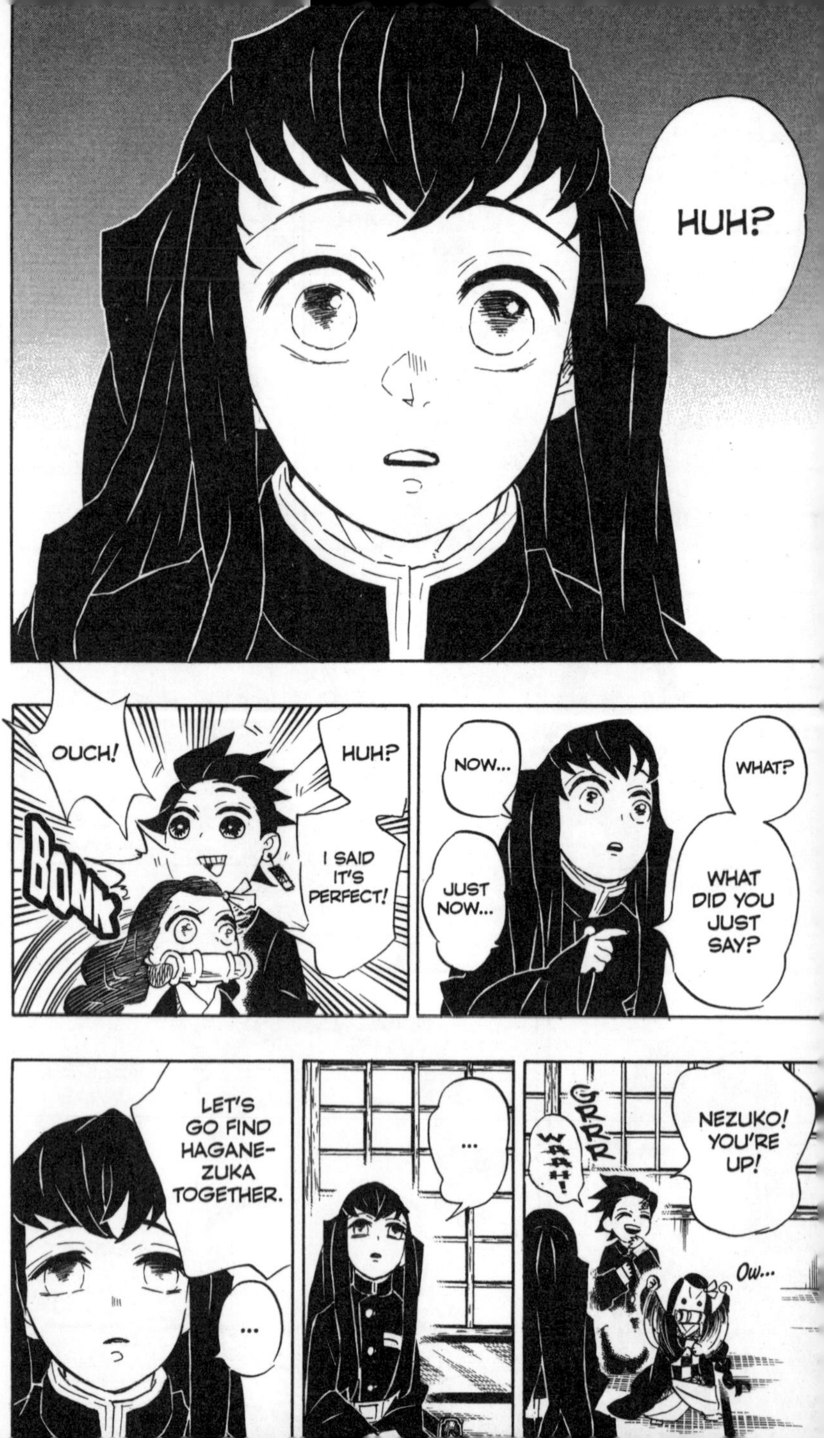
HUH?
WHAT?
NOW...
WHAT DID YOU JUST SAY?
JUST NOW...
HUH?
I SAID IT'S PERFECT!
OUCH!
BONK
NEZUKO! YOU'RE UP!
GRRR
WAAH!
Ow...
...
LET'S GO FIND HAGANE-ZUKA TOGETHER.
...

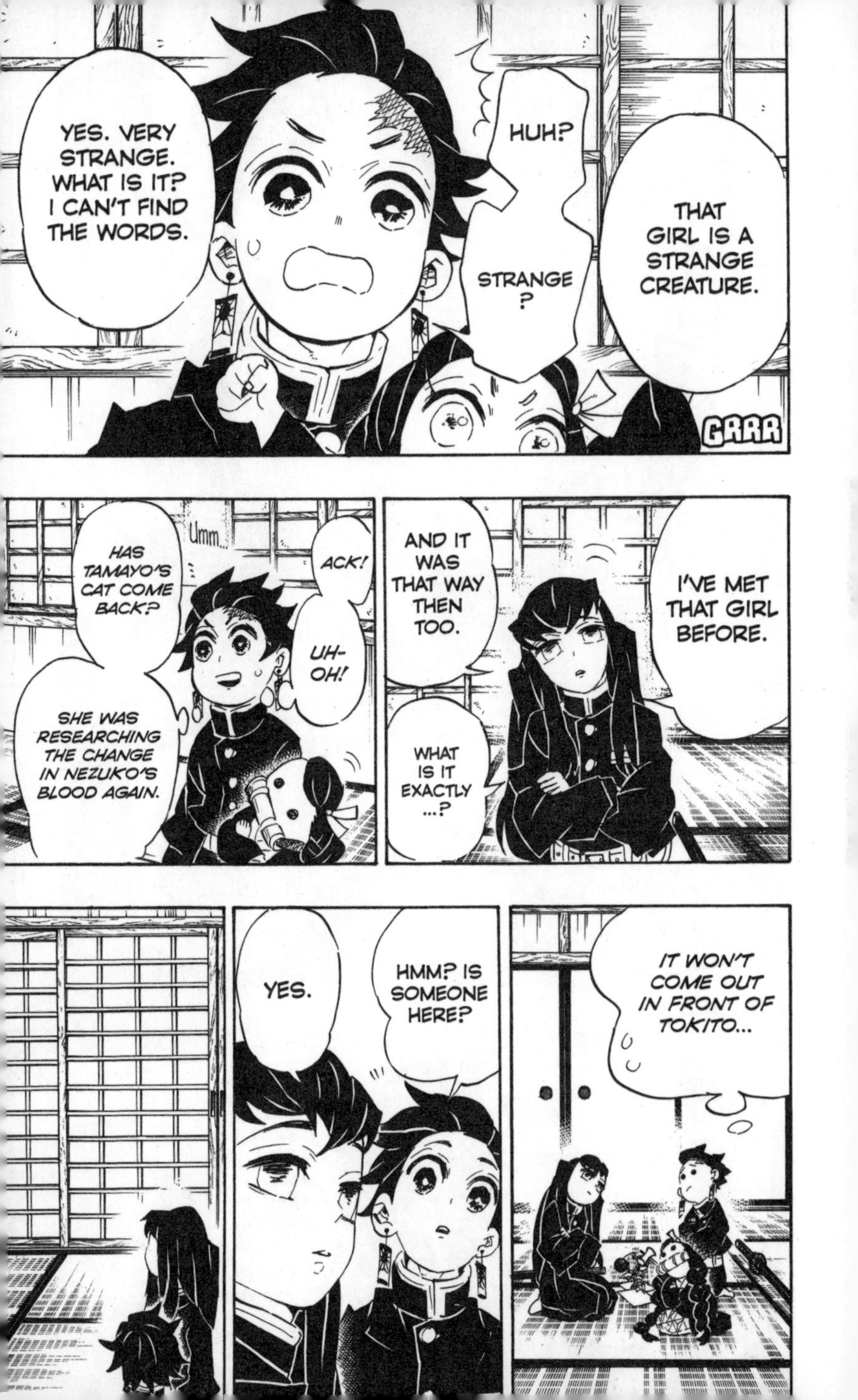
THAT GIRL IS A STRANGE CREATURE.
HUH?
STRANGE?
YES. VERY STRANGE. WHAT IS IT? I CAN'T FIND THE WORDS.
GRRR
I'VE MET THAT GIRL BEFORE.
AND IT WAS THAT WAY THEN TOO.
WHAT IS IT EXACTLY ...?
ACK!
UH-OH!
Umm...
HAS TAMAYO'S CAT COME BACK?
SHE WAS RESEARCHING THE CHANGE IN NEZUKO'S BLOOD AGAIN.
IT WON'T COME OUT IN FRONT OF TOKITO...
HMM? IS SOMEONE HERE?
YES.

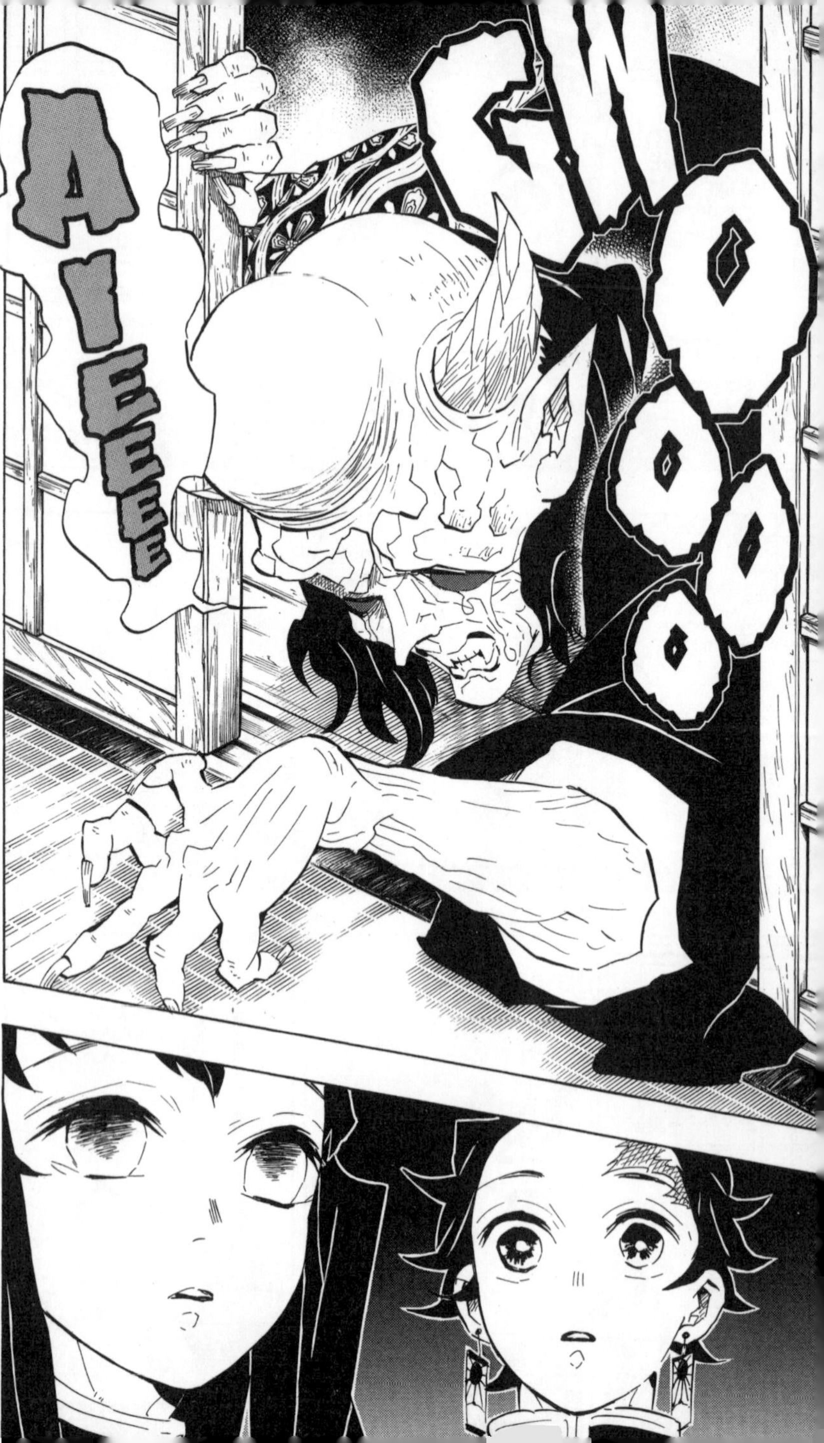
GWOOOO
AIEEEE

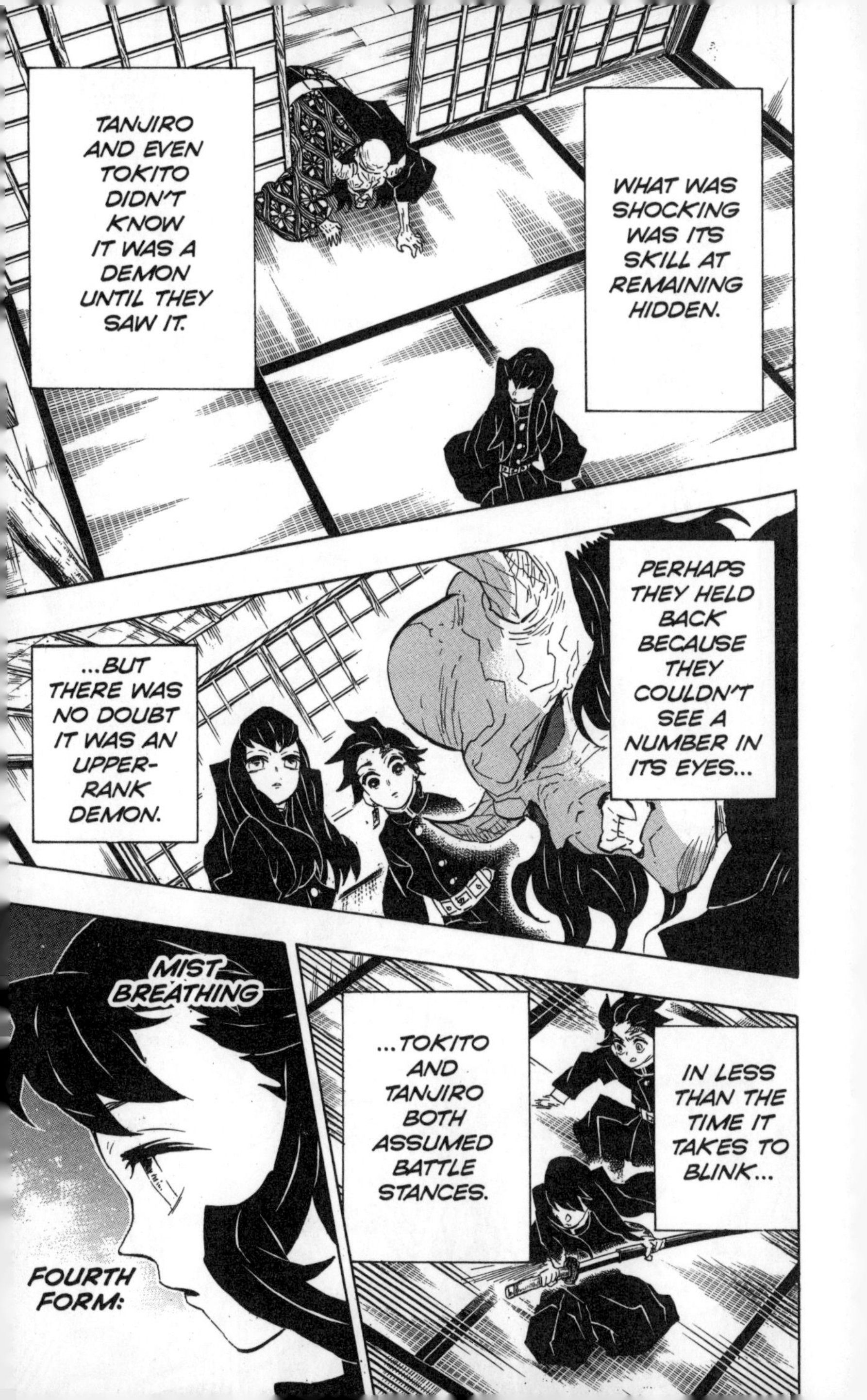
WHAT WAS SHOCKING WAS ITS SKILL AT REMAINING HIDDEN.
TANJIRO AND EVEN TOKITO DIDN'T KNOW IT WAS A DEMON UNTIL THEY SAW IT.
PERHAPS THEY HELD BACK BECAUSE THEY COULDN'T SEE A NUMBER IN ITS EYES...
...BUT THERE WAS NO DOUBT IT WAS AN UPPER-RANK DEMON.
IN LESS THAN THE TIME IT TAKES TO BLINK...
...TOKITO AND TANJIRO BOTH ASSUMED BATTLE STANCES.
MIST BREATHING
FOURTH FORM:

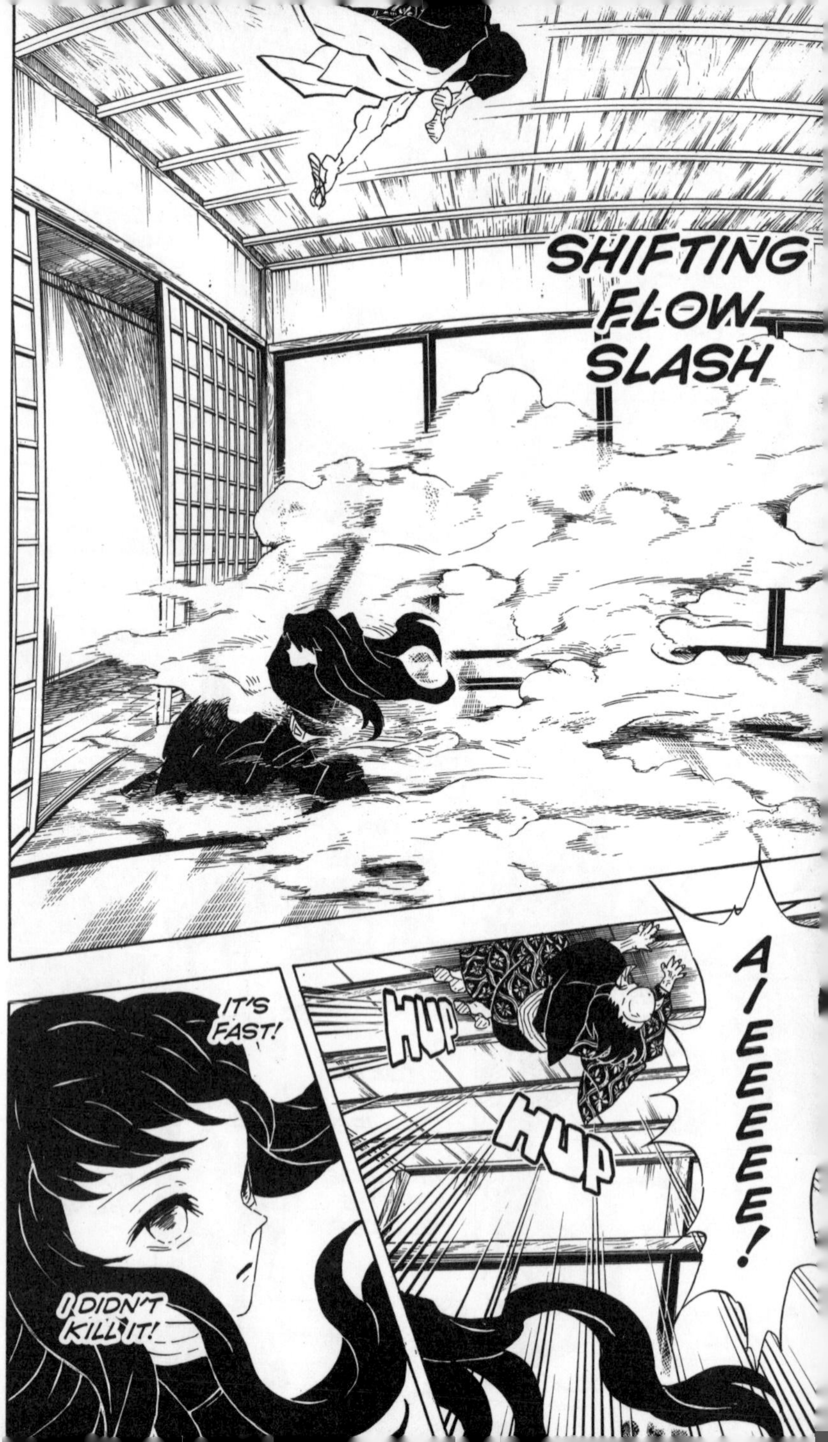
SHIFTING FLOW SLASH
AIEEEEEE!
HUP
HUP
IT'S FAST!
I DIDN'T KILL IT!

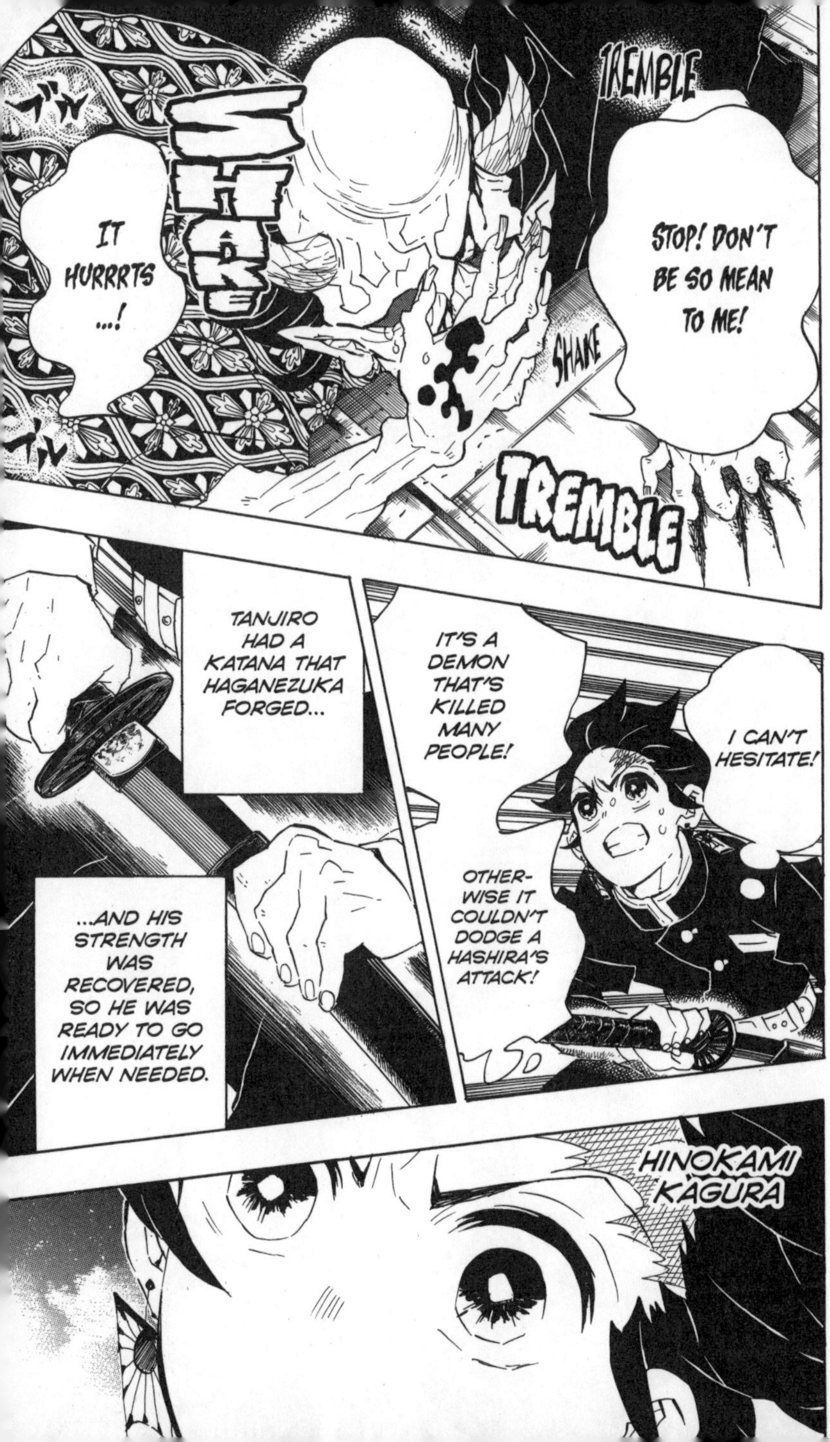
TREMBLE
STOP! DON'T BE SO MEAN TO ME!
SHAKE
TREMBLE
SHAKE
IT HURRRTS ...!
I CAN'T HESITATE!
IT'S A DEMON THAT'S KILLED MANY PEOPLE!
OTHERWISE IT COULDN'T DODGE A HASHIRA'S ATTACK!
TANJIRO HAD A KATANA THAT HAGANEZUKA FORGED...
...AND HIS STRENGTH WAS RECOVERED, SO HE WAS READY TO GO IMMEDIATELY WHEN NEEDED.
HINOKAMI KAGURA

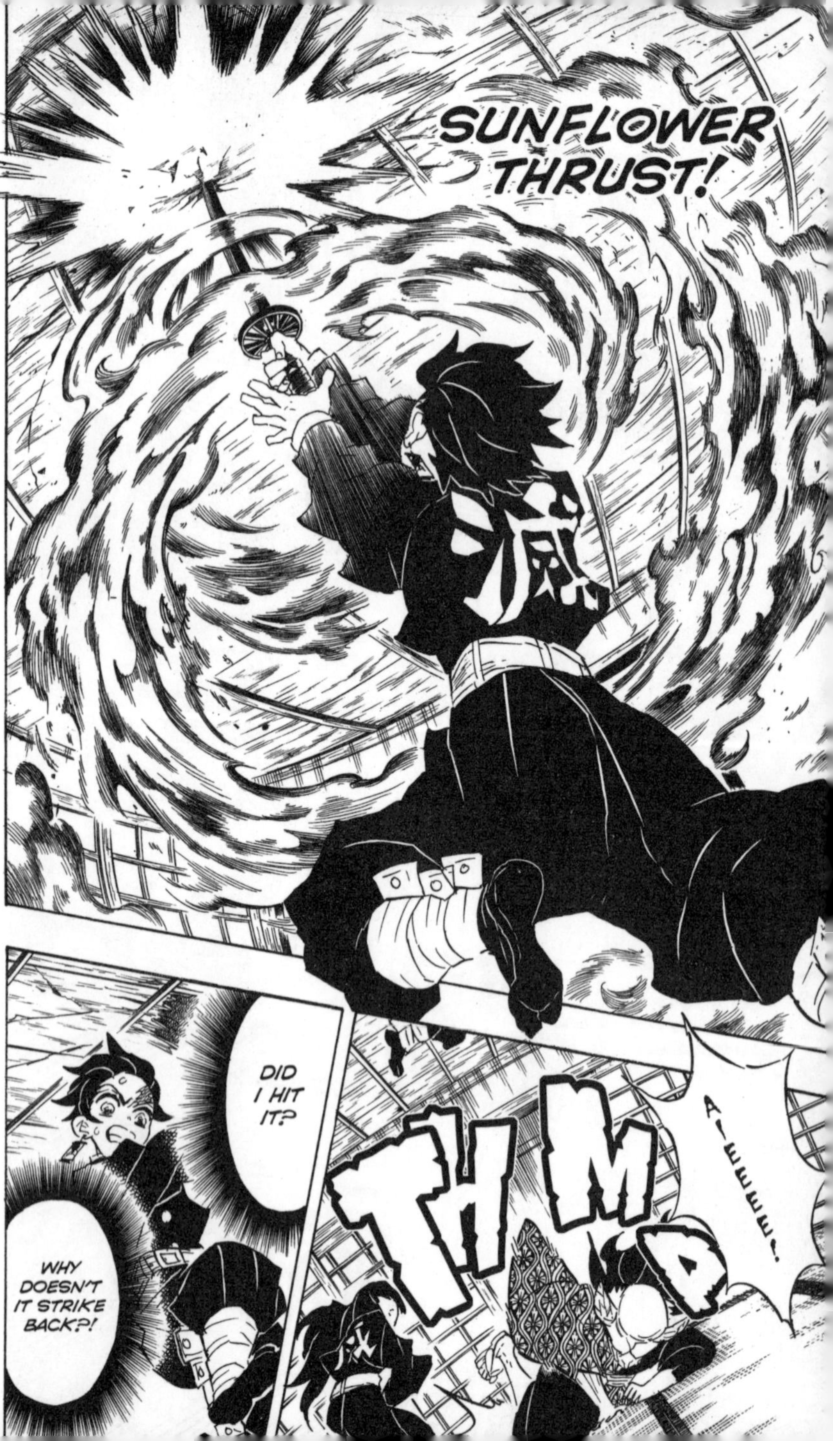
SUNFLOWER THRUST!
AIEEEEE!
THMP
DID I HIT IT?
WHY DOESN'T IT STRIKE BACK?!

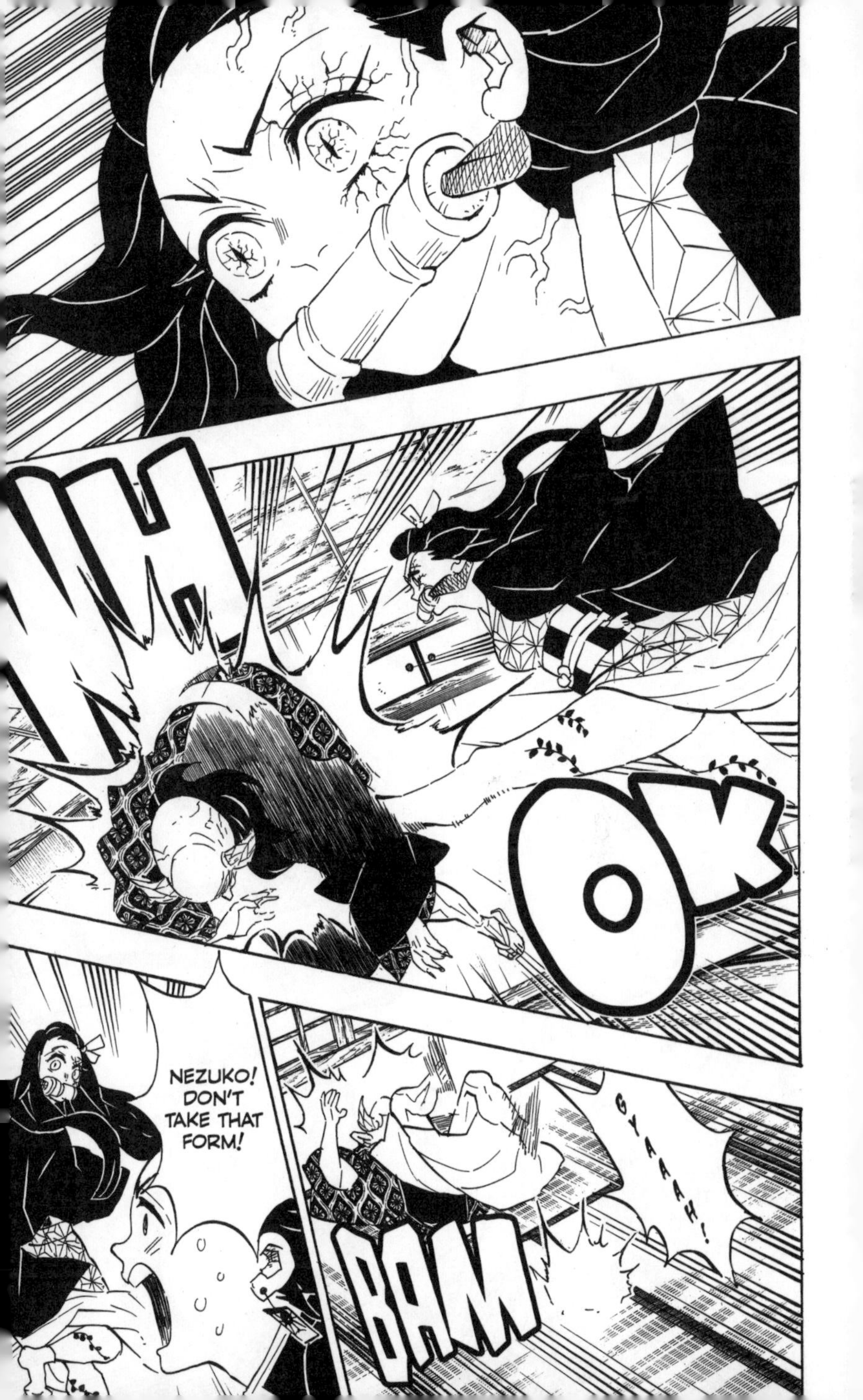

WH
OK
GYAAAAH!
BAM
NEZUKO! DON'T TAKE THAT FORM!

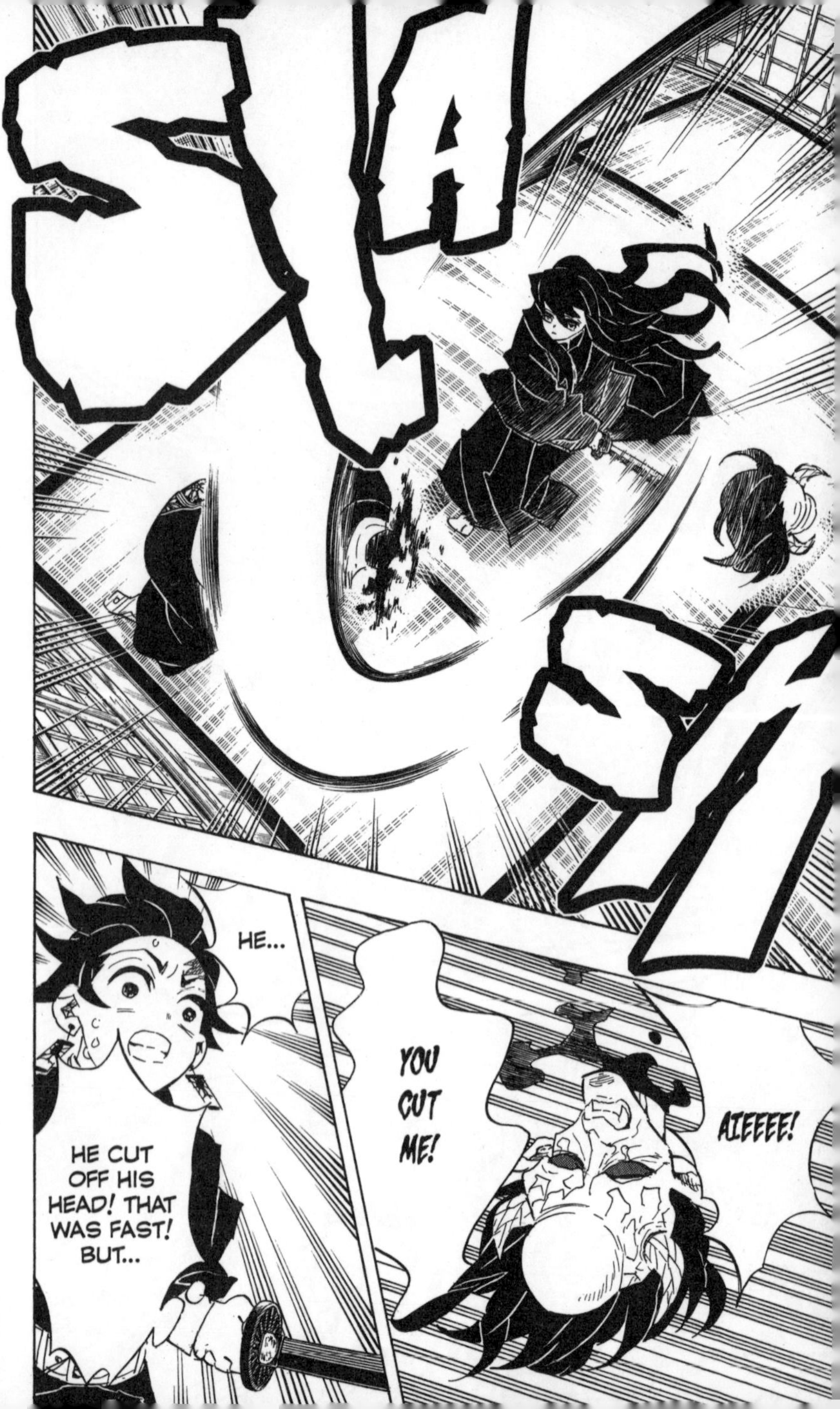
SLASH
AIEEEE!
YOU CUT ME!
HE...
HE CUT OFF HIS HEAD! THAT WAS FAST! BUT...

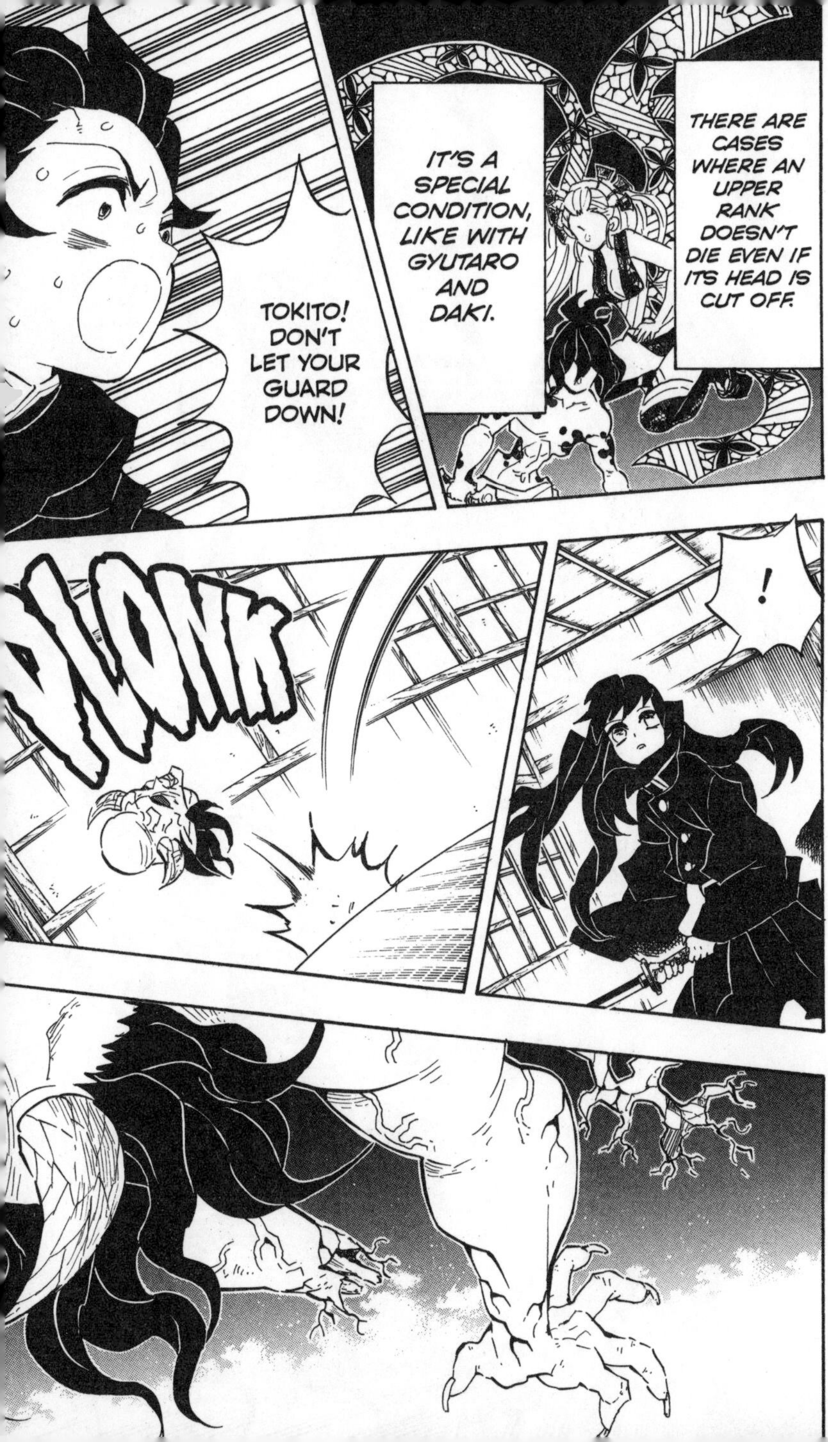
THERE ARE CASES WHERE AN UPPER RANK DOESN'T DIE EVEN IF ITS HEAD IS CUT OFF.
IT'S A SPECIAL CONDITION, LIKE WITH GYUTARO AND DAKI.
TOKITO! DON'T LET YOUR GUARD DOWN!
!
DONK

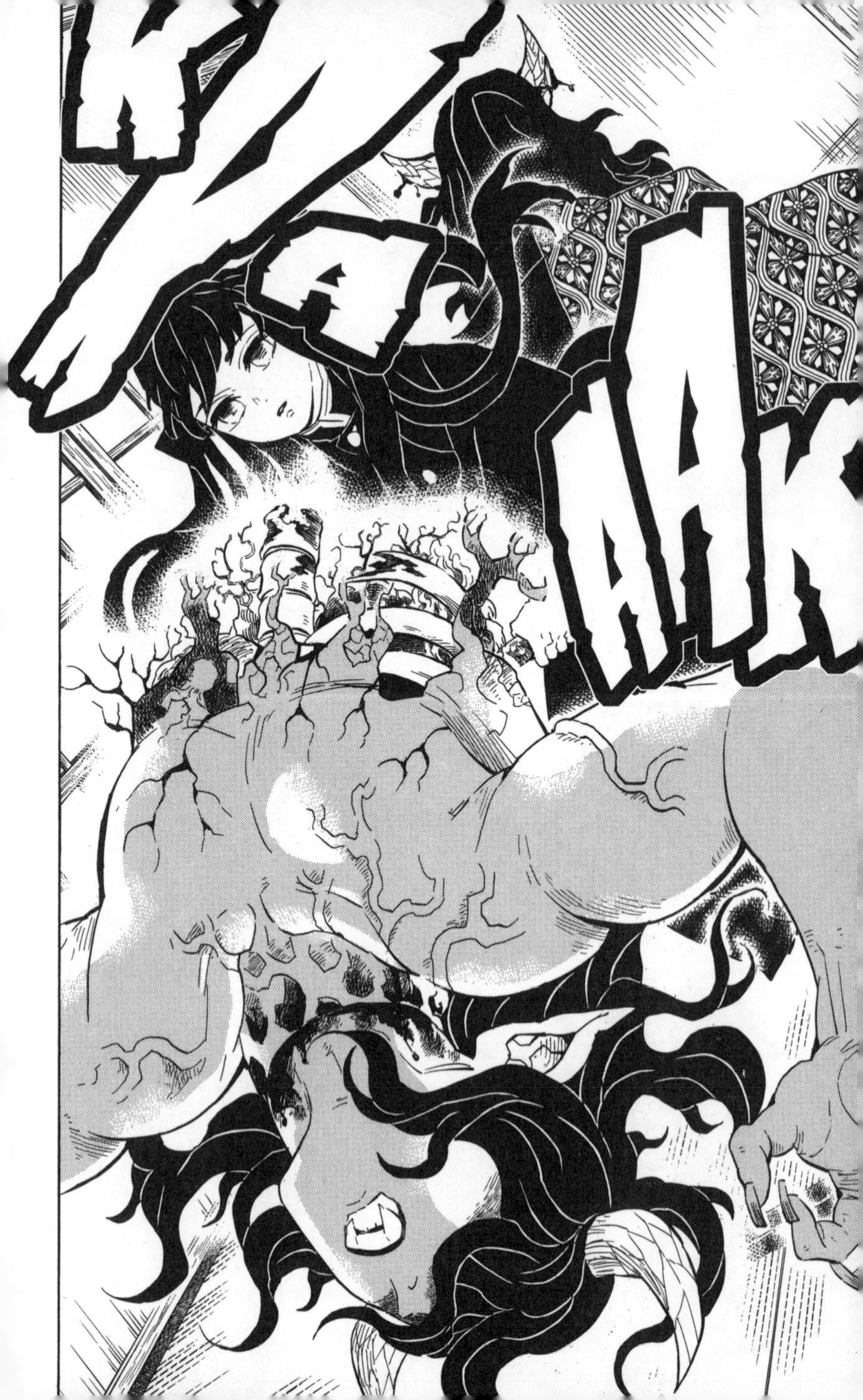
AAK

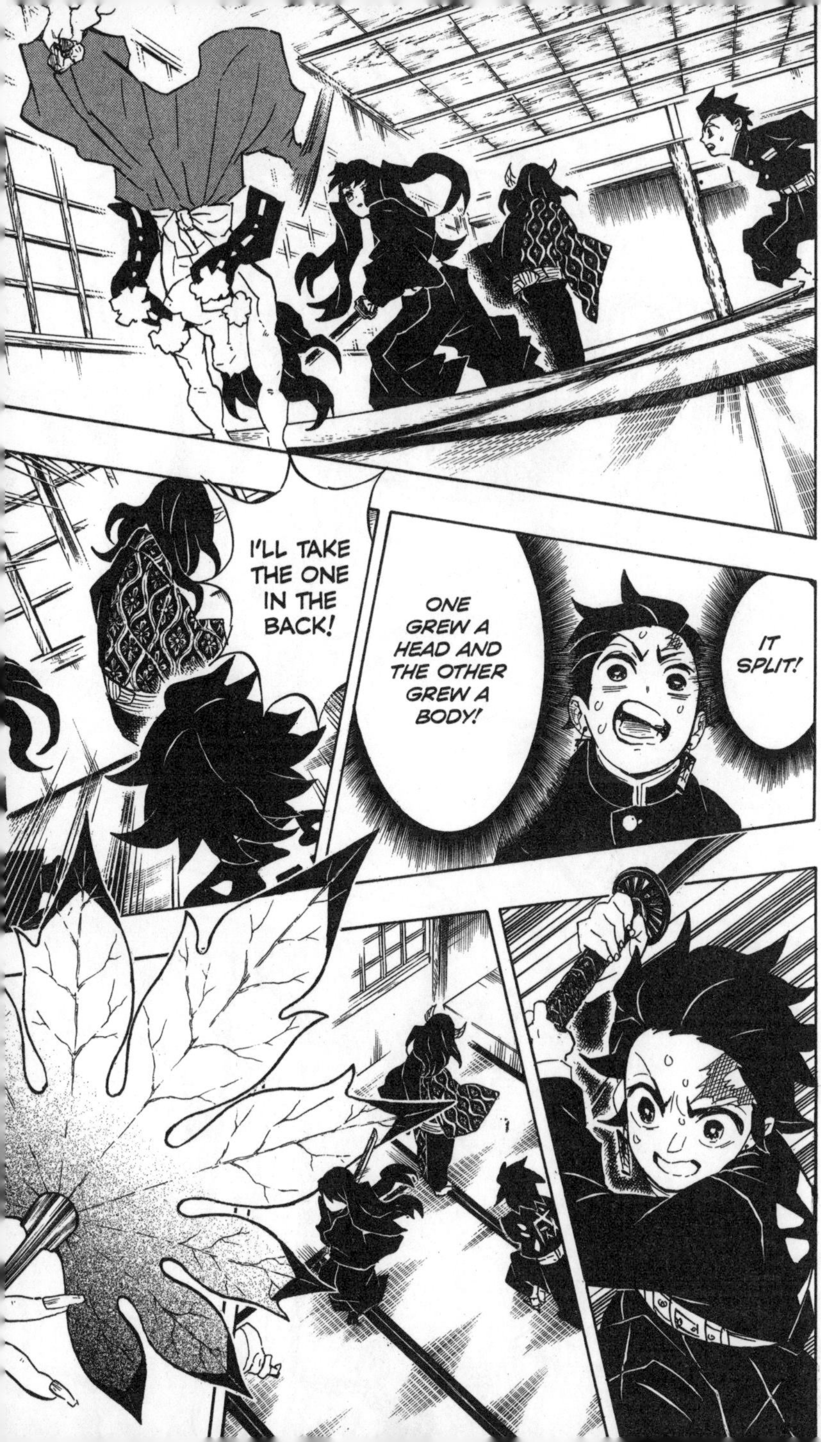
IT SPLIT!
ONE GREW A HEAD AND THE OTHER GREW A BODY!
I'LL TAKE THE ONE IN THE BACK!

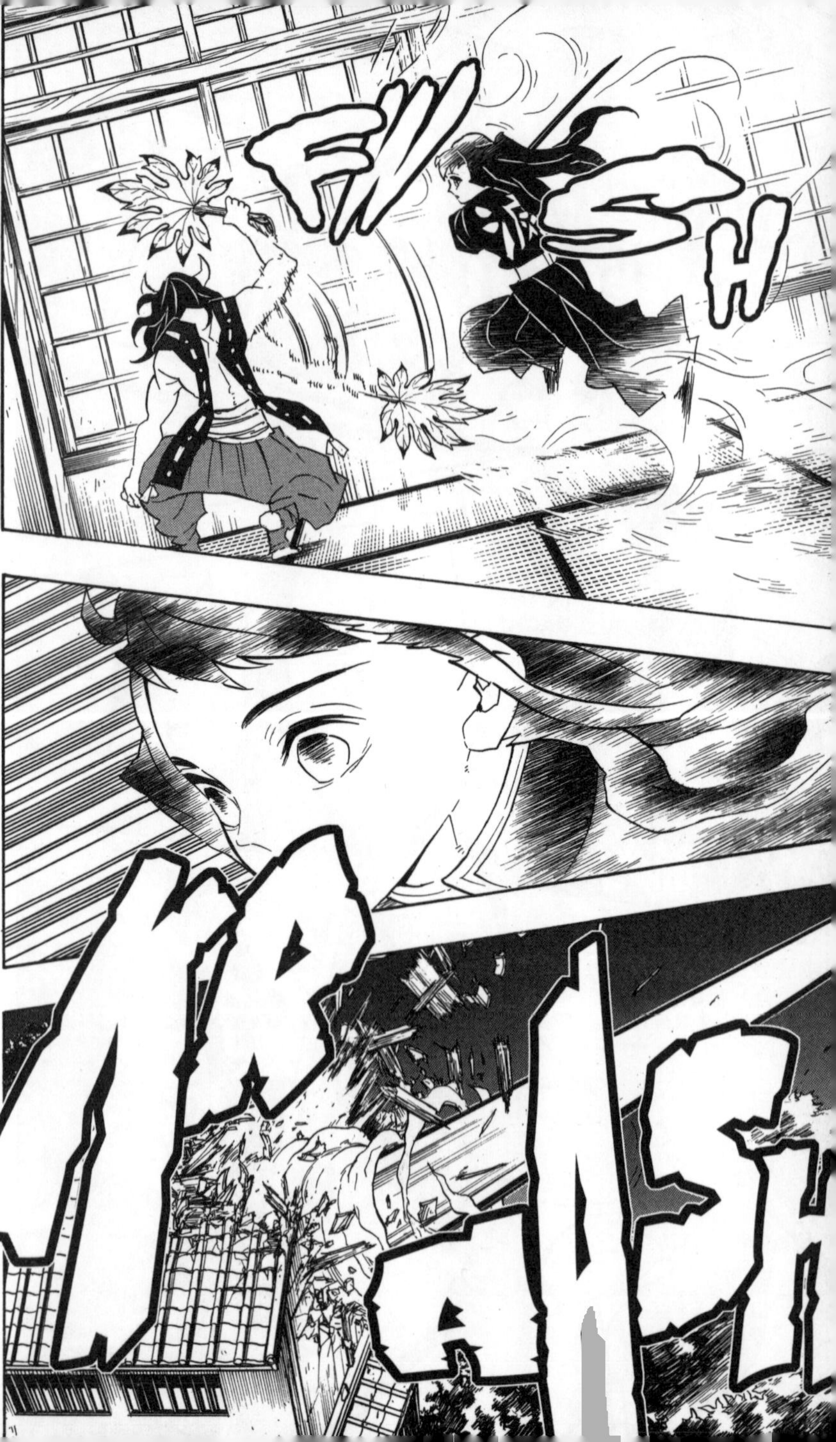
FWSH
KRASH

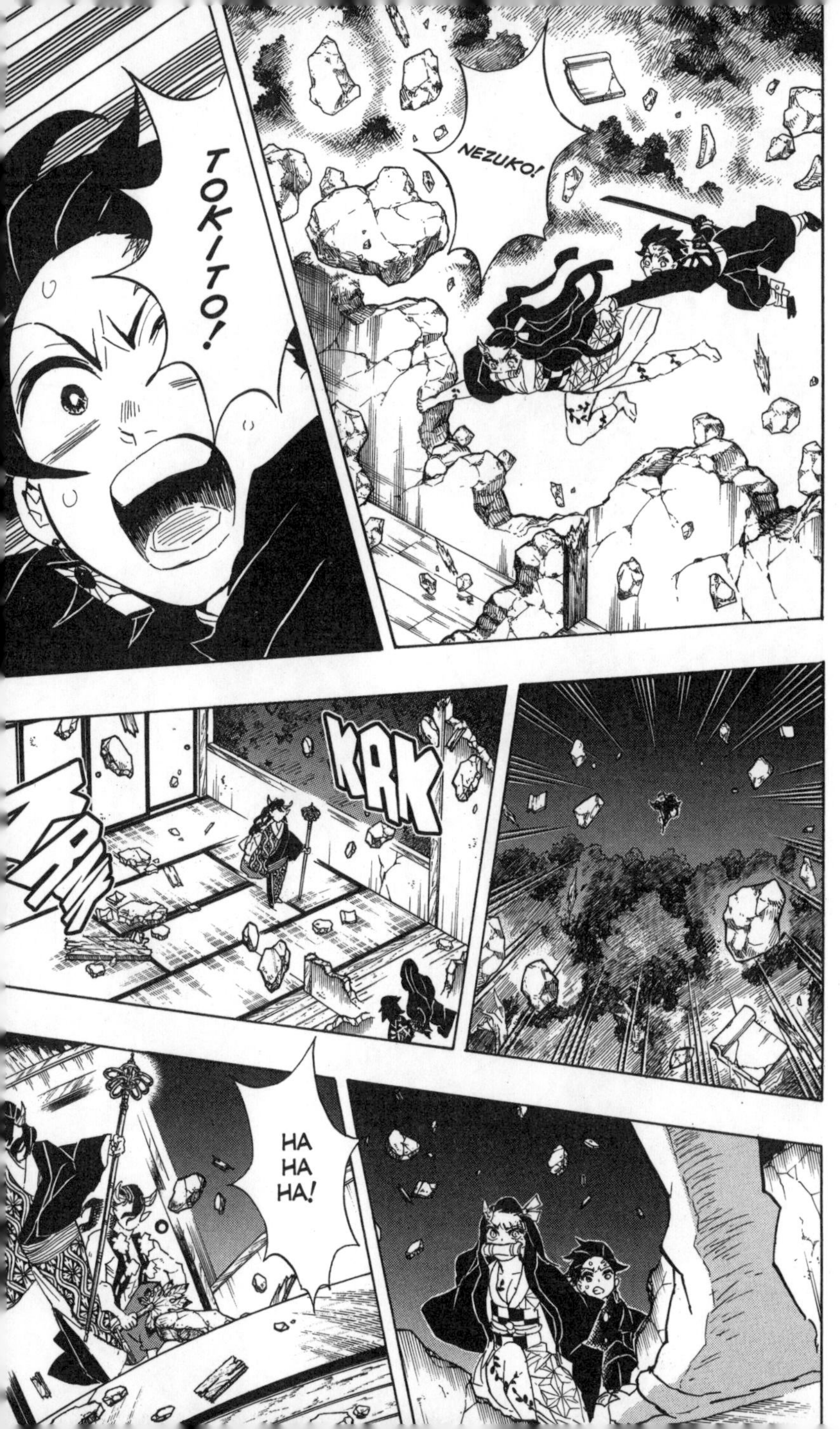
NEZUKO!
TOKITO!
KRK
HA HA HA!

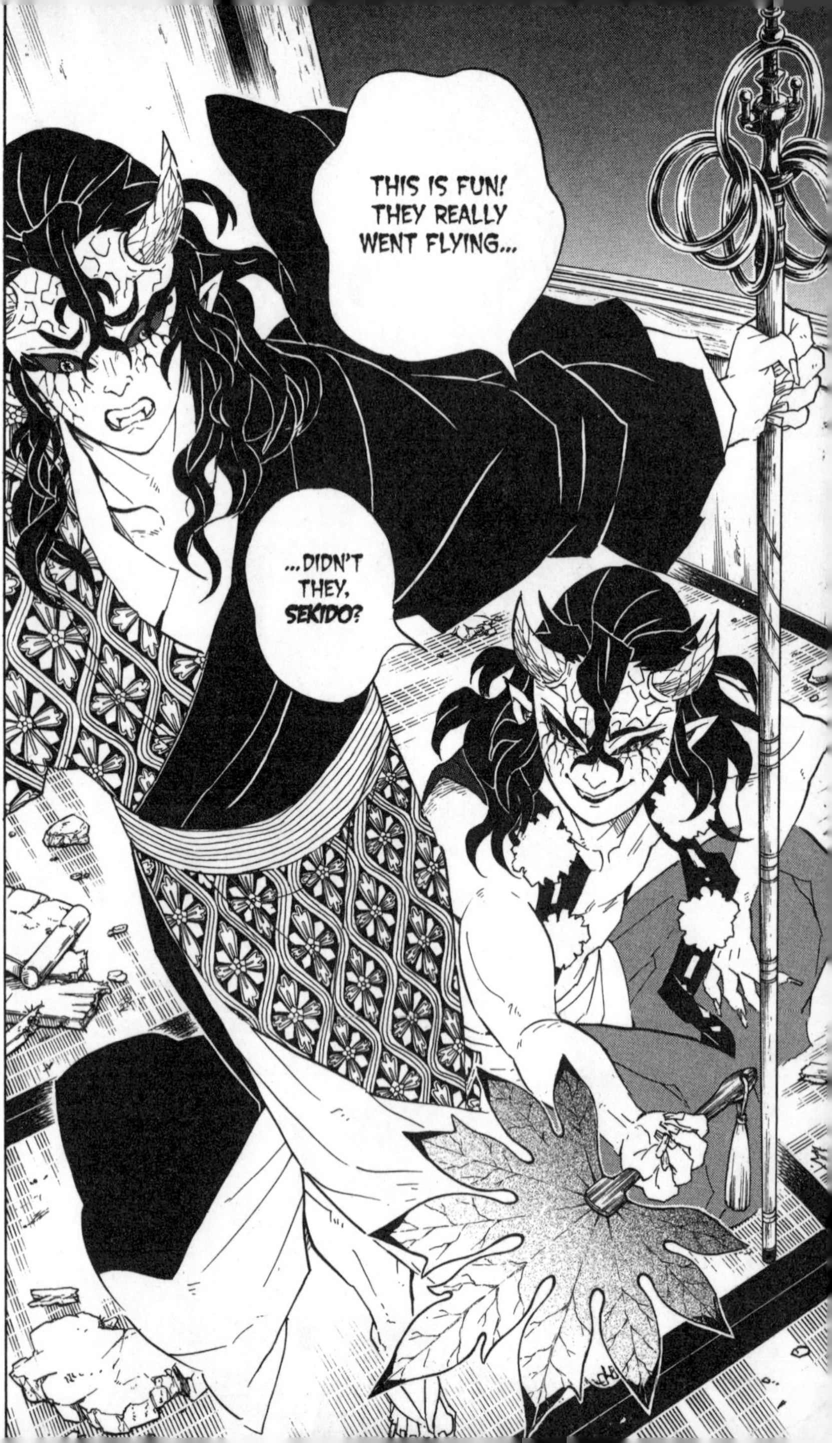
THIS IS FUN! THEY REALLY WENT FLYING...
...DIDN'T THEY, **SEKIDO**?

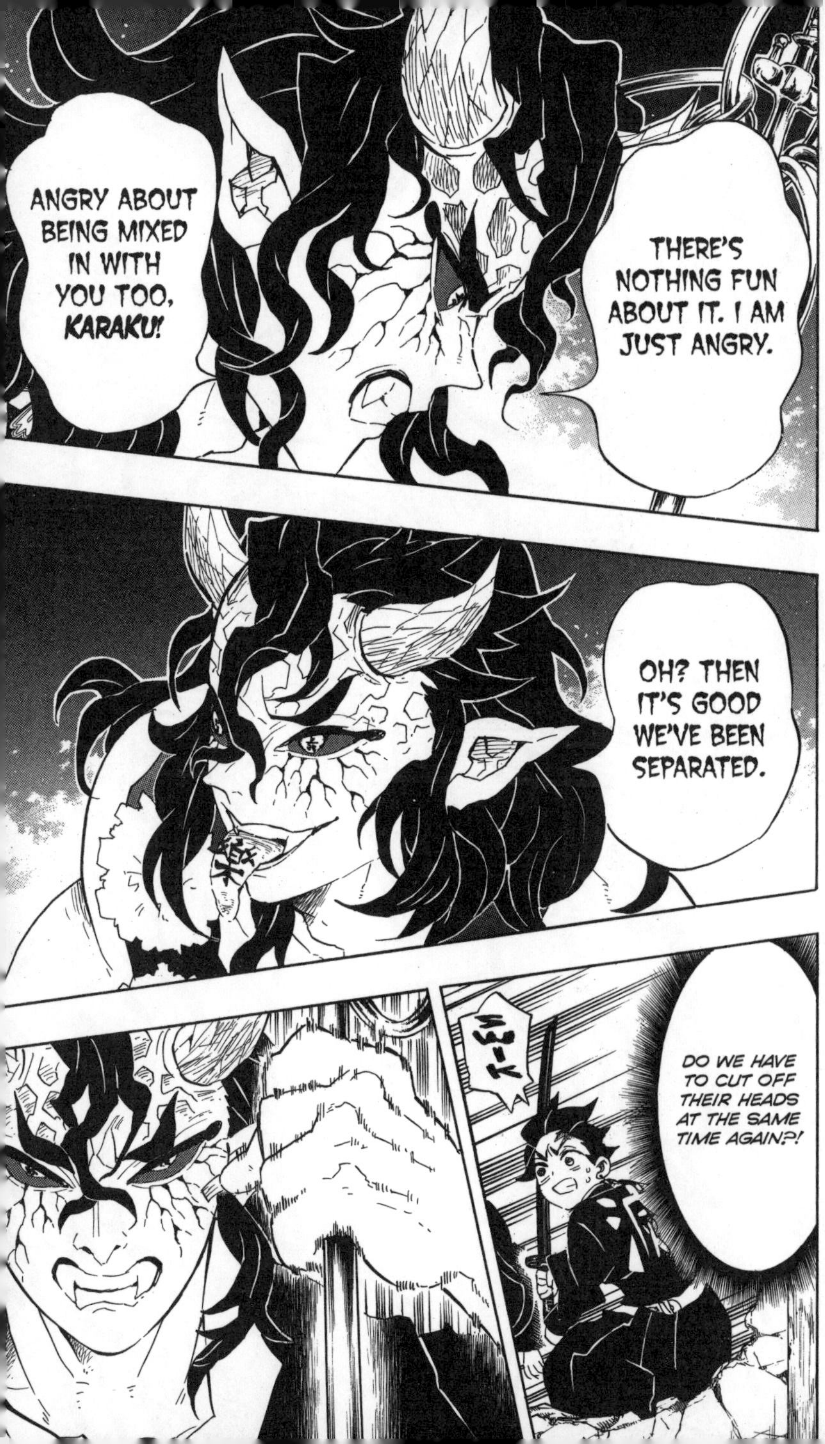
THERE'S NOTHING FUN ABOUT IT. I AM JUST ANGRY.
ANGRY ABOUT BEING MIXED IN WITH YOU TOO, KARAKU!
OH? THEN IT'S GOOD WE'VE BEEN SEPARATED.
DO WE HAVE TO CUT OFF THEIR HEADS AT THE SAME TIME AGAIN?!

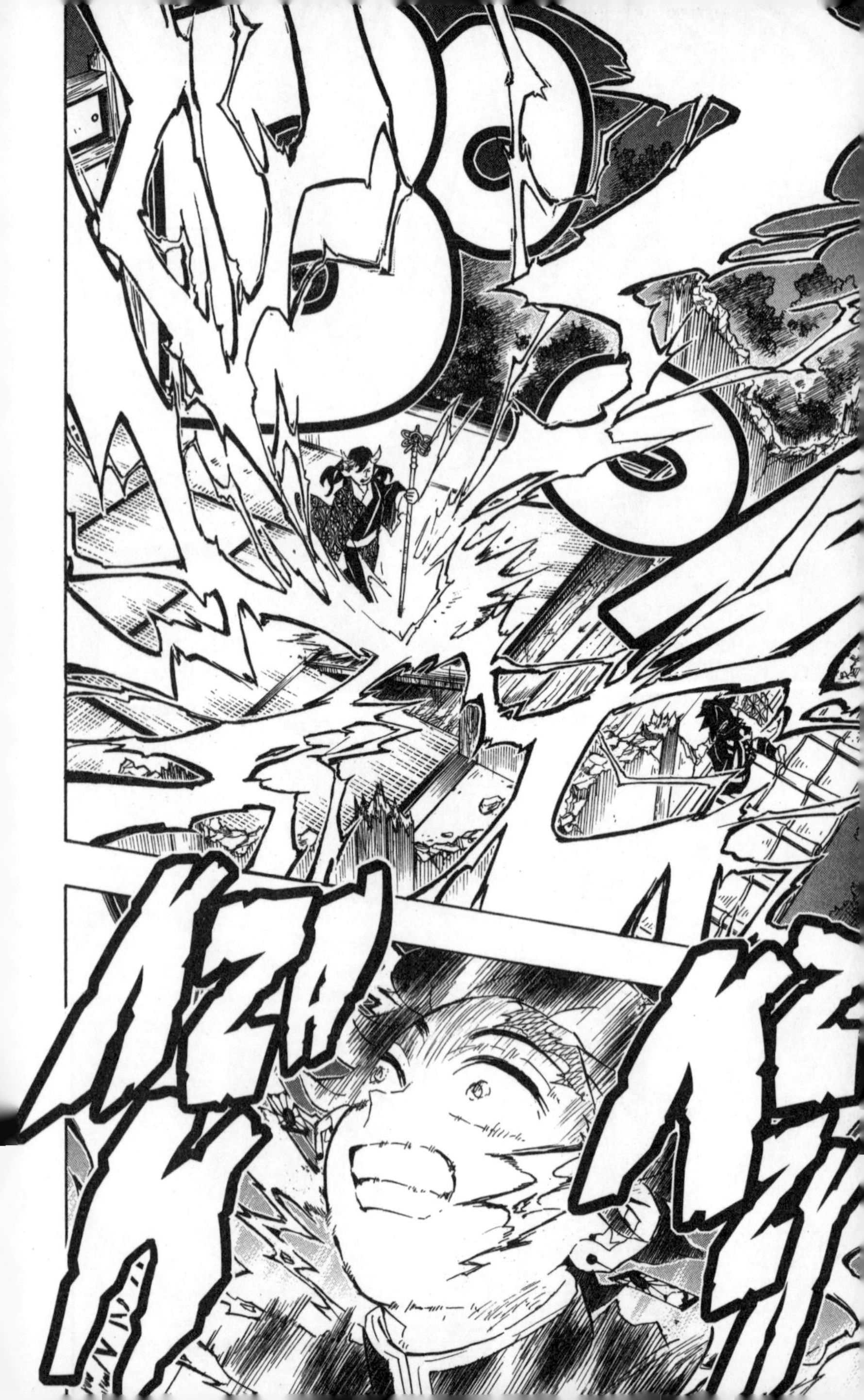

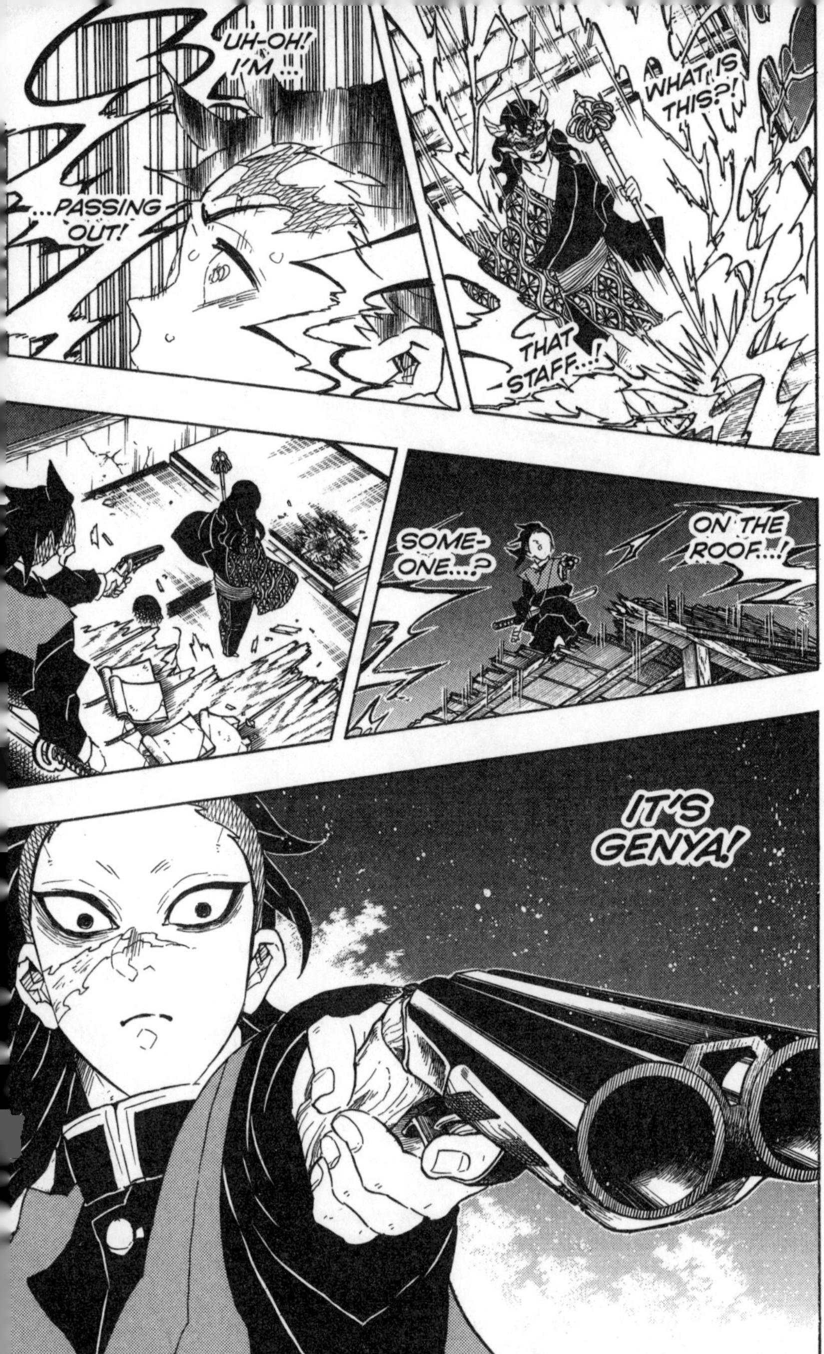
WHAT IS THIS?!
THAT STAFF...!
UH-OH! I'M...
...PASSING OUT!
ON THE ROOF...!
SOME-ONE...?
IT'S GENYA!

VOLUME 12—THE UPPER RANKS GATHER (THE END)

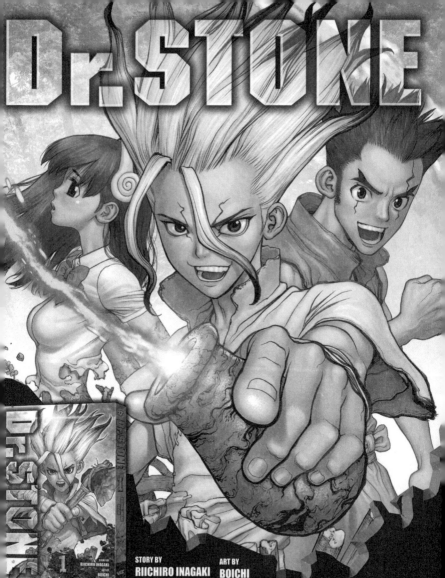

Dr. STONE

STORY BY
RIICHIRO INAGAKI

ART BY
BOICHI

One fateful day, all of humanity turned to stone. Many millennia later, Taiju frees himself from petrification and finds himself surrounded by statues. The situation looks grim—until he runs into his science-loving friend Senku! Together they plan to restart civilization with the power of science!

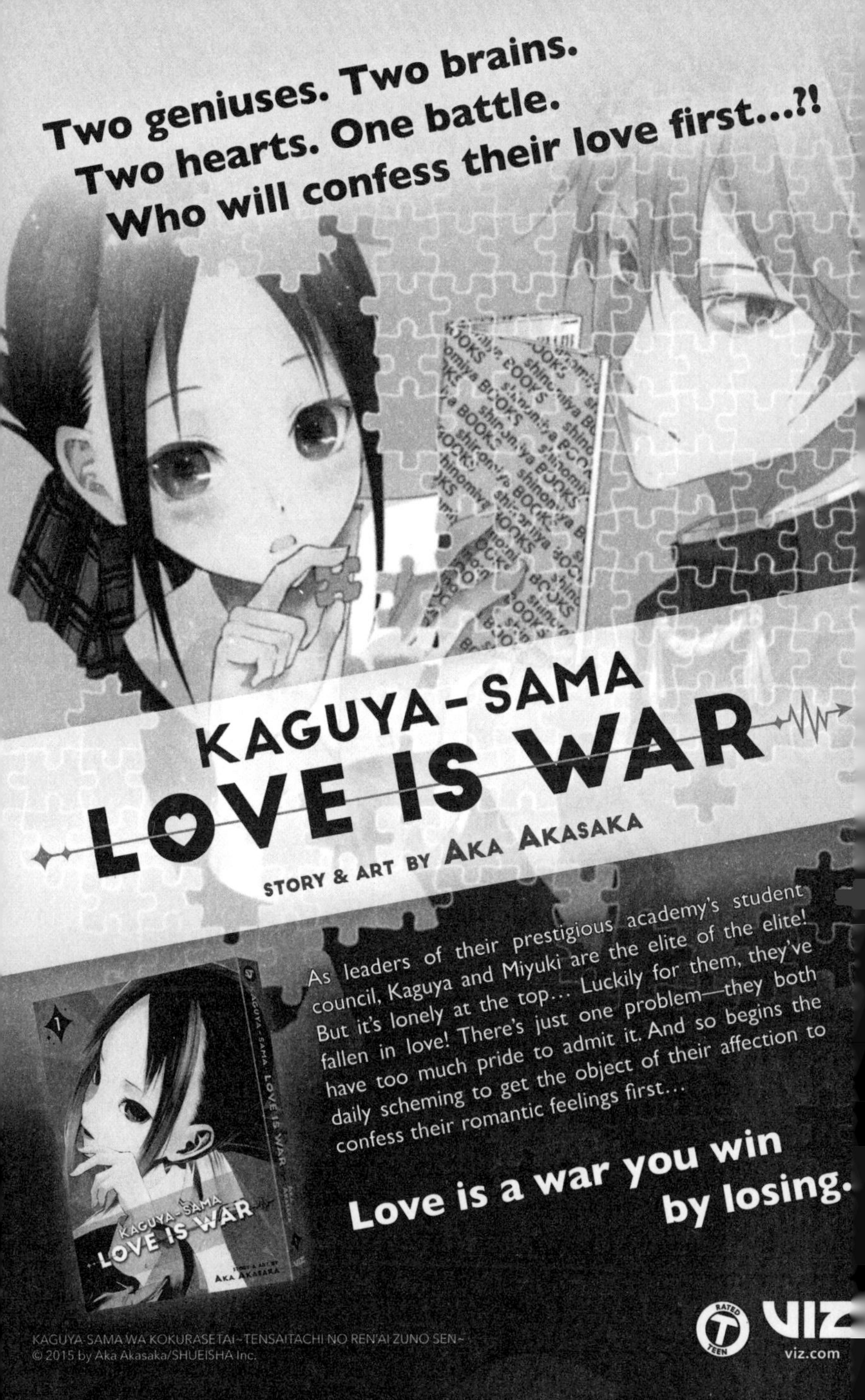
Two geniuses. Two brains.
Two hearts. One battle.
Who will confess their love first...?!
KAGUYA-SAMA
LOVE IS WAR
STORY & ART BY AKA AKASAKA
As leaders of their prestigious academy's student council, Kaguya and Miyuki are the elite of the elite! But it's lonely at the top... Luckily for them, they've fallen in love! There's just one problem—they both have too much pride to admit it. And so begins the daily scheming to get the object of their affection to confess their romantic feelings first...
Love is a war you win by losing.
KAGUYA-SAMA LOVE IS WAR
STORY & ART BY AKA AKASAKA
RATED T TEEN
VIZ
viz.com
KAGUYA-SAMA WA KOKURASETAI~TENSAITACHI NO REN'AI ZUNO SEN~
© 2015 by Aka Akasaka/SHUEISHA Inc.

YOU'RE READING THE
WRONG WAY!

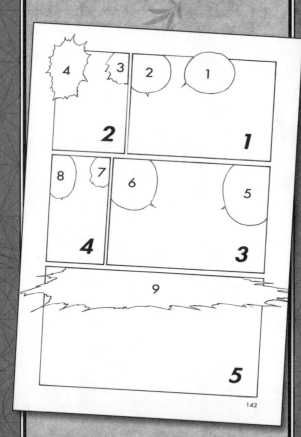

DEMON SLAYER: KIMETSU NO YAIBA reads from right to left, starting in the upper-right corner. Japanese is read from right to left, meaning that action, sound effects and word-balloon order are completely reversed from English order.